CW01653816

FRANCIS BACON

IN THE 1950S

YALE UNIVERSITY PRESS
NEW HAVEN AND LONDON

THE SAINSBURY CENTRE
UNIVERSITY OF EAST ANGLIA NORWICH

MICHAEL PEPPIATT

FRANCIS BACON

IN THE 1950S

First published to accompany the exhibition *Francis Bacon: Paintings from the 1950s*

Sainsbury Centre for Visual Arts
University of East Anglia, Norwich
26 September–10 December 2006

Milwaukee Art Museum, Wisconsin, USA
29 January–15 April 2007

Albright-Knox Art Gallery, Buffalo, USA
5 May–30 July 2007

Guest curator Michael Peppiatt

Sainsbury Centre curator Sara Cooper

Exhibition design by George Sexton Associates, Washington DC

This publication and exhibition have been made possible by the generosity of Lady Sainsbury and of the Robert and Lisa Sainsbury Charitable Trust

Copyright © 2006 Sainsbury Centre for Visual Arts
University of East Anglia
Norwich
www.scva.ac.uk

Copyright © Michael Peppiatt texts by the author

All works by Francis Bacon © Estate of Francis Bacon 2006. All rights reserved, DACS, London 2006

Photography and other copyright credits as given on page 196.

Michael Peppiatt asserts his moral right to be recognised as the author of this book

All rights reserved.
This book may not be reproduced, in whole or in part, in any form (beyond that copying permitted by Sections 107 and 108 of the U.S. Copyright Law and except by reviewers for the public press), without written permission from the publishers.

Designed by Paul Sloman

Printed in Italy by Conti Tipocolor

First published in hardcover by Yale University Press 2006

LIBRARY OF CONGRESS CATALOGING-IN-PUBLICATION DATA

Peppiatt, Michael.
Francis Bacon in the 1950s / Michael Peppiatt.
p. cm.
Includes bibliographical references and index.
ISBN 0-300-12192-X (CL : ALK. PAPER)
1. Bacon, Francis, 1909–1992–Criticism and interpretation. I. Title.
ND497.B16P48 2006
759.2–DC22

2006025519

The Sainsbury Centre for Visual Arts is supported with funds from:

CONTENTS

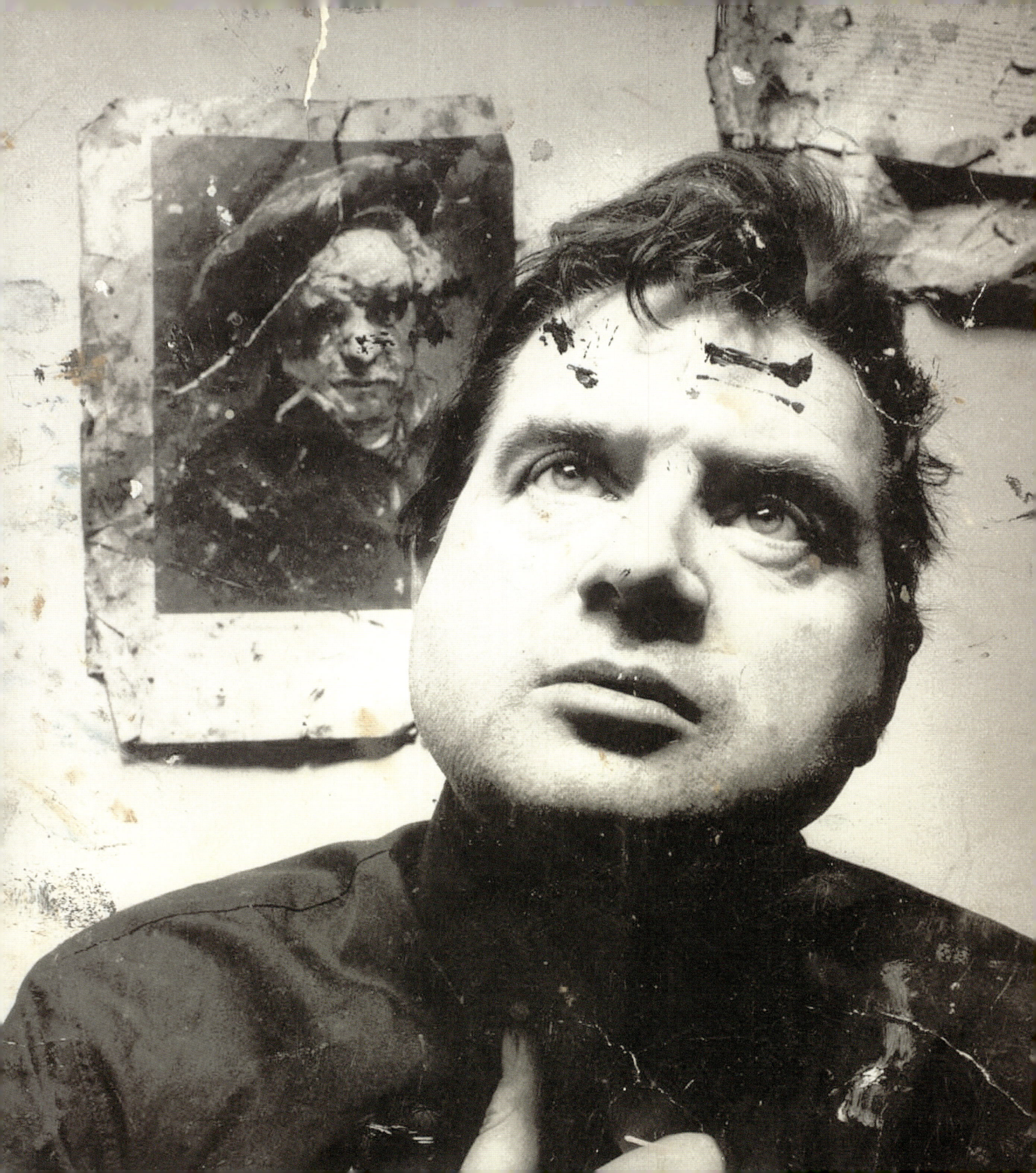

FOREWORD

The thirteen early works by Francis Bacon that offered the starting point for this exhibition lie at the heart of the collection of world art built by Sir Robert and Lady Sainsbury from the 1930s onwards, which was gifted to the University of East Anglia in 1973. The Sainsburys' relationships with living artists both informed, and were informed by, their collecting of art from cultures as diverse as those of pre-Columbian America and the west coast of Africa to the Pacific islands and prehistoric Japan. What holds the collection together is its root in a single and singularly personal vision.

Objects were added to the collection on the basis of what might best be termed their visceral appeal – and there can be few artists more visceral than Bacon. In the course of a developing friendship Bacon painted several Sainsbury portraits, all of which are displayed in the exhibition, and the Sainsburys' visits to his studio led to the purchase of further works. Since a self-imposed annual expenditure limit had always been set on the collection, the time came when the rising values of Bacon's work meant that no more were acquired, so at the Sainsbury Centre for Visual Arts we now have what is effectively a wonderfully concentrated 'snapshot' of Bacon at work in a distinct and formative period of his artistic and personal development.

To our own paintings have been added works from many other public and private collections, and we are particularly grateful to our lenders for allowing us to show works that are in almost constant demand – and are likely to be even more so in the years leading up to Bacon's centenary. That many have also agreed to extend their generosity to allowing us to tour the

Francis Bacon, London 1962, photo: Irving Penn. © 1963 Condé Nast Publications Inc.

exhibition to the Milwaukee Art Museum and to the Albright-Knox Art Gallery in Buffalo, New York, is particularly gratifying. For the production of this book we owe thanks to Gillian Malpass at Yale University Press, and to Paul Sloman for its design. Our thanks are also due to the Sainsbury Family Charitable Trusts, without whose support neither the exhibition nor the United States tour would have been possible, to the Estate of Francis Bacon and, of course, to our Guest Curator, Michael Peppiatt, for bringing together works that remind us yet again of the power and transformative energy of Bacon's vision.

Nichola Johnson
Director, Sainsbury Centre for Visual Arts

INTRODUCTION AND ACKNOWLEDGEMENTS

My interest in 'Francis Bacon in the 1950s' can be traced right back to the moment I met the artist, in 1963. At that time, Bacon had just had his first retrospective exhibition at the Tate, and his reputation was clearly in the ascendant (although no one then could have foreseen just how important and influential his work would become). What fascinated me during those first few months was not only the man and the artist I was interviewing and getting to know, but Bacon as he had been - in the tumultuous years leading up to this official success. I began to think from then on that in many ways the 1950s was the most fertile decade in Bacon's career, the period when he was at his wildest and most tormented, but also at his freest to invent and to destroy. As I analysed the artist's development in depth, I realized that this was the period when Bacon acquired the pictorial means he needed to bring forth his vision, before technical mastery started to absorb the rawness of what he conveyed.

In this exhibition we have included a couple of paintings from the 1940s and a few examples of Bacon's later work to give an idea of what happened before and what came after the 1950s. Bacon's genius was already apparent in the mid-1940s; he also went on to paint some of his most haunting works when advanced in age. 'Painting', as he liked to say, 'is an old man's métier'.

But by putting the focus of the present show on the 1950s, when the artist was in mid-career, we hope to show a little-known Bacon, a Bacon still searching for himself, eager to explore a wide variety of themes and to take all kinds of risks: Bacon before he became fixed on a single, grand, tragic vision. This is the first time that an exhibition has concentrated on a specific period in Bacon's career, and we are extremely fortunate to have been able to bring together works that have rarely or never been shown in public before.

*

By reading between the lines of the acknowledgments for an exhibition, one can derive some idea of how it all came together. In my experience, curating an exhibition (notably the exhibition of an artist as much in demand as Francis Bacon) is like entering a dark tunnel. For a long time after the loan requests have gone out, nothing happens and no works seem to be forthcoming; the curator simply blunders on, writing and telephoning; and it is not until months later that the first glimmerings of light, the first loans, appear. Then, and only then, the nightmare of bare white walls – an exhibition opening with no pictures – recedes, and the positive cycle of convincing the wary and persuading the recalcitrant begins.

For helping me locate works for the exhibition, I should like to give special thanks to Kate Austin, David Gordon, Andrew Kalman and Pilar Ordovás. Margarita Cappock, at the Francis Bacon Studio at the Hugh Lane Gallery in Dublin, generously helped in providing images from Bacon's studio for the catalogue and choosing actual working documents for display in the exhibition. John-Paul Stonnard stepped in to bring the bibliography up to date and to transcribe Bacon's letters to the Hanover Gallery. The librarians at the Tate Archive and the London Library could not have been kinder or more efficient.

I am especially indebted to Sara Cooper who has worked with me through every stage of this project with unfailing resourcefulness and good humour. I should also like to thank all her colleagues at the Sainsbury Centre who have contributed to the exhibition.

Many people helped in other ways, by their suggestions and their encouragement – or simply by their friendship. My warmest thanks to them all: Ida Barbarigo, Alice Bellony, André and Claude Bernheim, the late Valerie Beston, Tony and Glenys Bevan, Charles and Natasha Campbell, Marta Canals, Krzysztof Cieszkowski, Patrice and Mala Cotensin, Hamish Dewar, Adrian and Jamie Dicks, Fred and Diana Elghanayan, Christopher Eykyn, Colin and Sophie Gleadell, Cyrille de Gunzburg, Philip Herrera, Henry and Alison Meyric Hughes, Jill Lloyd, Olivier Lorquin, the late Marjorie Loggia, Gillian Malpass, Daniel and Nadine Milhaud, the late Zoran Music, Alexander Peppiatt, Clio Peppiatt, Kate Poole, John Richardson, Christopher and Carmel Shirley, Paul Sloman and Álex Susanna.

Michael Peppiatt

EXHIBITION LENDERS

INSTITUTIONS

Albright-Knox Art Gallery, Buffalo, New York, USA
Art Institute of Chicago, Illinois, USA
Dallas Museum of Art, Texas, USA
Dublin City Art Gallery The Hugh Lane (Francis Bacon Studio), Dublin, Ireland
Gemeentemuseum Den Haag, The Netherlands
Göteborgs Konstmuseum, Göteborg, Sweden
Hatton Gallery, University of Newcastle, Newcastle-upon-Tyne, UK
Hirshhorn Museum and Sculpture Garden, Washington DC, USA
Huddersfield Art Gallery, Huddersfield, UK
Museum of Modern Art, New York, USA
National Gallery of Canada, Ottawa, Canada
Sainsbury Centre for Visual Arts, University of East Anglia, Norwich, UK
Stedelijk Museum voor Actuele Kunst, Ghent, Belgium
Tate, London, UK
Walker Art Center, Minneapolis, USA
Whitworth Art Gallery, Manchester, UK
Yageo Foundation, Taiwan
Yale Center for British Art, New Haven, Connecticut, USA
Yale University Art Gallery, New Haven, Connecticut, USA

PRIVATE LENDERS

Aviva PLC, London, UK
Collection of Samuel and Ronnie Heyman, New York, USA
Private collection courtesy of the Galerie Beyeler, Basel, Switzerland
Private collection courtesy of the Crane Kalman Gallery, London, UK
Collection of Jan Krugier and Marie-Anne Krugier-Poniatowski, Geneva, Switzerland
Collection Jane Lang Davis

We should also like to thank those private lenders
who wish to remain anonymous.

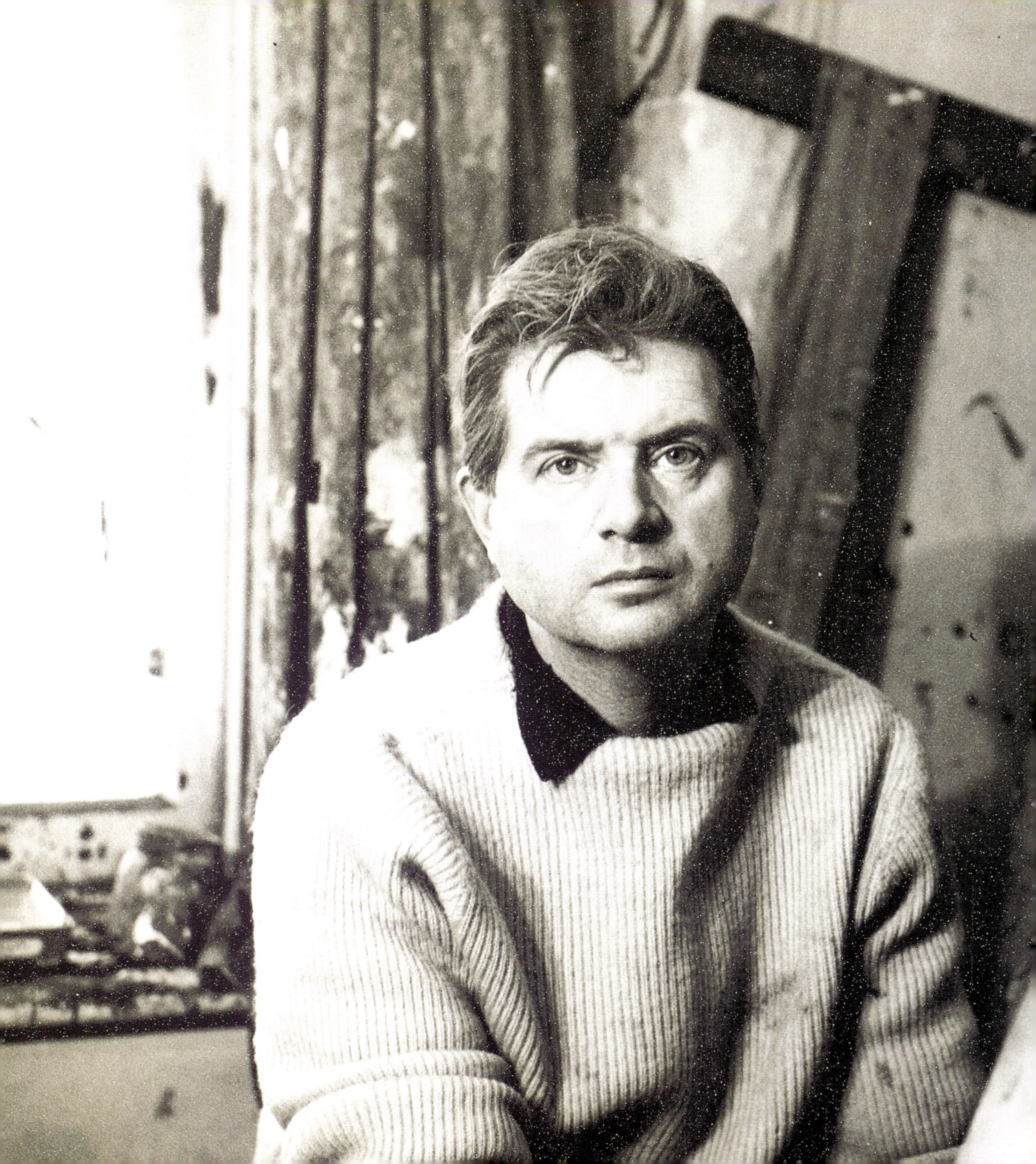

BACON'S EYES

Photographs of Francis Bacon as a very young man show an immaculately dressed youth with neatly parted hair and a fresh round face consumed by the intensity of his wide-set eyes. It is the gaze of a child surprised and fascinated by the mystery of the world. It both penetrates and receives: nothing is taken for granted. Years later, his look remains wide-eyed and astonished, its pure visual energy unclouded. Yet by the time Cecil Beaton photographs Bacon in the late 1950s, a wariness has crept into the eyes. The young man has lost his innocence, but not his wonder. The gaze turns now to the scream of pain and pleasure; the shudder of beast and man; the monkey in the cage; the couple in the grass; the grain of the paint; the blur of a snapshot. Having taken in so much of the world, the eyes harden. Later they will grow old in a young face. The smooth cheeks, the carefully tousled hair will continue to proclaim Bacon's uncanny youth, defying a lifetime of every excess. But like the portrait of Dorian Grey, the eyes will continue to absorb and record.

Whenever something caught Francis Bacon's attention, his normally genial gaze took on a cold, piercing intensity, like a bird suddenly spotting its prey. The look could come out of nowhere and at any time, provoked by a chance remark, a painting reproduced in an art magazine or the way a well-dressed woman had entered a restaurant. If you were unfortunate enough to have that look turned on you (and if you spent much time with Bacon, at some point it became inevitable), you had the sensation of being taken apart, swiftly and mercilessly. Whatever fear,

1 Francis Bacon, 1960, photo: Cecil Beaton, Cecil Beaton Studio Archive, Sotheby's.

guile or half-truth lurked within you had been analysed in a flash, minutely recorded and stowed away in a visual memory that forgot nothing, it seemed. It was the kind of scrutiny that took years to come to terms with, leaving you painfully self-aware, as if you had been scrutinized, once and once only, to the bone.

What went on in the pale blue depths of that unwavering stare? Although he could be cruel and occasionally treacherous, Bacon was not a malevolent man. To the people he liked, he went out of his way to be generous and supportive; and those he disliked, he generally disregarded until they dropped away from his life. Nevertheless, there was something completely pitiless in that gaze. Was it the drive to tear off every veil, to lift appearance and look behind – the need to stare the starkest of facts from advanced skin diseases to dead meat in the face? Did Bacon feel that only the intensity of that look – the 'mirada fuerte' that John Richardson mentions in relation to Picasso – could pierce the surface and lead him to a deeper, underlying truth? Certainly Bacon trusted his eyes to tell him everything he ever wanted to know; a look came into them at times like that of a child picking a toy or an insect to pieces to find out how it worked. Talking and reading, both activities that Bacon did with great appetite and flair, had proved to be extremely useful and illuminating, but it was what he saw that counted. Vision was where all the senses and all experience converged in their most complete and potent form. However much he enjoyed the company of friends, a *bon mot* or the first frosted bottle of Chablis, Bacon existed through sight. And as I write this, I remember the look of terror that flashed through Bacon's eyes (it was in Marseilles in 1976, the day after his exhibition had opened at the Musée Cantini) when we bumped abruptly into a blind man with dark glasses and a white cane tapping his way round a dark side street corner behind the old port.[1]

Those eyes, of course, spent a long lifetime dissecting everything that came within range. They had taken in animal and human life at an early age on a horse-training farm in Ireland, where the spectacle of thoroughbreds copulating was counterpointed by the couplings with his father's grooms, but they found their true focus in the densely populated centres of great metropolises. London, Paris, Berlin, and later to some extent Madrid, were the places that offered the most varied and abundant prey. There was no need for open landscape and the eruption of wild life when human nature could be caught in its essential bestiality trapped in the confines of a room. Bacon had, in fact, lived his life to excite and satisfy the hunger in his eyes as quickly and completely as he could. Love begun in bars, lulled in champagne, could only be fulfilled in the sadomasochistic arena, with its variety of harsher delights. There, more than anywhere, in the confusion of extreme pleasure and extreme pain, Bacon found access to a reality – the rawest emotion, the undisguised scream – that most situations in life disguised. And later, in his own version of 'emotion recollected in tranquillity', Bacon was free to flay his lovers and himself on canvas with an abandon that would have proved fatal in reality, drawing with supreme cynicism on medical textbooks, scientific photography and the entire history of figure- and flesh-painting in Western art.

Bacon's eyes took in not only the extreme situation, but the whole sweep of daily existence. 'What I love most in the end,' he said to me once, when he was already quite old, 'is simply being conscious. And all I ask of life these days is a body that will get me from place to place, and a mind that works.' He watched with fascination as people's faces – above all, those he knew well – were transformed: contorted in hate, loosened by drink, intensified by desire. And from his portraits, I think it is clear that if he watched intently, like a predator, it was also with undiminished fellow feeling and tenderness. Unsparing though he could be in his criticism of other people's art or characters, he was very indulgent towards the weaknesses and follies of those he cared for. Thus when the high-flown *Sturm und Drang* of sadomasochistic homosexual love proves overwhelming, Bacon aficionados are able to turn for relief to the compassionate intimacy and insight with which the artist portrayed his circle of close friends.

'I am like a grinding machine,' Bacon famously observed. 'I look at everything, and everything goes in and gets ground up very fine.' Along with photography and the history of art came almost everything that had a visual existence, from newspaper print to desert boots and lipstick. I recall Bacon becoming transfixed, for instance, by a puddle of milk on a café table; he lifted his finger, as if to draw in it, then rather reluctantly abstained. And I remember thinking at the time (we were sitting appropriately enough at the Coupole in Paris) how vital the discovery of surrealism had been to Bacon. With its insistence on the significance of the unconscious and its fascination with the 'chance encounters' of quite disparate things, surrealism – including Picasso at his most surrealist – was no doubt the single most important influence on his development, however much he distanced himself from the whole phenomenon thereafter. But, as with his other 'borrowings', Bacon rapidly absorbed surrealist attitudes and techniques and turned them into something unmistakably his own.

Nor was it of course only visual phenomena that attracted Bacon's interest. Everything, in a sense, from an Edith Piaf song to a line from one of Yeats's late poems went in and was ground up very fine; and there is a whole study to be made of the effect literature had on Bacon. But more mundane things – the chance shape of that puddle of milk, the colour of bad wine drunk late at night, lamplight on teeth or a scar – also left their traces. And from this extraordinary commingling all Bacon's images were born – chaotically and by the promptings of chance, but with a comprehension of the human condition that continues to probe our sense of ourselves.

*

What Bacon saw and how his imagination ground it up we will only ever know in part. That is surely one of the fundamental reasons why his images continue to haunt and taunt us. But the archive of his eye had a quantifiable, material existence in the studios he used, most notably in the studio in Reece Mews, in South Kensington, which remained the centre of his working life for thirty years. In many reµspects the two ran in parallel, the studio operating as a repository for what the eye had seen and selected, with old images serving to refresh the memory and trigger off new ones. And when the artist was alive, the experience of going in there, if only for a few minutes, was electrifying. The aura it derived from the scores of memorable paintings that had been created there was heightened by the sense that others still to come hung palpably in the air. It was almost as if the studio, set like a trap with every kind of suggestive mark and document, were itself capable of engendering new pictures.

Once I got to know it, having been allowed in for brief periods both during the day and at night, the studio began to fascinate me almost as much as did Bacon. The Reece Mews studio came to seem like the artist's other self. It complemented all kinds of things that Bacon had told me about his work and his life; tantalizingly, its jumbled contents promised to fill in some of the many missing pieces in the jigsaw. If Bacon really had no interest in this or that painter, for instance, then why was an exhibition catalogue or reproductions of his work lying on the studio floor? Which new model, or lover, or both, were those fresh and barely crumpled photographs of, and why would a Greek phrase book have suddenly erupted out of the paint-encrusted rubble underfoot?

What Bacon said could often be evasive or subject to a passing mood or whim; he was also very aware, even when his guard seemed down and he was far gone in drink, of the impression he was making. In that sense, the studio was more reliable. It was a record of countless mornings of work, in elation or despair; the repository of so many sources; the mirror of the artist's mind. While Bacon was alive, I made extensive notes about the studio and wrote several factual descriptions of it. The following, written over twenty years ago, is still confidently couched in the present tense:

> Bacon's London studio, inauspicious enough on the outside, is situated in a quiet, cobblestoned mews in South Kensington. Having negotiated a staircase to the upper floor as steep as a ship's ladder, with a waxy ship's rope bolted as a handrail to the wall, the rare visitor finds himself in an ordinary rectangular room in no way predisposed for use as an artist's working space. It is just big enough to allow the painter to concentrate on one large canvas at a time; for this inveterate painter of triptychs, one might reasonably have expected a space three times as large, in which several paintings could be kept going simultaneously. Similarly, the light coming through the smallish opening overhead and one side wall hardly seems sufficient for the artist to gauge his acid suavity of colour. Many grander studios have been offered to him, but Bacon has not moved. He works best in that modest, familiar, cluttered room.
>
> Sheer omnipresence of paint is what impresses most as one enters this highly fraught space. Coloured marks – accidental splats, brush wipes, trial runs of one hue against another – rainbow or cascade over the walls, turning them into giant palettes. Another pattern of chance blobs and trickles extends in an intricately coloured net over the book- and photo-strewn floor. Sticky masses of half-spent tubes, thickets of coagulated brushes rear up on all sides,

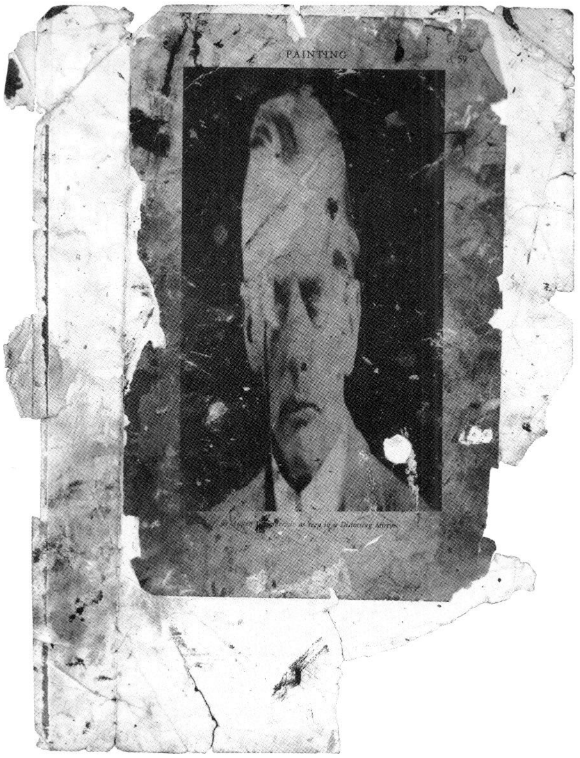

2 Studio document. Leaf from Amédée Ozenfant, *Foundations of Modern Art* (London, 1931), showing Sir Austen Chamberlain in a distorted mirror. Dublin City Gallery, The Hugh Lane.

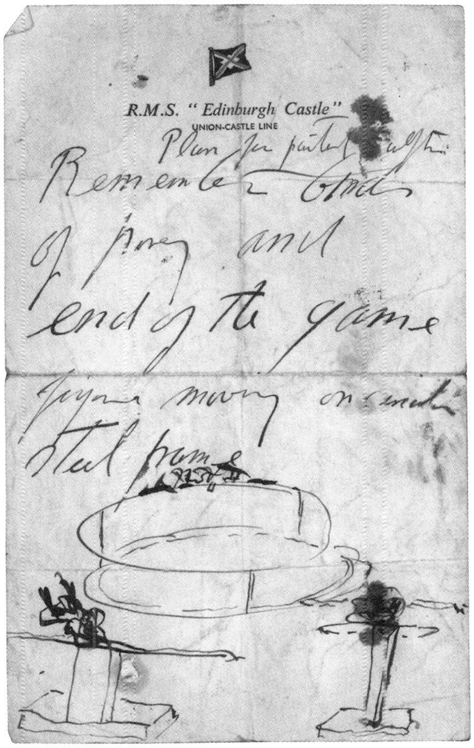

3 Studio document. A sheet of notepaper with a sketch by Francis Bacon. Dublin City Gallery, The Hugh Lane.

amid old plates and pans used to mix colour, rollers, rags, tins and jars of every description. An out-of-date passport or a single, shiny shoe occasionally heaves into sight like a drowning man, and is lost. Pinned to the wall are reproductions of Bacon's own, immaculate paintings, sprung out of this daunting mess. But the intense confusion also has something hilarious, even cheering, about it because it conveys utter disrespect for the ordinary rules of living and breathes a rare sense of freedom.

Then what catches the eye is the chaos carpeting the studio floor, which can be read as a kind of sourcebook for Bacon's imagery. In it, paint-smeared and trampled, are newspaper items, books ranging from pre-Socratic philosophy to manuals on ape behaviour, an old T-square and dustbin lid, as well as several paint-soaked sweaters which Bacon has used to press on canvas so as to obtain a ribbed, chromatic effect. Above all, there are photographs of a spectacular diversity: snaps of friends, reproductions of works by Michelangelo, Velázquez and Rembrandt; scenes of disaster, car crashes and war reportage; studies of ani-

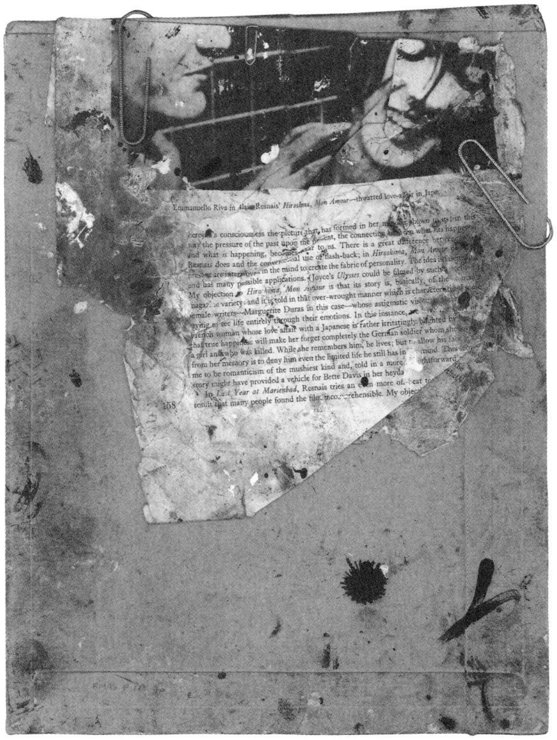

4 Studio document. Mounted leaf with black and white still of Emmanuelle Riva in Alain Resnais's film *Hiroshima mon amour* (1959). Dublin City Gallery, The Hugh Lane.

mals or athletes in motion; pictures of the Third Reich; Polaroid portraits of the artist himself. This image-jumble becomes most riveting when the artist moves from one end of the littered studio to the other, kicking up half-buried images that stay at the top of the heap for an instant to give new evidence – and perhaps fresh inspiration.

Yet to know that photographs of Goebbels lie cheek by jowl with the tragedies of Aeschylus, or that boxers stare into a page of T. S. Eliot, tells something only about the raw ingredients that may at some time, in some mingled or sifted form, have gone into Bacon's imagery. The essential, and most difficult, problem lies in determining how they have been transformed. Bacon has, after all, had the opportunity and the voracious visual appetite to look at virtually everything in existence; and his imagination has to the highest degree the power to blend the consciously remembered with chance recall of the kind that stalks our sleeping or daydreaming minds.[2]

*

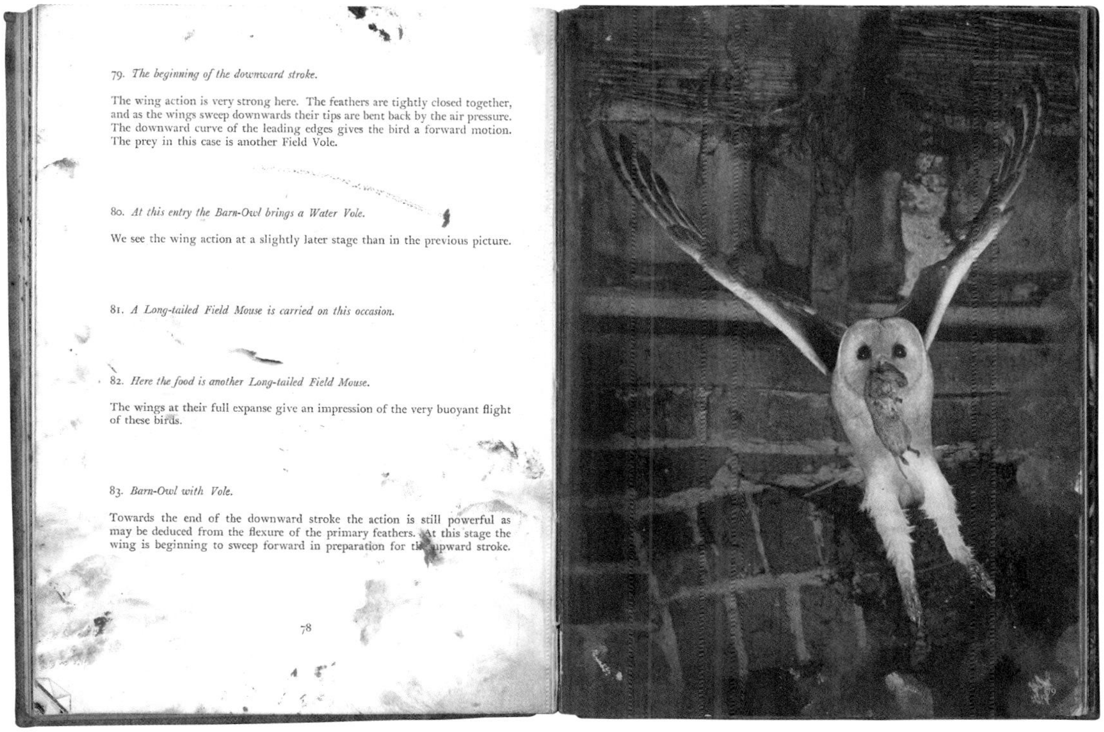

79. *The beginning of the downward stroke.*

The wing action is very strong here. The feathers are tightly closed together, and as the wings sweep downwards their tips are bent back by the air pressure. The downward curve of the leading edges gives the bird a forward motion. The prey in this case is another Field Vole.

80. *At this entry the Barn-Owl brings a Water Vole.*

We see the wing action at a slightly later stage than in the previous picture.

81. *A Long-tailed Field Mouse is carried on this occasion.*

82. *Here the food is another Long-tailed Field Mouse.*

The wings at their full expanse give an impression of the very buoyant flight of these birds.

83. *Barn-Owl with Vole.*

Towards the end of the downward stroke the action is still powerful as may be deduced from the flexure of the primary feathers. At this stage the wing is beginning to sweep forward in preparation for the upward stroke.

78

5 Studio document. Pages 78–79 of Eric Hosking and Cyril Newberry, *Birds in Action* (London, 1949). Dublin City Gallery, The Hugh Lane.

Since his death in April 1992, Bacon has rarely been out of the press. Indeed, he often seems to be more alive than ever, with the mythology surrounding him growing more extravagant by the year, as if his existence had been transformed, like that of a Pharaoh, into a vast archaeological dig, with 'finds' being made regularly and reported to an eager public. Numerous paintings long thought lost or destroyed have now come to light; others have been found missing and must at least currently be catalogued with the chilling phrase: 'Present Whereabouts Unknown.' The paintings lost and found have, however, received nothing like the attention accorded to the voluminous batches of drawings that have surfaced. Here the shades of Bacon have been taken to task since, throughout his lifetime, the artist made a special point of repeating in interviews and to all those who would listen in private that he 'never' drew. This was indeed somewhat misleading, but mostly because Bacon tended to talk in absolute terms; what he meant essentially was that drawing had no real relevance to the way in which he made images. True, Bacon roughed out odd sketches on scraps of paper and the end pages of books as a way of testing or noting down a potential image. More significantly, he often 'drew' the outline of his central image with a paintbrush on the canvas as a run-up to actually engaging with a new picture. But unlike, say, Giacometti, for whom drawing was a central activity and the daily touchstone of his art, Bacon considered his drawings at best as notes, without interest or merit.[3] A mere fraction of these posthumously discovered 'drawings' have actually been accepted as authentic and acquired by the Tate in London. The rest, including large numbers of overpainted photographs, continue to linger in limbo, despite widespread publicity, with a large question mark as to their provenance in some cases and their authenticity in others.

Another great upheaval in Bacon's posthumous world was the removal lock, stock and barrel of his studio from the South Kensington mews where he had worked for the last thirty years of his life to Dublin, the city where he had been born but to which he had no subsequent attachment. One result of this unexpected transfer has been the publication of numerous documents that once formed part of the great shifting sea of materials which Bacon kept underfoot as he worked. Many of the photographs and sources thus revealed were already known or resembled other documents previously recorded in the artist's possession. Certain others, however, offer new insights into the way Bacon's visual imagination gathered the most disparate fragments and used them either quite literally or – seasoned practitioner of surrealist techniques that he was – blended so closely with others as to become almost unrecognizable.

Among the thousands of studio items that have now been catalogued is a curious book containing photographs of 'paranormal' experiences. I knew that Bacon, for all the scorn he poured on any form of 'mysticism', had been intrigued by W. B. Yeats's spiritualism; but I had put that down to his admiration for Yeats as a poet. I also remember him referring, with what seemed like amused scepticism, to Madame Blavatsky, the Russian-born theosophist celebrated for her psychic powers. But there may have been more to it than that since some of these photographs, reportedly taken in mid-séance, reappear barely changed in certain of Bacon's paintings, one of them notably on the left-hand side of the central panel of *Triptych 1974*, a partly obscured head that also puts one in mind of Sigmund Freud. And while we are talking about this particular painting, it would be worth adding that, to my almost certain knowledge, the other head in this panel is a portrait of the writer Michel Leiris, the poet and former Surrealist who became a close friend of Bacon's, while the horses cantering down the beach are clearly inspired by a similar scene by Bacon's much-beloved Degas.[4] But Bacon's mind worked in unpredictable ways, and it was certainly not because an image caught his attention that he believed in its underlying substance. Who might have thought, for instance, that among the artist's proven sources was a manual entitled *Fundamentals of Soil Science*? Transposing – not to say 'lifting' – an image from it into a painting did not presuppose an expert knowledge of (or conviction in) irrigation techniques![5]

Such clues to Bacon's imaginative processes and working methods will no doubt continue to emerge for many years to come. This is, after all, the stuff art history is made of, and it is both fascinating and extremely useful, allowing better-documented insights and interpretations ofa work to evolve. At the same time, all the sources in the world, neatly analysed and cross-referenced, will never do more than illuminate the matrix out of which a powerful work of art has emerged. That is no doubt why Bacon remained quite secretive (locking certain key documents in a sea-chest he kept specifically for that purpose) not only about his occasional sketches but also the full range of his interests and borrowings; he feared that his pictures might be reduced to the sum of the influences they had absorbed.

It already seems clear, despite the wealth of posthumous revelations outlined above, that Bacon's paintings resist this kind of interpretation, with the core of their mysteriously independent existence untouched; and this is a sign of their enduring fascination and power as painted images – what the painter and critic Lawrence Gowing once called 'pigment-figments'. But beyond their manifest and less apparent appropriations, how do these images function? Ultimately, they seem folded in on themselves, like images in words that other words cannot undo. One thinks of Eliot at the end of the *Four Quartets*: 'When the tongues of flame are in-folded / Into the crowned knot of fire / And the fire and the rose are one.' Or the intricate imagery of the great Jacobean poets, in which the entire universe is ransacked to stretch a particular thought or sensation into its fullest expression. Bacon was vauntingly ambitious. He had no interest in producing paintings that could be interpreted as having a specific, and hence necessarily limited, meaning. On the contrary, Bacon aimed at universality, at creating images that would infiltrate the imagination at every level and so perhaps, eventually, take their place beside the most evocative and potent paintings of the past.

This essay is a revised version of a text that appeared in the exhibition catalogue 'Francis Bacon und die Bildtradition', published by the Kunsthistorisches Museum, Vienna, and the Fondation Beyeler, Riehen/Basel, 2003.

1 The incident was made more memorable by what followed. Bacon and I had been talking in English. The moment he picked up on our conversation, the blind man waved his stick at us and began railing against 'les sales étrangers' ('filthy foreigners'). I remonstrated in French, politely enough. But that only fuelled the man's fury, and he began hitting me over the shoulders with his cane. We moved quickly on and did not talk for a while. Neither of us ever referred to the incident again, but I think we were both struck by its suddenness and its curious implications.

2 This extract comes from an essay published in the *Connoisseur* (New York, September 1984), pp. 84–90.

3 In some of the restaurants Bacon used to frequent, particularly in Paris, the chef would sometimes appear and intimate that if the 'maître' (a form of address Bacon detested) had enjoyed his cooking he might like to leave a little drawing as a souvenir. 'But I simply don't draw', Bacon would reply with some exasperation, then double the already excessive tip.

4 An antiquarian bookseller in Paris tracked down a copy of the Lemoisne catalogue raisonné of Degas's work that I had ordered knowing it might be one of the few gifts Bacon would welcome. Coming to London some months later and seeing the rare powder-blue volumes back-broken, paint-smeared and strewn all over the studio floor was dismaying until I accepted how useful a source book it had become for the artist.

5 The image in question illustrates 'irrigation by the corrugation method'; and it reappears in a relatively little-known painting by Bacon, *Two Men Working in a Field* (1971).

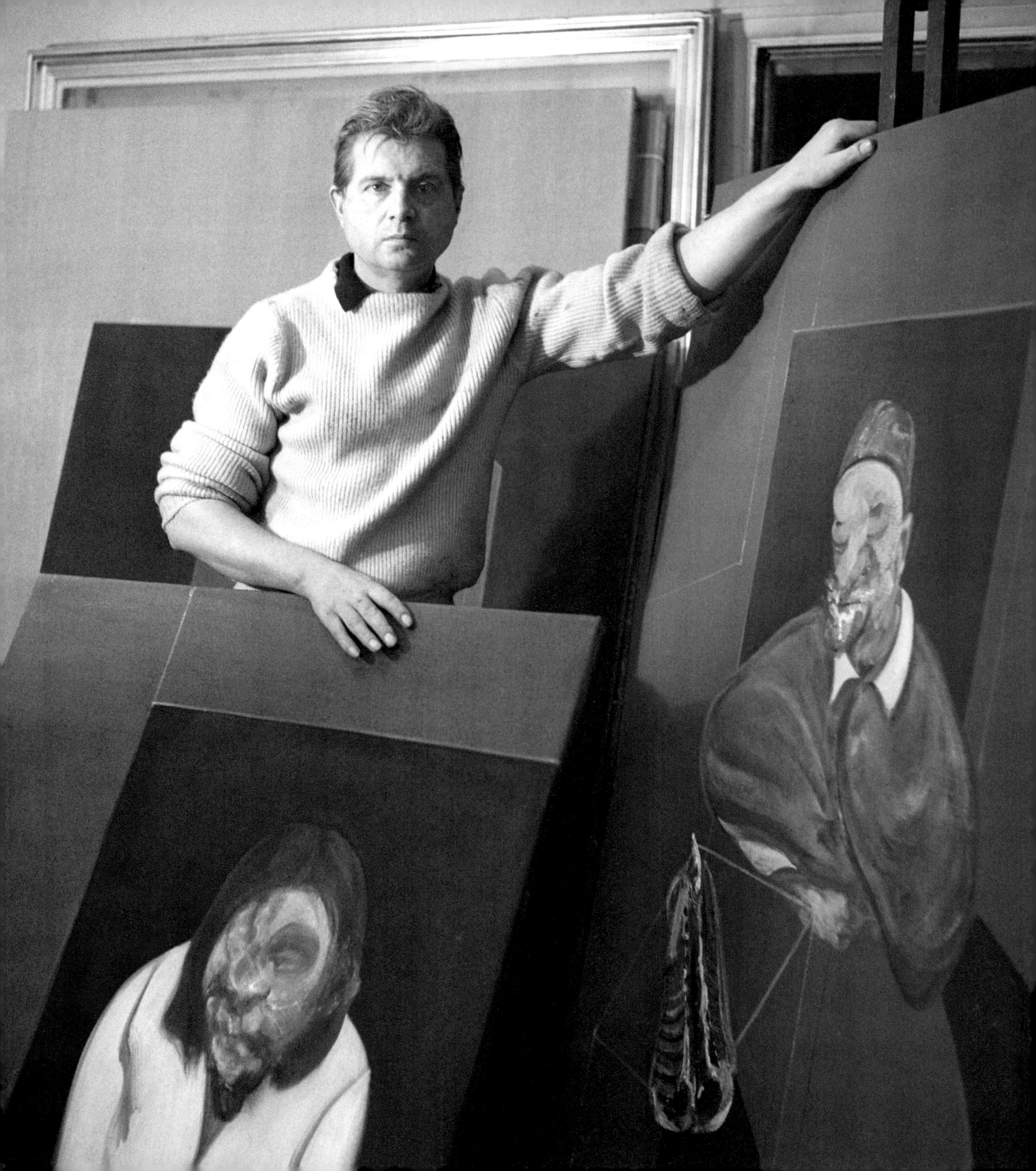

FRANCIS BACON IN THE 1950S

Like a wound, we all carry within us an obsession with the period preceding the major events that mark our lives. It may be the time immediately before we were born: the hinterland, both familiar and mysterious, of our parents and the way life was then. It may be the encounter with a great figure of the past, a poet or visionary, who transforms our present and whose beginnings we seek to identify with. Or again, it may be a period that we ourselves have lived through, but that we relive differently, more meaningfully, through the vivid existence of someone else.

When I first met Francis Bacon in the early 1960s, he was flush with the success of his retrospective at the Tate. I see him now, pink with drink, in a blue-and-white check shirt and a grey flannel suit, turning at the bar of the French House on Dean Street, his arms opened wide to welcome the young, uncertain student that I was. With his gambler's luck, Bacon was then on the crest of a wave. He had a new notoriety – a rebel artist lying half in the arms of the establishment, half in the drinking clubs, gambling dens and pick-up places of Soho. He also had a new studio (after years of wandering from room to room), a powerful new gallery, and a new, if hapless and confused, lover. Moreover, he had new money, thanks to a few brave collectors, and he was not slow in spending it, on old friends and new friends, on rounds of champagne and on the treacherous turn of the roulette wheel. Francis Bacon was on the threshold of a

6 Francis Bacon, 1960, with *Red Cardinal (Seated Figure)* and *Head of a Woman*, photo: Cecil Beaton, Cecil Beaton Studio Archive, Sotheby's.

career as one of the most successful, most disturbing and most hotly debated artists of the twentieth century.

Yet, at that particular time – which, for me, revolved around Soho's pubs, restaurants and drinking clubs in the summer and winter of 1963 – the work that had gained Bacon his sulphurous reputation came entirely from the late 1940s and the 1950s. As I went around with him, increasingly drawn into the power and charm of his company, these were the images that came repeatedly to mind, like an unresolved nightmare: the screaming heads and snarling chimpanzees, the early Popes and portraits of van Gogh, the anonymous figures trapped, against blue velvet curtains, in tortured isolation. These were the works that had made Bacon's 1962 retrospective so unforgettable. They were raw in a way that went far beyond the extremities of pain and outrage that the howling mouths and contorted flesh intimated. It was the actual texture of the image scraping across the nerve that thrilled and anguished even those visitors who already had some experience of Bacon's work. Here, in a London still in thrall to its memories of wartime fears and privations, was an almost unbearable fluency in new modes of suffering and humiliation. In that unwelcome, macabre revelation, not only the human figure but pigment itself had never before looked so naked and vulnerable – as if the skin of the paint had been peeled back to reveal the potential for pain beneath. Alongside it, other contemporary English art paled into pleasantness. You could live comfortably with a coolly refined Ben Nicholson, or even a spiky Graham Sutherland and a skeletal Henry Moore; but how to accommodate one of Bacon's screams in your drawing room? The exhibition marked a watershed not only in English art, but in the English sensibility. Once this outrage had been put on public display in the country's premier modern museum, the limits of what was acceptable in visual art would never be quite the same again.[1]

One of the many things that intrigued me when I began going round with Bacon was how my generous, jovial, admirably well-mannered new friend could have fathered such a race of deformed, howling brutes. Where was the dark, angst-ridden artist in this affable, elegant boulevardier, whose only concerns appeared to be whether the Chablis had been sufficiently chilled and the waiters properly tipped? What suffering did his constant laughter and endless, exuberant, Edwardian toasts ('Champagne for my real friends, real pain for my sham friends!') conceal? If this was a man in torment, racked by the enigmas of existence, how could he wine and dine half of Soho every evening, then play roulette for vertiginous stakes until dawn?

Part of the answer, it seemed to me then, as it does all the more clearly now, lay embedded in the 1950s. In that decade – for me the mysterious hinterland that he had inhabited so fully just before I met him – Bacon came of age as a painter. It was during those years, filled with rebuffs and reversals of fortune, but also with extraordinary invention and daring, that Bacon began to explore in depth all his great themes while trying out a number of others that he eventually discarded. It was, in my view, the most fertile single decade of his career. Never again would the Baconian world be so rich and diverse. In animal life alone, there were not only mon-

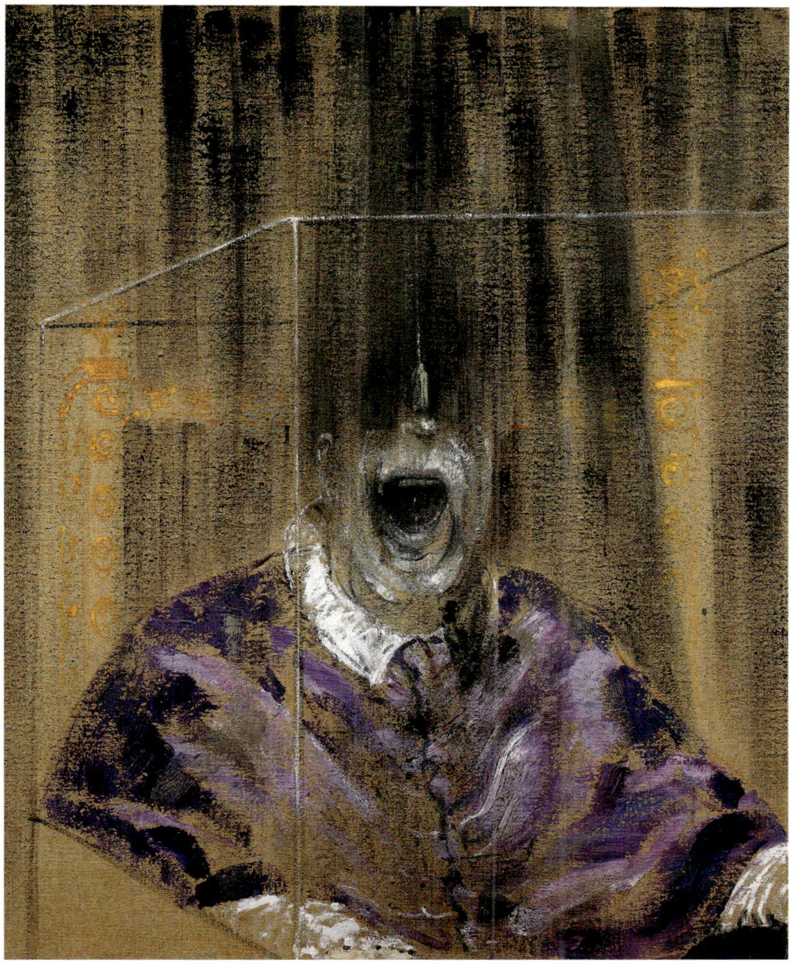

7 *Head VI*, 1949, 93 × 77 cm, oil on canvas. Arts Council Collection, Hayward Gallery, London.

keys, but dogs, owls and elephants. Between the supreme pontiff and the soberly suited men howling out their pain, their fear or their pleasure, there were also Sphinxes and ghostly heads of William Blake, female nudes and even children, self-portraits and portraits of friends. Even more surprising in a painter whose imagination was later confined to airless interiors, there were glimpses of landscape – recollections of Africa and the Côte d'Azur so vivid that one wonders at the painter of exotic atmospheres that Bacon might have been.

As the decade opened, Bacon already possessed the necessary technical prowess to express his vision, but he was still not fully in command of his disturbing images, which appear at times to rise from some dark well of the unconscious. As a result there remains in the pictures of the 1950s a violence and an almost clumsy urgency, transcending all formal or pictorial problems, that began to fade once Bacon grew more experienced and technically adept. In these early imaginings of man and beast pushed to the limits of endurance, the artist appears overwhelmed by the extreme situations he has brought forth, as if he has become a medium for a force beyond himself and had not yet come to terms with the strangeness and weight of his calling.[2]

Very occasionally, Bacon touched on this mysterious area, notably when he said once: 'I think that the best works of modern artists often give the impression that they were done when the artist was in a state of not knowing – for example, Picasso and Braque in those very late analytical-cubist pictures, where the whole thing seems totally inexplicable . . . and you sense that the artist didn't know what he was doing, that he had a kind of rightness of instinct and that only instinct was operating and that somehow he was working beyond reasoning.'[3]

This most fruitful yet most mysterious period of Bacon's career corresponded to the most tumultuous and despairing years of the artist's unsettled existence. For most of the time, Bacon was without a fixed address, borrowing rooms and changing studios with bewildering frequency, as if he were in headlong flight, both from himself and his destiny. Nevertheless, it was also during this decade that the artist established his lifelong routine – a still point strictly adhered to in a turning world – of waking and working early in the morning, then spending the rest of the day and much of the night talking and drinking in the bars and clubs of Soho, or in whatever other louche place he happened to find himself. Bacon spent long periods of these *Wanderjahren* abroad, gambling in Monte Carlo or visiting his ill-fated lover, Peter Lacy, in Tangier. If the decade had begun in relative security, it was to end in emotional chaos and disaster.

A LATE BEGINNER

One of the abiding enigmas about Bacon is the exponential jump his work makes from very early cubist and surrealist pastiches to the violent figure studies of the immediate post-war period. It seems well-established (in part by Bacon himself) that this was not, as long believed, as a result of the impact of the war and existential despair on what would otherwise have remained a remarkably genteel vision of the world. One cannot simply dismiss these pale essays 'in the manner of' simply as a young man's fumblings to find his own style – because there is nothing in them at all to herald the 'terribilità' to come. So, if it was not the horrors of war, what did transform Bacon, the young society designer who did dainty paintings on the side, into the monstrous visionary with a terrible truth to tell, scourge of his and successive generations?

By all accounts, Bacon was a late beginner. Looking through his early work (including the so-called 'abandoned' and 'destroyed' paintings listed in the catalogue raisonné), it is clear that he did not even start to hit his stride until the mid-1940s.[4] Bacon himself dated his artistic coming of age to the *Three Studies for Figures at the Base of a Crucifixion* of 1944 and imposed the orange triptych (now famous, but which Eric Hall, Bacon's companion, had trouble persuading the Tate to accept as a gift) as the *fons et origo* of everything he had painted. Thenceforth by order of the artist no works prior to 1944 were allowed into the canon – although Bacon had been painting for some twenty years previously. His commentators fell in, to a man. John Russell's perceptive monograph begins with the *Three Studies*, and the interviews that David Sylvester conducted and edited brilliantly make only the briefest mention of anything that happened before. Similarly, in later life, Bacon insisted that all retrospectives should show nothing prior to 1944.

Now that we are free to say it, there is a great deal to say about the late beginner's work before he claimed to have begun. Very little has in fact been written about this highly revealing, early section of Bacon's work. I mention it here simply to give one indication of how far Bacon studies still have to go.[5] It is also to make a subsequent point which leads directly into Bacon in the 1950s. In Bacon's mind and thenceforward in everyone else's, the *Three Studies* was his breakthrough painting, the 'masterpiece' which announced his arrival on the artistic scene. But was it? The three panels, Bacon said in 1959, were 'sketches for the Eumenides (the Greek Furies) which I intended to use as the base of a large Crucifixion which I may do still'.[6] These 'studies', in other words, were conceived as a kind of predella to a larger 'altarpiece'. Bacon was a very deliberate kind of person, and if he had such a scheme in mind, he would have pursued it intently. I think he did. He painted the large Crucifixion, but for reasons he never gave and we will never know, he did not accept it as the work he wanted. Single-minded though he was, Bacon remained full of doubts and second thoughts throughout his career (that is, after all, an integral part of being an artist). He destroyed or rejected large numbers of his paintings, even though some of them were amongst the best he ever did. Like those discarded works, the 'Crucifixion' did not come up to Bacon's impossibly demanding standards. Having completed the base, he dreamt of a picture beyond anything he had ever accomplished: a Crucifixion at once as grand as an Old Master and as profane as a street hoarding, an image that tore away the false comfort of religion and exposed once more the human condition as it always will be: no more grand or meaningful when crucified than an animal carcass hung in a butcher's shop. That was, of course, *Painting 1946*, a work infinitely more powerful and successful than the 'Three Studies', and Bacon's real first masterpiece – which came about, the artist later said, as 'a series of accidents mounting on top of each other'. For conservation reasons, *Painting 1946* has almost never left its home at the Museum of Modern Art in New York (one of Alfred Barr's most inspired acquisitions, sold to him by Bacon's far-sighted dealer, Erica Brausen, who in her correspondence actually refers to the picture as the 'Crucifixion'). Will anyone ever dare the clash of orange and magenta – the dissonance of a true challenge to accepted belief – and hang *Painting 1946* over the predella? And is it still too early to see in Bacon, the author of abattoir Crucifixions and demented Popes, as the most searchingly religious painter of the twentieth century?[7]

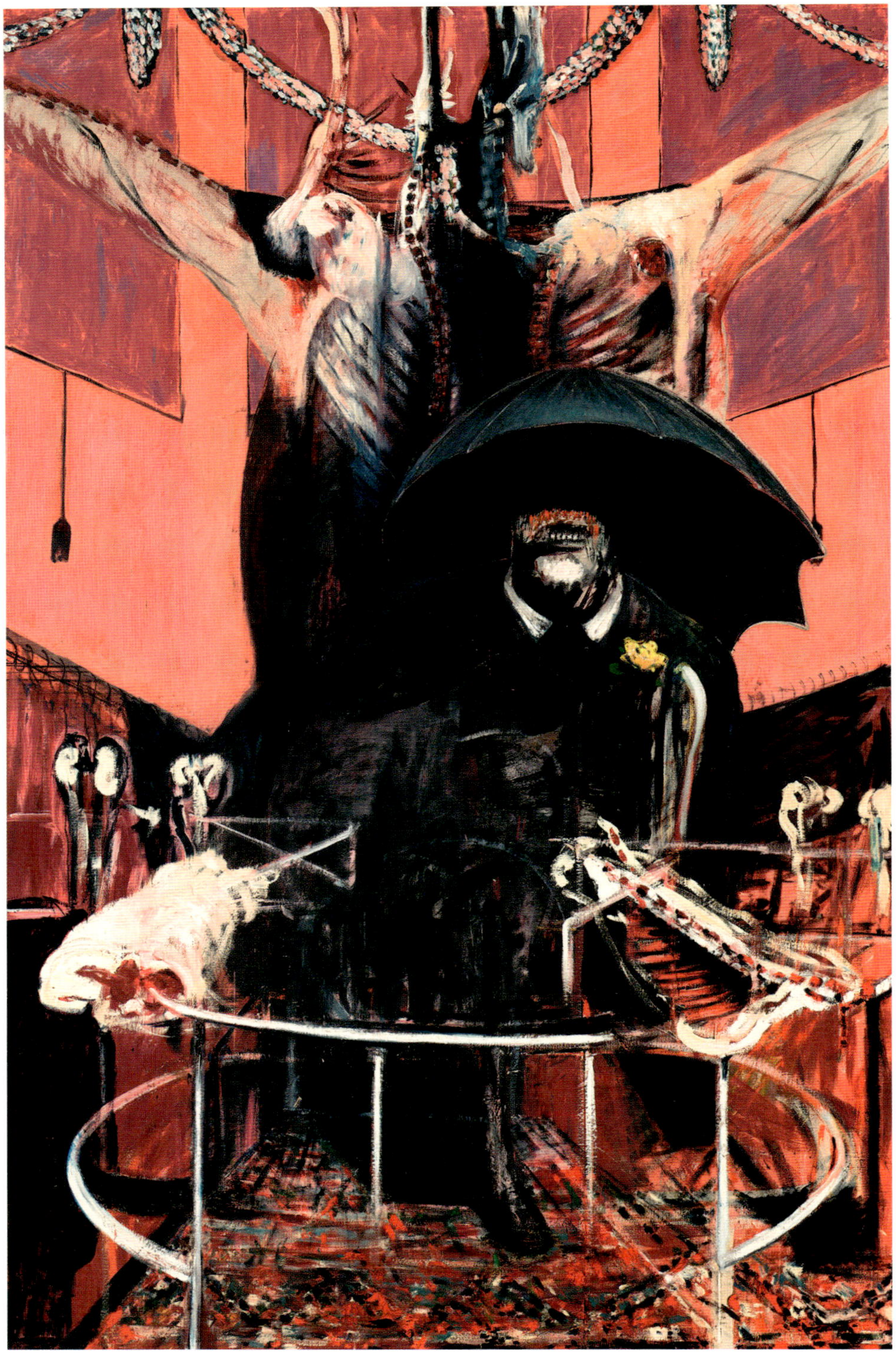

8 Francis Bacon, *Painting 1946*, 1946, 198 × 132 cm, oil and pastel on linen.
Museum of Modern Art, New York.

DRÔLE DE MÉNAGE

One sure explanation for Bacon's ability to make the shift from pale imitation to the first awkward, forceful utterances of his own was that, for the first time since he was ejected from his parents' house, he had found a secure emotional and domestic situation.[8] Comforting as that sounds, it could also hardly have been more bizarre. For years Bacon had been sharing his rackety existence with his old nanny, a spirited and resourceful woman called Jessie Lightfoot, to whom he had always felt closer than to his own mother.[9] Then, of Bacon's many male conquests, one – a prosperous and respectable married man named Eric Hall – decided to set up house with the wayward young artist and his 'nan'. Together they took a lease on the ground-floor flat in what had been the painter John Everett Millais' house in Cromwell Place.[10] At the back of the flat was a large, top-lit space, once used as a billiards room, that would become Bacon's studio. Having visited Bacon there in the late 1940s, the painter Michael Wishart left this evocative description both of the studio and of his friend's style of life at the time:

> The dowdy chintz and velvet sofas and divans with which the cavernous room was sparsely furnished gave it an air of diminished grandeur, a certain forlorn sense of Edwardian splendour in retreat. Later I came to realize that this atmosphere reflected the touch-and-go richesse and weary glamour of those hotels in and around Monte Carlo where Francis had spent so much time during a period of disillusion and self-doubt, during which he painted only sporadically. He was happier among the ghostly clients of the casinos, whose life-styles, conditioned by the crazy whim of a little ball, veer from extravagant opulence to abject poverty. The glimmer of two vast Waterford chandeliers produced the mysterious illumination of the room.[11]

Scandal can never have been far from this curious domestic set-up. Quite apart from the outraged disbelief that Bacon's paintings were beginning to stir up, there was the fact that Hall had abandoned wife and family to live in an openly homosexual relationship – a situation that was hardly made less unorthodox by the presence of an elderly female retainer whose skills included shop-lifting when funds grew low and dispensing regular advice, much appreciated by Bacon, as to which of his many passing gentlemen friends might provide them with the most income.[12] Although painting had now become the focus of Bacon's life, it did not prevent him from throwing wild parties. Michael Wishart captures the whole, rather blasé, post-war spirit of the time when he recalls the party given for his marriage to Anne Dunn in the Cromwell Place studio's faded grandeur:

> We bought two hundred bottles of Bollinger for two hundred people, and soon had to send out for more, as our gate-crashers snowballed. Francis astonished everyone by painting his two large chandeliers crimson, and his face a more delicate colour. I hired a hundred gold chairs and a piano. For three nights and two days we danced. We had two very good pianists.

One was the painter Ruskin Spear, the other our stockbroker Granny Blackett. We knew Granny from the nightclubs where he liked to improvise and sing, in a dated Cowardesque voice, his parodies such as:

> You stepped out of the train
> With your tiara on
> And your mascara on . . .[13]

Deliberately and persistently breaking the rules in life as in art, Bacon also held regular gambling sessions in the studio. Like homosexual relations, gambling was strictly illegal and, if detected, severely punished. When the private casino was in full swing, a few lookouts disguised as house painters, with ladders and buckets, were posted round Cromwell Place to warn Bacon of any possible raid. Nanny Lightfoot came into her own during these gaming sessions, looking after hats and coats and plying the guests with enough food and drink to keep them clustered around the roulette wheel. The venture not only went undetected (due in large part to the mixture of daring, charm and worldly wisdom that Bacon already brought to the management of his chaotic, day-to-day existence); it also brought in substantial takings which helped to finance the young painter's love for champagne, grand hotels and extravagant hospitality. It was, Bacon recalled many years later, 'a lovely life'.

SUNNY PLACES FOR SHADY PEOPLE

Despite the parties and the gambling sessions, postwar London continued to have a pinched and dreary look. Rationing was still in operation, with spam and powdered egg making all too frequent an appearance on the daily menu. Sensuous and greedy, Bacon had always been interested in good food and drink; even at the end of his life, he would remember particularly delicious dishes he had consumed. With Eric Hall as his companion and mentor, Bacon was able to indulge these appetites with greater discernment, since Hall had travelled more widely and become something of an epicure. Both men adored France, and since gambling came high on their list of pleasures, they left London ('so dreary, so dreary,' as Noel Coward sang, 'everything's in grey and brown') as often as they could for the brighter colours and climate of the Côte d'Azur. Taking advantage of the strong pound, the two men made their way along the coast, staying in the best hotels. Bacon's daily life was spartan: up at first light (whatever the carousings of the night before), he went straight to work in a bare, comfortless studio. But when he was not grappling with a new image, he loved to sink into luxury; what attracted him, he told me once, was the distance and contrast between the two. One of his chief delights during these long trips with Hall was to sit in cafés and bars and, as described earlier, watch the antics of other people – above all, the con men, the drifters, the gigolos and heiresses that congregated along the coast. His keen sense of the fundamental futility of life, which he transmitted so powerfully in his paintings, found plenty to feed on. 'The barmen in those places were fascinating,' Bacon reminisced much later:

> They were really like nursemaids. People would come in and draw up a seat and pour their life stories out. And the barmen would keep filling up their glasses and telling them what to do. It was simply mad, and after a while the boredom was so extraordinary you simply sat there and couldn't believe it. And then I remember one woman got so bored she just went up to her room and threw her dog out of the window. Well, it landed on that thing, the awning, below, and somebody had to be sent to rescue it. Everyone loved that, naturally. It gave them something new to talk about and relieved the boredom, just for a moment.[14]

Bacon's real passion, however, was gambling, which meant that once they had played the tables at Nice and Cannes, the two men went straight for Monte Carlo, where the great Belle Epoque casino with its plush, private rooms drew the biggest players and highest stakes. Here Bacon found an ambience, both highly sophisticated and highly artificial, that attracted him so powerfully it became an addiction. He had already enjoyed the mystique of roulette in a variety of casinos, moving expertly from table to table in a kind of trance, placing his jetons very deliberately on an intuitive sequence of numbers and rarely hedging his bets. But in the salons privés the whole ceremony took on a vastly increased allure. Not only was there the elegance of the space and the polished metal rails encircling the roulette tables (a decorative element he had always loved, incorporating similar rails both in his pictures and in the interiors he designed); there was also the magnificent futility of gambling heightened by watching a gorgeous afternoon fade over the Mediterranean – of feeling the artificiality of winning and losing on the spin of a wheel more keenly against the magnificent backdrop of mountainous coast and sea. Bacon approached gambling exactly as he approached painting – as an activity that depended on inspired luck. He was excited by the terrific highs and lows that gambling, like painting, procured. 'You can't understand the tremendous draw gambling has unless you've been in that kind of position where you terribly need money and you manage to get it by gambling,' he told me once, going on to give a memorable vignette of his experiences in Monte Carlo:

> I had a really marvellous win at one point. I was playing on three different tables and I kept thinking I could hear the numbers called out before they came up – as if the croupiers were actually calling them out. I had very little money and I was playing for small stakes. But by the time I'd finished I'd got sixteen hundred pounds, which was a very great deal for me then. And I went out and took a villa and stocked it with food and drink and invited a lot of people to come and live there. . . . I adore the atmosphere of Monte Carlo. It has a kind of grandeur, even if you might call it a grandeur of futility. There's something so beautiful about the view you get from the casino when you look out on to the bay and the curve of the hills

> behind. I love that kind of landscape. That, and just desert. I love the feeling of all that space with nothing in it. It sounds ridiculous, liking a landscape from behind a window, but I actually can't stand the countryside. After a day or two, I long for streets and people and just to be able to walk and see them. . . . Those places like Monte Carlo fascinate me too because of all the odd people who seem to be able to exist there and nowhere else. You know, the curious kinds of doctors with their promises of rejuvenating you who at that time I suppose could only practise in those sorts of places, and all the incredible old women who queue up in the morning for the casino to open.[15]

But the more frivolity seemed to dominate, the more closely Bacon day-dreamed and tracked new images. The fun – whether it was losing sums large enough put him under pressure or participating passively in sadomasochistic sex – actually allowed the paintings to form, like a façade of protective frivolity. Bacon loved extremes: to paint by day and gamble by night kept him in the state of nervous tension that enabled him constantly to push back the boundaries. Only by living and working on the edge, he believed, could he go far enough to innovate; or, as he himself put it, 'you have to go too far to go far enough – only then can you hope to break the mould and make something new.'[16]

In his letters to his friend and dealer Erica Brausen during this period, Bacon describes the delight he found in the Mediterranean landscape and light ('days hot and trembling like the middle of summer'), while making frequent references to the work which, despite the many distractions, he was managing to accomplish. Like his letters to Graham Sutherland in the previous decade (1943–47), Bacon's correspondence with Erica Brausen provides a lively record of his thoughts, plans for pictures and movements throughout the 1950s, charting his progress from his visits to his mother in South Africa to various stays in Monte Carlo, Tangier and the more homely Wivenhoe. These letters, tantalizingly sporadic and fragmentary as they are, form the single best source of written information to have been preserved about Bacon during this key period of his life and work (they are published in full on pp. 141–161).

SNARLING MONKEY, SCREAMING POPE

> I saw him open his mouth wide – it gave him a weirdly voracious aspect, as though he wanted to swallow all the air, all the earth, all the men before him.
>
> Joseph Conrad, *Heart of Darkness*

Although Bacon found the pleasures too intense and the light too bright to paint successfully in the various villas and hotel rooms, that he, Eric Hall and Nan Lightfoot occupied at different moments in and around Monte Carlo, haunting images had been building up in the artist's

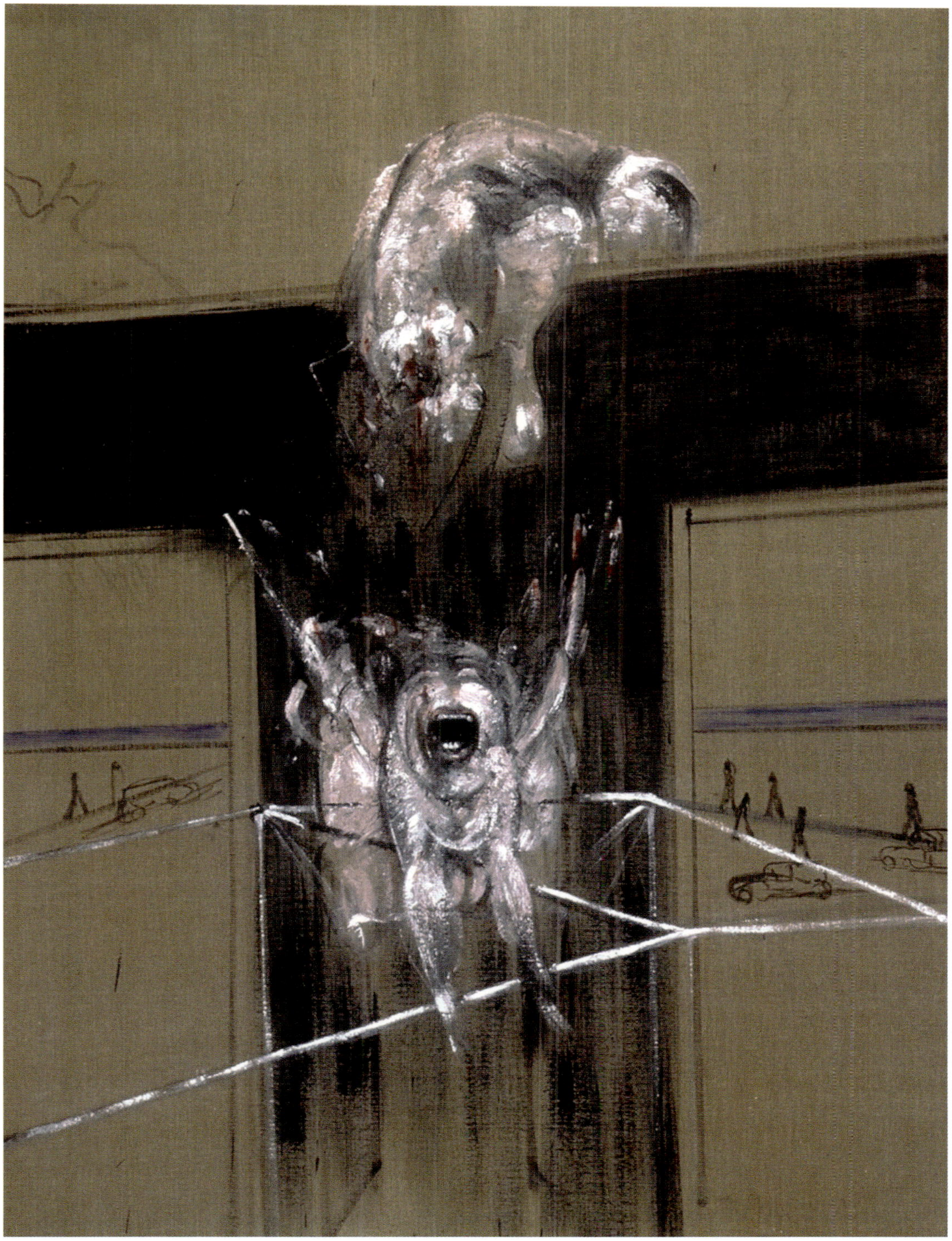

9 *Fragment of a Crucifixion*, 1950, 140 × 108.5 cm, oil and cotton wool on canvas.
Collection Van Abbe Museum, Einchoven.

imagination. He would have tried them out frequently in rooms darkened against the Mediterranean sun, only to destroy them or simply leave them behind. (Around this time, when he began painting on the rough, unprimed side of the canvas, Bacon would give batches of these discarded paintings to artist friends to use for their own work; not surprisingly, most of these canvases were preserved for their own sake and have since reappeared on the market.)[17] Bacon strongly believed that images were 'handed' to him ready-made; that he only had to day-dream to get 'one image after another dropping into my mind like slides'. And when he returned to the relative calm and stability of the Cromwell Place ménage, the images would tumble out of him in a 'furor pingendi' that enabled him in concentrated bouts of work to complete a picture within a couple of days, even though (and on rare lucky occasions, because) he might be too drunk or emotionally disturbed to function coherently. It was in this way that Bacon's masterpieces of the late 1940s and early 1950s were produced: through constant trial and error, elation and destruction, technical awkwardness absorbed and made suddenly effective by sheer force of invention. With the imagery built up from this inner pressure, it is no wonder that almost all the heads, both of man and monkey, are open-mouthed with the sudden release. In one fell swoop, by focussing on what was most animal in man – the primal scream – Bacon had found the single image which was to define his vision.

The open mouth became central to Bacon's iconography from very early on; in some of his first, recorded paintings – notably *Abstraction from the Human Form*, dated *c.*1936 – it already has a distinct presence, although the subject is more a precise delineation of lips and teeth rather than the representation of a scream.[18] By the early 1950s, however, it had become obsessive, dominating all other concerns; and it would be no exaggeration to say that, if one could really explain the origins and implications of this scream, one would be far closer to understanding the whole meaning of Bacon's art. Was it linked to his own desperate, open-mouthed struggle to breathe as a chronic asthmatic, brought up in a household filled with just the right amounts of horse and dog hair to trigger off regular attacks? And did this early fixation on the open mouth draw Bacon quite naturally to the screams in Poussin's *Massacre of the Innocents* and Eisenstein's *Battleship Potemkin* as well as to a study of diseases of the mouth, delicately reproduced in hand-coloured plates in a clinical manual which Bacon purchased as a young man in Paris and kept thereafter as a source book in his studio? Was his fascination with the mouth ('the beautiful colours of the mouth and the glitter of the teeth') sexual, as he slyly suggested in an aside in his interviews with David Sylvester (but which Sylvester never followed up)? Was it a revolt against the conventions of his upper-class, Anglo-Irish upbringing, with their partitioning of life into what was and what was not done? Or a revolt against the father, the strict, tough and good-looking Captain Eddy Bacon, formerly of the Durham Light Infantry and, throughout Francis's youth, a horse-trainer with a weakness for military discipline at home and highly polished boots abroad? Or indeed, as the roar from the open mouth grew louder and more fearless, against all father figures?

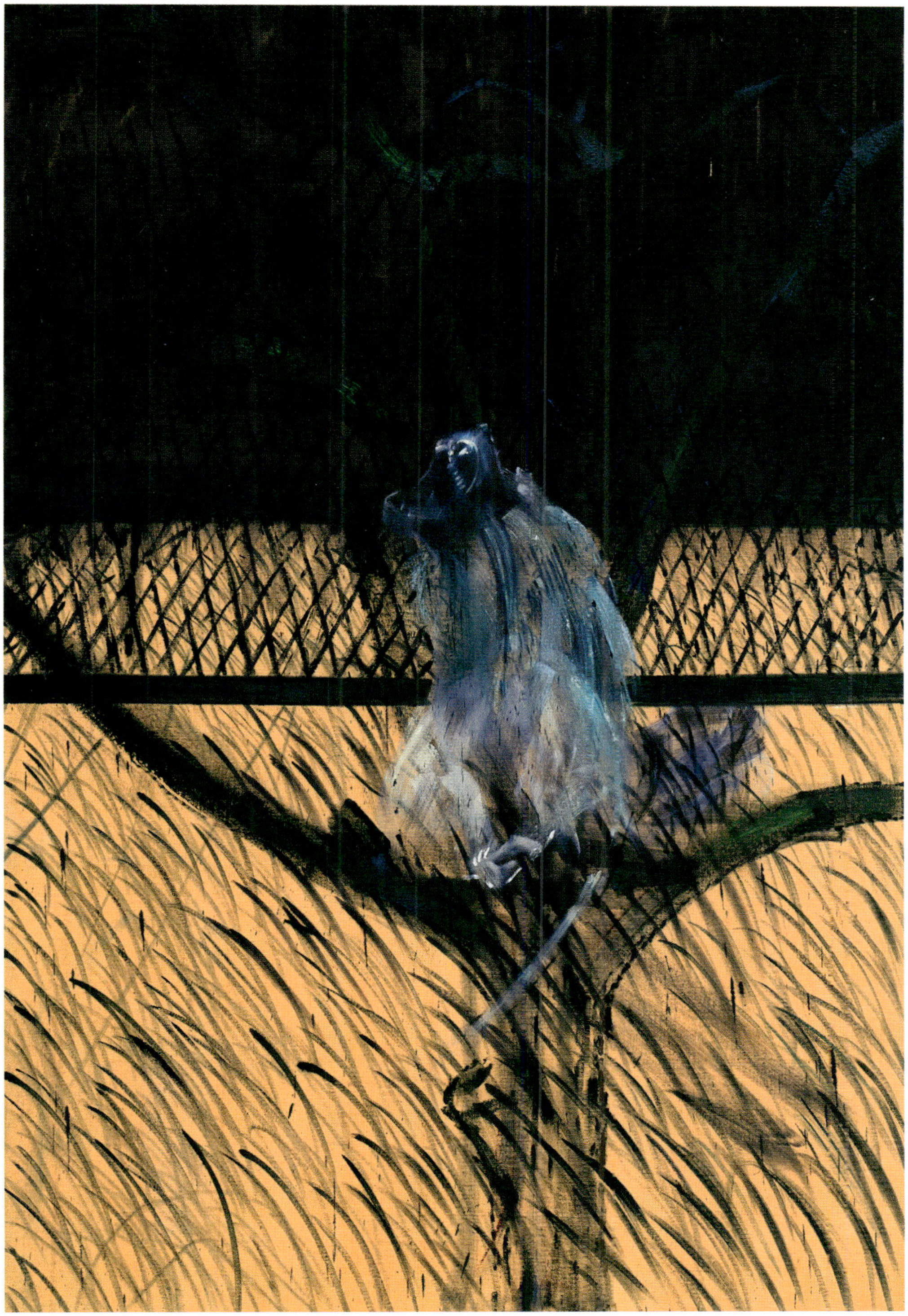

10 *Study of a Baboon*, 1953, 198.3 × 137.3 cm, oil on canvas. Museum of Modern Art, New York. James Thrall Soby Bequest.

As he grew towards manhood, Bacon was catapulted into a world where all the sons worth their salt were rising up against their fathers' generation and the catastrophes following the First World War. Bacon's genius was to have found a single image through which he could express the whole range of his most extreme emotions: fear, disdain, hate, lust and even a fierce kind of love. Although he shunned the hunt (thereby earning his sportsman father's disappointment and scorn) and avoided all contact with domestic animals, being only too conscious of how swiftly both triggered off an acute asthma attack, Bacon remained fascinated by animals. One of the reasons he visited his mother – first in 1950, then in 1952 and 1957 – in her new surroundings in South Africa was because he wanted to watch and to photograph the wild life, notably in the Kruger National Park. 'I felt and memorized the excitement of seeing animals move through the long grass', Bacon declared on his return: and out of these trips came several memorable animal and landscape pictures, notably *Elephant Fording a River* (see CAT 12) and *Rhinoceros*, also painted in 1952 and shown in Bacon's third exhibition at the Hanover Gallery later that year.[19] What interested Bacon most about watching animals was that he could see 'instinct' – the primal impulses and reactions shared with human beings – clearly at work, and not disguised by the veneers of civilization. This key notion in Bacon's art, that man is an animal, was explored in numerous paintings throughout the 1950s in which humans and monkeys are depicted as interchangeable, if not almost indistinguishable: both imprisoned in dark cages with their mouths opened in screams.

Whether in man or monkey, the scream was the moment of truth, the moment at which all pretence and false-seeming fall away. This goes to the heart of what Bacon strived to achieve: to remove the layers of convention and camouflage by which he believed we all live and reveal the basic and unalterable facts of existence. However he himself camouflaged his purpose, affecting a dandyish *désinvolture* and proclaiming that his art 'meant' nothing, Bacon was driven to proclaim this truth again and again. Ultimately, it was the subject of every picture he made, and he once touched (very lightly) on this essential point when he said: 'We nearly always live through screens – a screened existence. And I sometimes think, when people say my work looks violent, that perhaps I have from time to time been able to clear away one or two of the veils or screens.'[20]

Having established this disturbing parity between man and animal, Bacon vastly increased the stakes when, in place of the anonymous heads, he first enclosed the screaming features within the paraphernalia of the Pope. This one transformation shows Bacon's genius more sheerly than any other. To have commingled jungle cry and medical malformation, the dictator's harangue and the lover's orgasmic release, Poussin and Eisenstein in one image already constituted a remarkable imaginative feat, a big, subtly layered metaphor with multiple associations. But the real master stroke was to hit as high up on the human scale as it was possible to go, incorporating into this monstrous hybrid not only Velázquez but all the implications of the Supreme Pontiff on his throne. In any one period, there are only a finite number of images with

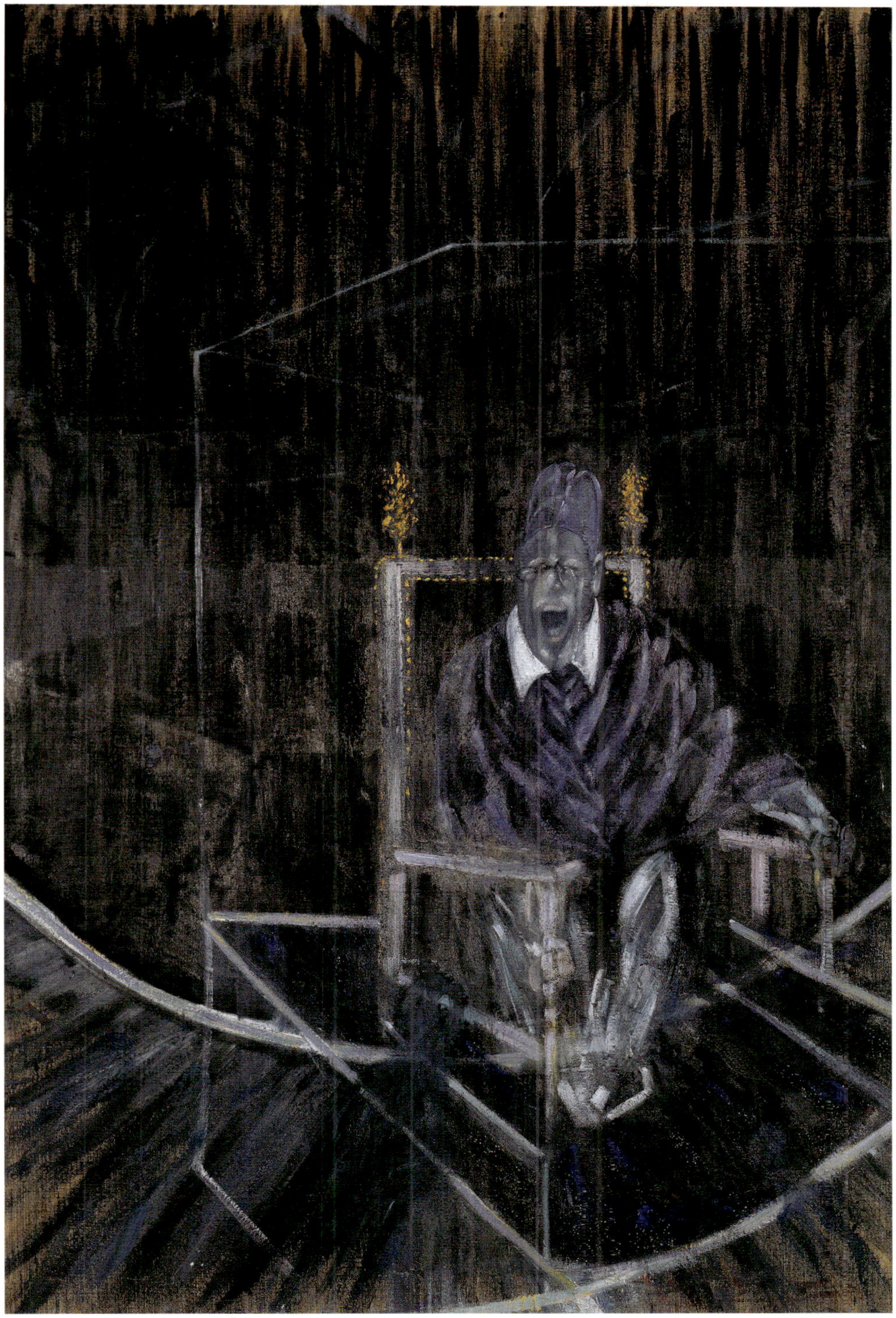

11 *Pope II*, 1951, 198 × 137 cm, oil on canvas. Kunsthalle, Mannheim.

almost limitless connotations. In our time, along perhaps with Picasso's *Demoiselles d'Avignon*, Duchamp's *Le Grand Verre* and a Giacometti *Femme debout*, Bacon's *Popes* are not only the centrepiece of all his paintings in the 1950s but a centrepiece of the whole of twentieth-century art.

There could be – and in time there no doubt will be – a book-length study devoted entirely to Bacon's *Popes*. The theme dominated Bacon's imagination throughout the decade and beyond, with the result that he did no fewer than fifty variations on Velázquez's great *Portrait of Pope Innocent X*. Having at last found his subject par excellence, the one image in which he could sum up so many others, Bacon appeared not to want to relinquish it, as if there were still more paraphrases to bring to the surface before he had managed to get the theme fully out of his system. Ironically, the footnote to this obsession was that when he eventually visited Rome, Bacon declined to go to the Palazzo Doria Pamphilii (where the picture still hangs today) claiming that he was too embarrassed to look at it after all the 'stupid' things he had done to it; he also cited his emotional dramas with Peter Lacy as overshadowing their whole time in Rome. The truth is both simpler and more telling: Bacon did not want to see the original picture because he found reproductions, being already at one remove from reality, more manipulable and therefore closer to his purpose. As a seasoned gambler, Bacon was not likely to put his winning streak at risk by such a simple-minded eyeball-to-eyeball at the shrine.

One other characteristic of Bacon's *Popes* that is too rarely considered is how exquisitely they are painted. All the sound and fury that ushers them in, from the profanation of the papal image and the ransacking of a great Velázquez to the cry emanating from what should be the ultimate orifice of traditional authority and calm, easily allows one to overlook the technical brilliance from which these images derive their power. One need only look at the delicacy with which the gold finials are fashioned on the papal throne, or the milky translucence of the pontiff's lower garments (other associations entering here), or the painterly elegance of the pleated curtains that create the backdrop to the fiercely projected, almost disembodied scream.

NO FIXED ABODE

It would be reassuring to imagine that these provocative images were recollected in the relative tranquillity provided by the Cromwell Place studio; that in the all too evident turmoil of his life the artist had a secure place to paint. But for Bacon, a man now in his early forties, that cosy arrangement with Nan and Eric – a chosen second mother and father – had never been likely to last. Bacon's innate independence and his affairs with other men (whom Nan chose for him) had doubtless eroded the relationship with Hall. But what killed off the ménage, brutally and definitively, was the death in April 1951 of Jessie Lightfoot. Michael Wishart, in his memoirs, recalls Bacon's grief at her death being so intense ('Francis looked as if he wanted to die') that

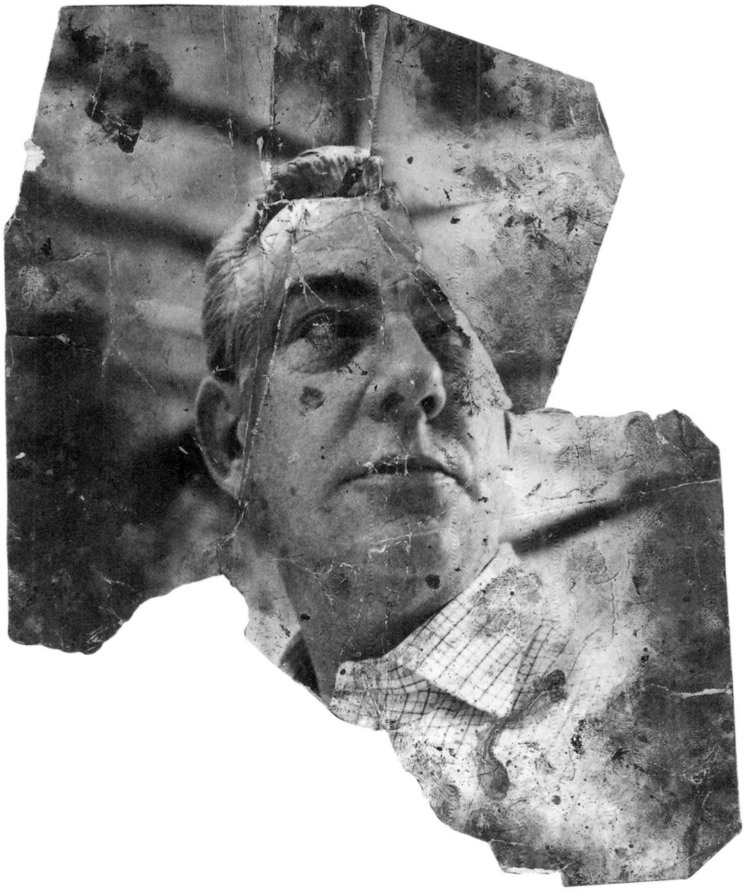

12 Studio document. Peter Lacy, late 1950s–early 1960s, photo: John Deakin. Dublin City Gallery, The Hugh Lane.

he wondered whether she had not, in fact, been his real mother. Highly unlikely though this is, Bacon was certainly more attached to his old nurse, who had shared his life so fully, than to his whole family. Devastated by the loss and possibly filled with guilt because he had been away gambling in Monte Carlo when she died, Bacon underwent a complete crisis: he terminated the relationship with Hall, sold the remaining lease on the Cromwell Place studio to a fellow-painter and began living from room to room, never staying in any one place for long.[21] Although he talked freely about the misfortunes of his life, Bacon very rarely mentioned this period or Jessie's death, possibly because it remained more private and more painful even than Peter Lacy's death a decade later.

Bacon's footloose existence lasted for several years, taking him through numerous makeshift arrangements. After an initial stay at Carlyle Studios just off the King's Road, Bacon moved to a room not far away at 6 Beaufort Gardens. Then, improbably enough, he rented a country cottage outside Henley-on-Thames and subsequently took a room at the Imperial Hotel in Henley itself, before returning to the Kensington and Chelsea area (which he rarely forsook while living in London), first to a house by the Thames at 9 Apollo Place, where the critic David Sylvester was also living, then briefly to lodgings at 19 Cromwell Road almost overlooking the old haunt he had shared with Eric and his nan. This odyssey was completed by stays in a flat off Sloane Square and a studio in nearby Mallord Street. The wanderings were not limited to England, however. There were also trips to South Africa and Rome, then, more and more frequently through the second half of the 1950s, to Tangier. And it was not until 1955 that Bacon came to have some semblance of a semi-permanent address when he moved into the flat shared by his friends, Peter Pollock and Paul Danquah, at Overstrand Mansions in Battersea, where he stayed and worked, at least intermittently, until 1961.

Curiously, these constant migrations and the upheavals caused by his new lover, Peter Lacy, did not prevent Bacon from working. It may be the prerogative of genius to find stimulation in adversity, order in chaos or whatever other dissonant coupling, but in the midst of this peripatetic existence, bedevilled by more gambling debts, homosexual bust-ups and other chaos than we will ever know, Bacon produced some of the most haunting images of his entire career – while destroying or abandoning many more. Unlike a writer, who can work with paper and pencil on a café table or in a train, a painter has an absolute need of space, light and an array of materials. Bacon improvised. He taught briefly at the Royal College of Art (while his friend, the artist John Minton, was travelling abroad) and managed to fit in some painting while he was there.[22] Later, another friend, the painter Rodrigo Moynihan, lent him his own studio at the College; from time to time, other acquaintances obliged. Whenever he did work, Bacon painted at considerable speed, usually to produce new canvases for a show that was imminent; then, as later, he reckoned that if a painting was going to come off at all, it would come quickly and decisively. His working pattern, particularly during the early and mid-1950s, was erratic: he would 'drift' (to use the term he favoured) for weeks on end without a painting routine, then shut himself away for a while and work more or less non-stop. Bacon needed the spur of a new show not only to oblige him to supply the promised number of works, but also to prevent him from destroying a large part of his production.

The Hanover Gallery, which laid the foundations of Bacon's success both in London and abroad, pressed him regularly for a new exhibition; and much of the artist's work to have survived from the 1950s was made in response to the gallery's demands.[23] Bacon tended to work right up to the last moment, so much so, that when he exhibited his first Popes, two of them were delivered still wet to the Hanover just before the show opened. Bacon and Brausen had a closer relationship than most artists have with their dealers. The fact that both were homosexual was one bond, but the friendship was based on an appreciation of each other's qualities.

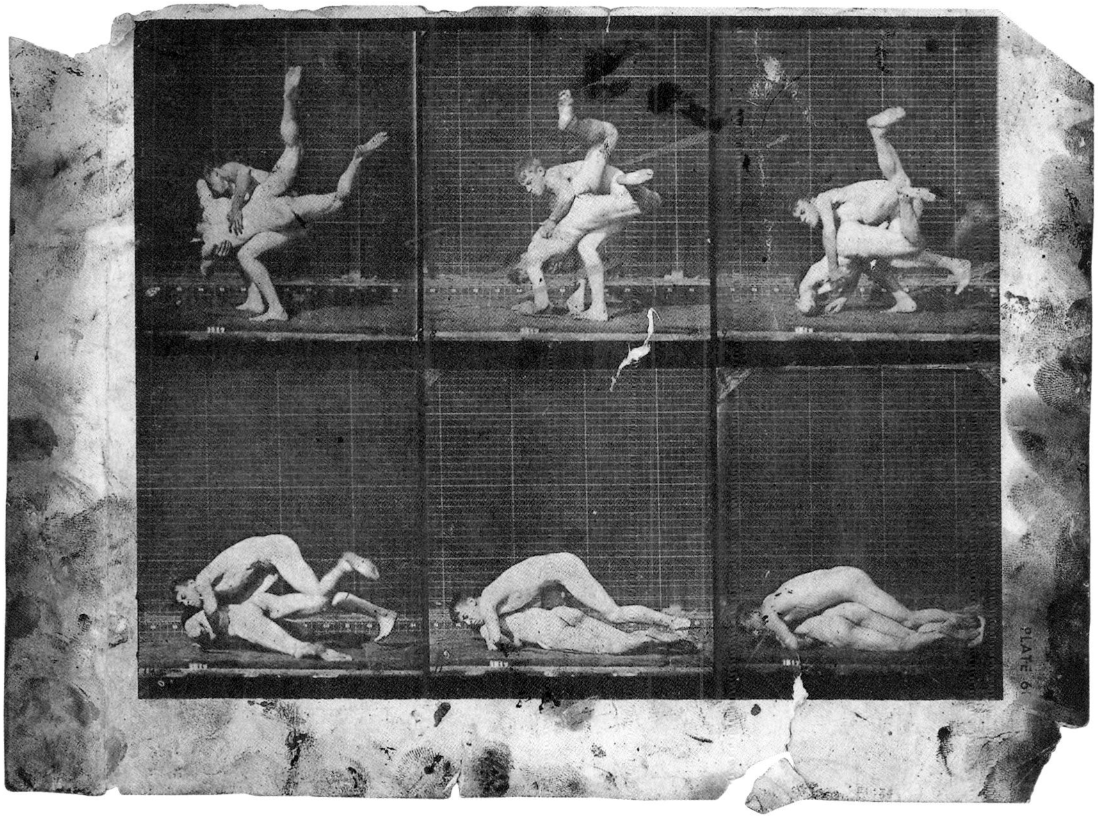

13 Studio document. Leaf from Eadweard Muybridge, *The Human Figure in Motion* (Philadelphia 1887, London 1901). Dublin City Gallery, The Hugh Lane.

Brausen was the first dealer to realize just how unusual a person and how outstanding an artist Bacon was, and she risked her gallery's slender means on supporting him at a time when his work was considered virtually unsellable. For his part, Bacon liked Brausen's cosmopolitan background, her independence and, of course, her willingness to take a gamble on him. The relationship was frequently tense, however. In addition to having to hang wet pictures just as an exhibition opened, Brausen found herself on the receiving end of images so potentially scandalous that she feared – realistically enough, given the laws and the moral attitudes of the 1950s – a police raid. Thus, although she was courageous enough to accept Bacon's highly homoerotic *Two Figures* of 1953 as part of an exhibition, she half-hid it away on the mezzanine floor of the gallery. (That particular work was inspired by Muybridge's photographs of naked wrestlers, which prompted Bacon to remark to me later: 'the thing is, unless you look at those Muybridge figures with a magnifying glass, it's very difficult to see whether they're wrestling or having sex.')[24]

Brausen also helped establish Bacon on the international scene. In 1953, Bacon was given his first show outside London, at Durlacher Bros in New York. This exhibition of thirteen canvases, mostly painted within weeks of being shipped, laid the foundation for Bacon's reputation in the US since several notable collectors bought works. Seymour Knox presented his *Man with Dog* to the Albright-Knox Art Gallery in Buffalo, while William Burden and his wife gave *Study for Portrait VII* to the Museum of Modern Art in New York; later it also received the magnificent 'Baboon' which the influential art critic, James Thrall Soby, had acquired at the time. In the following year, Bacon was invited, with Ben Nicholson and Lucian Freud, to represent Great Britain at the Venice Biennale. The Tate lent its 'Three Studies' of 1944 and *Figure in a Landscape*, to which were added *Pope I* and *Pope II* of 1951 and the very recent *Three Studies of the Human Head* and *Sphinx* of 1954, so that this showing at the British Pavilion amounted to Bacon's first, albeit minor, retrospective.

Other foreign shows took place later in the decade at the Galerie Rive Droite in Paris, the Galleria Galatea in Turin, the Galleria dell'Ariete in Milan and l'Obelisco in Rome, thereby initiating the fascination with Bacon's work that continued to thrive thereafter in both France and Italy – the two countries that responded to Bacon's achievement first and, in many respects, most perceptively.[25] Nearer home, Bacon's career underwent a very positive change, and his life a visible improvement, when two of England's most prominent collectors, Bob and Lisa Sainsbury, began to take an interest in his work. Bacon had already enjoyed a certain amount of patronage, but never on the level that the Sainsburys provided. His work had come to their attention via Erica Brausen, of whom they were already clients. Their relationship began when Lisa commissioned Bacon to do a portrait of her husband. Lisa then sat to Bacon (she was one of the last people to do so before Bacon decided he would only work from photographs of his sitters); and no fewer than eight portraits of her got under way, three of which survive. Many years later, Lisa Sainsbury remembers these sittings, and the conversations before and after them, with particular pleasure because she and Bacon developed a very lively friendship, full of mutual confidences and amusing gossip. Not the least benefit for Bacon from this relationship was the fact that, throughout a period when he was constantly short of money, the Sainsburys first advanced him cash, then guaranteed an overdraft on his bank account. Over the following few years, several other Bacon works were acquired – some bought, others gifts from the artist – until the Sainsburys owned no fewer than thirteen works.

A GILDED-GUTTER LIFE

For all the rootlessness and confusion that trailed Bacon throughout the first half of the 1950s, his career seems to have progressed as if it had a life of its own. Despite the obvious disadvantage of not having a permanent studio where he could build up a momentum of work, for instance, he managed in the course of 1953 to produce over twenty pictures (or considerably more, if one counts the works destroyed) in an *annus mirabilis* as inventive as it was prolific. It was a year that began with the exquisite, small *Study of a Nude* (now in the Sainsbury collection), then included all eight Papal studies for portraits, the sublimely sensuous *Two Figures* as well as a couple of haunting Sphinxes, and ended on a series of magnificent screaming heads. In the following two years he produced several masterpieces, including *Figure with Meat*, giving rise to the inevitable question: if Bacon was so distraught and subjected to such insecurity, flitting from debt to debt, digs to digs, how did he find the inner resource to drag these terrifying and majestic images up from a dark, tortured psyche into the light of day? I think that in his very nature – in what he would have called his 'instinct' – Bacon was made up of extremes and was driven to seek them out, living between order and chaos, luxury and penury, brilliant success and crushing defeat; and only in those circumstances, when his whole being was on the rack and stretched to an extent most of us would find unbearable, could he in fact obey the dictates of his inner demon.

Similarly, there was another deep and apparently unbridgeable contradiction between this creator of terrifying images, a drunken, farded sodomite swaying nocturnally through the lowest dives and gambling dens of Soho, and the debonair charmer who made 'séduire, c'est tout' his motto, blending effortlessly with the most exalted social circles. Again, it was the contrast of extremes. There was nothing Bacon enjoyed so much and handled so well as leaving a gang of toughs he had got drunk with in an East End pub to have tea in a Knightsbridge drawing-room or dinner with collectors at the Ritz. He might relish the atmosphere of grand restaurants, treating his friends to caviar and Krug when he could least afford it, but when he went 'home' he was confronted by a comfortless mess in a temporary space. He might cut himself off for days, seeing no one and leaving the telephone unanswered, then reappear as the most gregarious man in London, with friends at every level of society, and often in the most surprising places. A variety of new bars and private drinking clubs opened during the 1950s, especially in Soho, and Bacon became a veritable Virgil in these infernal regions, since he habitually stayed out until very late at night and loved to drift from one curious and often illicit establishment to another. Some of these clubs, which were essentially backrooms fitted with a bar, catered specifically to homosexuals and had cosy names like the 'Piano Bar' or the 'Maisonette'. Others, like the Colony Room (also known as Muriel's, after its formidable proprietress, Muriel Belcher), attracted a wide mix of artists, writers, Soho characters and other oddballs; it was here that Bacon earned a useful ten pounds a week for bringing in his many acquaintances and other punters to spend their money at the bar; it was also here, fatefully, that he met the greatest and most disastrous love of his life, Peter Lacy. One of the club's writer-members, Colin MacInnes, caught the peculiar, Soho seediness of Muriel's (which he calls 'Mabel's') in his novel, 'England, Half English':

> To sit in Mabel's, with the curtains drawn at 4pm on a sunny afternoon, sipping expensive poison and gossiping one's life away, has the futile fascination of forbidden fruit: the heady

> intoxication of a bogus Baudelairian evil. As the gin slips down your throat, and the dim electrics shine on the potted plants and on Mabel's lurid colour scheme of emerald green and gold, you feel like the fish in the tank above the cash-register – swimming aimlessly among artificial water weeds, mindless in warm water.[26]

If the Colony Room was one essential port of call for Bacon, the Gargoyle Club was the other. Designed by Henri Matisse, with countless pieces of antique glass set in the walls and a sweeping gold and silver staircase, the Gargoyle was the place where everybody who was anybody in the arts or in upper-class bohemia would meet to drink, dance and generally 'carry on', from Dylan Thomas to Jean-Paul Sartre, Augustus John to Tallula Bankhead. It was 'a place made for rows', Bacon claimed years later, and as a hawk-eyed observer of human passions, he adored the nightly parade of intrigue and jealousy, caught and reflected round the room from a thousand fragmented mirrors.

But, in one further contradiction (the stuff, ultimately, out of which both Bacon's life and his art were woven), while Bacon seemed to everybody in the bars and restaurants of Soho to be carousing every day until the small hours, he was in fact painting hard, usually from first light until noon, while his fellow-revellers lay comatose in bed. Moreover, since he was singularly articulate and quick to turn a memorable phrase, Bacon began to be interviewed and to be asked to condense his thoughts about art. In 1953 John Rothenstein, then Director of the Tate Gallery, had the inspired idea of getting him to write a tribute to Matthew Smith, whose painting he knew Bacon admired, for the catalogue of a retrospective of Smith's work. Not surprisingly, the text turned out to be more illuminating about Bacon's own approach to art; and it can be reread today as the artist's first 'manifesto'.[27] For Bacon was conscious of the need to place his work – which was still the preserve of a small circle of connoisseurs and admirers – in a wider, more comprehensible context. Subsequently, he also availed himself of the chance to put forward his views in an 'Artist's Statement' in a catalogue published in 1955 by the Museum of Modern Art in New York.[28]

A number of influential writers had already been won over to Bacon's cause, nevertheless. Wyndham Lewis had led the way with a review of the artist's first show at the Hanover Gallery that was so far-seeing it can still be read with benefit today.[29] Robert Melville, David Sylvester, John Russell and several other prominent critics wrote remarkably perceptive texts throughout the decade on an artist whose work could be counted on to raise hackles or meet with blank incomprehension even in the most cultivated circles in Britain of the 1950s. Sensing that Bacon was in many ways his own most illuminating commentator, Sylvester began a series of fascinating interviews with Bacon which, once completed, were to become the official source for future interpretations of his work; they were a huge success, with Graham Greene putting them on a par with Delacroix's 'Journal'. For all his nightly roistering and dubious dalliance, Bacon's sense of purpose had never wavered. Having painted the pictures, he also supplied the glossary by which they could be explained. The practitioner had become his own theorist, the oracle its own interpreter.

FATHER FIGURES

Bacon thus proved as skilful in talking about his pictures as he was in painting them. He knew how to give out just enough information to make the work more vivid, intensifying its allusiveness as well as the impenetrability of its enigma (of which the material correlative is the Old Master gilt framing and the glazing he insisted his paintings should have). He talked to scores of critics and journalists, philosophers and film-makers, in English and in French, drunk or sober, but he always talked around his work, brilliantly and evocatively, thus avoiding the most leading and lasting questions. When asked about the cry that resounds through his painting as its central theme, its leitmotif, Bacon evaded the point disarmingly by saying he had really wanted to paint the smile but failed, or that he had always been attracted by the beautiful colours of the mouth.

It is curious that while Bacon's two acknowledged sources for the scream are women (the mother in Poussin's *Massacre of the Innocents* and the nurse in Eisenstein's *Battleship Potemkin*), it is, in Bacon's own work, men who scream (the only exception being precisely *Study for the Nurse in the Film 'Battleship Potemkin'*, 1957). It is also interesting to note that, while the two women are screaming over the loss of a child, Bacon's protagonists are screaming for no apparent reason; often boxed in and pressed up against the picture plane, they are screaming in a tight, airless void. It may be, as we have seen, that this asphyxiated sensation is directly connected to Bacon's own chronic asthma and to the way, during a bad attack, he had to fight to get breath; or related, as Bacon himself suggests in an interview, to the sexual implications of the open mouth; and of course it refers quite explicitly, in certain works featuring two figures, to the release of orgasm.[30]

But this cry, which echoes from one end of Bacon's work in the 1950s to the other, must have had its origin in some specific experience, even if it was to take on all kinds of other associations subsequently. The rages of Captain Bacon, terrorizing the household with his outbursts and barked-out, military-style orders, may well have been the source. Bacon père had died in 1940, but memories of his threatening, tyrannical presence would not have faded, all the more so because, as Francis freely admitted, the brutal Captain had been the first man to arouse his sexual feelings.[31] Other implications immediately crowd in if one accepts the apocryphal story of the father's having had his asthmatic son horse-whipped by the stud-farm grooms.[32] Would this experience – pain and humiliation that led to an exquisite release – not have awakened the sadomasochism that later defined Bacon's sexuality; and was he not thereafter forever in search

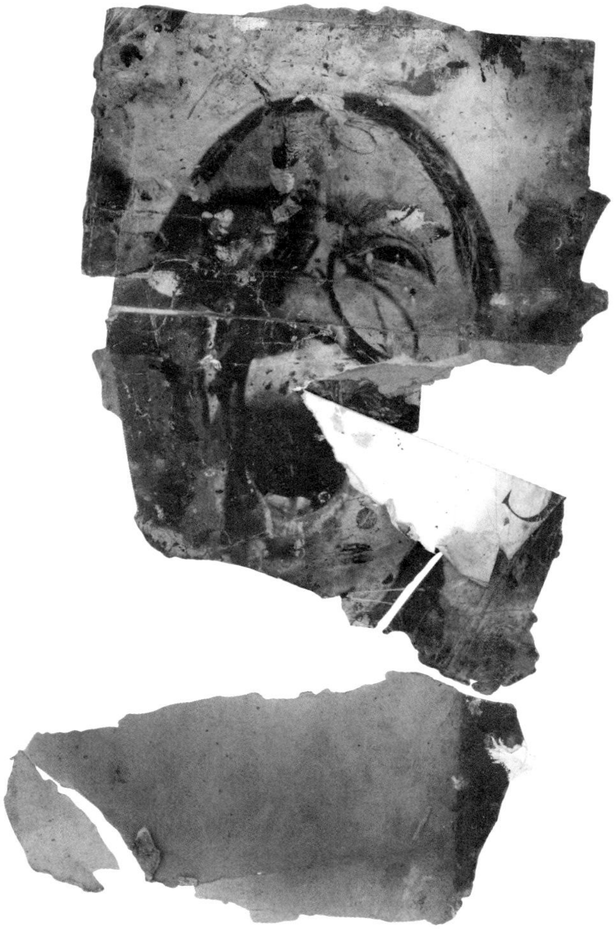

14 Studio document. Black-and-white illustration of the screaming nurse in Eisenstein's film *Battleship Potemkin*. Dublin City Gallery, The Hugh Lane.

of a 'cruel father'? It was this instinctive quest to return to the origin of so much pain mixed with pleasure that must have led him to Velázquez's masterly portrait of Innocent X, an image that had such an inexplicable hold over him that he once likened it to the crush a schoolboy might have on an older pupil. The Pope, whether commemorated in the great Renaissance portraits or shown being borne aloft in a sedia gestatoria above the crowds around St Peter's in more contemporary photographs, was of course the supreme temporal authority – the ultimate Papa. In many of Bacon's Popes one may find the heavy, brooding face of his own father; overlaid or mixed in (as so many elements and memory traces are in Bacon's images) one may also detect the rather brutal features of Peter Lacy, the man whom Bacon loved most because he made him suffer more than any other.

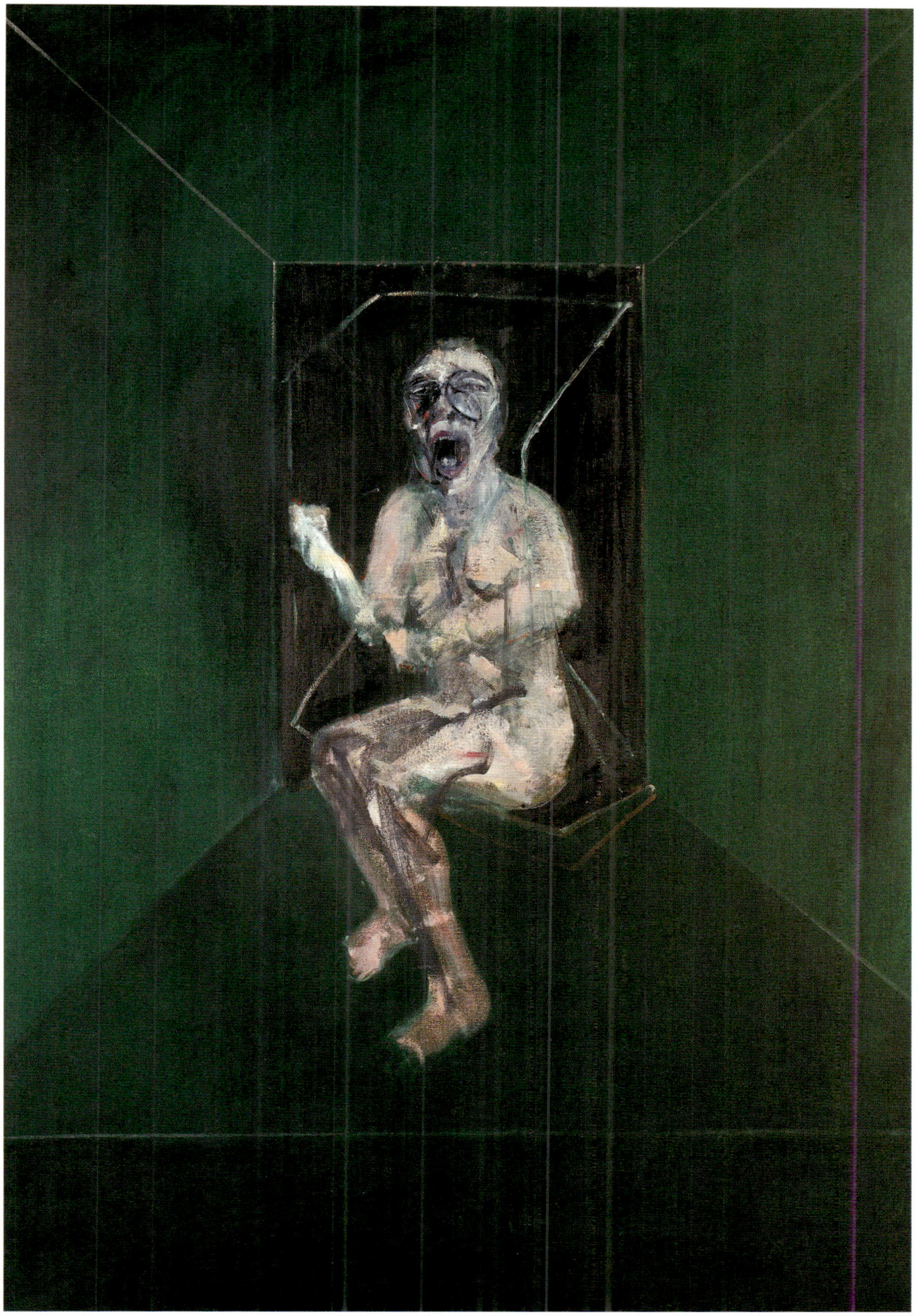

15 *Study for the Nurse in the Film 'Battleship Potemkin'*, 1957, 198 × 142 cm, oil on canvas.
Städelsches Kunstinstitut, Frankfurt-am-Main.

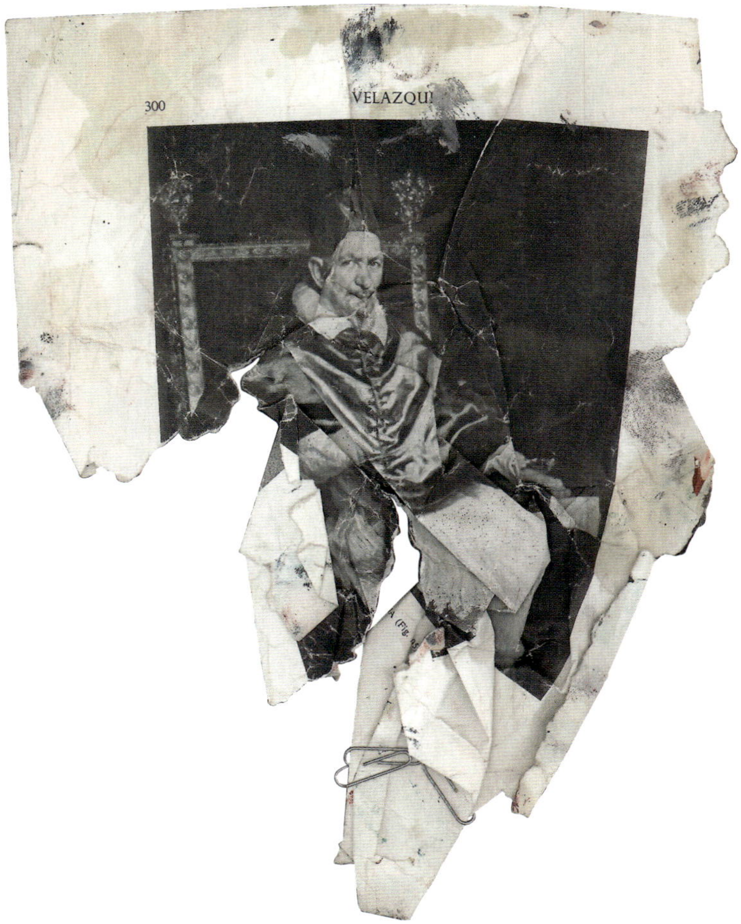

16 Studio document. Illustration of Velázquez's *Portrait of Pope Innocent X*, 1650. Leaf from unidentified book. Dublin City Gallery, The Hugh Lane.

Father figures of one kind or another dominated Bacon's sexual and emotional life until he himself was well into middle age. It was as though, having been banished from home by his father at the age of sixteen, he felt impelled to restore the original relationship, however traumatic, with an older man. With the 'uncle' who took him to Berlin very soon thereafter, Bacon succeeded briefly: as tough and unsentimental as his own father, the man took him to his bed (a sumptuous four-poster affair in the Hotel Adlon), then left him to make his own way through the capital's array of erotic satisfactions. Bacon soon realised that by offering himself as a 'companion' to older men, he could survive virtually anywhere. Thus began a lifelong pattern of 'drifting', as he put it, 'from bar to bar, and from person to person'. Beneath the drifting, how-

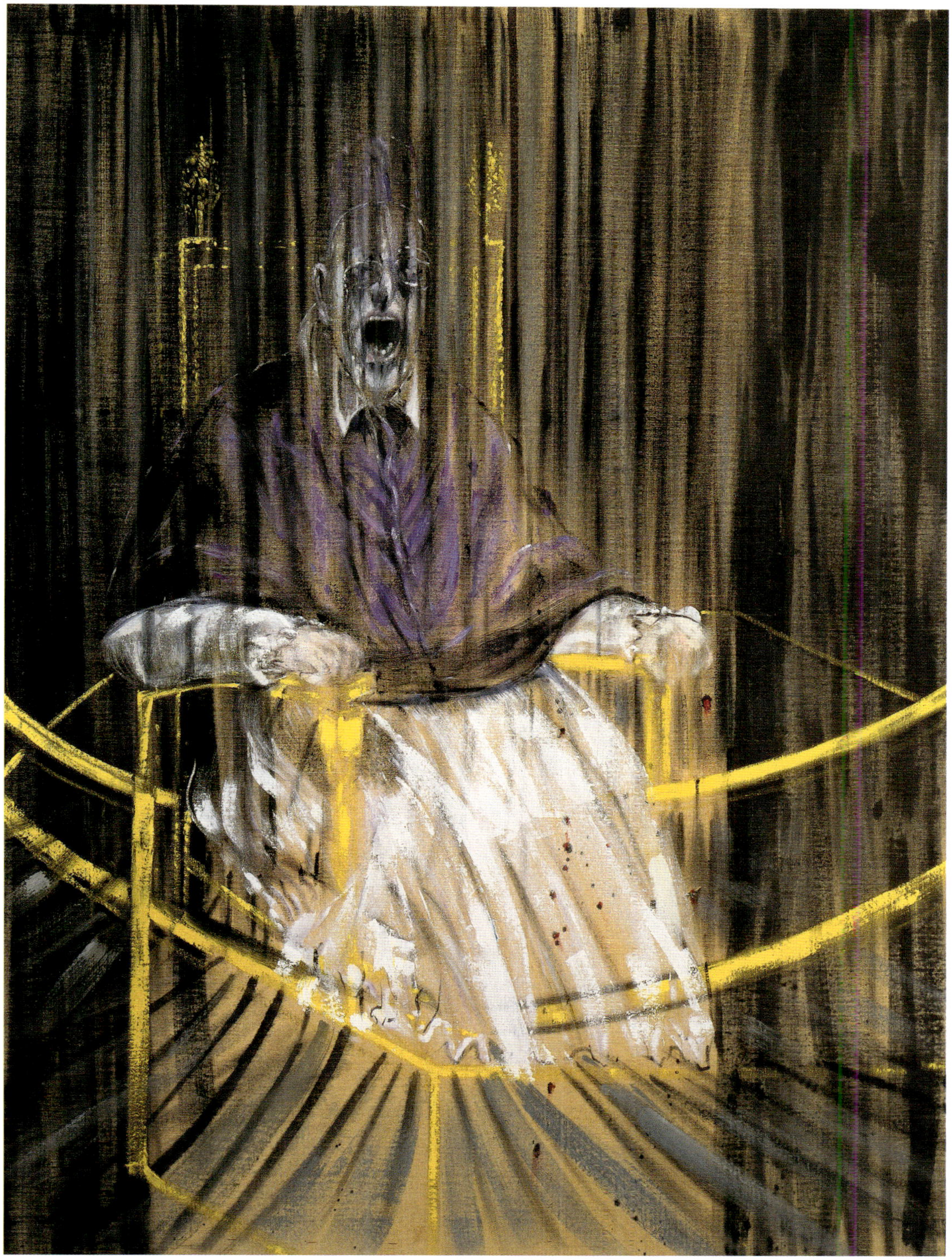

17 *Study after Velázquez's Portrait of Pope Innocent X*, 1953, 153 × 118 cm, oil on canvas.
Des Moines Art Center. Purchased with funds from the Coffin Fine Arts Trust;
Nathan Emory Coffin Collection of the Des Moines Art Center.

ever, there was a powerful sense of vocation; and gradually Bacon began to develop relationships with older men who could help him specifically to pursue his career. From Roy de Maistre, the Australian artist, he absorbed in no time the basic knowledge and techniques that he needed to launch himself as a painter; and from Eric Hall, he derived both a valuable *savoir-faire* and the unconditional support that helped him, as we have seen, to bring forth the monstrous vision that had lain hidden itself beneath the delicate pastiches of Picasso and surrealism that characterized his very early work. But neither man was 'cruel': on the contrary, they were highly civilized and considerate, and thus destined to leave a relatively superficial imprint on Bacon's life.

It is symptomatic that while Bacon never painted either de Maistre or Hall, his devoted lovers and mentors, he never ceased painting Peter Lacy throughout the 1950s. Indeed one might say that, such obvious exceptions as the Sphinx and the van Gogh paintings apart, most of the figure paintings and portraits of the 1950s are either wholly or indirectly inspired by Lacy; even behind the Popes and the life masks of William Blake one senses the menacing, self-destructive presence of the former Spitfire ace. Intense and violent, the relationship between the two men was doomed from the start. They met at Muriel's bar, the Colony Room, in Soho. It could have been any casual encounter: two alcoholic homosexuals passing in the night. But Bacon, for the first, and possibly only, time in his life, fell helplessly in love. Lacy was the first man he had ever met who seemed even tougher than he was – able to drink more and take more punishment. He was entranced by Lacy's natural wit and his ability to play any number of hits, old and new, on the piano. Yet he was aware, and this only increased the attraction, that they would seek to destroy one another. Lacy liked younger men, and although Bacon had maintained an improbably youthful look, he was in fact older than Lacy. 'Being in love in that way, being absolutely physically obsessed by someone, is like an illness,' Bacon said to me many years later. 'It's like a disease, a disease so ghastly I wouldn't wish it on my worst enemy.'

In Lacy Bacon certainly found the cruel father he had been seeking. When the two men attempted to live together, in the unlikely surroundings of a country cottage at Hurst, near Henley-on-Thames, Lacy dictated the terms. He wanted (at least in the version of events that Bacon gave me) to have his lover chained to the wall, living like an animal on a bed of straw. Bacon was not given to indiscretions about his sexual modus operandi, but he did mention once that Lacy had a whole collection of rhino whips and that, when they were together, they enjoyed exploring the further reaches of sadomasochism. Part of Lacy's cruelty was his attitude to Bacon's painting, which ranged from indifference to active animosity. At regular intervals, having beaten the artist badly, Lacy would proceed in a drunken rage to destroy his clothes and then as many of his canvases as he could find. Violent quarrels, full of physical and verbal abuse, would sometimes lead to reconciliations which Lacy and Bacon then celebrated with such epic benders in the local pubs that sooner or later a new full-scale dispute was bound to erupt. Their on-and-off life together in the English countryside was later summed up by Bacon, with a bitter simplicity, as 'four years of continuous horror, with nothing but violent rows'.

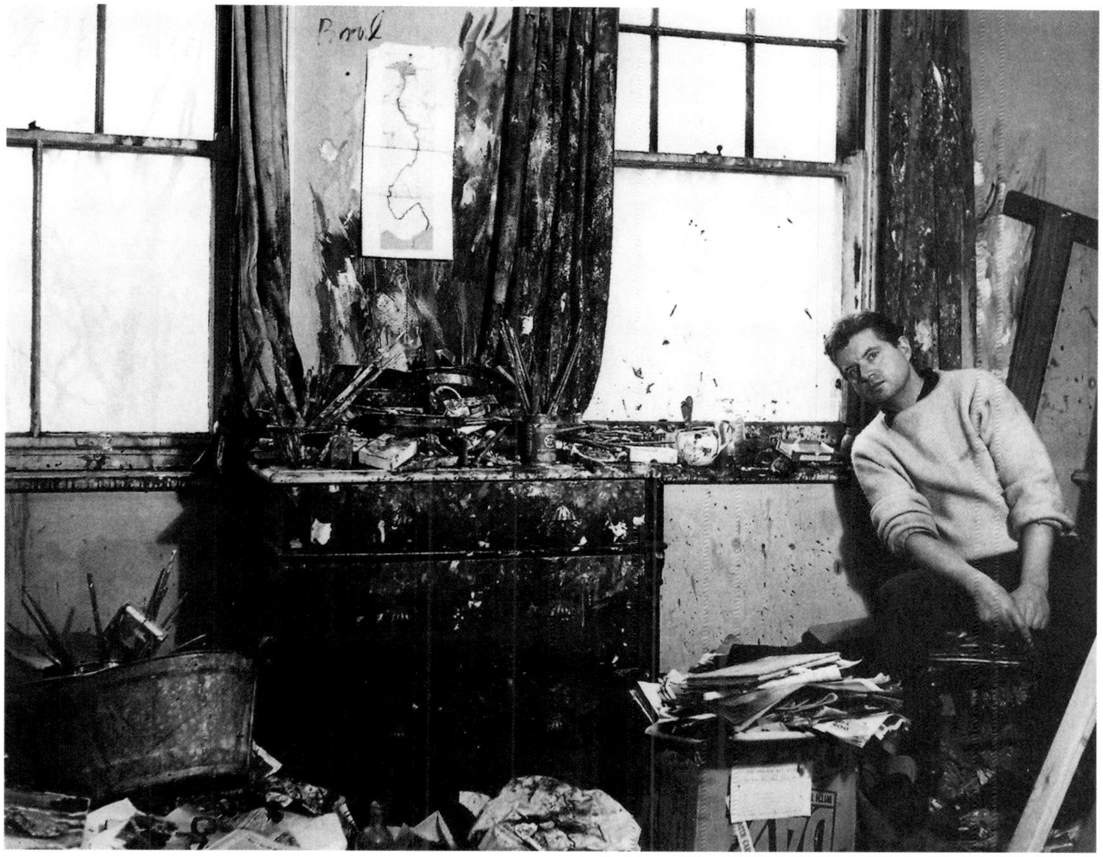

18 Francis Bacon, 1960, photo: Cecil Beaton, Cecil Beaton Studio Archive, Sotheby's.

But Bacon could not break away. No one had dominated him so effectively since his father, and he appeared literally entranced by the punishment meted out, even though Lacy's rages became so violent at times that Bacon had to flee. It was almost impossible for him to work in these circumstances and at times he felt overwhelmed with difficulties and despair, as a letter sent to Erica Brausen from a temporary address (the Imperial Hotel at Henley-on-Thames) clearly suggests: 'I am not able to finish any paintings at the moment,' Bacon writes, 'so will you please put off the exhibitions. I am terribly sorry about this but as you know these things happen with work. I will let you have the paintings I owe you as soon as I possibly can but please do not have a show of the things you have got in the gallery of mine. I think it would be a great mistake to show them both for you and for me as you know. I want to replace most of them when I can. Also there have been too many shows of mine. I am desperate and completely broke and am going to try to get a job for a time. I am terribly sorry about this but will let you have the pictures as soon as possible. I hope before the end of the year. Please forgive me but I cannot finish the work at the moment.' (See complete letters to Erica Brausen on pp. 141–153.)

Fortunately, Bacon had an alternative base, having by now moved into the Battersea flat shared by his friends Peter Pollock and Paul Danquah, an amiable gay couple who knew every twist and turn of Bacon's plight and who were always on hand to patch up a wound or hear about the latest row. It was here, in the small, chaotic room that his friends had lent him to work in, that Bacon painted out the traumas of his life with Lacy, since not the least attraction of the relationship for the artist was that it compelled him to work: painting alone allowed him to survive the physical and mental battering. Nevertheless, it was not all storm and stress. The cry that had begun with the father and taken on more force through the anguish of an impossible love affair also allowed instances of gentleness, such as the portraits Bacon did of Lacy in repose or asleep. There can be no doubt, looking at these rare moments of tenderness in Bacon's work, how deeply attached he had become to Lacy. 'It was like the song,' Bacon ruefully concluded once. 'I couldn't live with him, and I couldn't live without him.' Given the extremes they had already reached in country cottages, it would have been better for both men if the relationship had ended there and then. But the hunger for self-destruction was too strong in each of them to be satisfied with anything less than disaster.

INTERZONE

> Minarets, palms, mountains, jungle... Hipsters with smooth copper-coloured faces lounge in doorways twisting shrunken heads on gold chains . . . people eaten by unknown diseases watch the passer-by with evil, knowing eyes.
>
> William Burroughs, *Naked Lunch*

Quite as decadent as Monte Carlo and definitely more exotic, Tangier gained a reputation during the 1950s as a 'free zone' where drugs were readily available and homosexuality tolerated, if not openly encouraged. Numerous American writers, from Paul Bowles and Tennessee Williams to the Beat poet Allen Ginsberg, all gay to a man, either settled there or visited at length. Not surprisingly, Bacon appears to have met them all. Bowles noted perceptively that Bacon seemed to him like 'a man about to burst from internal pressures'. More randomly and flamboyantly, Ginsberg described Bacon at that time as having the look of an English schoolboy and the soul of a satyr who 'wears sneakers and tight dungarees and black silk shirts & always looks like going to tennis . . . and paints mad gorillas in grey hotel rooms drest in evening dress with deathly black umbrellas – said he would paint a big pornographic picture of me & Peter (Orlovsky)'. Ginsberg also later recorded that Bacon had told him that the only way

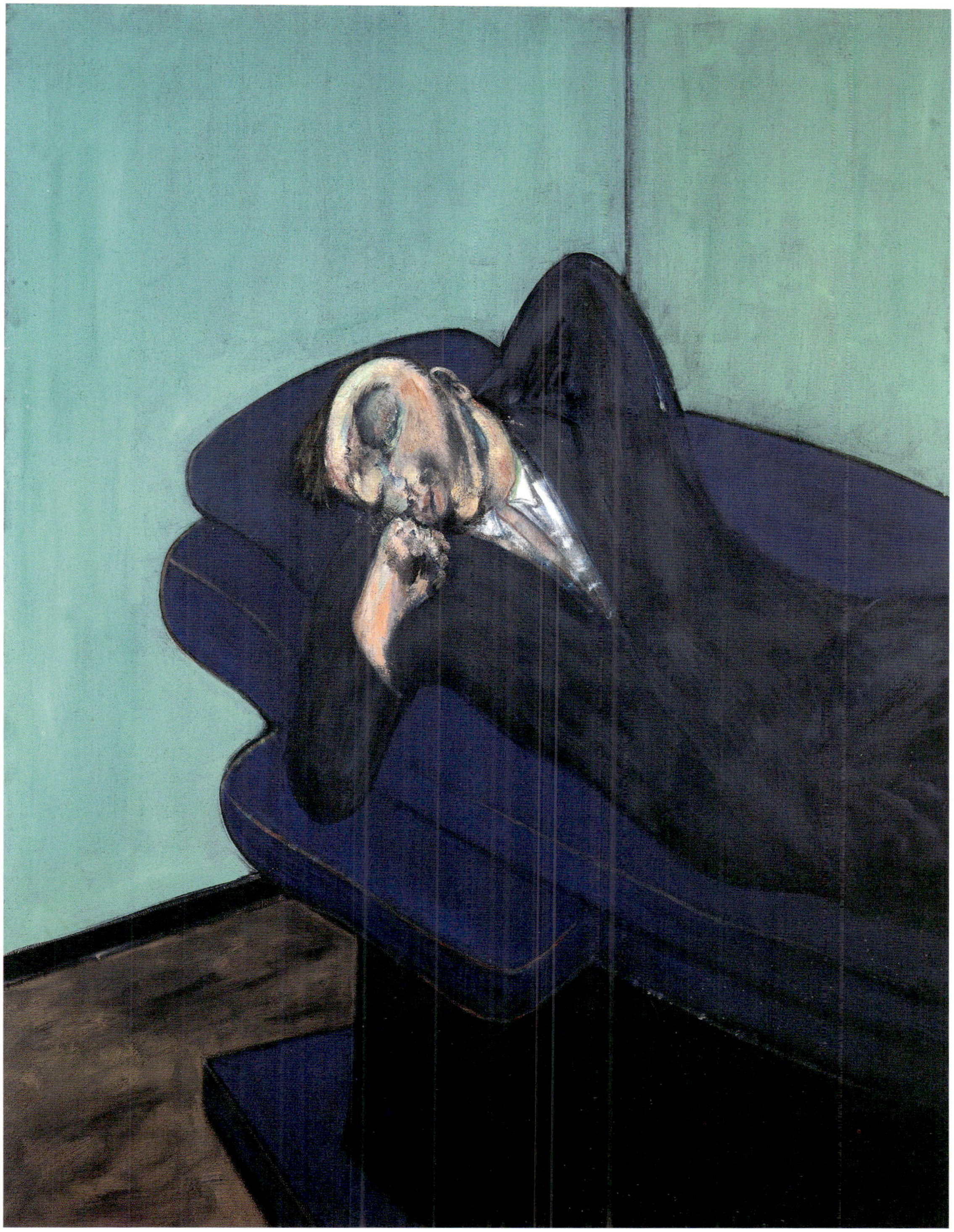

19 *Lying Figure*, 1958, 153.5 × 119.5 cm, oil on canvas.
Bochum Museum, Bochum.

he could complete a painting was 'with a chance brushstroke that locked in the magic – a fortuitous thing he couldn't predict or orchestrate'.[33]

By the time Peter Lacy moved to Tangier around 1956, the city had long been host to a fully fledged international community, with its own bars and social structure, which found the relaxed moral attitudes, the climate and cost of living more congenial than London, Paris or New York. Although he had (by Bacon's account) come from a wealthy family, Lacy seems to have entered a definitive downward spiral shortly after arriving in the Moroccan port. With his nerves shattered by his wartime experience as a fighter pilot, Lacy had little in the way of skills beyond a ready wit, an unmistakeably English look and a gift for playing the latest hits on the piano all through the night. Coupled with his alarming alcohol consumption (which Bacon, a reliable guide in the matter, put at a regular three bottles of spirits a day), Lacy soon found himself with the job from hell. The bar most favoured by the gay expatriates was called Dean's, after its improbable owner, a mysterious character, variously described as Jamaican or Egyptian, with an upper-class English accent and hints of fallen grandeur. In a letter to his wife, Ann Fleming (a close friend of Bacon's), the novelist Ian Fleming calls Dean's 'a sort of mixture between Wiltons and the porter's lodge at White's', adding: 'There's nothing but pansies, and I've been fresh meat for them.'[34] In order to settle the bar bill he had rapidly run up there, Lacy agreed to a devil's pact with Dean to play the piano until Dean's closed in the early hours. Since Lacy continued to drink heavily through the night, his bar bill could never be paid off, with the result that by the time Bacon arrived on his first visit to Tangier in the summer of 1956, Lacy was already indentured to Dean's and soon thereafter almost literally chained to the bar's piano, playing until he collapsed from drink and exhaustion.

As an habitué of the easy-come easy-go lifestyle of Monte Carlo and the other casinos on the Côte d'Azur, Bacon took to Tangier's cosmopolitan mixture of crooks (which included the leading figures of London's underworld), queers, hopheads, fugitives and remittance men as though he were coming home. 'Francis Bacon is due next week to live with his pansy pianist friend,' Fleming reported waspishly to his wife; and from the first of his many sojourns in the city, Bacon knew instinctively how to fit in at every level, from the Arab bordello to the garden parties put on by the resident grandee, David Herbert, the younger son of the Earl of Pembroke (whom Fleming nicely characterized as 'a kind of Queen Mum' reigning over the motley expatriate crew). Bacon also struck up some important friendships during these stays, most notably with Bill Burroughs, whose cut-up techniques in *Naked Lunch* (written mainly in 'Interzone', as he named Tangier) especially interested the English artist, for whom the way of making art always remained as essential as its content. At one point their mutual friend Allen Ginsberg suggested that Bacon painted as Burroughs wrote, but Burroughs corrected him sharply: 'Bacon and I are at opposite ends of the spectrum. He likes middle-aged truck drivers and I like young boys. He sneers at immortality and I think it is the one thing of importance. Of course, we're associated because of our morbid subject matter'.[35]

This social suaveness did nothing to abate the raging quarrels that flared up once more between Bacon and Lacy, each of them further incensed by the other's frequent infidelities with the local youths, who appeared to be in endless supply.[36] Bacon took rooms and flats of his own, and despite the strong light which he had always found singularly unconducive to painting he managed to produce impressive batches of work. 'I hope to come back with about twenty or twenty-five paintings early in October,' he wrote at one point to his faithful dealer, Erica Brausen. Lacy's fury and Bacon's self-doubt nevertheless put paid to most of these – if they were in fact ever painted (Bacon's claim to be 'full of work' often preceded a plea for money, although several abandoned canvases, left to another painter living in Tangier, have since come on to the market). Along with the destruction of most of his paintings, Bacon underwent such bad beatings that he was found several times wandering in an alarming condition through the streets at night. The British Consul alerted the Chief of Police in Tangier who investigated the matter, then replied laconically: 'Pardon, Monsieur le Consul-Général, mais il n'y a rien à faire. Monsieur Bacon aime ça.'

Although he painted little in Morocco and kept even less (even *Man Carrying a Child*, so patently inspired by North Africa, was in fact executed in London), Bacon had drawn a perverse strength from the decadence of Tangier and the poignant spectacle of his lover killing himself with drink. Decadence and disaster were, in the end, what his paintings fed off. The stronger the chaos and misfortune, the more beautiful and telling his images became. However much Bacon claimed to admire the 'happiness' of Renoir landscapes and to have sought to paint the smile rather than the scream, any form of contentment was anathema to his art. Although it took a while to absorb, the brilliance of Moroccan light and colour also led him to reconsider his entire palette. Tangier was both the end of an affair and the catalyst for a renewed, painterly vision.

PHANTOMS OF THE ROAD

. . . somewhere in the sands of the desert
A shape with lion body and the head of a man,
A gaze blank and pitiless as the sun,
Is moving its slow thighs, while all about it
Reel shadows of the indignant desert birds.

W. B. Yeats, 'The Second Coming'

Distraught by the destructive relationship with Peter Lacy, Bacon had long periods during which he was unable to work. But the pressure of images built up inside him, as well as the pressure from the Hanover Gallery for more shows, so that from time to time he shut the door of whatever makeshift studio he had and executed a whole series of pictures without pause.

Man in Blue, a mysterious figure met (and possibly seduced) while Bacon was staying at the Imperial Hotel in Henley-on-Thames, gave rise to just such a rapid series, with all seven versions on the theme painted one after another in 1954, and all but the last one shown together (with a *Sphinx*) in Bacon's fifth exhibition at Erica Brausen's gallery in June and July of that year. These enigmatic, dark blue figures emerging from a dark blue ground stand out by their precisely delineated, almost clinical composition and deliberately restrained, cold colour, as if Bacon were making in his art a conscious attempt to regain the control he had lost so spectacularly in his life. The man in question has all the immobility and much the same aura of enigma with which Bacon had endowed his series of *Sphinxes* (exemplifying the artist's ability to conjoin myth and the everyday); whereas the great suite of eight *Popes*, conceived as stills from a film, and the other figure studies of the same period give off an alarming charge of pent-up hysteria. To take a screaming *Pope* or writhing figure and set it beside a *Man in Blue* or an unearthly head of William Blake is to sense the new power that Bacon had acquired as an artist. There is a range and complexity in these works that marks them apart: one can sense a sinister calm beside the cry, a more subtle interlocking of the central image and its surrounding structure, a more knowing manipulation of the paint itself as well as of warm and cold tones. While his personal life was in shreds, and the contact with Lacy brought Bacon himself to the border of madness, his art apparently assumed its own course, deepening its compositional resources, testing the emotional complexities of colour, cooling the hysteria until it took on the more insidious hues of generalized threat.

Now in his mid-forties, Bacon had enough work behind him, and a sufficient body of support amongst the brighter critics, dealers and museum people, as well as amongst the art students and the young, to push his experiments out in several directions. What he had already discovered about his natural capacities was that he worked best in variations on a theme; and almost his entire output during the 1950s can be resumed into a number of distinct, thematic categories. Perhaps the main reason that Bacon became so drawn to working in series was his fascination with movement – with the way not only that appearance changes instant by instant into something completely unforeseen, but that the medium of oil paint, as if in counterpoint, constantly metamorphoses, suggesting an infinity of different choices from the moment it is applied. This is what both delighted and exasperated Bacon in his chosen medium, which he described so well in his tribute to Matthew Smith: 'That is why real painting is a mysterious and continuous struggle with chance – mysterious because the very substance of the paint, when used in this way, can make such a direct assault on the nervous system; continuous because the medium is so fluid and subtle that every change that is made loses what is already there in the hope of making a fresh gain.' (For complete text, see n. 27).

Bacon's new confidence and fluency also allowed him to take on commissioned portraits, such as those of Robert and Lisa Sainsbury, the adventurous young collectors whom, as we have seen, he met through Erica Brausen. The portrait of Robert Sainsbury (see CAT 20) remained in

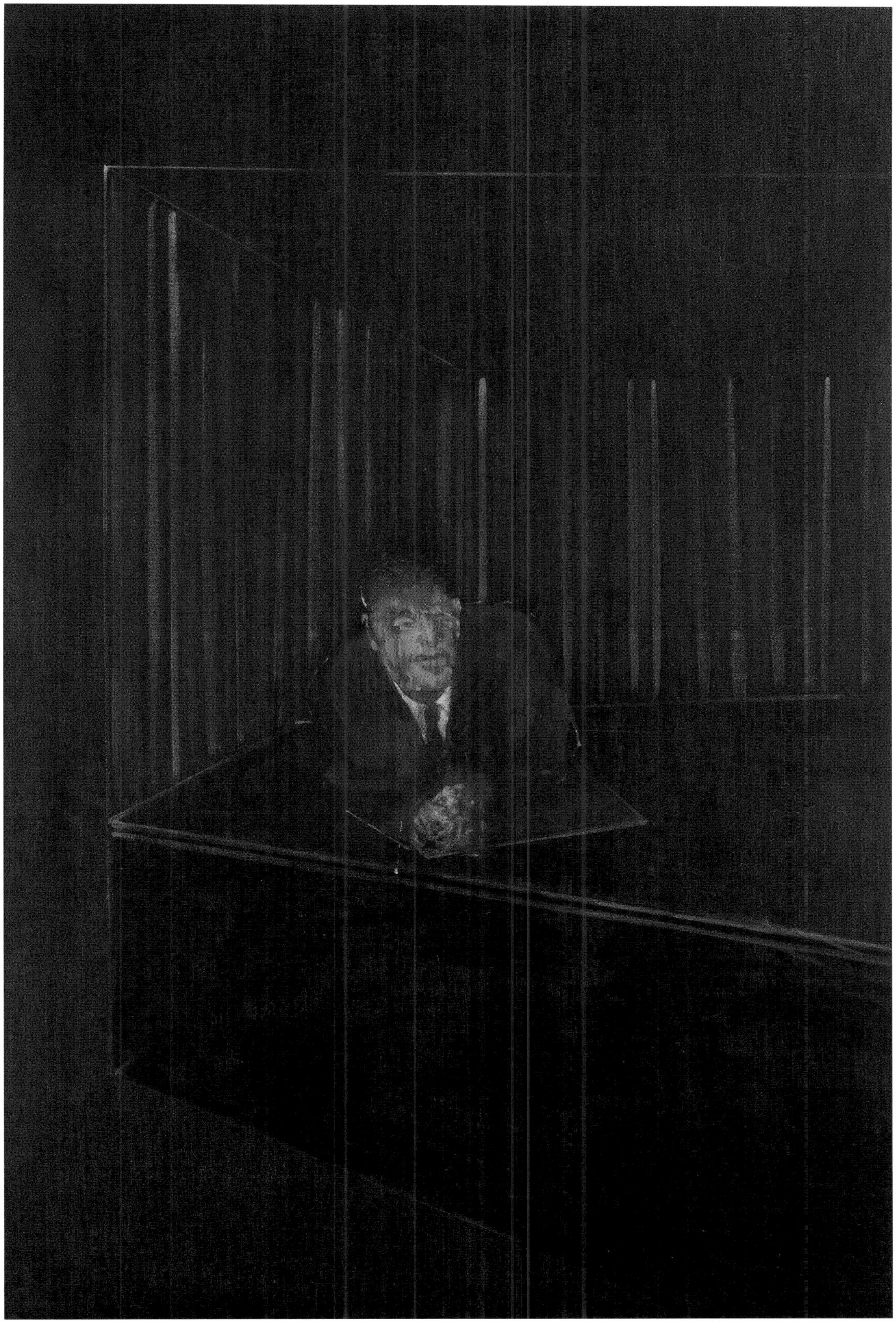

20 *Man in Blue IV*, 1954, 198 × 137 cm, oil on canvas. Museum Moderner Kunst, Stiftung Ludwig, Vienna.

the cool, controlled mode of the 'Men in Blue' and the heads of Blake: intriguing, distant and as if captured just as the image were about to fade into the dark void of picture ground behind. In the case of Lisa, with whom he struck up a lively friendship, Bacon produced some eight studies, of which he destroyed all but three. Here, again, one senses how Bacon was intent on bringing together a maximum of widely differing associations in a single image: they are portraits of Lisa, but also paraphrases of famous Egyptian heads and even of certain African masks as well as of portraits in the grand European manner. If Bacon returned to portraits of Lisa so assiduously, it was both because he was fascinated by the structure of her face and intrigued by her quick mind and decisive personality; for her, equally, the mornings spent sitting to Bacon were made memorable by the talk, which moved easily from the grand themes of art, love and death to gossip; but it was also because the Sainsburys played a key role in his life at this moment, as can be seen from the letters he wrote to them during the 1950s (published in their entirety on pp. 141–159).

Under the dual influence of a darkly disturbing love affair and the brilliance of North African light and colour, Bacon's way of painting as well as his subject matter was about to take a dramatic new turn. Even as a very young artist, Bacon had been fascinated by van Gogh. 'When I started out, Cézanne was the god,' Bacon told me once, 'but for me the very great artist of that period has always been van Gogh.' It was not only the uniquely vivid art of van Gogh that impressed Bacon, but also his poignant life story and his letters to his brother Theo, which Bacon kept as a bedside book. Where Velázquez and Picasso had been fathers to Bacon, van Gogh ('le suicidé de la société', in Artaud's words) was more like an older brother with whom he began to identify all the more closely as his relationship with Lacy grew increasingly fraught and obsessive.

Even in the work of artists he admired, Bacon tended to like above all only a particular segment or phase: it would be the pastels of Degas, the drawings of Giacometti, the Picassos of the Dinard period that would be singled out for special and repeated praise. With van Gogh, he was drawn mostly to the early work, particularly to the *Potato Eaters* and the *Pair of Shoes*, which the young Dutch painter completed before leaving Nuenen for Paris. It was then, Bacon felt, that van Gogh, still clumsily grappling to express the force of his vision, communicated most directly and powerfully and came closest to his own dictum (which Bacon had instinctively made his own) that 'real painters do not paint things as they are, after a dry and learned analysis. They paint them as they themselves feel them to be.' But there were nevertheless several later van Goghs that he was strongly drawn to, and none more than *The Painter on the Way to Tarascon*, painted in Arles in mid-summer 1888. Bacon had visited the area round Arles several times on visits to France, and having got to know the local landscape he particularly admired the way van Gogh had managed to capture what he called its 'living quality'. Another aspect that perhaps attracted him to this painting – and which no doubt in his eyes added to its poignancy – was that it had been destroyed when the museum that owned it in Magdeburg was bombed during the final phase of the Second World War. Thus Bacon could only know it, like

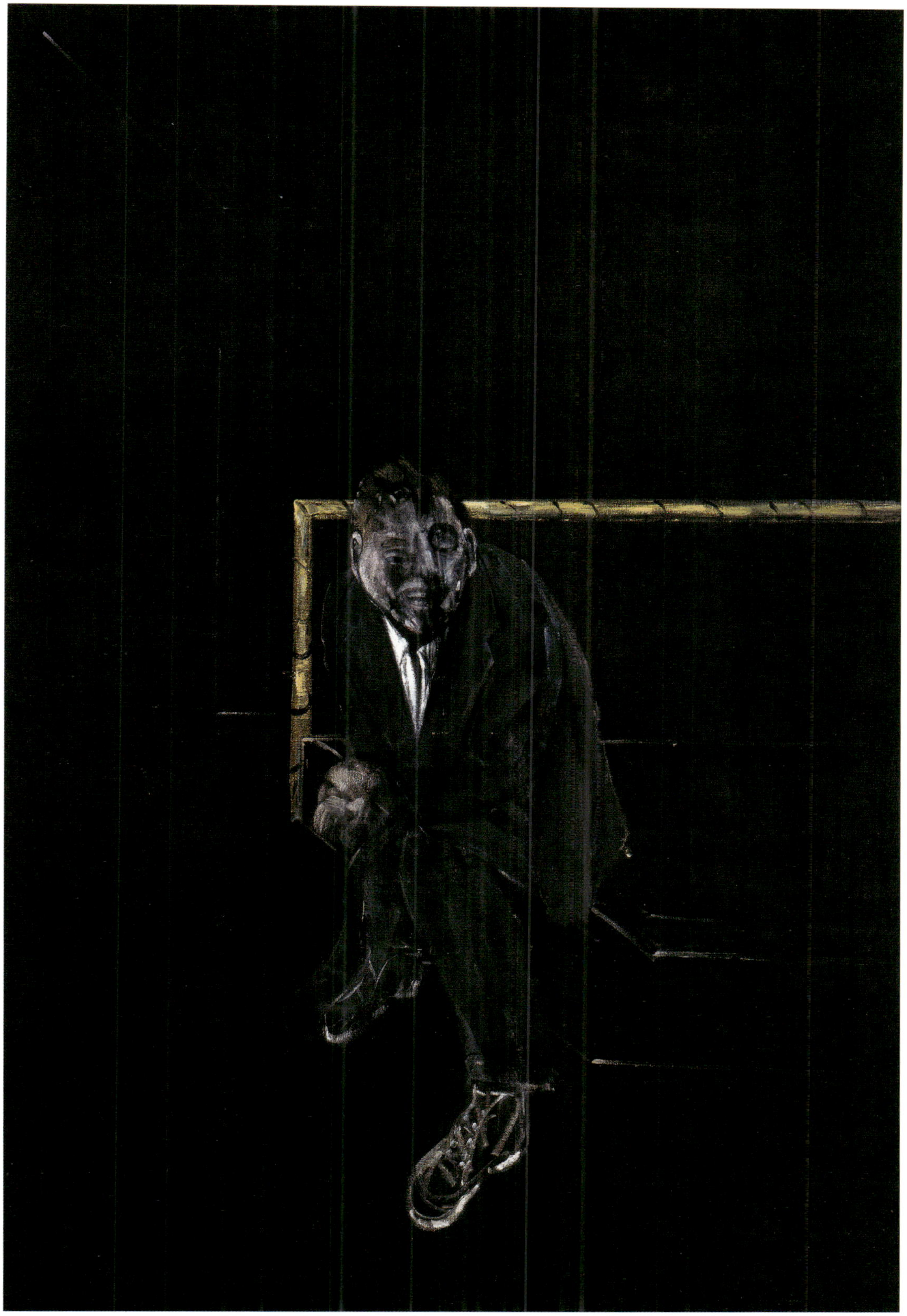

21 *Self-Portrait*, 1956, 198 × 137 cm, oil on canvas. Collection of the Modern Art Museum of Fort Worth, Gift of The Burnett Foundation in honour of Marla Price, acquired in 2002.

Velázquez's *Portrait of Pope Innocent X* that had previously inspired him, from reproductions. Indeed, even more than the Velázquez, which existed even if Bacon chose not to go and look at it when he visited Rome, the fact that the original van Gogh was no longer there undoubtedly made him feel freer to do whatever he wanted with it.

After a disastrous stay in Tangier in 1957 and faced with an imminent show at the Hanover for which no paintings were ready (although Brausen had already advanced him money on them), Bacon had no alternative but to produce the contents of an entire exhibition in short order. The heat, light and colours of Morocco, coupled with the alienation Bacon felt wandering round Tangier trapped in his unhappy love affair, put him in mind of the terrible isolation van Gogh experienced on his way to the 'motif', mocked and occasionally set on by the local children. Bacon had already produced his first *Study for Portrait of van Gogh* in 1956 – just after his first *Self-Portrait*, appositely enough – but there had been no sign that the subject would extend into a series of eight paintings, with three variations on other van Gogh themes to follow (notably *Head of a Man – Study of Drawing by van Gogh* of 1959 and *Homage to van Gogh* of 1960). Although the theme had been dormant for a full year, new paraphrases suddenly crowded his imagination. 'I'd always loved that picture – the one that was burnt in Germany during the war – and as nothing else had gone right I thought I'd try to do something with it,' Bacon explained later to John Russell. 'Actually I've always liked early van Gogh best, but that haunted figure on the road seemed just right at the time – like a phantom of the road, you could say.'[37]

Once begun, the van Gogh series came quickly, with three of the new canvases (II to IV in the series) being put straight into the Hanover show of March–April 1957, and two others (V and VI) being added, while still wet, during the course of the exhibition. Compared to the Bacon paraphrases, the van Gogh original looks controlled, mild and autumnal. Where the Dutch artist has golds, browns and greens, Bacon brings a discordant, writhing mass of metallic reds, yellows and blacks. Where the figure of the artist in van Gogh has a lonely but plucky solidity, in Bacon it becomes ridiculed – an ape or a drudge strapped in its painter's paraphernalia like a sandwich-man trudging meaninglessly under the broiling sun. Or in other versions, the substance of the isolated painter has seeped out of his body into his shadow, which accompanies him like a mocking double on the hot road. It seems reasonable to suppose – since the love of his life had rejected and destroyed his paintings – that Bacon's van Gogh paintings commemorate an artist who has lost his bearings in existence. From picture to picture, the painter's enterprise comes across as horribly meaningless: slouched beneath the tools of his trade, the lone figure makes his painful way through alien country charred by the sun to nowhere and nothing. If the van Gogh series echoes Lacy's derision, it also shows Bacon's capacity to take self-laceration further. Here, in the wild (often too wild and unresolved) chaos of colour contrasts, Bacon auto-destructs: the subject is no longer van Gogh moving towards his tragic end, but the futility of art and the futility of life. Under that implacable sun there is a sense of barely concealed

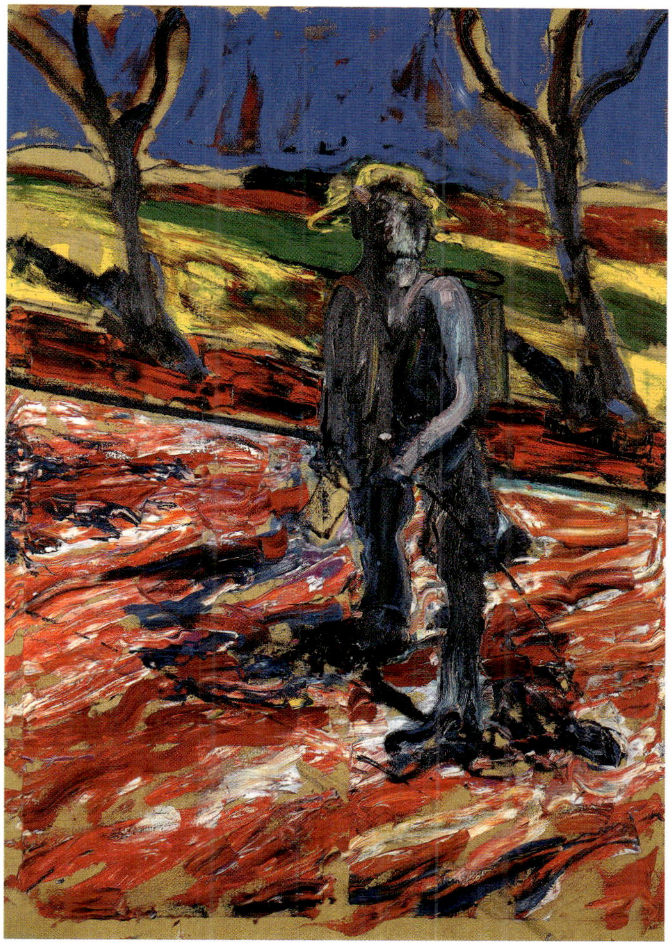

22 *Study for a Portrait of van Gogh III*, 1957, 198.4 × 142.5 cm, oil and sand on linen. Hirshhorn Museum and Sculpture Garden, Washington DC, Gift of the Joseph H. Hirshhorn Foundation, 1966.

madness. Having just emerged from the blue-black gloom of his claustrophobic interiors, Bacon at first seems freer: the ghosts kept in their cages against neatly pleated drapes have been banished, and a brighter vision seems at hand. But this scorched planet quickly turns out to be more frightening by far. Seeing van Gogh stripped of his last vestiges of dignity in a desert of malignant colour makes the airless interiors in which Bacon had hitherto acted out his dramas seem positively desirable. Man's inventions may be bad enough but, in Bacon's eyes, nature is infinitely worse.

These pictures, which caused quite an uproar both for and against when they went on show, are particular examples of the way all Bacon's paintings are in fact autobiographical. In many of the works, it is not so obvious. But here, in the van Gogh series, one senses a man, thrashed by his own inner contradictions and pushed to his absolute limits. If he had not possessed an unusual fortitude and sense of purpose, Bacon might well at this point have taken the same route as van Gogh, or indeed Peter Lacy.

THE MAGPIE EYE

On his return to London after one of the last trips he took to Tangier in the 1950s, Bacon received a telephone call from Lacy, who said to him: 'From now on, consider me dead. Consider me dead.' Bacon knew by now that nothing would stop Lacy from destroying himself. In the first few years of their relationship, the sense of danger had excited him. He had always sought out disaster, in his life as in his art, impelled by his own vitality and the conviction that the closer you got to it the more clearly you saw the reality of existence, itself forever hovering on the brink of extinction. Once in a situation, particularly in an intimate situation, Bacon could not help himself from pushing it to the edge. 'Only by going too far can you go far enough,' he would say about art; and he took the same attitude as vigorously towards life. The extended crisis with Lacy had not prevented him from starting other affairs, which could only add to the tensions between the two men. And as if he needed more complications, Bacon had begun going around in Tangier with Ronnie Kray, the notorious gangster, who had taken a distinct liking to the ease of homosexual relations in the Arab port.

In part because he had unequivocally dominated him during their relationship, Lacy was to remain the great love of Bacon's life. Bacon was devastated as he saw Lacy slip further into alcoholism and doomed entanglements with faithless Arab boys. But he was conscious that Lacy, incoherent with drink by mid-morning, had lost the 'toughness' he had so admired. He was also aware that the dying love affair had badly disrupted his whole capacity for producing powerful images. Compared to the score or so of new works painted in a good year, Bacon could show only a mere half-dozen for 1958, and most of them portraits of Lacy. Meanwhile, another crisis, of a different kind, was looming. Bacon's career, which he cared about and controlled a great deal more than he let on, had begun to stall. He was irritated by Erica Brausen's insistence on holding shows of his work so frequently – 'rushed affairs', as he called them, at the rate of almost one a year – and was somewhat disappointed that the gallery was not attracting a wider circle of private collectors and museum directors, even though Brausen had recently been able to sell a *Study for van Gogh* for £600 (a handsome sum at that time for a work by a still relatively little-known and 'difficult' painter). Bacon was also heavily in debt to the Hanover; so that when an ambitious gallery with the equally established-sounding name of Marlborough Fine Art offered him an agreement that would pay off all his debts, including

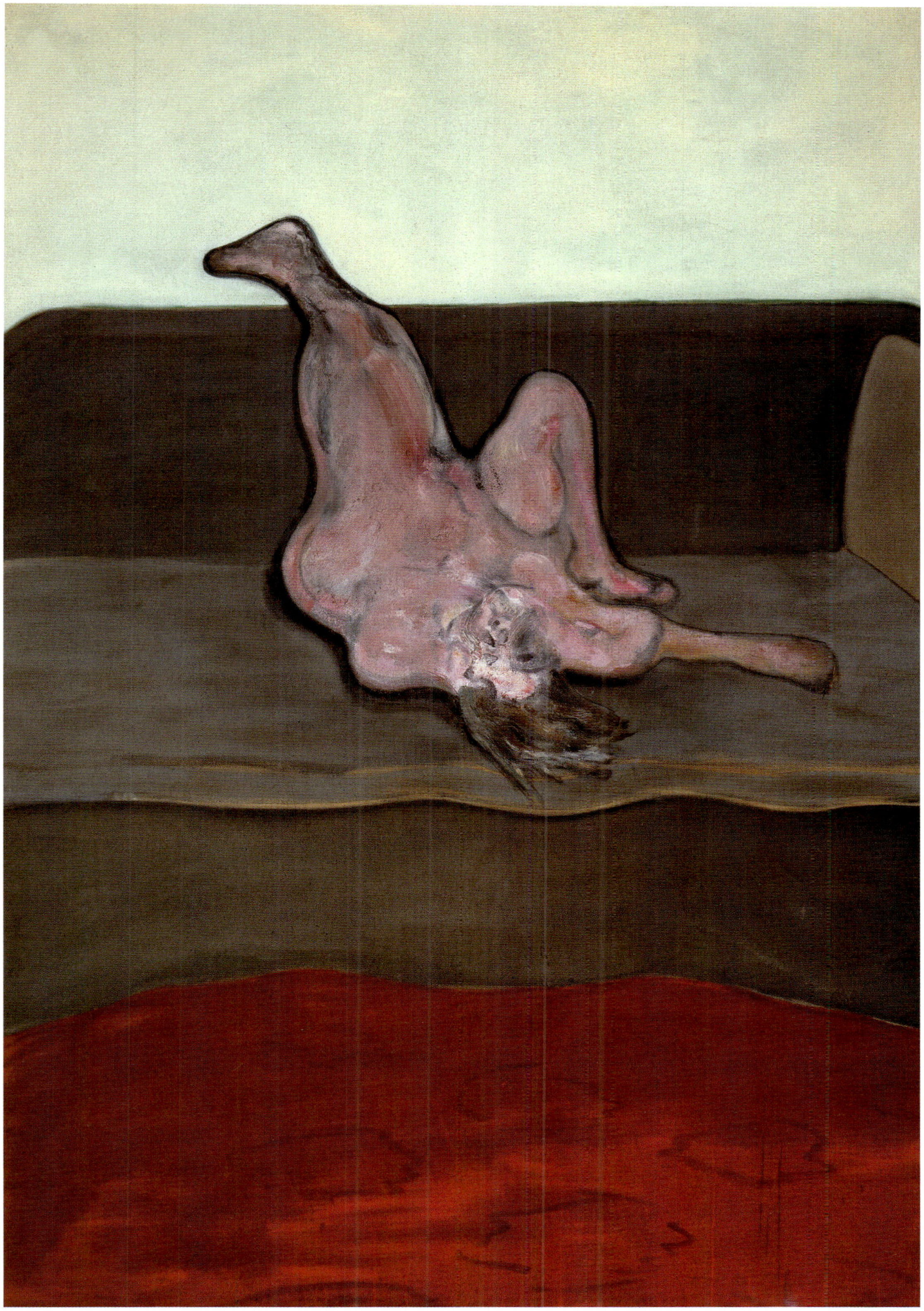

23 *Reclining Woman*, 1961, 199 × 142 cm, oil on canvas.
Tate, London.

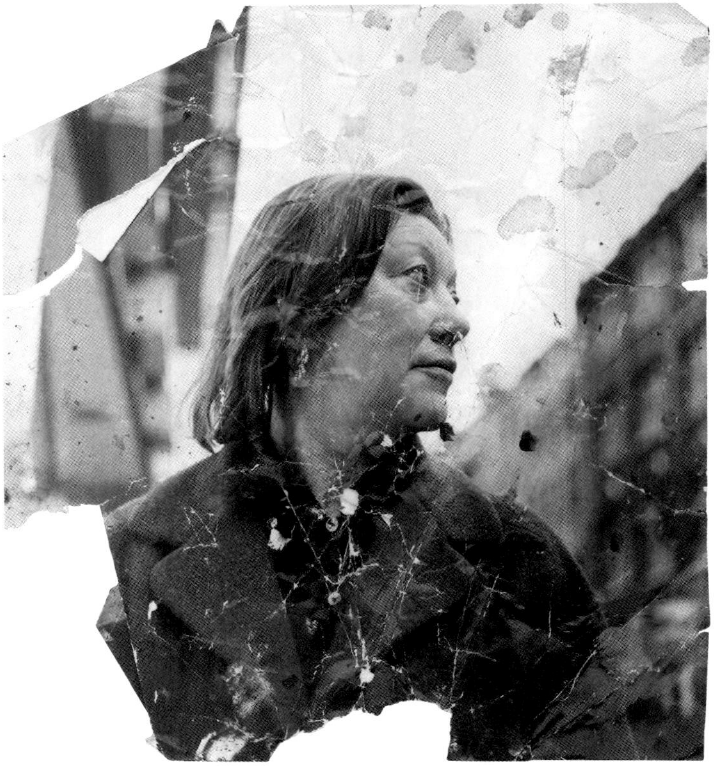

24 Studio document. Isabel Rawsthorne in Dean Street, Soho, 1960s, photo: John Deakin. Dublin City Gallery, The Hugh Lane.

some pressing gambling losses, he did not hesitate to accept. Mindful as he was of Brausen's flair and much-tested loyalty, Bacon would have immediately seen that the Marlborough, also founded by talented Jewish refugees, was capable of taking his reputation and the prices of his paintings to new levels.[38]

As a result of the new arrangement, 1959 proved more fruitful. There were new heads and new figures, a new *Pope* and several studies of women, including a portrait of Bacon's great friend and ally, Muriel Belcher, removed from the smoky confines of the Colony Room and pinned in an imperious sweep of red and pink against a vivid emerald background. Bacon's need to work that year dictated a decision that would otherwise seem completely out of character: in the early autumn of the year, he took himself off to St Ives. Later in life, it was all but impossible to pry Bacon out of a metropolis. When not in London, he could usually be found in Paris or Madrid, or occasionally in Nice, Monte Carlo or other haunts of his youth. That he moved not only outside London but to an artists' colony (anathema to the solitary creator he had

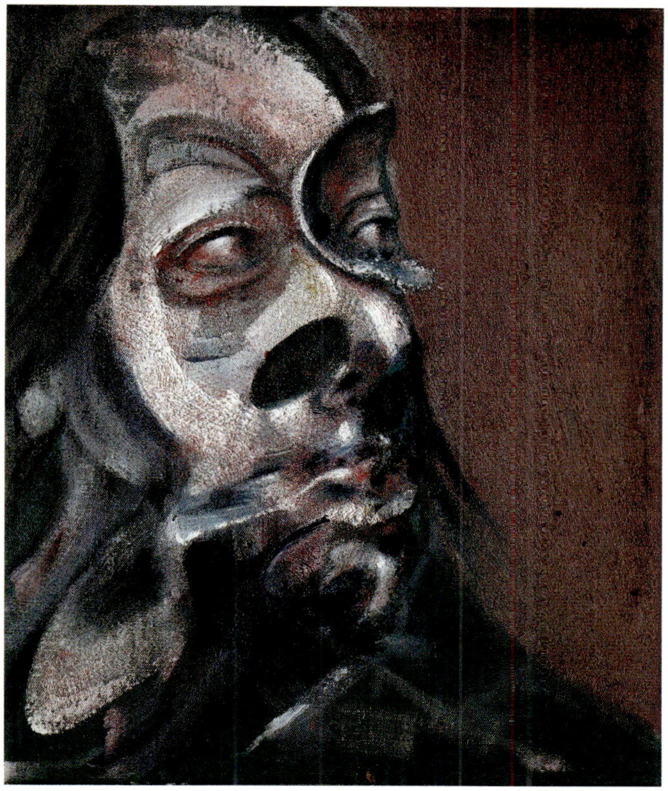

25 *Study of Isabel Rawsthorne*, 1966, 35.5 × 30.5 cm, oil on canvas. Musée d'art moderne, Centre Georges Pompidou, Paris. Donation Louise and Michel Leiris, 1984.

always been), moreover of the abstract tendency that he had publicly derided, seemed a total contradiction more dangerous in its way than consorting with the Krays. Yet, with his charm at the ready and his extraordinary capacity for survival, Bacon turned what should have been a season in hell mostly to his advantage.[39] Having rented a decent space at Porthmeor Studios, which looked out over the beach towards St Ives Bay, Bacon soon found the best places to eat and drink and quickly set about making himself agreeable to the local community (as he had done in Tangier), from Barbara Hepworth, the reigning grande dame, down – sidestepping the criticism of such militant abstractionists as Patrick Heron (whom Bacon sarcastically dubbed 'the Prince of Colours') to concentrate on intense bouts of work.

In a little over three months, Bacon in fact produced no fewer than twenty canvases, more than twice his recent annual yield, although before leaving St Ives he destroyed all but six of them. Those that remain show a radical change not only in palette and composition but in the application itself of paint. We are already a long way from the expressionistic violence and heated colour of the recent 'van Gogh' series. It is as though Bacon had walked through a wall into a cold, almost icy light – as indeed he had; there is no doubt that the landscape and the luminosity, the great sweep of sea and sky, had brought a completely new chromatic register to Bacon's paintings (and it is interesting to reflect that an artist so closely associated with shuttered interiors and artificial light was in fact this sensitive to nature). But the cooling of Bacon's palette came perhaps even more from a change of inner climate and the fact that he was no longer emotionally distraught; he had closed a door and gone into another place, where his companions might arouse his scorn in the bars at night with talk of the greater purity and freedom of abstract form, but where he was able to review his own art in relative peace and isolation. However, this did not prevent Bacon – with the magpie eye, quick and ravenous, that had absorbed so many styles and sources – from noting what might serve his purposes in the abundance of abstract experimentation going on daily in the studios all around him.[40] Throughout his development as a painter, Bacon had been visibly seeking effective ways to articulate his pictorial space. Having eschewed classical perspective early on, he fell back regularly on such devices as a transparent frame or a receding couch or chair to suggest compositional depth. Having taken a close look at the Abstract Expressionists, then perceived to be very much at the cutting edge in Europe, Bacon lifted the use of broad, horizontal bands of colour as a means of creating a background for his figures. It was the kind of sleight of hand at which Bacon was especially adept; and he incorporated the new scheme into a couple of coolly controlled figure paintings – *Reclining Woman* (1961) and *Seated Figure on Couch* (1962) – before abandoning it.

If we know what Bacon looked like at the end of the 1950s, when he himself had just turned a youthful fifty, it is primarily thanks to the society photographer Cecil Beaton, who took numerous shots of Bacon in various poses in the tiny Battersea studio. Since Beaton (whose own effeminacy belied a steely will to succeed) sat to Bacon and published copious, chatty memoirs about the outstanding people he knew, we also have a unique verbal sketch of how Bacon came across as well as how he worked at the time. Although it gives an excessively cosy picture of the brilliant, wayward artist, the account does convey how seductive Bacon's presence could be. Having flatteringly described the painter's 'lithe' physique, Beaton sets the scene by explaining that Francis 'had just returned from a winter in Tangier where he had been too harassed and ill to paint. But he was then recovered and full of the joy of London life. He was bursting with health and vitality, in his extraordinarily messy, modest drawing room studio in a most unlikely block of scarlet brick flats'. Bacon got to work on the portrait 'with great zest, excitedly running backwards and forwards to the canvas with gazelle-springing leaps . . . He did not seem interested in my keeping still, and so I enjoyed looking around me at the incredible mess of his studio – a converted bedroom no doubt: so unlike the beautiful, rather conventional "artist's abode" that he had worked in in South Kensington when I first knew him! Here the floor was littered in a Dostoevsky shambles of discarded paintings, rags, newspapers and every sort of rubbish, while the walls and window curtains were covered with streaks of black and emerald green paint.’

The sittings were interrupted by Beaton’s travels, but when he returned to Bacon’s studio in 1960 to see the half-finished and now abandoned portrait he was alarmed to find that it depicted ‘a monster cripple – a nude figure, with no apparent head, but with four legs’. Once Bacon had sat him on a kitchen chair and got going on a second portrait, Beaton noted ‘among the rubbish of old discarded suede shoes, jerseys, and tins on the floor, one or two very costly art books on Egypt and Crete’. As the two men chatted (with Bacon mentioning that he had just had a tooth knocked out), Beaton took time to fill in the background for his readers: ‘Francis had spent the winter in Cornwall. But it hadn’t worked out as there had been such terrible quarrels and he got behind-hand with his work. It was the same in Tangier: such upsets! Rows and getting thrown out of the window! He had done no work. Then a talk about Tangier – Francis’ Tangier, a close intimacy with the Arab world, with the brothel life, and the freedom that can be found only in certain Mediterranean countries where access to women is difficult.[40]

Perhaps predictably (with the photographer already worried about how the emerald background of Bacon’s canvases would look against his rooms’ existing colour-scheme), the second portrait proved to be even more disturbing: ‘an enormous, coloured strip-cartoon of a completely aged – nay senile – businessman’, with a ‘swollen mass of raw meat and fatty tissues’ for the face. Bacon himself thought the portrait ‘one of the best things I’ve done’, but as soon as he sensed Beaton’s dismay he destroyed the picture without further ado.[41]

At this juncture, Bacon could ill afford to destroy his work so readily. The Marlborough had proved quite as demanding as the Hanover by planning his biggest exhibition thus far – over thirty paintings, all dated 1959–60 – for the Spring of 1960; and he was anxious to fulfil his new gallery’s expectations of him. ‘Highly acclaimed by the younger generation’, as Beaton noted, and ‘satanically influential’, as Robert Melville wrote rather breathlessly in an introductory text, Bacon was beginning to find himself subjected to all the pressures of fame. The extreme emotional chaos, the extravagant freedom and footlooseness of the 1950s would now no longer rule his life. From being a Rimbaud of the art world – hugely inventive and disruptive, fervently admired or dismissed but still little-known – Francis Bacon was about to become one of its brightest stars.

ENVOI

There are moments in everyone’s life – a crisis, a crossroads, a Rubicon – when forces or events come together to produce an irrevocable change. As the 1960s got under way, Bacon knew that nothing would be the same. The 1950s had been the best of times (to paraphrase Charles Dickens) and they had been the worst of times. Bacon had struggled with his life and with his art as he was never to struggle again. With Peter Lacy, he had experienced the most exalted and

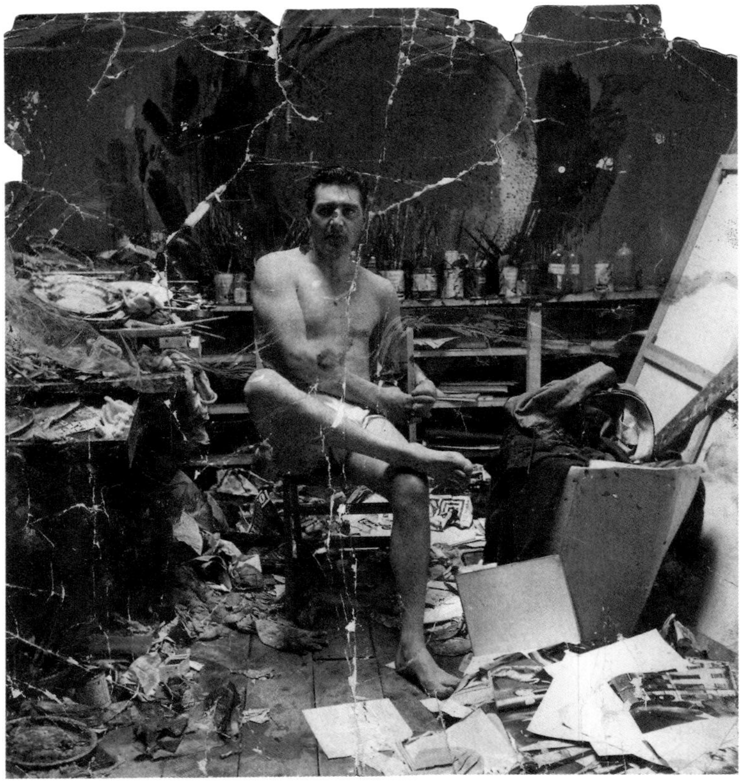

26 Studio document. George Dyer in the Reece Mews Studio, *c.*1964, photo: John Deakin. Dublin City Gallery, The Hugh Lane.

most destructive love affair he was ever to know. In Erica Brausen, he had found the most understanding and devoted dealer, even if she did not have the financial backing and commercial drive to take him to the next stage in his career. But he had broken away from these two poles of his existence; and now, as in a play where one act closes and another opens, he had to reaffirm his identity and find his bearings again.

Most of all, during these years, Bacon's work had gone through transformation after transformation. It had begun the decade with a roar, and there was no whimper at the end of it but a kind of contained or internalized violence, all more disquieting in that it no longer screamed and showed its teeth but lurked in the very grain of the swirling paint, permeating not only the livid or ruddily distorted flesh but the ominous dark blue and ambiguous emerald green backgrounds as well. The sense of menace, as pervasive in Bacon's paintings as it is in Graham Greene's novels of the same period, had gone underground. It raged under closed eyelids or lay in wait in cages and behind neatly pleated background drapes.

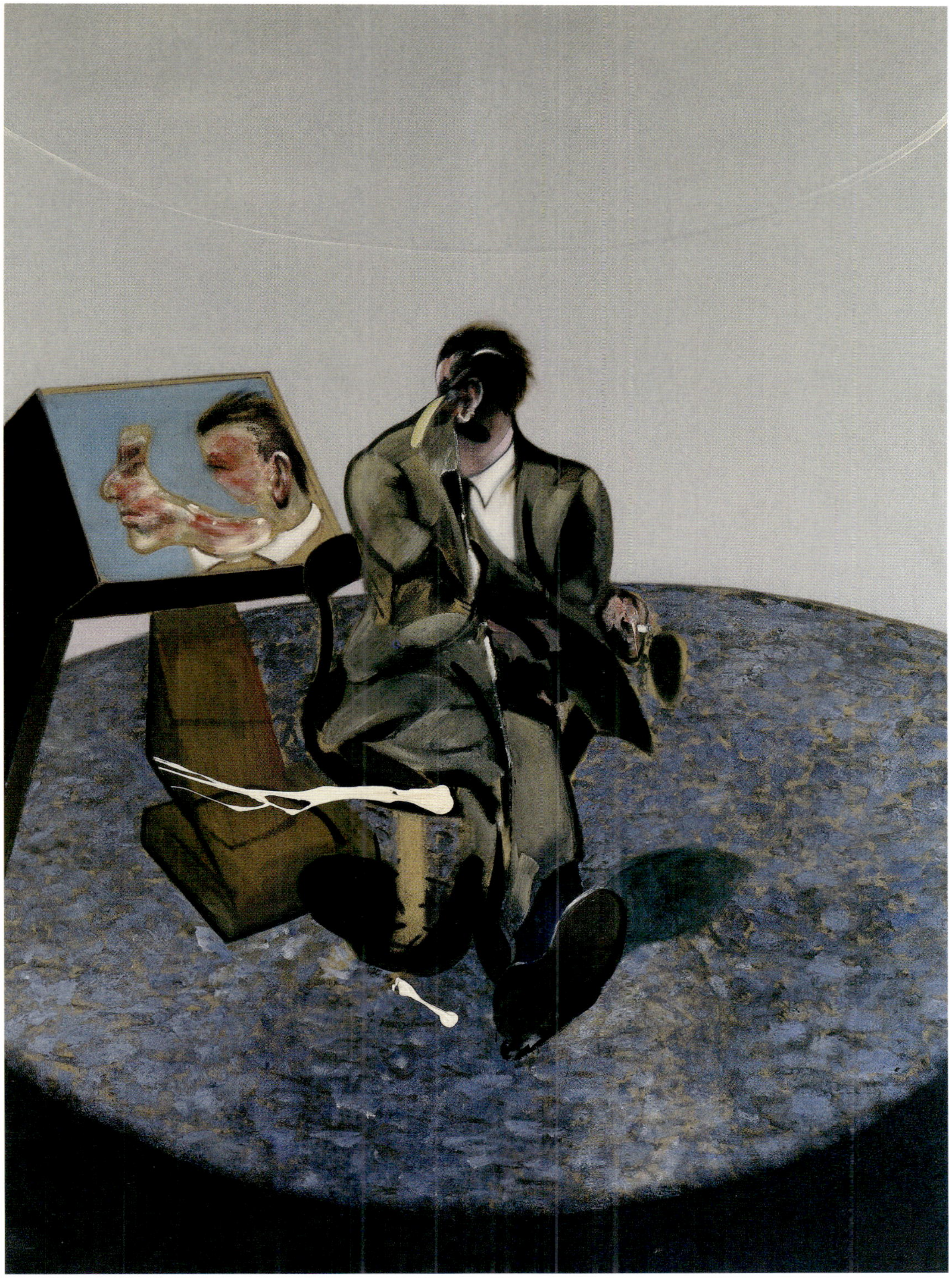

27 *Portrait of George Dyer in a Mirror*, 1968, 198 × 147 cm, oil on canvas.
Museo Thyssen-Bornemisza, Madrid.

Through the 1950s Bacon had in fact pushed out into more directions than he was ever to engage with again: his focus shifted constantly from animal to man, interior to landscape, Pope to Sphinx, van Gogh to Blake, Hurst to Zimbabwe, Monte Carlo and Tangier to Cornwall, Mediterranean to Atlantic light, mythical to contemporary, the poetic to the recognizably everyday banal. He had moved in his inspiration and subject matter from Renaissance masterpiece to war photo and newsreel, from the day's reportage to the 'long call from antiquity', from Aeschylus to Eliot. He had alternated dramatically between cold and hot colours, testing their power to evoke different emotions and moods. At the same time, Bacon had experimented ceaselessly with the medium of oil paint, juxtaposing highly controlled, thinly applied passages with areas of impasto full of apparently random effects. He had also tried out numerous compositional and perspectival devices, from shadows and tubular furniture to cages and receding boxed-in spaces, to create structures for his virtuoso effects (although the ability to organize pictorial space convincingly was to remain a constant problem in his work and no doubt his greatest abiding weakness as a painter).

A series of events precipated Bacon out of the 1950s, with their pinched postwar aura opening up into a more durable, more pleasurable peace time. One was, of course, his first exhibition with his new gallery in the spring of 1960. Modest as it looks now, the catalogue to *Francis Bacon: Paintings 1959–60*, with its mauve cover and numerous illustrations, was clearly a significant publication in the London art world of the time. It contained a short biography, a Cecil Beaton portrait of the artist in the studio, a list of Bacon's previous exhibitions and an elliptically allusive introduction by Robert Melville, one of Bacon's most subtle commentators. The show included a large number of *Lying Figures* and *Heads*, but it was dominated by four studies for *Popes*. 'Francis Bacon has a refined and mocking flair for grandeur,' Melville concluded, 'and his paintings sometimes provide a remote and bitter after-taste of Venetian sumptuousness: but what he always, inexplicably, achieves is an eerily erotic collusion between the substance he manipulates and the psychic content of the image it tries to deface.'[42]

Quite as important a change to Bacon as his new gallery, which went on to organize scores of shows of his work worldwide, was his new studio in Reece Mews, a cobblestone passage lined with former stables just off the Old Brompton Road. A man whose chaotic, bohemian ways were firmly anchored in a fixed discipline, Bacon was to live there until he died. Nondescript and comfortless as the space itself remained, Bacon (who was unusually sensitive to the atmosphere of rooms) had sensed that he could work well there; and because of the paintings produced within its paint-splattered walls and the visually stimulating clutter that grew ankle-deep on the floor, the studio was to become a bizarrely hallowed space that deeply impressed the few people that Bacon ever allowed in to see a new picture before it was removed by his dealers.[43]

In choosing a studio in this part of South Kensington, Bacon was also quite consciously recreating a link with his past. Reece Mews lay just behind and parallel to the studio in Cromwell Place which, some ten years earlier, Bacon had abandoned after the death of Jessie

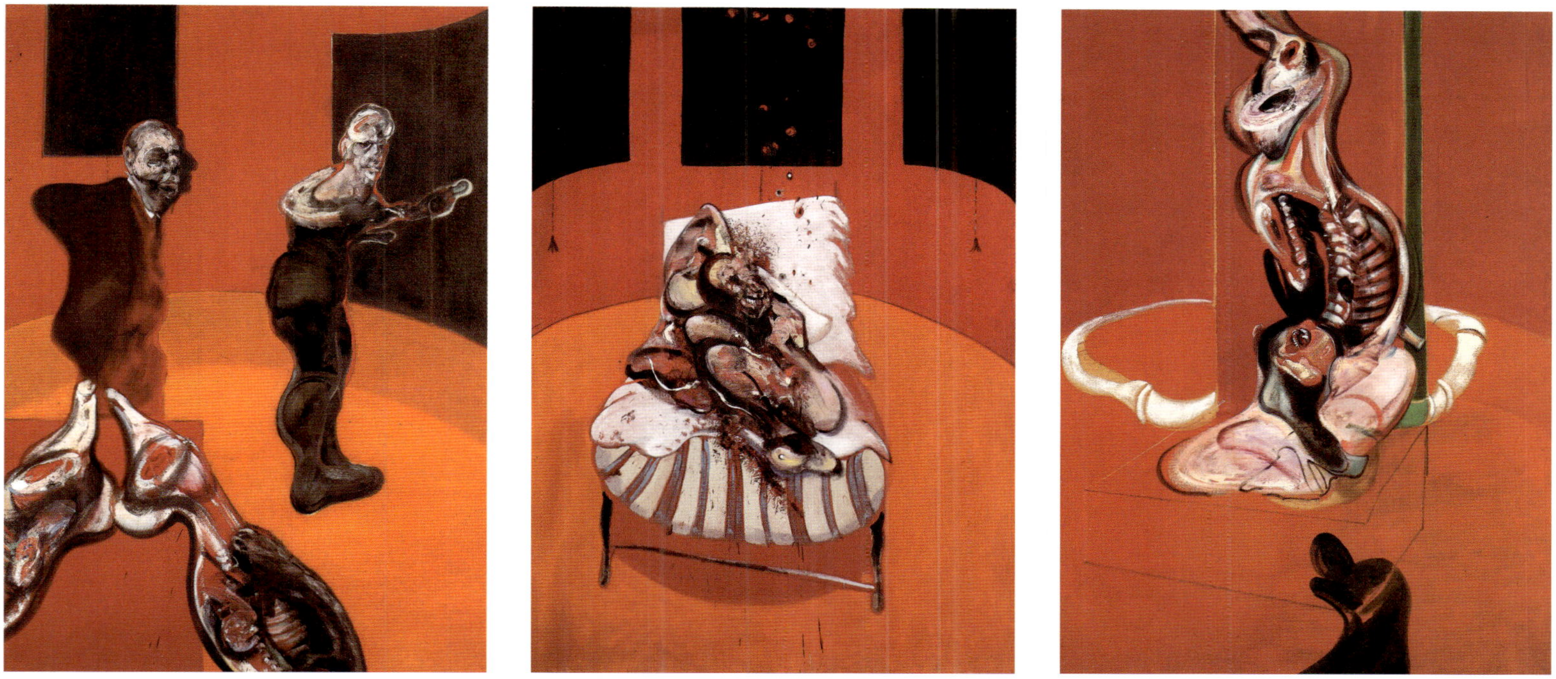

28 *Three Studies for a Crucifixion*, March, 1962, 198.2 × 144.8 cm, oil and sand on canvas. Solomon R. Guggenheim Museum, New York.

Lightfoot. For that whole period – almost the entire 1950s – he had been, as we have seen, to all intents and purposes homeless. Having returned to his old haunts and old habits in this area, with its partly French population and flavour, Bacon was never to leave – even though he did try out other studios, notably in the East End and in Paris.

One further event that went far in projecting Bacon into this new phase of his career was the retrospective held at the Tate Gallery in the early summer of 1962. The exhibition comprised ninety-one paintings – just under half Bacon's oeuvre at the time, according to the catalogue – ranging from the earliest Crucifixions of 1932–33 to the *Three Studies for a Crucifixion* (1962) which Bacon completed especially for the event. This startlingly violent triptych, which arrived still wet at the Tate, marked a decisive moment in Bacon's career and also, more importantly, in his whole psychological development. It is likely that the painting, which was done rapidly and while Bacon was often badly drunk and not in control, contains an implicit narrative – one of obvious importance to Bacon, since he went to some lengths thereafter to deny that it contained any kind of 'story'. Read very briefly from left to right, it appears to recount Bacon's expulsion from the family home by his father through a traumatic sexual encounter (possibly in Berlin) to an inverted Crucifixion (no doubt of Bacon himself) in the last panel, where the body has been split open like a side of meat in the abattoir.[44] However exaggerated or self-dramatizing, this picture of humiliating exile and suffering acted as an exorcism. It commemorated in a passionate outburst of rage the end of Bacon's complex subjection to father figures.

As if to underline this finality, Bacon received amongst the telegrams of congratulations at the opening of the Tate show one from Tangier informing him that Lacy had just died. Seeking masochistically to intensify the pain that Lacy's disappearance caused him, Bacon insisted that it was a suicide – that Lacy had deliberately and systematically drunk himself to death. The mixture of pain and guilt that Bacon felt for many years after the death fed into his paintings. But a whole new range of subjects, he discovered, was close at hand. 'When I was younger,' Bacon told me once, 'I needed extreme subject-matter for my paintings. Then, as I got older, I realized I had all the subjects I needed in my own life.' Always intense and varied, Bacon's social life reached epic dimensions as his legend and his fame as a painter grew in the wake of his Tate retrospective. Having devoted the morning to painting, the artist felt free to devote the rest of the day and much of the night to eating, drinking and generally carrying on with his wide circle of friends and even wider circles of admirers, drifters and spongers. Old friends took on a special importance as he realized that his feelings about them were as vivid and as transmutable into art as his feelings about any grand theme from the Greek tragedies to Yeats, the cave paintings to the Crucifixion, Michelangelo to Muybridge. Long in thrall to the great stories of civilization, Bacon suddenly found the myths he had pursued through art, poetry and religion in the everyday. The heroes and heroines of tragedy, the Orestes and Othellos, the Clytemnestras and Lady Macbeths, were all around him in the bars and clubs of Soho. If you had the power and conviction to raise then into myth, then Lucian Freud and George Dyer, Isabel Rawsthorne, Muriel Belcher and Henrietta Moraes, with their striking looks and strange trajectories through life, were very literally the stuff of which legends are made.

Bacon set about portraying them, with the fury and flair of a man who gave everything to friendship but disciplined himself to get little in return. He subjected his friends to the vertiginous roller coaster of his own sadomasochistic drives, flaying them alive with the force of his love. But because his will to live was always stronger than the worst punishment that portrayal could mete out, they lived on: bloodied heroes cut down to the bone, reeling against the painted sky, survivors in a world where it was taken for granted that the gods kill for their sport. Forever mindful of the great moments of history, Bacon realized that by mythologizing his inner circle, he could create a gallery of characters that typified a certain side to London, and more precisely to mid-century Soho, as memorably as any portraitist or novelist before him. Bacon was also about to find a new lover, young enough to be his son, in the guise of the hapless, ill-fated George Dyer. There were other voices and other doors opening. However disastrously, a new decade beckoned Bacon on.

1 The other exhibition being held at the Tate at the same time as the Bacon retrospective was an infinitely less disturbing 'Ecole de Paris' group show.

2 Despite his virulent atheism and his detestation of anything he thought smacked of mysticism, Bacon maintained a lifelong (and perfectly contradictory) interest in spiritualism. He kept a book purporting to have recorded and photographed séances and the subsequent apparition of spirits (*Phenomena of Materialisation* by Baron von Schrenk-Notzing) in his studio, and he incorporated the ectoplasm shown issuing from the mouths of mediums into numerous paintings.

Bacon also showed a great interest in oracles. In a letter to me dated 5 December 1984, he mentions the notion of 'enigma' and wonders out loud whether 'at Delphi the Sibyls still give it out'. In conversation he also once said to me: 'Often in my work I feel that I am following a long call from Antiquity'.

3 David Sylvester, *Interviews with Francis Bacon* (London: Thames and Hudson, 1993), p. 100.

4 The catalogue raisonné was compiled by Ronald Alley and published in London in 1964. Two appendices at the back of the catalogue list 'Abandoned pictures' and 'Destroyed pictures'. Since the catalogue was published, several 'abandoned' and a good number of so-called 'destroyed' paintings have come back into circulation.

5 The only study of Bacon's early works that I am aware of was published nearly thirty years ago. It is Hugh Marlais Davis, *Francis Bacon: The Early and Middle Years, 1928–1958* (New York, 1978).

6 Alley, *Francis Bacon*, p. 35.

7 For a detailed analysis of Bacon's religious views, see my essay 'Francis Bacon: The Sacred and the Profane', in *Francis Bacon – Le Sacré et le profane,* exh. cat., in French and English (Paris: Musée Maillol, 2004).

8 Bacon's father ordered him to leave the family house in Ireland after he surprised the sixteen-year-old boy trying on his mother's underwear.

9 It seems likely that Bacon joined up with his old nanny when he returned from Paris to London in 1928. From then on, they appear to have lived mostly together until her death in 1951.

10 Millais House currently houses the offices of the National Art Collections Fund.

11 Michael Wishart, *High Diver* (London: Quartet Books, 1978), pp. 61–62.

12 Bacon would regularly advertise his services as a gentleman's 'companion' in the personal columns in *The Times* (which then occupied the whole front page of the newspaper). The replies, he recounted gleefully, pored in; and Nanny Lightfoot, with unerring accuracy, would choose the gentleman likely to benefit the Bacon ménage most.

13 Wishart, *High Diver*, p. 68.

14 Quoted in Michael Peppiatt, *Francis Bacon: Anatomy of an Enigma* (London: Weidenfeld & Nicolson, 1996 and New York: Farrar, Straus & Giroux, 1997), pp. 120–21.

15 Peppiatt, *Anatomy of an Enigma*, pp. 121–22.

16 In conversation with the author.

17 There is a useful study to be made about the canvases which Bacon 'abandoned' in the various studios, in England and abroad, that he occupied. Essentially, if Bacon wanted to destroy a work, he did so in no uncertain manner, cutting it or having someone cut it, to shreds. On the other hand, if he had second thoughts about a picture but did not destroy it, leaving it behind him as he changed studios, then he basically wanted it to survive.

18 In Alley, *Francis Bacon*, this picture is listed as destroyed.

19 The 'Rhinoceros' painting is catalogued in Alley, *Francis Bacon*, as 'destroyed' (D8).

20 Sylvester, *Interviews*, p. 82.

21 Bacon sold the lease to the portrait painter, Robert Buhler, who was teaching at the Royal College of Art, at that time located just round the corner on Exhibition Road.

22 Bacon later presented the Royal College of Art with a painting for their collection: first, it was *Study for Bullfight 1* (1969), which Bacon then substituted by *Study of Human Body (Man Turning on the Light)* (1973). Since so little information is available about Bacon's time at the Royal College of Art, the following account is worth publishing in full. Written by the painter Albert Herbert, a student at the College at that time, this memoir, entitled *Francis Bacon at the Royal College of Art 1951–52*, is kept at the Tate Archive (under the reference TGA 991/47):

In 1951 John Minton inherited some money and went to Jamaica giving his teaching time to Francis Bacon. Professor Moynihan let Bacon use his studio to work in. This was the room in which Moynihan had painted the large group portrait of the College Staff. You might have thought that the students would have been excited by this new artist working in the College but I don't recall that being so. I was one of the very few who were really interested in Bacon's painting.

I first saw him in the students wash room, stripped to the waist, washing oil paint off his shoulders. I was too shy to comment on this, but at some point I did tell him that oil paint on raw canvas was supposed to rot it. He just shrugged and said 'Degas did it'.

He was quite affable and smiley but made no attempt at all to do any teaching. I once saw him peering at one of my paintings so I went up and stood by it, but he then walked away.

He was not secretive. He left the door of his studio ajar and during his very long lunches I often went in to see what he was doing. There were about 20 canvases, perhaps about 4 × 3 feet stretched the wrong way round. At one stage he filled a bucket with black house paint and with a broom from the corridor splashed it over the canvases. It also went over the walls and the ceiling. I noticed he drew on the canvas with chalk and pastel – working out compositional lines in a traditional way. These lines were of course eliminated when he painted over them. He was not quite so spontaneous as he later said. I am certain I remember this correctly because I copied the idea myself. Most of these paintings were of naked men in the grass. One day he slashed many of them and gave me some of the fragments to paint on, which I did - (this now seems surprising, but he was not at that time very famous, and only recall painting over smudgy paint – like the standing grass in the backgrounds).

At the end of one term (probably Christmas) Robert Buhler persuaded him to give a 'sketch club' criticism. Students hung their work on the walls and he was expected to discuss them. He paced up and down in a bouncy way in his thick crepe soles smiling amiably and said 'I am afraid I just can't think of anything to say about these paintings. I am told I should give three prizes but as they all appear equally dull I can't do that'. He then began to walk out of the room until Buhler said 'Perhaps you could answer some questions Francis?' So he stood smiling confidently at us, rather like an actor, apparently unaware that he now had a hostile audience, most of whom did not value him as an artist much anyway.

1st question 'Why are all these paintings so dull?'

'Because they are all based on someone else's painting.'

'Mr Bacon, in your last show all the paintings were based on a Vélasquez. How do you answer that? Why are you painting the Pope?'

I am afraid I just can't recall all of this but it quickly became an intense argument in which Bacon seemed to lose his cool and began to justify his work with impulsive, sometimes absurd explanations that he seemed to be making up under the stress of the questions. For example – he said he painted the Pope because he wanted to use purple paint – it was as if there was an aspect of his work he was anxious not to reveal or else he really did not know consciously what he was doing.

I was immensely impressed by this long heated discussion – the most significant lesson of my time as a student. Every other artist or teacher had spoken of painting as if it was a craft which one went about in a rational controlled way – Francis was demonstrating that this was not so.

Looking back now it is possible that I understood it like that – real artists are driven by unconscious motives – just because I intuitively wanted to believe that. I once discussed this with my exact contemporary, Michael Andrews (who was at the Slade then) who had a similar feeling about Bacon.

That was in 1951. I feel that Bacon soon began to turn himself into a professional artist, with a public image and more like a craftsman.

23 *Time Magazine* noted in its review of the 1949 Hanover show that Bacon had already destroyed 700 paintings.

24 Bacon began consulting Muybridge's photographs of animals and human beings in motion in the late 1940s, probably at the Victoria and Albert Museum just across the road from his Cromwell Place studio. During the 1950s Muybridge became one of his prin-

cipal sources – or 'triggers of ideas', as Bacon put it. Having looked so intently and for so long at Muybridge's images and Michelangelo's drawings (another influential source), Bacon was later to claim that he could no longer distinguish Muybridge's influence on his work from Michelangelo's.

25 Due in part to his work having been included in the Venice Biennale and shown in several galleries around the country, the Italians were the first people on the continent to admire and collect Bacon; and a number of important paintings from the 1950s are still in Italian collections today. The French took longer to admit Bacon into their canon of great, living artists; but after the Bacon retrospective held at the Grand Palais in Paris in 1971, no country remained as appreciative and enthusiastic.

26 Colin MacInnes, *England, Half English* (London: MacGibbon and Kee, 1961), p. 73.

27 The whole text, published in the catalogue of the Matthew Smith retrospective at the Tate Gallery in 1953, runs as follows: 'Because I very much admire Matthew Smith, I am delighted to have been asked to write something about him, although I know I will not be able to do him justice. He seems to me to be one of the very few English painters since Constable and Turner to be concerned with painting, that is, with attempting to make idea and technique inseparable. Painting in this sense tends towards a complete interlocking of image and paint, so that the image is the paint and vice versa. Here the brush-stroke creates the form and does not merely fill it in. Consequently, every movement of the brush on the canvas alters the shapes and implications of the image. That is why real painting is a mysterious and continuous struggle with chance – mysterious because the very substance of the paint, when used in this way, can make such a direct assault upon the nervous system; continuous because the medium is so fluid and subtle that every change that is made loses what is already there in the hope of making a fresh gain. I think that painting today is pure intuition and luck and taking advantage of what happens when you splash the bits down, and in this game of chance Matthew Smith seems to have the gods on his side.'

28 Four of Bacon's paintings had been included in a show entitled 'The New Decade: 22 European Painters and Sculptors', and the artist produced the following statement for the accompanying catalogue: 'Art is a method of opening up areas of feeling rather than merely an illustration of an object. . . . A picture should be a recreation of an event rather than an illustration of an object; but there is no tension in the picture unless there is the struggle with the object. I would like my pictures to look as if a human being had passed between them, like a snail, leaving a trail of the human presence and memory trace of past events as the snail leaves its slime.'

29 Wyndham Lewis wrote: 'Of the younger painters none actually paints so beautifully as Francis Bacon. I have seen painting of his that reminded me of Velásquez and like that master he is fond of blacks. Liquid whitish accents are delicately dropped upon the sable ground, like blobs of mucus – or else there is the cold white glitter of an eyeball, or of an eye distended with despairing insult behind a shouting mouth, distended also to hurl insults. Otherwise it is a baleful regard from the mask of a decayed clubman or business executive – so decayed that usually part of the head is rotting away into space. But black is his pictorial element. These faces come out of the blackness to glare or to shout. I must not attempt to describe these amazing pictures – the shouting creatures in glass cases, these dissolving ganglia the size of a small fist in which one can always discern the shouting mouth, the wild distended eye. In the *Nude*, in front of not the least ominous of curtains, about to enter, the artist is seen at his best. Bacon is one of the most powerful artists in Europe today and he is perfectly in tune with his time. Not like his namesake 'the brightest, wisest of mankind', he is, on the other hand, one of the darkest and most possessed.' Wyndham Lewis, 'Round the London Art Galleries', *The Listener*, 17 November 1949.

30 'I've always been very moved by the movements of the mouth and the shape of the mouth and the teeth. People say that these have all sorts of sexual implications, and I was always very obsessed by the actual appearance of the mouth and teeth, and perhaps I have lost that obsession now, but it was a very strong thing at one time. I like, you may say, the glitter and colour that comes from the mouth, and I've always hoped in a sense to be able to paint the mouth as Monet painted a sunset.' Sylvester, *Interviews*, pp. 49–50.

Release is very explicit in *Two Figures* (1953) and *Two Figures in the Grass* (1954), but the motif of open mouth and orgasm can be found in much later paintings, such as *Two Figures* (1975).

31 In answer to David Sylvester's question as to what his feelings about his father were, Bacon replies: 'Well, I

disliked him, but I was sexually attracted to him when I was young. When I first sensed it, I hardly knew it was sexual. It was only later, through the grooms and the people in the stables I had affairs with, that I realized it was a sexual thing towards my father.' Sylvester, *Interviews*, pp. 71–72.

32 The story was told to Daniel Farson by the writer Caroline Blackwood, who had got to know Bacon well when she was married to Lucian Freud in the 1950s. As a member of the Guinness family, Blackwood would have been familiar with the Anglo-Irish background of Bacon's childhood, and the fact that she tells this story gives it more credibility. However, Farson notes that Blackwood herself had first heard it from a third person, a 'homosexual friend'. If it is true, one wonders why no one ever heard it from Bacon himself, who was not above telling stories which showed him in a dramatic light.

33 Quoted in Ted Morgan, *Literary Outlaw: The Life and Times of William S. Burroughs* (London: The Bodley Head, 1991).

34 *The Letters of Ann Fleming*, ed. Mark Amory (London: The Harvill Press, 1985), p. 197.

35 Morgan, *Literary Outlaw*, p. 267.

36 At one point Bacon apparently took up with an alarming-sounding Moroccan known simply as 'the Gorilla'. See Daniel Farson, *The Gilded-Gutter Life of Francis Bacon*, London, 1993, p. 162.

37 John Russell, *Francis Bacon* (New York: Thames and Hudson, 1993), p. 51.

38 Although, as a general rule, he was unusually considerate of other people's needs and wishes, Bacon could sometimes be ruthless, and even treacherous.

39 Bacon's boundless self-reliance and optimism (however rooted in nihilism) comes over nicely at the very end of his conversations with Sylvester. When Sylvester asks him whether he would prefer the torments of hell to annihilation, Bacon replies unhesitatingly: 'Yes, I would, because if I was in hell I would always feel I had a chance of escaping. I'd always be sure that I'd be able to escape'. Sylvester, *Interviews*, p. 200.

40 Bacon would also have seen the 'New American Painting' exhibition which opened at the Tate Gallery in February 1959. A 'magpie' eye is in itself of little interest; it is what it does with its finds that counts, of course. Since Bacon drew so little and did not bother to conserve his drawings, we have scant indication as to how the magpie eye worked and how the artist's images took first shape. In the late 1950s, however, Bacon made a series of notes for future paintings that can be read almost in lieu of drawings. They were written on the endpapers of a book devoted mainly to photographs of monkeys that Bacon kept in the studio (*Introducing Monkeys* by V. J. Stanek). Dated between December 1957 and January 1959, the notes contain quite detailed indications of what kind of images were running through Bacon's mind during this period. It is worth quoting a few of these here (in no particular sequence), not least since some of them have a direct bearing on the pictures Bacon went on to produce around that time or even much later in his career:

> Man pulling screaming child in centre of circle
>
> use figure volante of Rodin on sofa arms raised
>
> Upside-down figure in centre of room on sofa
>
> The bed of crime in centre of circular room
>
> Camel lying down in middle of circle of sand
>
> Chimpanzee standing in middle of carpet
>
> Figure at wash basin with boxing figure in circle
>
> landscape with old newspapers

Some of the notes are more general (such as the exhortation: 'Turn the local image + movement into ritual image') while others contain precise technical directions, notably when Bacon makes the following memo to himself: 'against dark background made of alizarin crimson + Winsor green keep background as simple as possible with blinds or radiator'). These notes can be consulted in Matthew Gale's book on Bacon's drawings, *Francis Bacon: Working on Paper* (London: Tate Gallery Publishing, 1999, pp. 76–80).

41 Cecil Beaton, *The Restless Years* (London: Weidenfeld & Nicolson, 1976), pp. 100–106. Beaton probably asked for his portrait to be painted after having taken so many photographs of Bacon. There is a telling little coda to the story. When Beaton visited Augustus John (also for a sitting) shortly after the second portrait séance with Bacon, he complained that 'Francis Bacon had painted me like a piece of raw offal against an emerald green background.' 'You deserve it for sitting to him,' Augustus said and then, with infinite sarcasm: 'These idiosyncracies are the perogative of genius.' Beaton, *The Restless Years*, p. 107.

42 Robert Melville's text was originally published in the catalogue to the fifth Bienal of São Paulo, which included a one-man show of Bacon's paintings, in 1959.

43 Having got to know the studio quite well during my frequent visits to Reece Mews (where visitors usually got no further than the spartan bed-sitting room which occupied the remaining space), I used to think of this little work-space as the key to the mysteries of Bacon's images since it contained so many paint traces and such an archive of books and photos consulted. I put down some of my impressions of this memorable space in my biography of Bacon (*Francis Bacon: Anatomy of an Enigma*) and also in an essay entitled 'Francis Bacon At Work', in *Francis Bacon: A Retrospective*, exh. cat. (New York: Harry N. Abrams, Inc., in association with The Trust for Museum Exhibitions, 1999), pp. 25–37, and brought out in French as a small book, *Francis Bacon à l'atelier* (L'Echoppe, Paris, 1999). Several other studies have taken the studio as their focus, the most complete being Margarita Cappock's *Francis Bacon's Studio* (London: Merrell, 2005).

44 I have analysed the significance of this triptych and of Bacon's whole attitude towards the Crucifixion in the catalogue to the exhibition (Peppiatt, *Francis Bacon – Le Sacré et le profane*), which was shown at the IVAM in Valencia (2003) and at the Musée Maillol, Paris (2004).

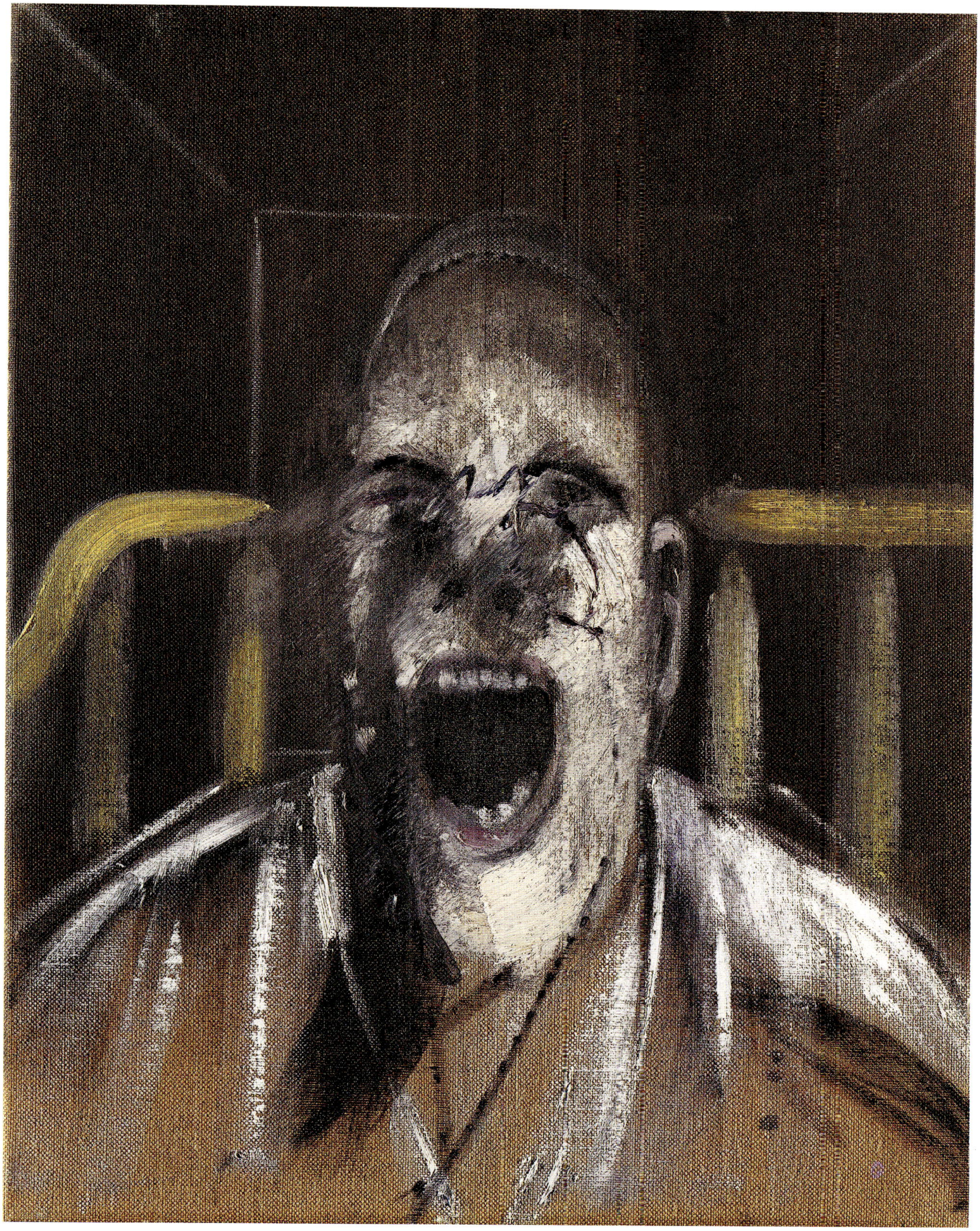

CAT 1 *Study for the Head of a Screaming Pope*, 1952, 67.9 x 57.8 cm, oil on canvas. Yale Center for British Art, New Haven, Gift of Beekman C. and Margaret H. Cannon.

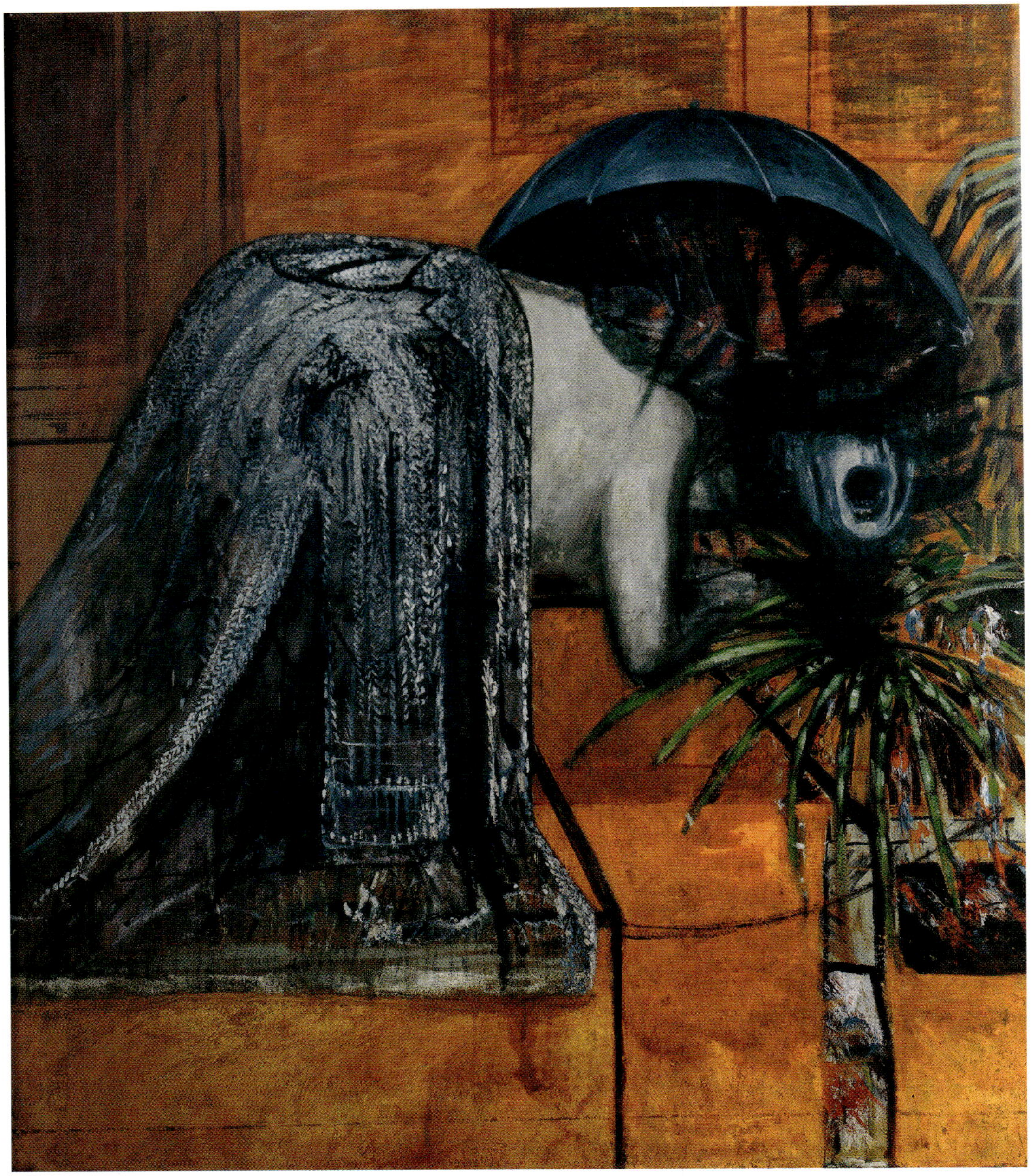

CAT 2 *Figure Study II*, 1945, 145 × 128.5 cm, oil on canvas. Huddersfield Art Gallery, presented by the Contemporary Art Society to Batley Art Gallery, 1952.

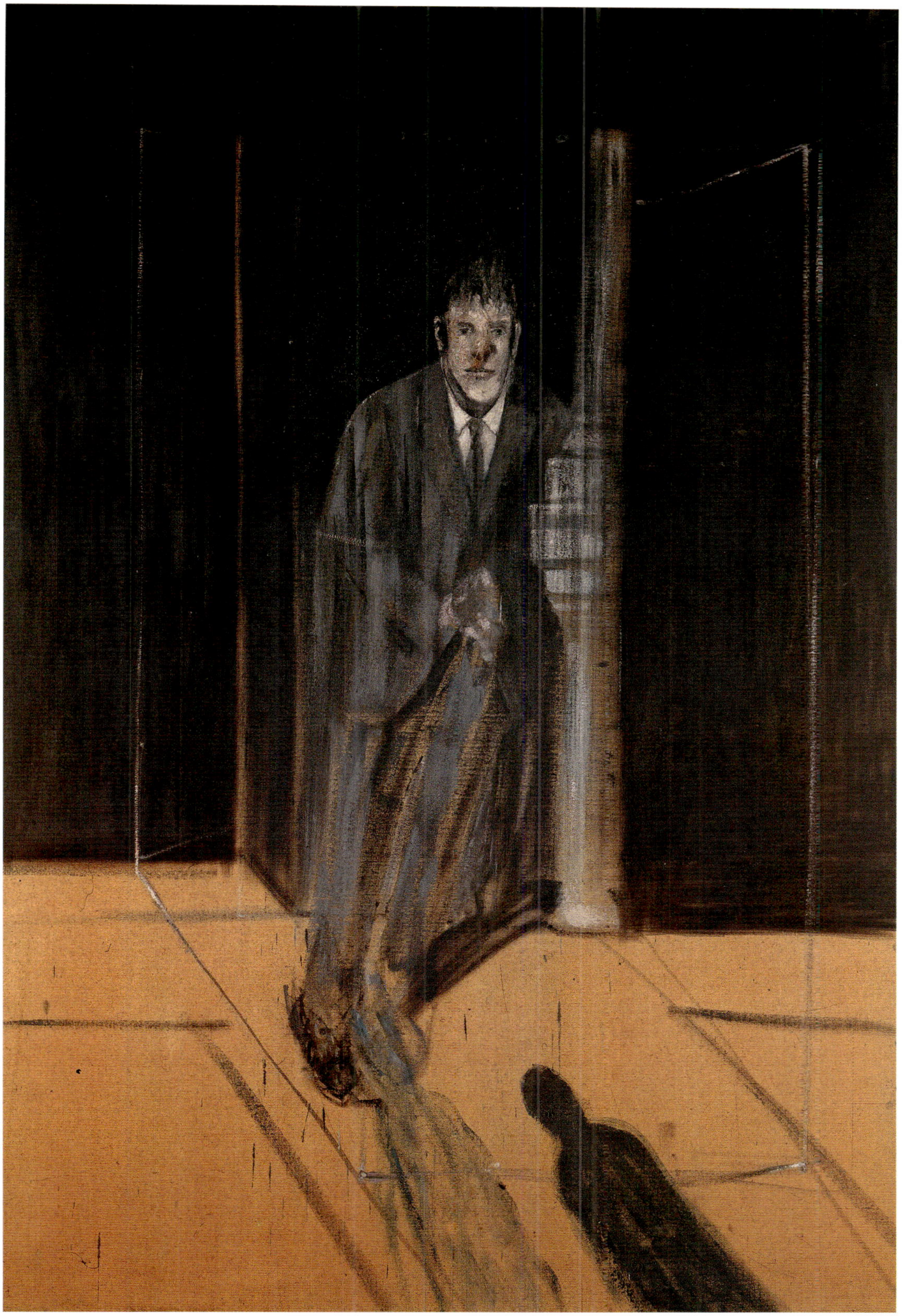

CAT 3 *Portrait of Lucian Freud*, 1951, 210.2 × 149.4 cm, oil on canvas. The Whitworth Art Gallery, University of Manchester.

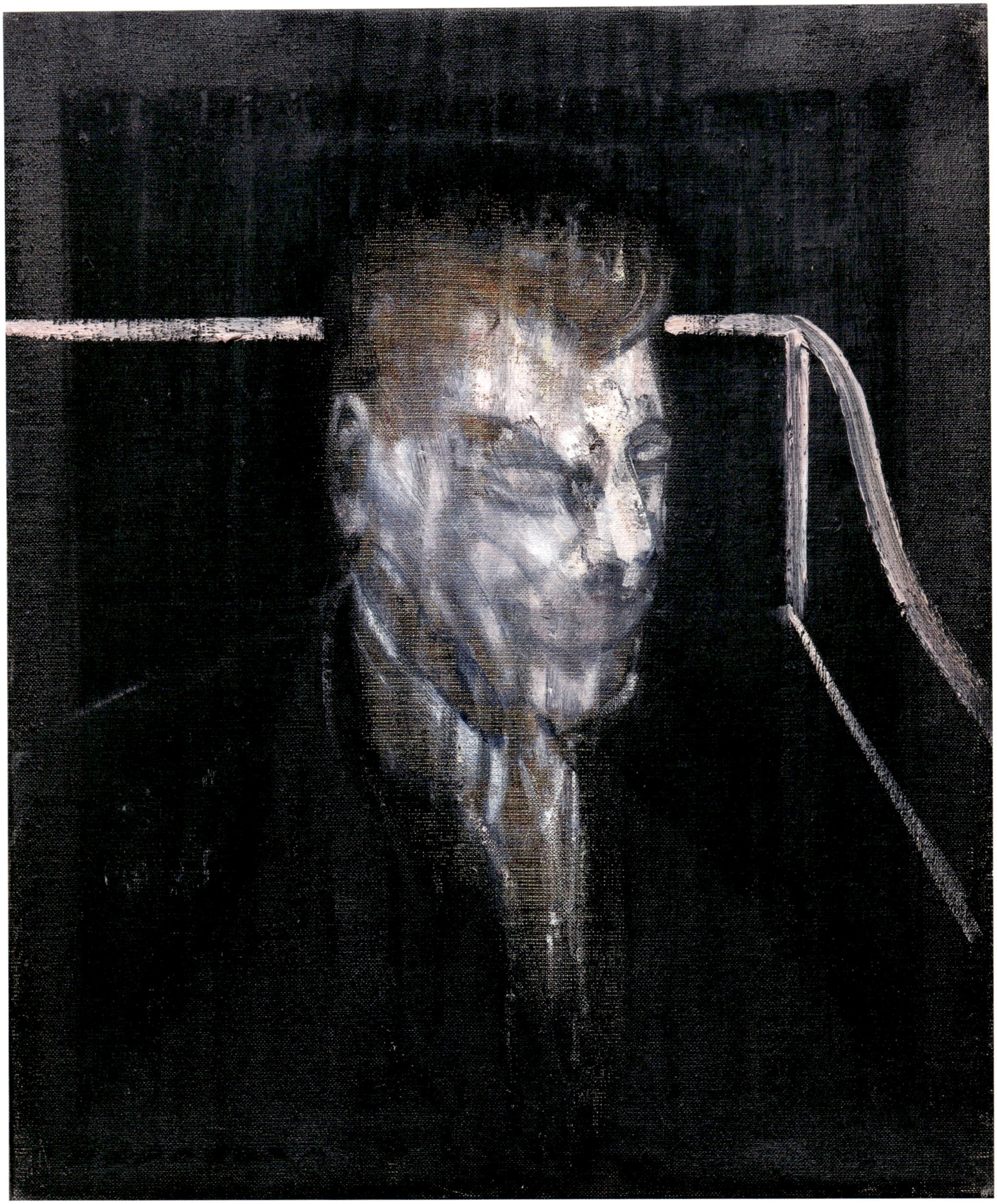

CAT 4 *Head in Grey*, 1955, 70 × 61.25 cm, oil on canvas. Collection Walker Art Center, Minneapolis.
Donated by Mr and Mrs Edmond R. Ruben, 1995.

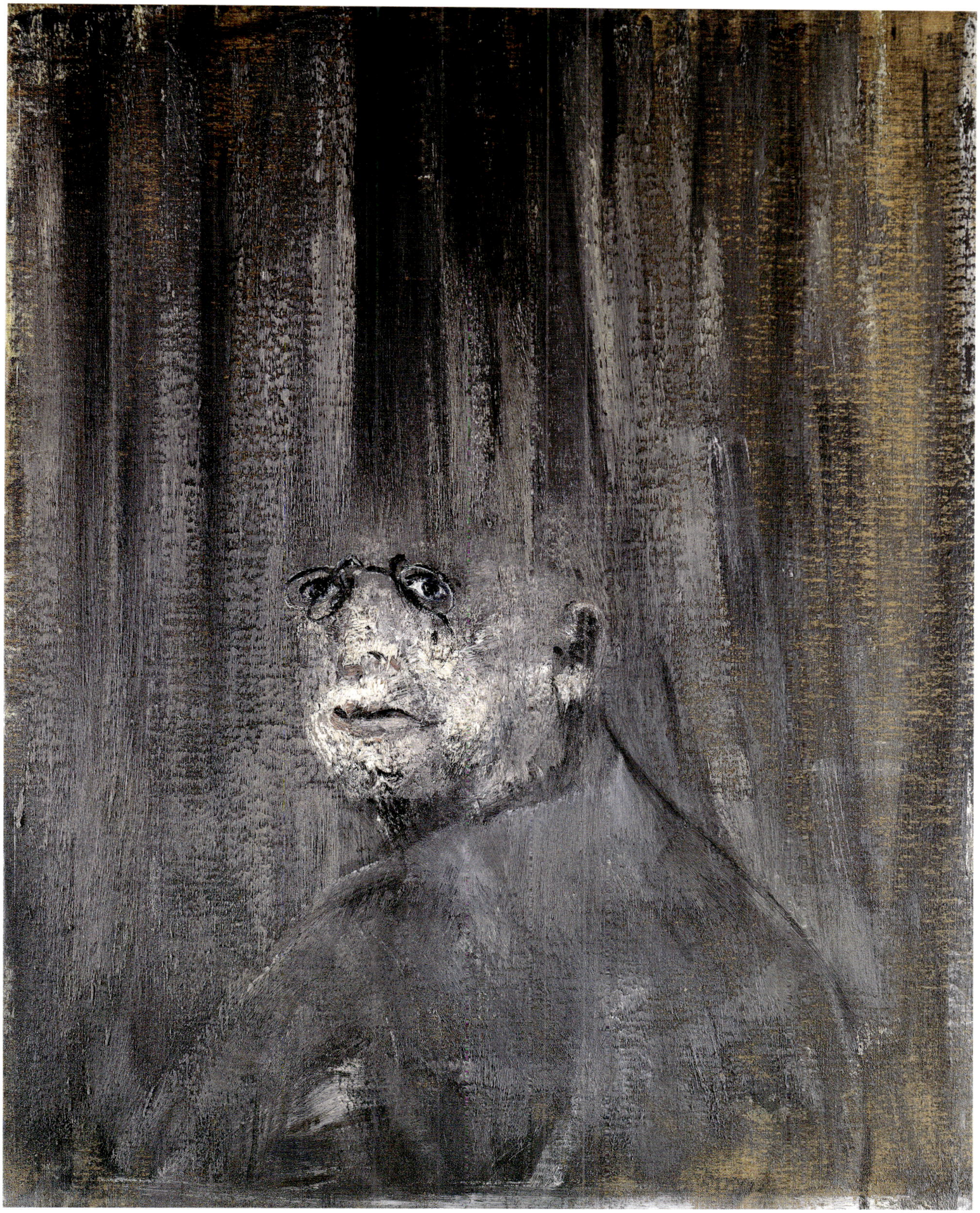

CAT 5 *Head III*, 1949, 81.3 × 66 cm, oil on canvas. Private collection.

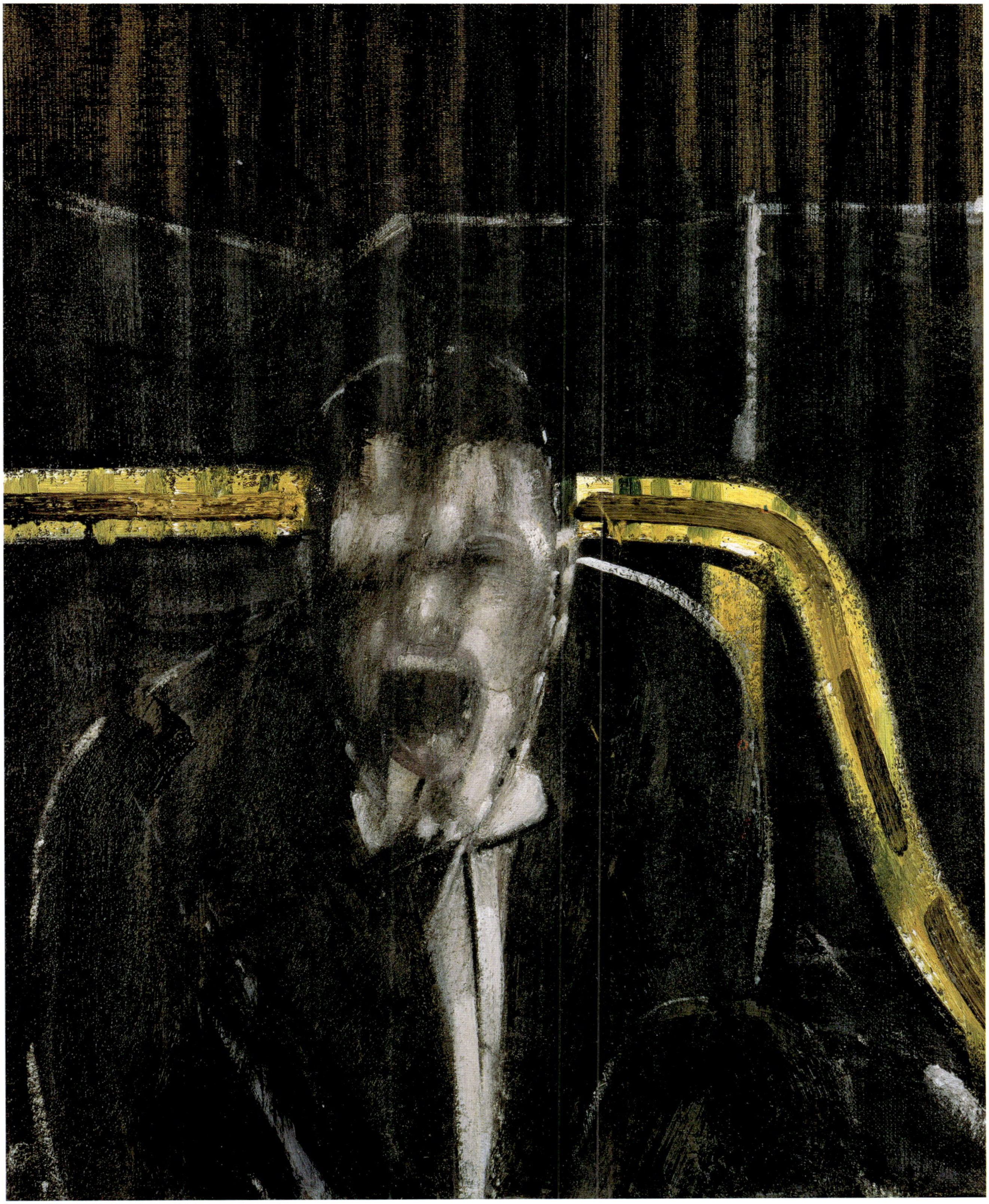

CAT 6 *Screaming Man*, 1952, 75 × 66 cm, oil on canvas. Private collection.

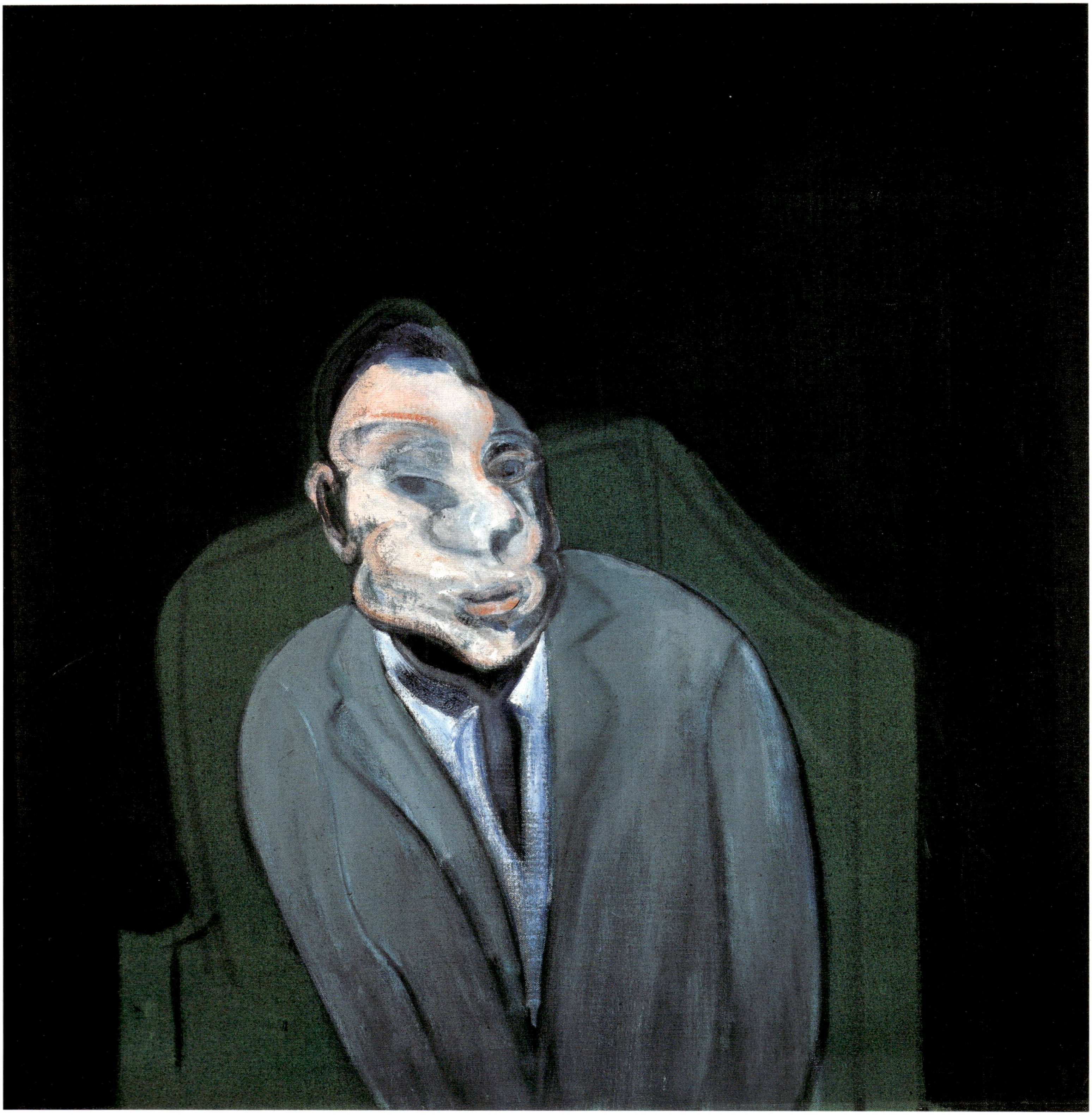

CAT 7 *Head of a Man*, 1960, 89.2 × 89.2 cm, oil on canvas. Robert and Lisa Sainsbury Collection, University of East Anglia, Norwich.

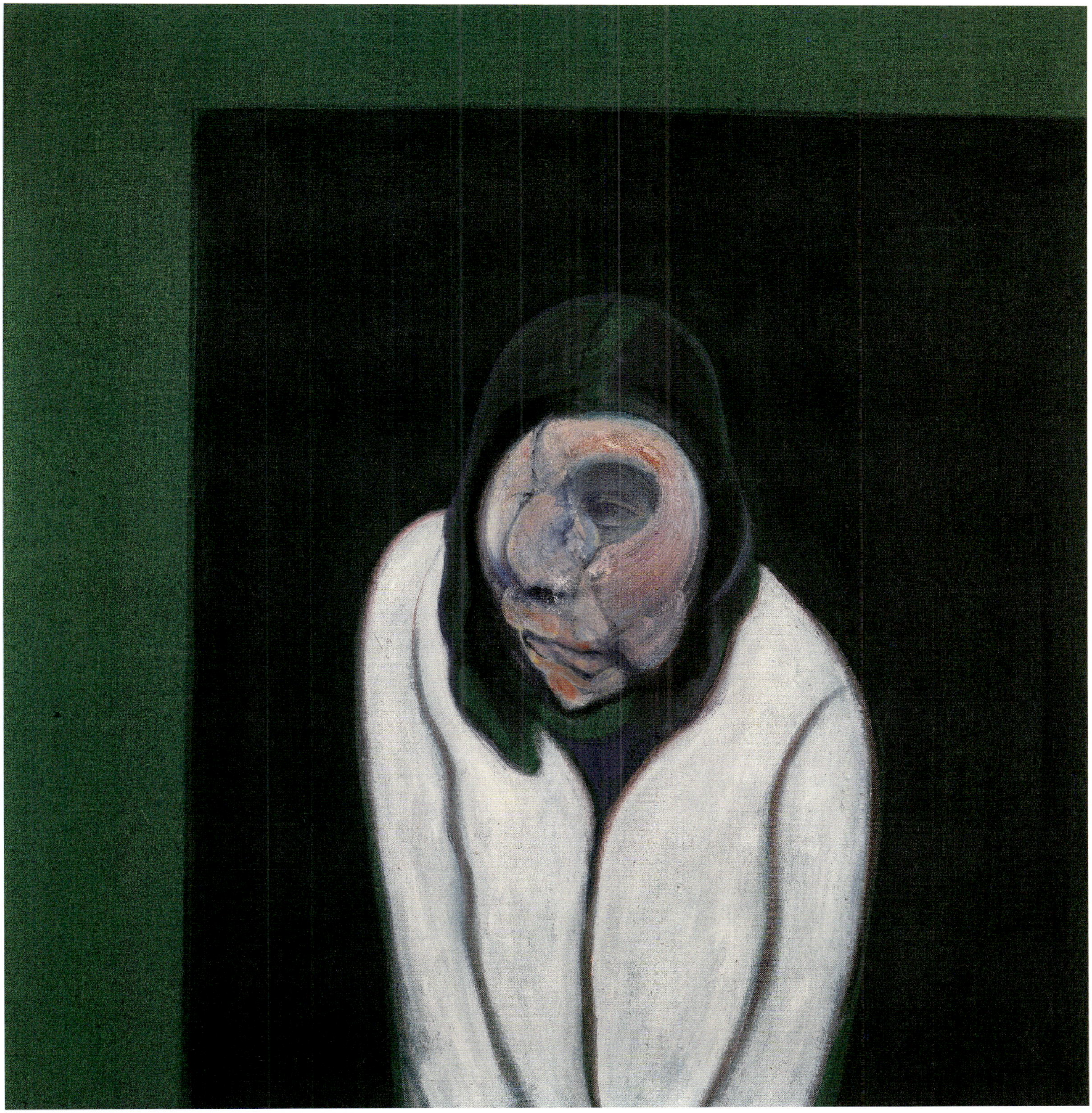

CAT 8 *Head of a Woman*, 1960, 89.2 × 89.2 cm, oil on canvas. Robert and Lisa Sainsbury Collection, University of East Anglia, Norwich.

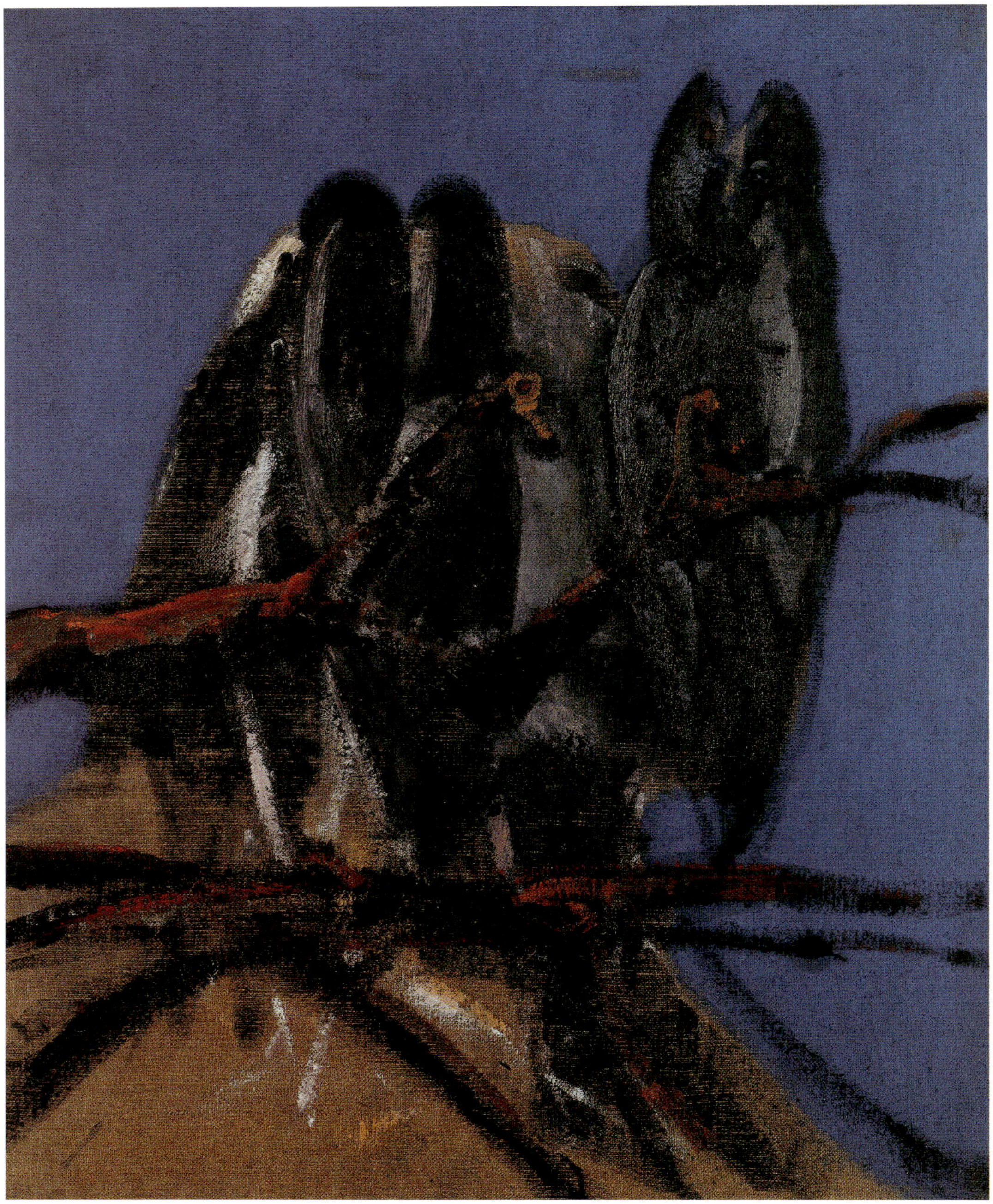

CAT 9 *Owls*, 1956, 74 × 64 cm, oil on canvas. Private collection.

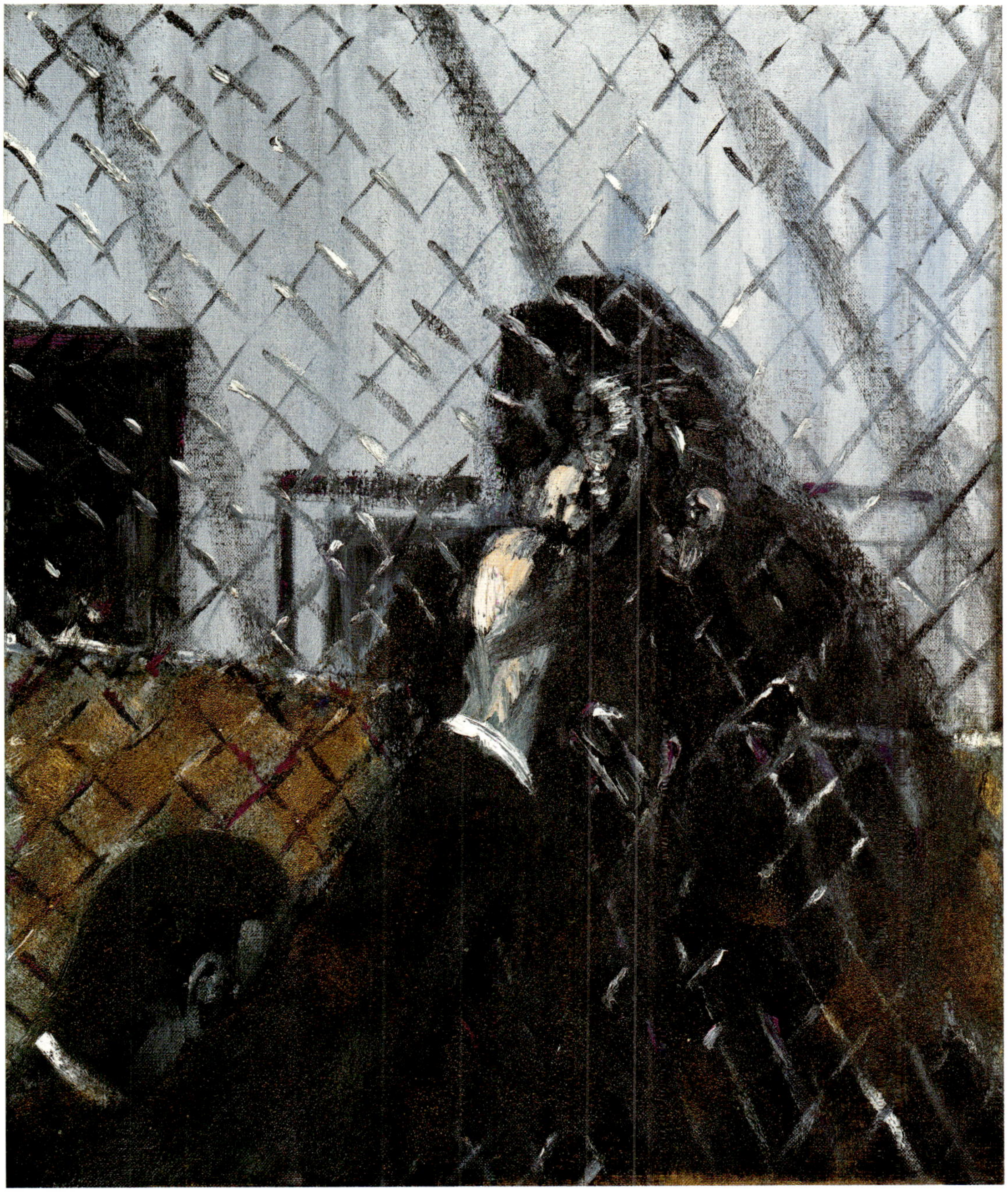

CAT 10 *Figure with Monkey*, 1951, 85 × 75 cm, oil on canvas. Private collection.

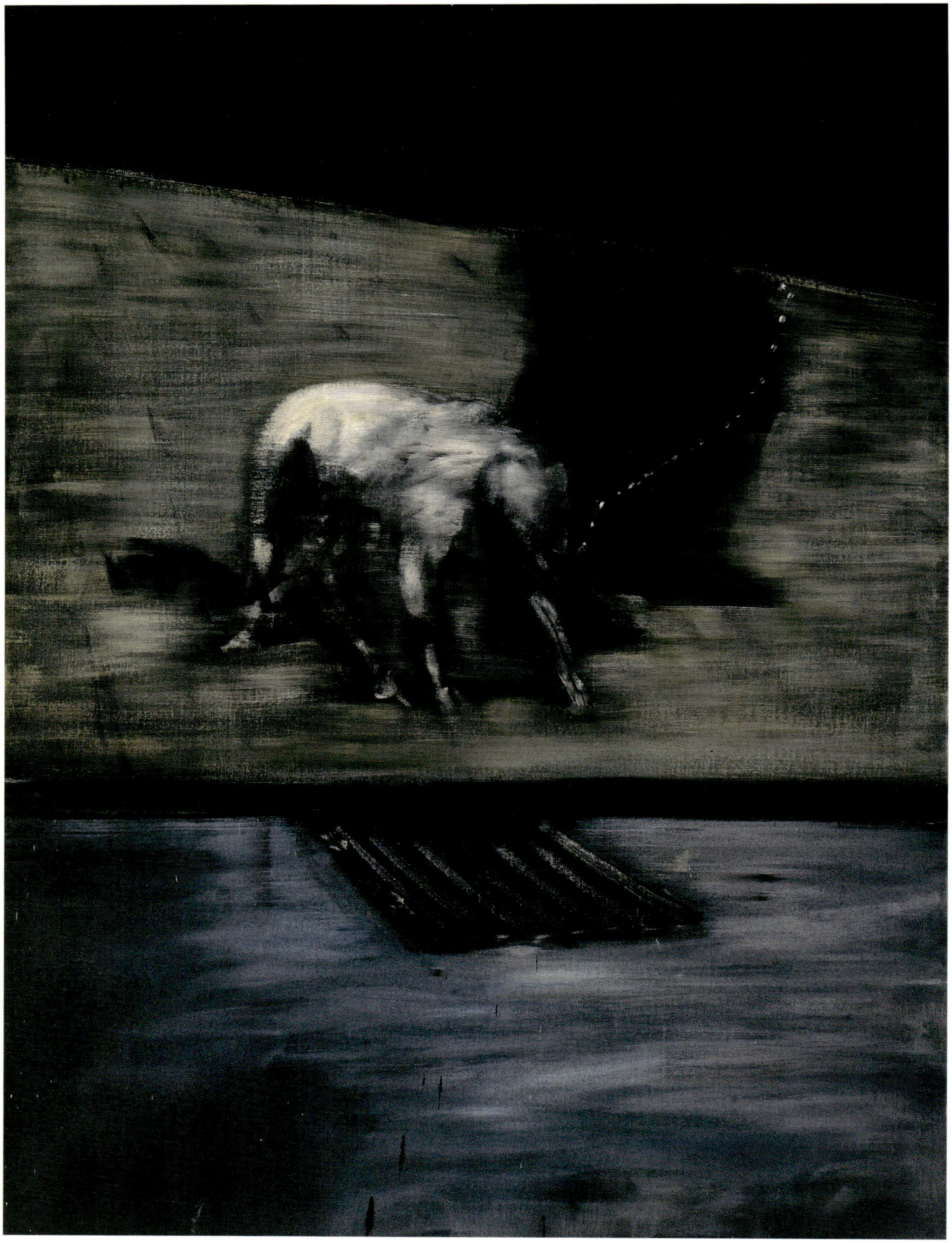

CAT 11 *Man with Dog*, 1953, 153.1 × 118.1 cm, oil on canvas. Albright-Knox Art Gallery, Buffalo, New York. Gift of Seymour H. Knox, Jr., 1955.

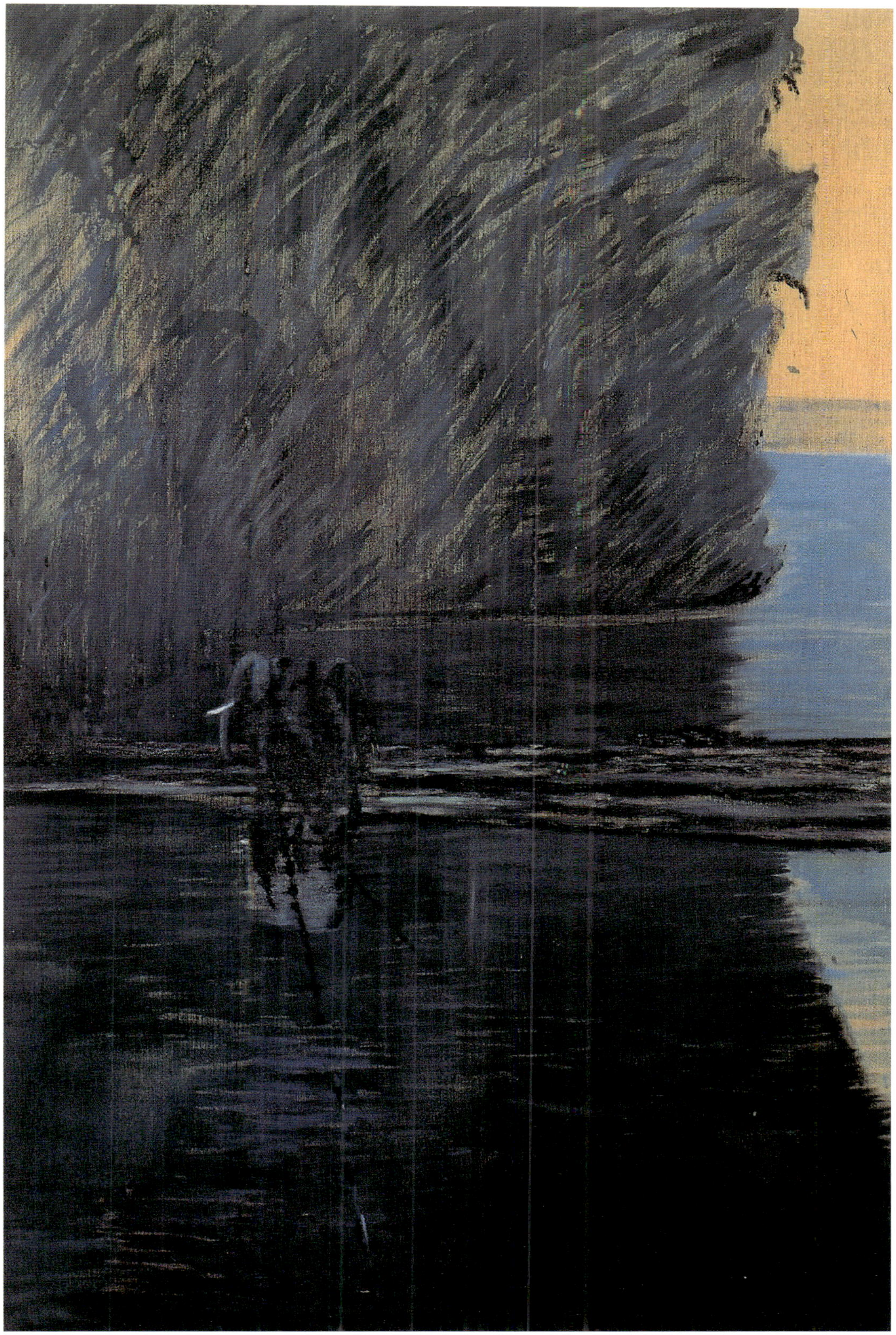

CAT 12 *Elephant Fording a River*, 1952, 198 × 137 cm, oil on canvas. Private collection, courtesy Crane Kalman Gallery, London.

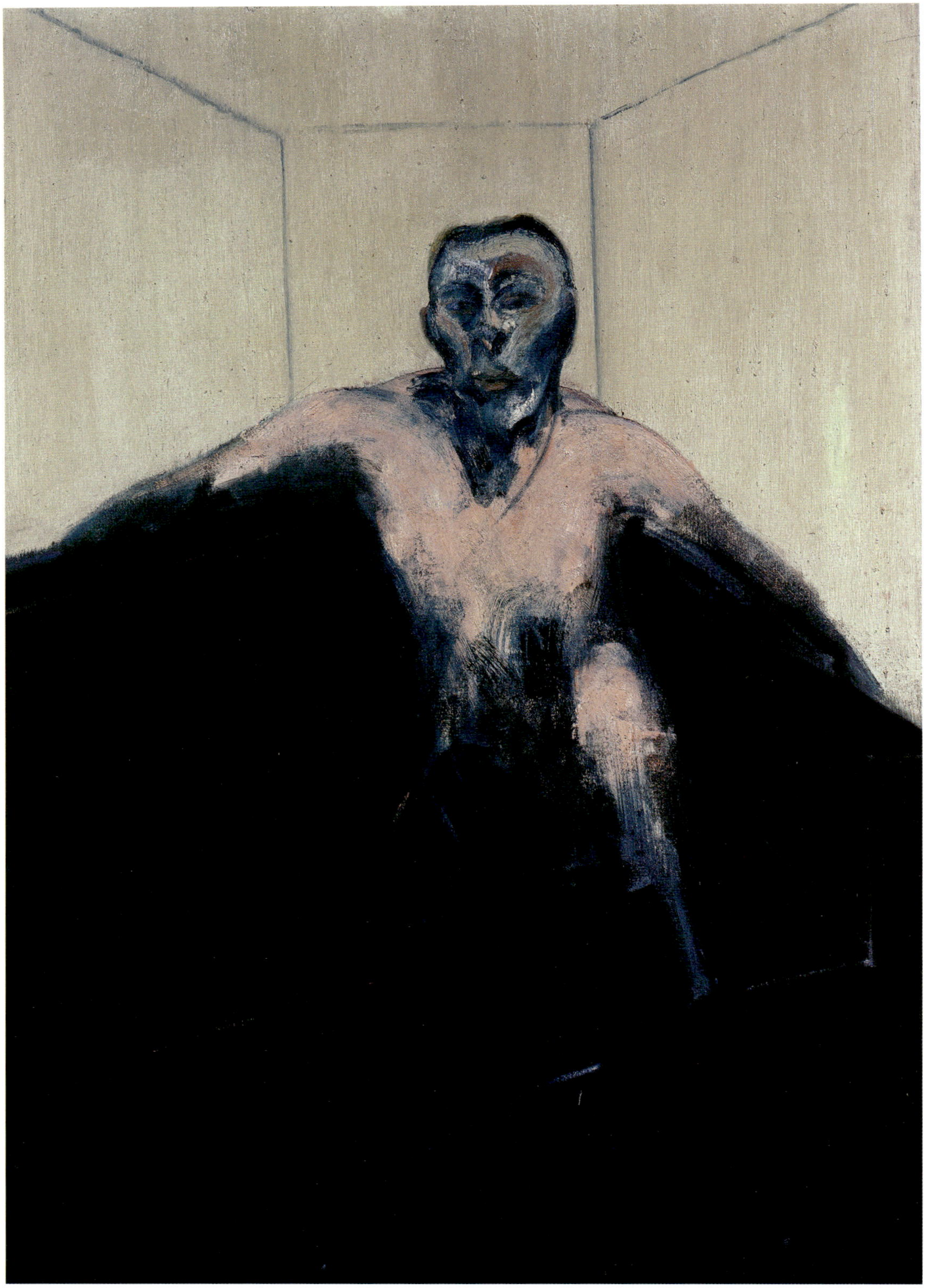

CAT 13 *Study for Portrait of P. L., no. 2*, 1957, 151.8 × 118.5 cm, oil on canvas. Robert and Lisa Sainsbury Collection, University of East Anglia, Norwich.

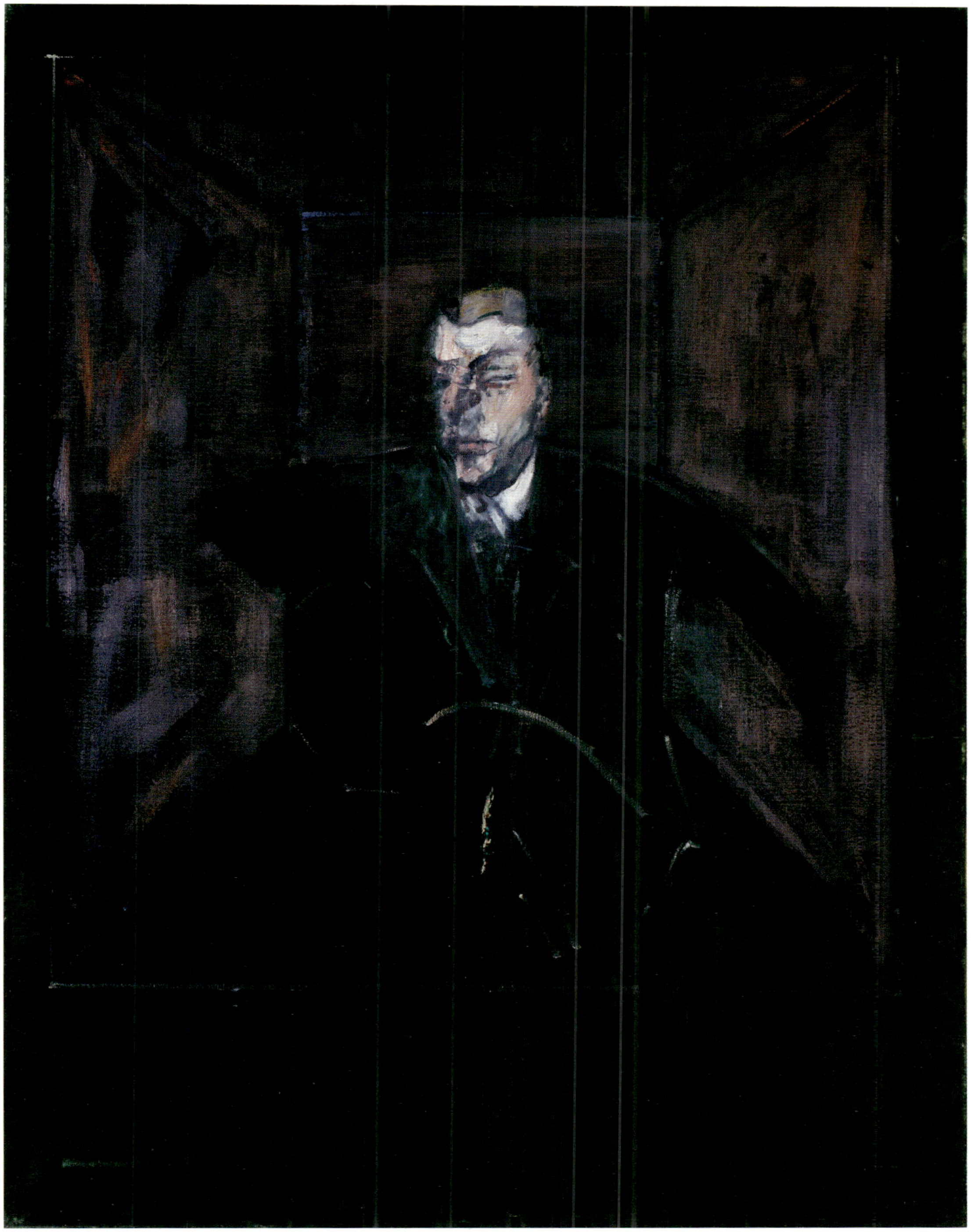

CAT 14 *Study for Figure VI*, 1956/7, 155 × 122 cm, oil on canvas. Hatton Gallery, University of Newcastle.

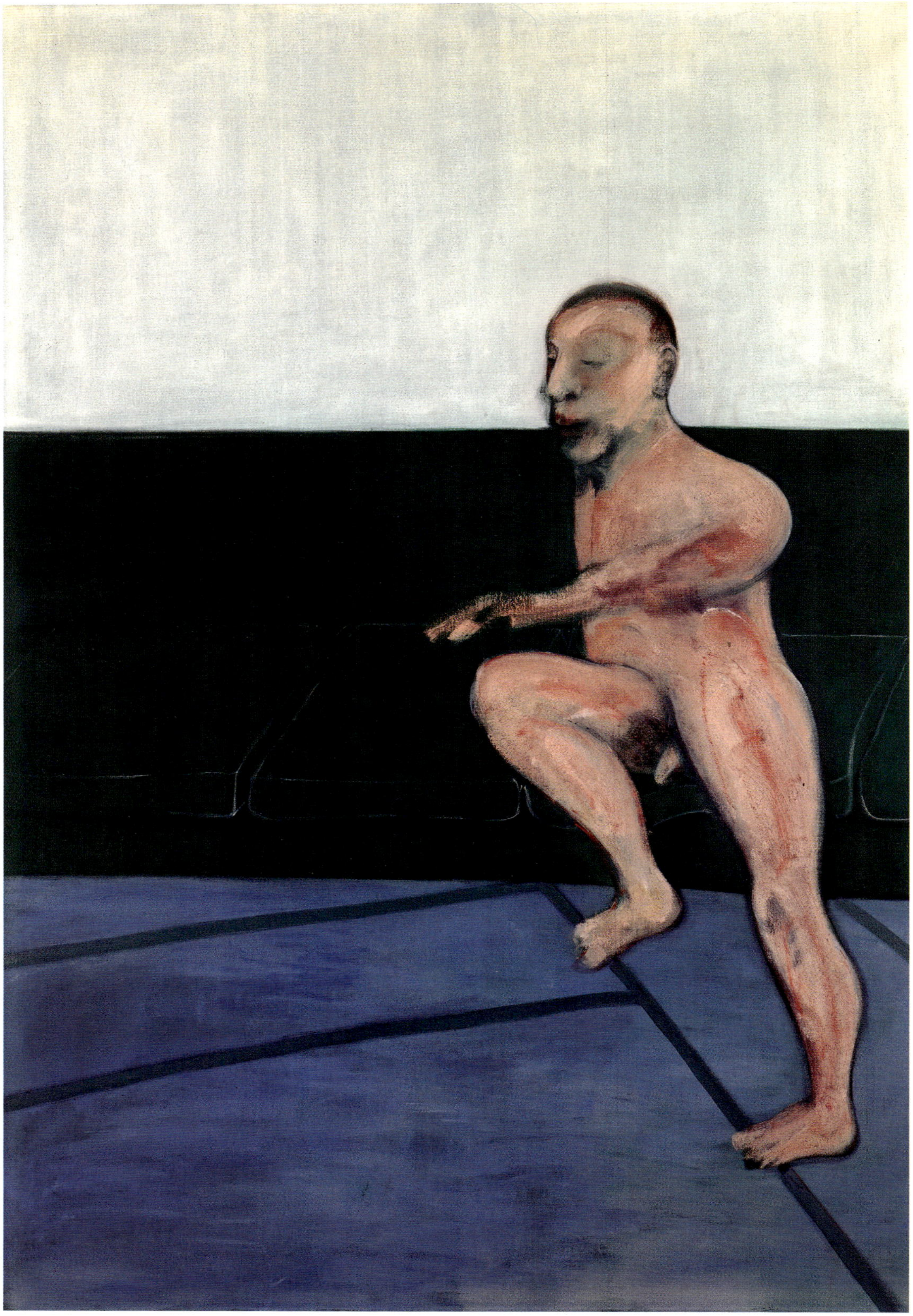

CAT 15 *Seated Figure on Couch*, 1959, 198 x 141.5 cm, oil on canvas. Private collection.

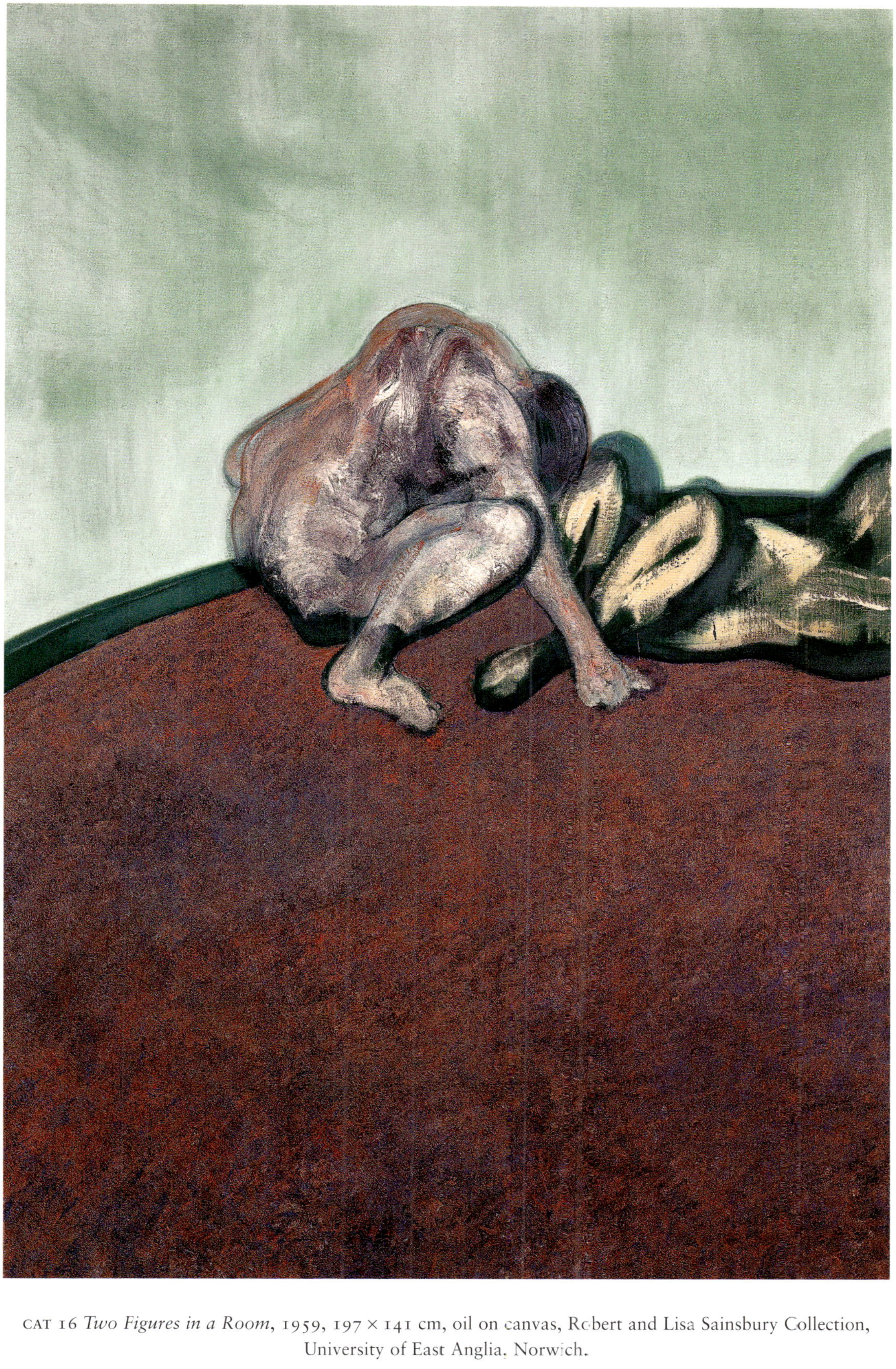

CAT 16 *Two Figures in a Room*, 1959, 197 × 141 cm, oil on canvas, Robert and Lisa Sainsbury Collection, University of East Anglia, Norwich.

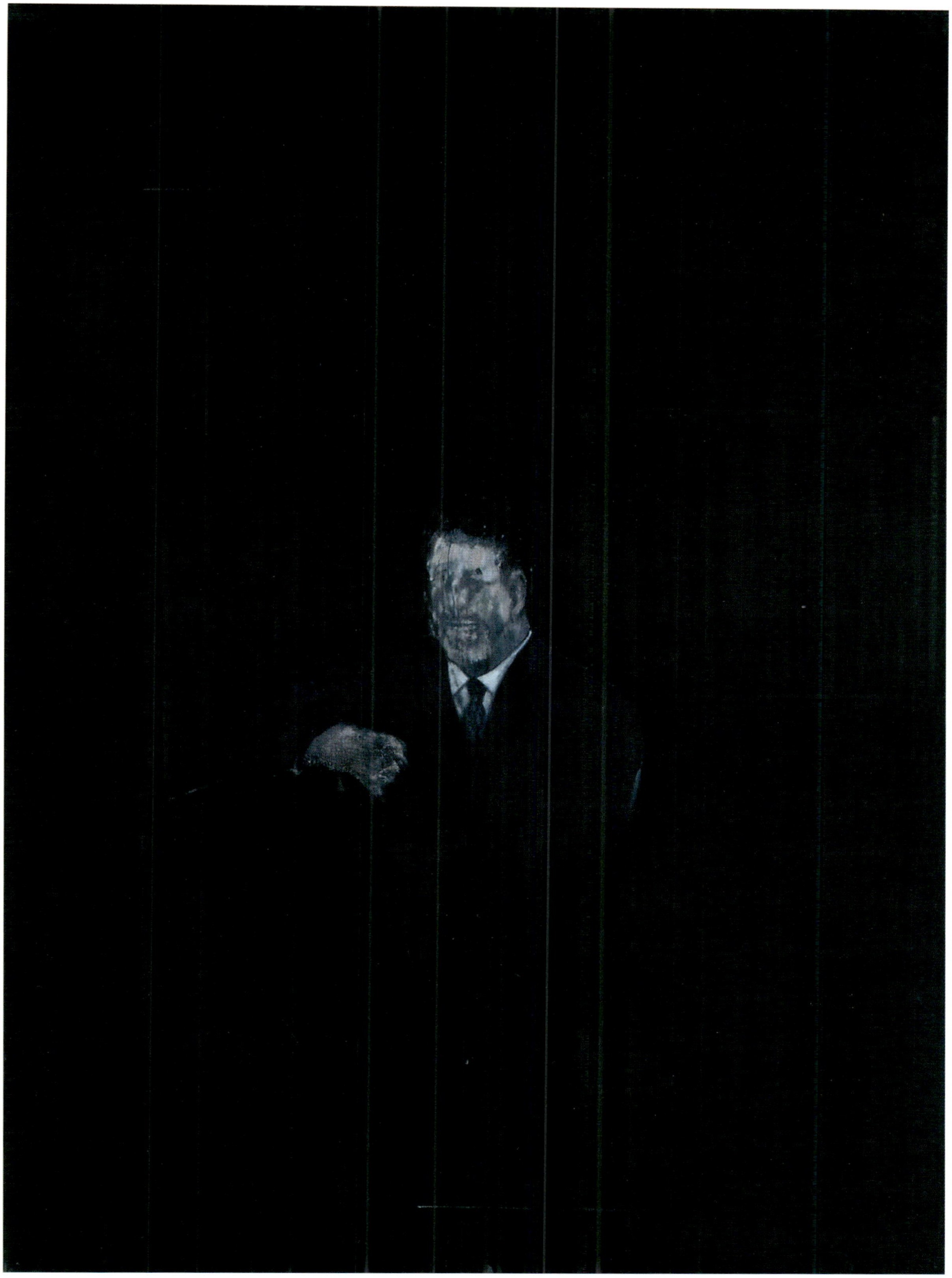

CAT 17 *Man in Blue* VI, 1954, 198 × 137 cm, oil on canvas. Aviva PLC.

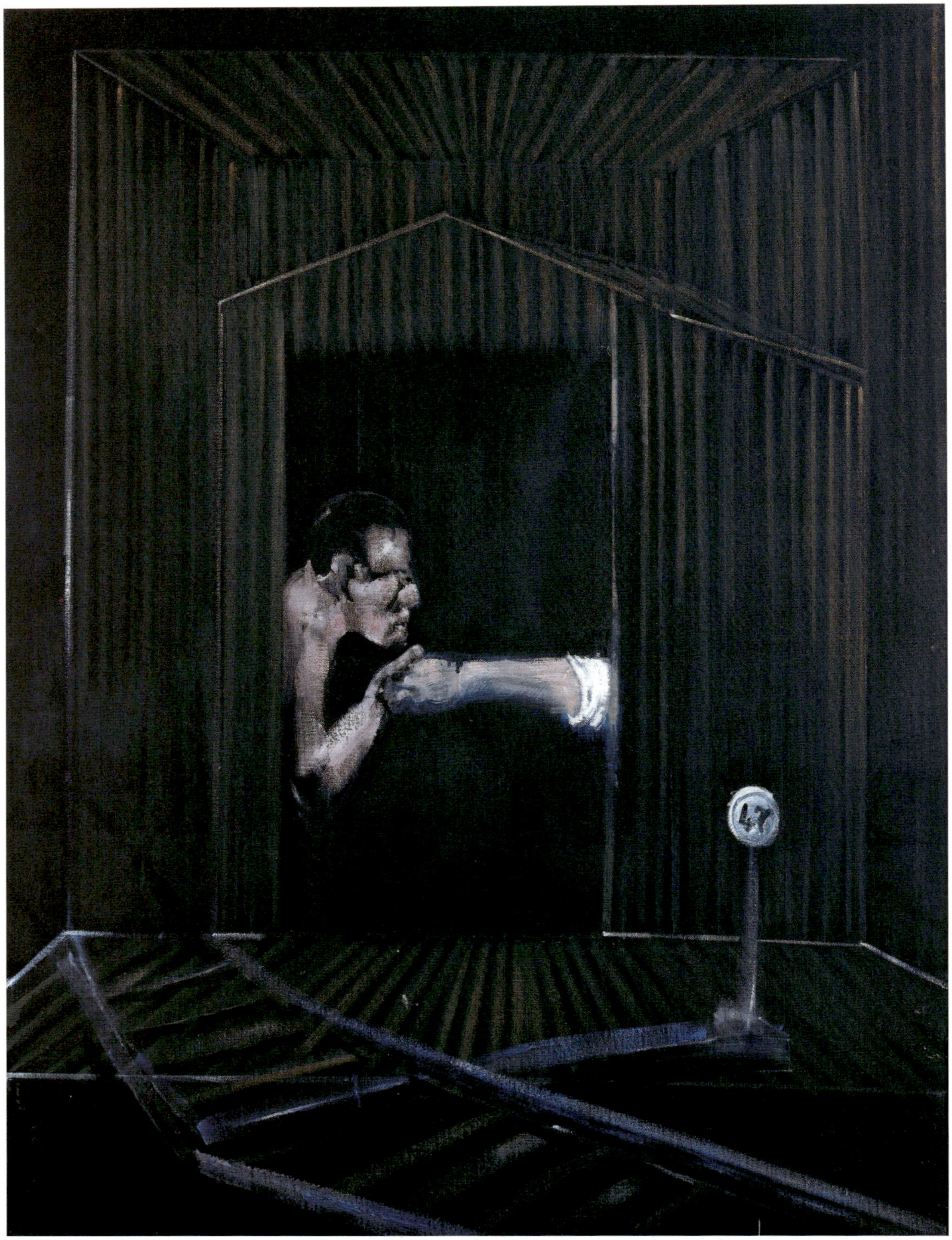

CAT 18 *End of the Line*, 1953, 152.4 × 116.8 cm, oil on canvas. Collection of Samuel and Ronnie Heyman.

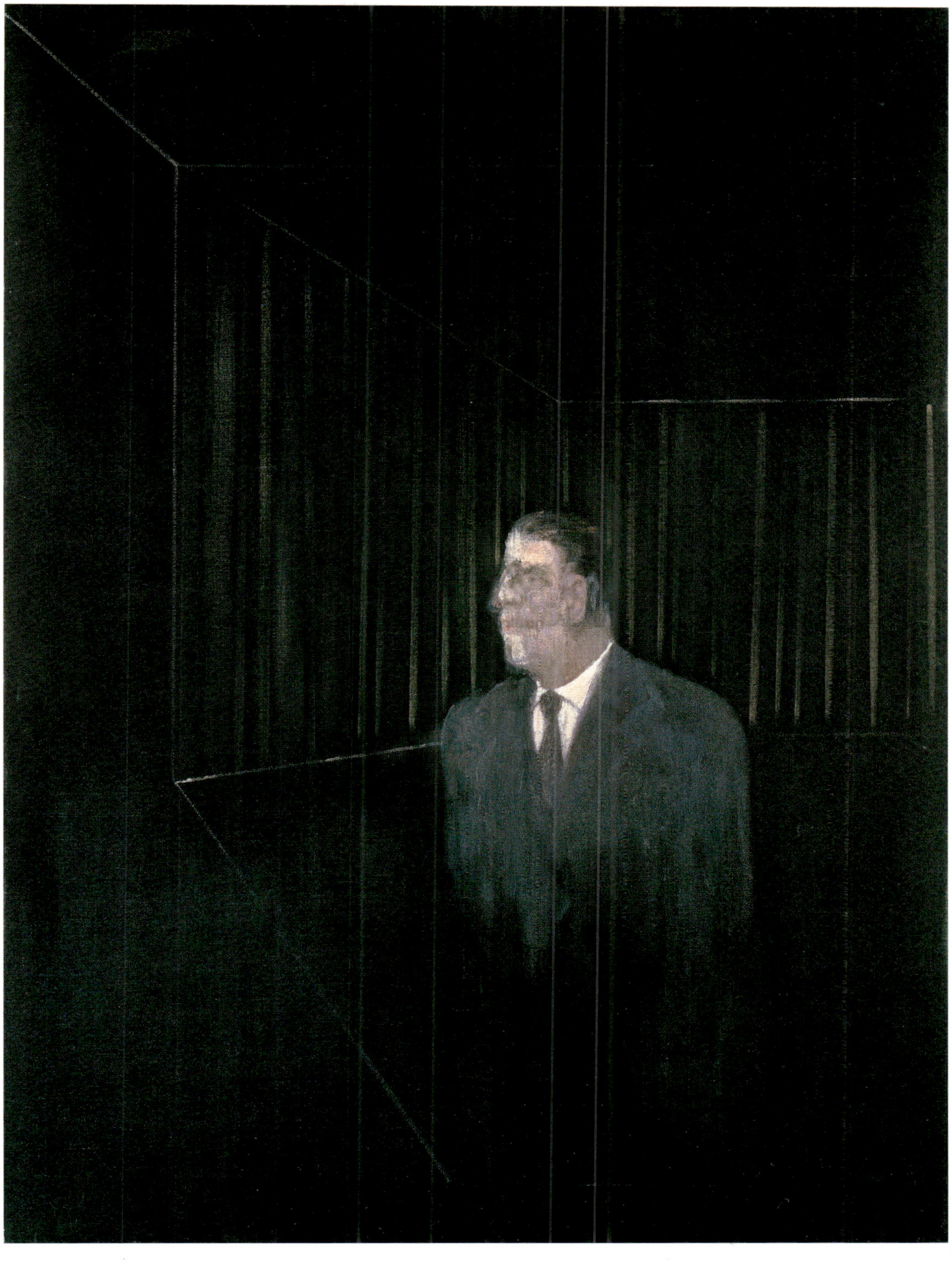

CAT 19 *Man in Blue II*, 1954, 152 × 117 cm, oil on canvas. Private collection, courtesy Galerie Beyeler, Basel.

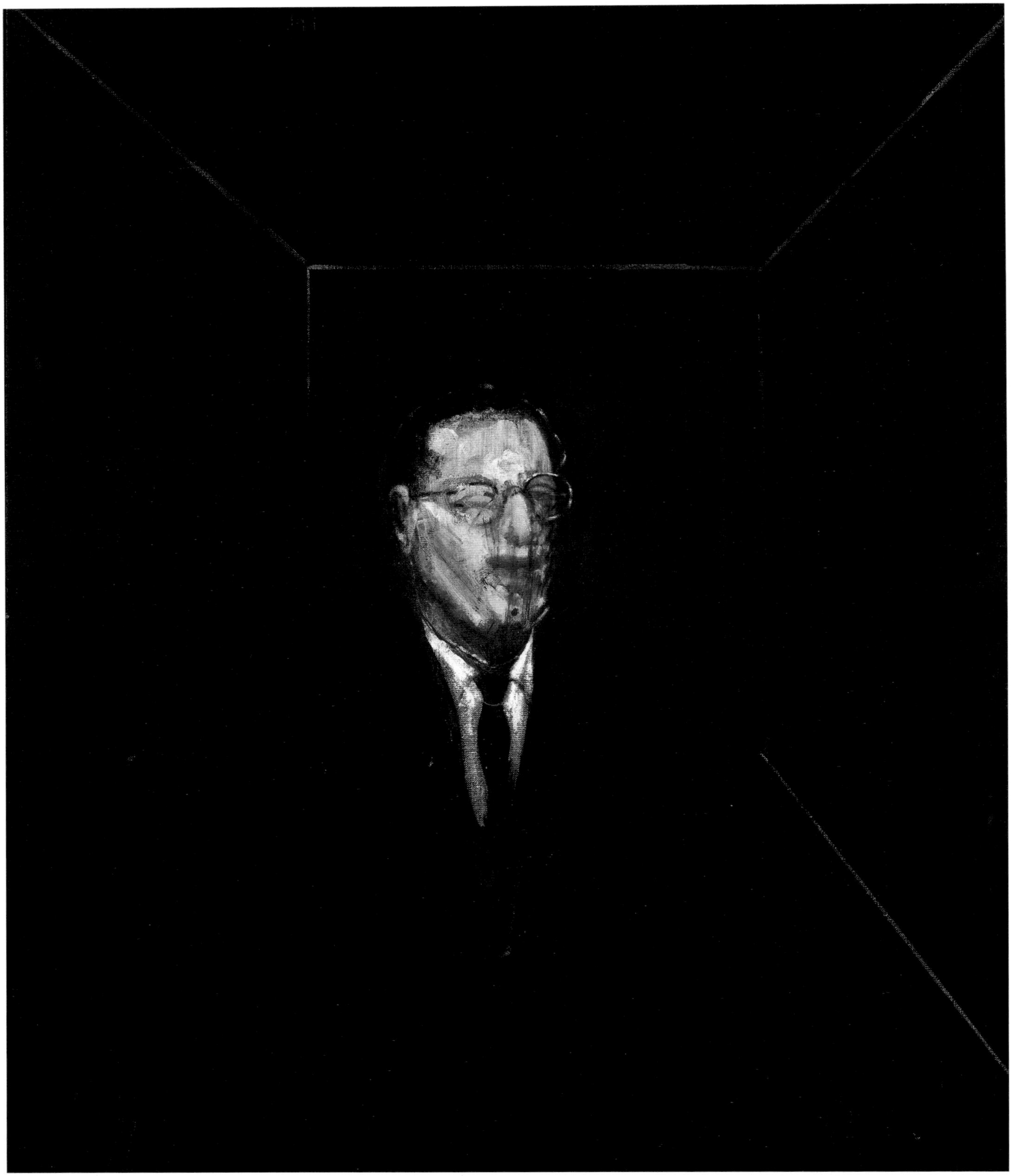

CAT 20 *Portrait of R. J. Sainsbury* (Robert Sainsbury), 1955, 114.7 × 99.3 cm, oil on canvas. Robert and Lisa Sainsbury Collection, University of East Anglia, Norwich.

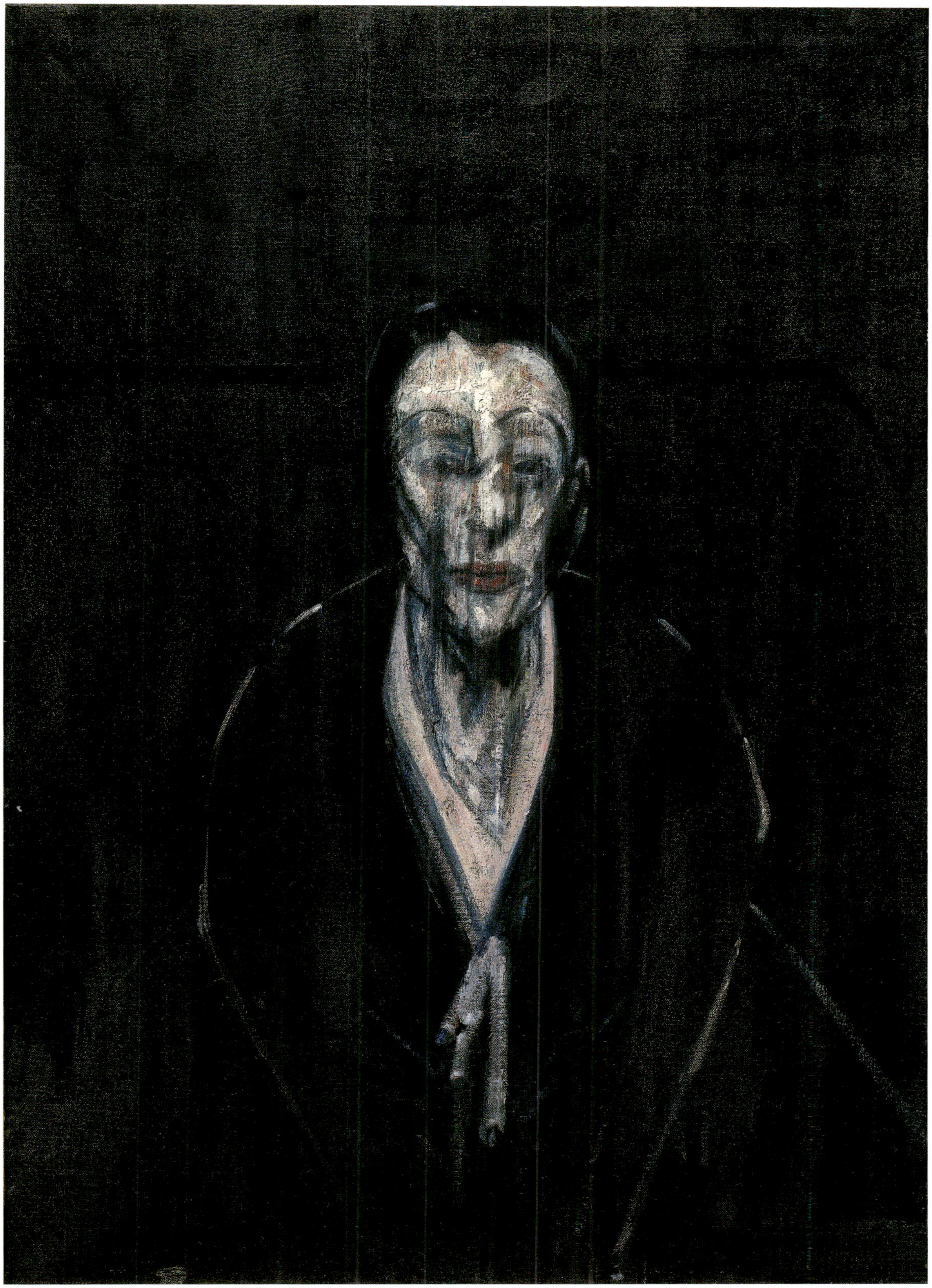

CAT 21 *Portrait of Lisa*, 1956, 100.6 × 72.7 cm, oil on canvas. Robert and Lisa Sainsbury Collection, University of East Anglia, Norwich.

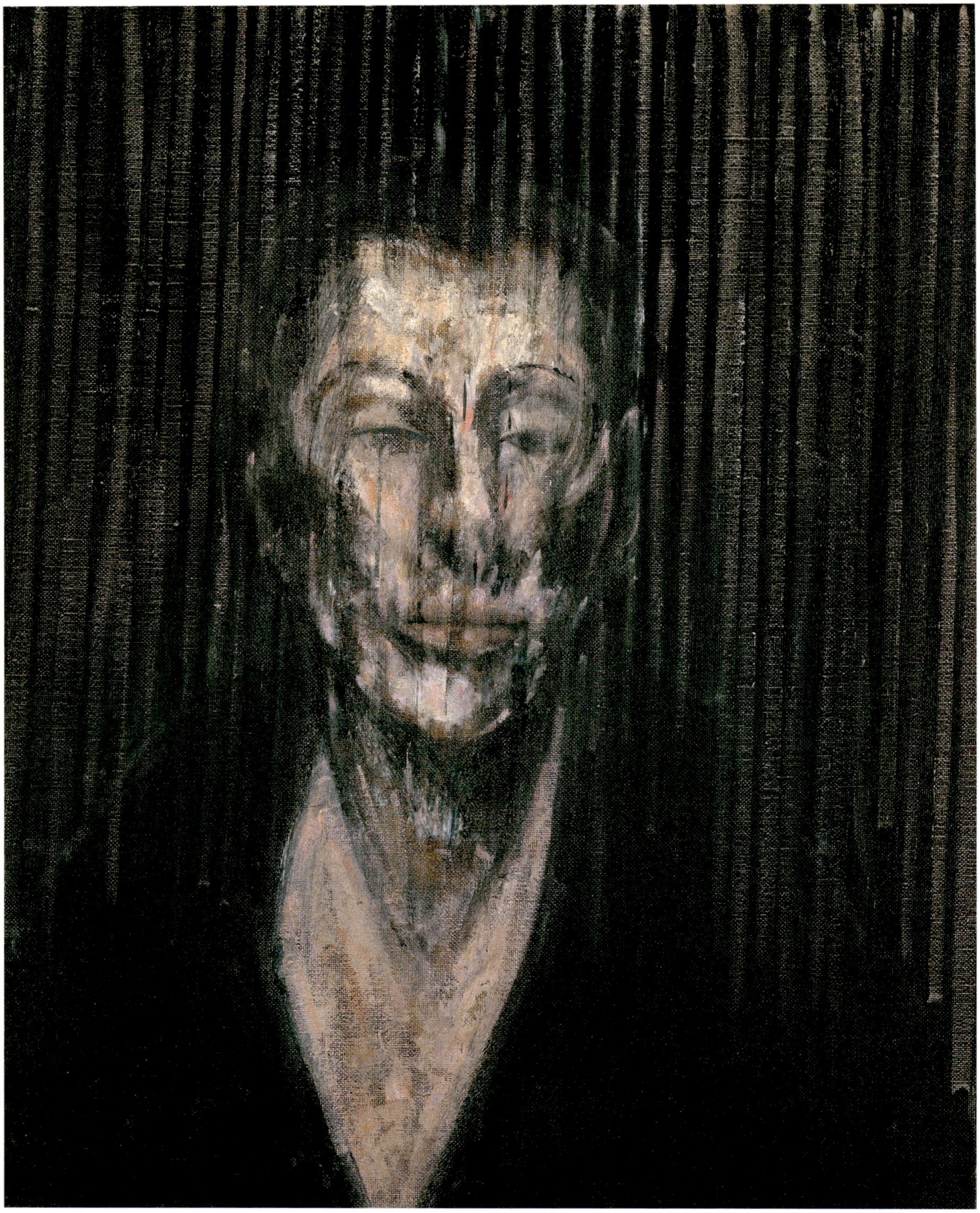

CAT 22 *Sketch for a Portrait of Lisa*, 1955, 61 × 54.9 cm, oil on canvas. Robert and Lisa Sainsbury Collection, University of East Anglia, Norwich.

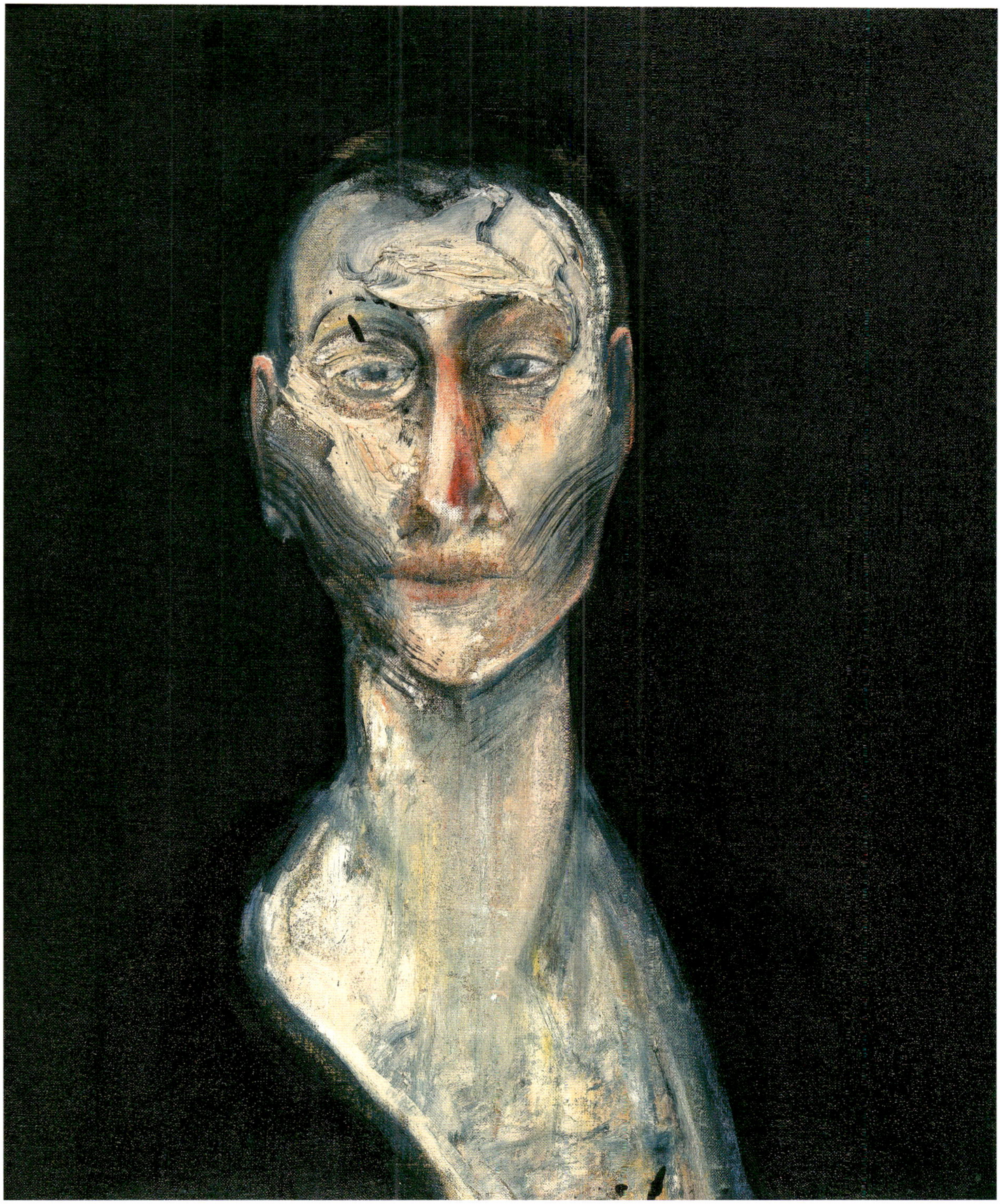

CAT 23 *Portrait of Lisa*, 1957, 73.5 × 64 cm, oil on canvas. Robert and Lisa Sainsbury Collection, University of East Anglia, Norwich.

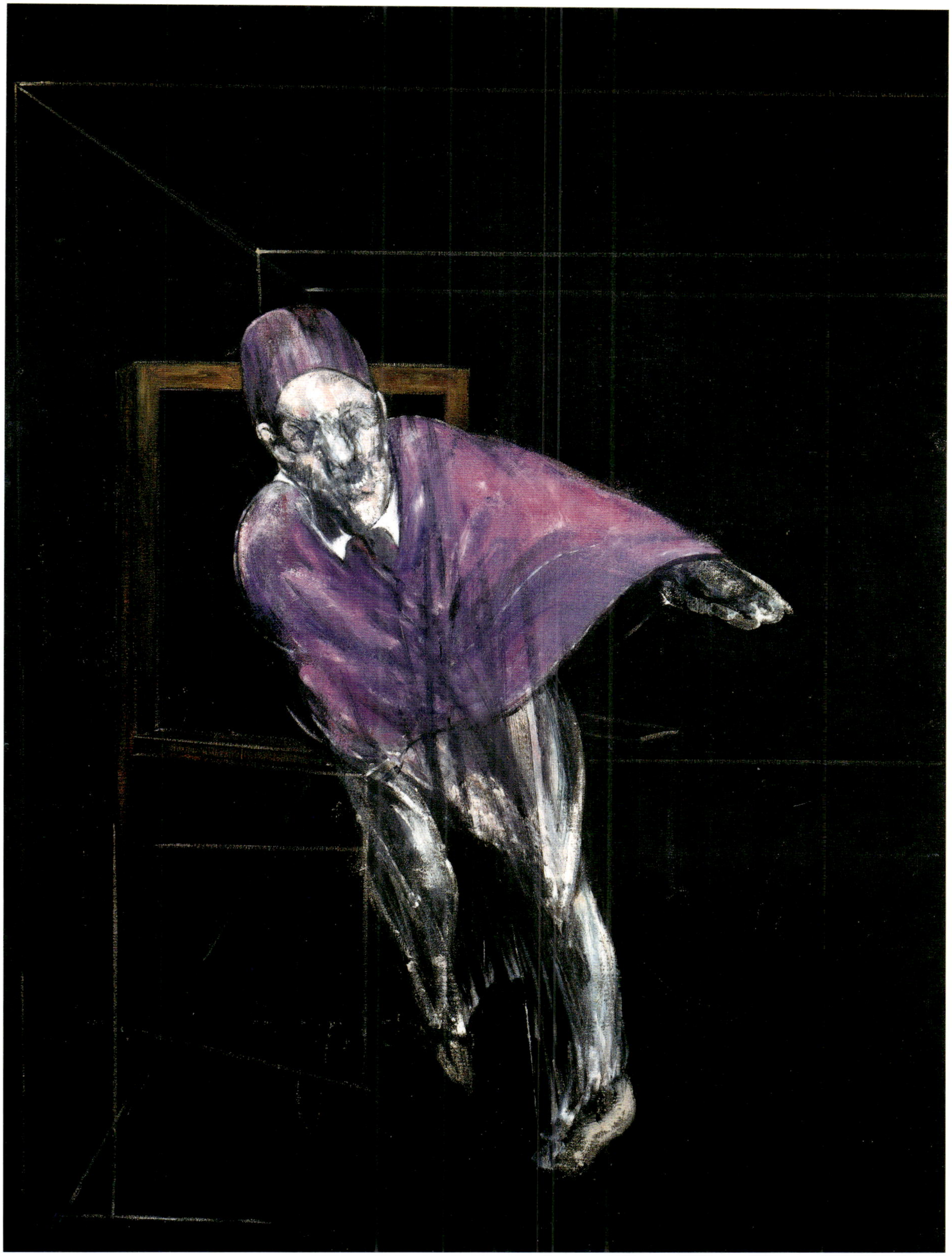

CAT 24 *Study for a Pope*, 1955, 170 × 135 cm, oil on canvas. Collection Jan Krugier and Marie-Anne Krugier-Poniatowski, Switzerland.

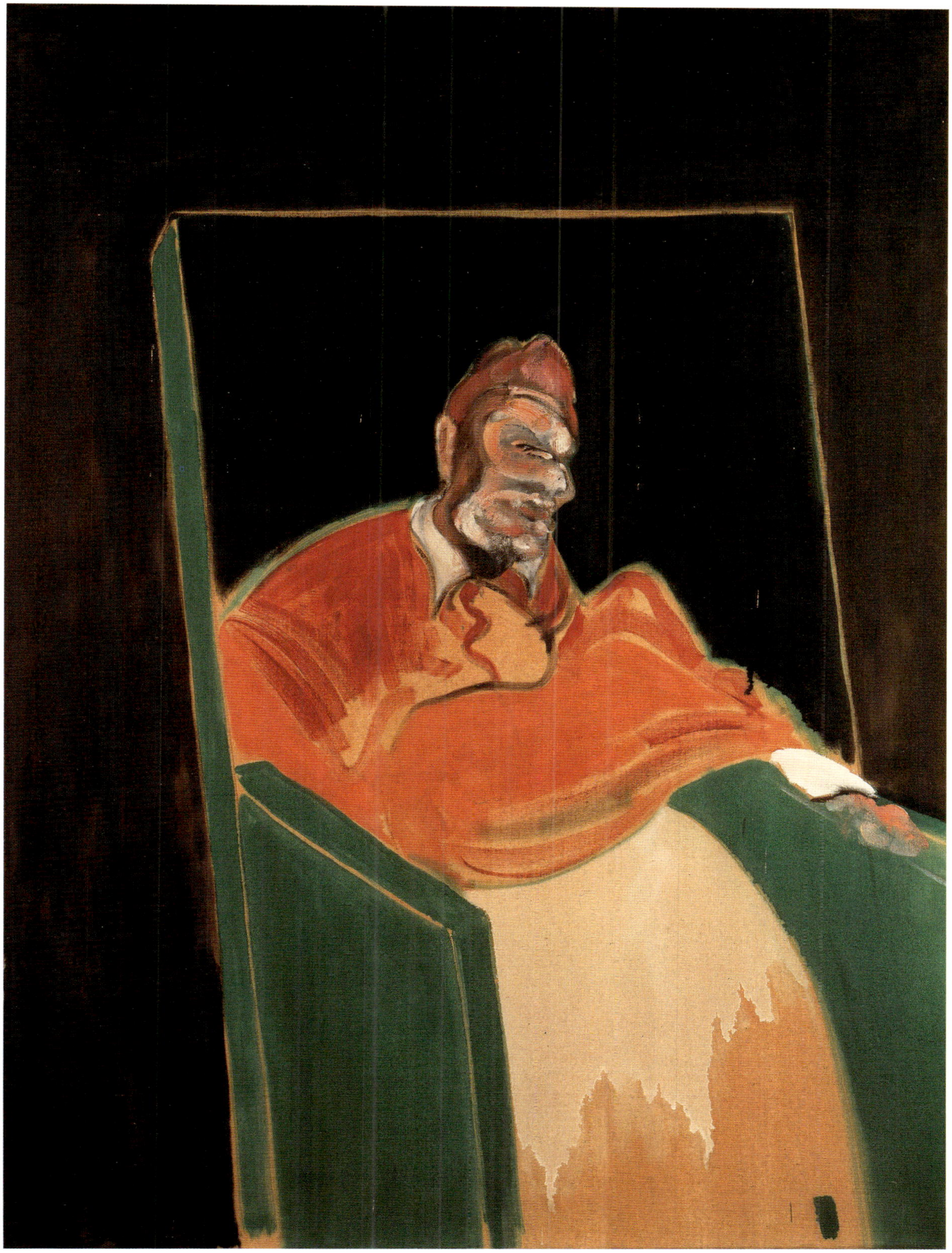

CAT 25 *Study for a Pope VI*, 1961, 152.4 × 116.8 cm, oil on canvas. Yageo Foundation, Taiwan.

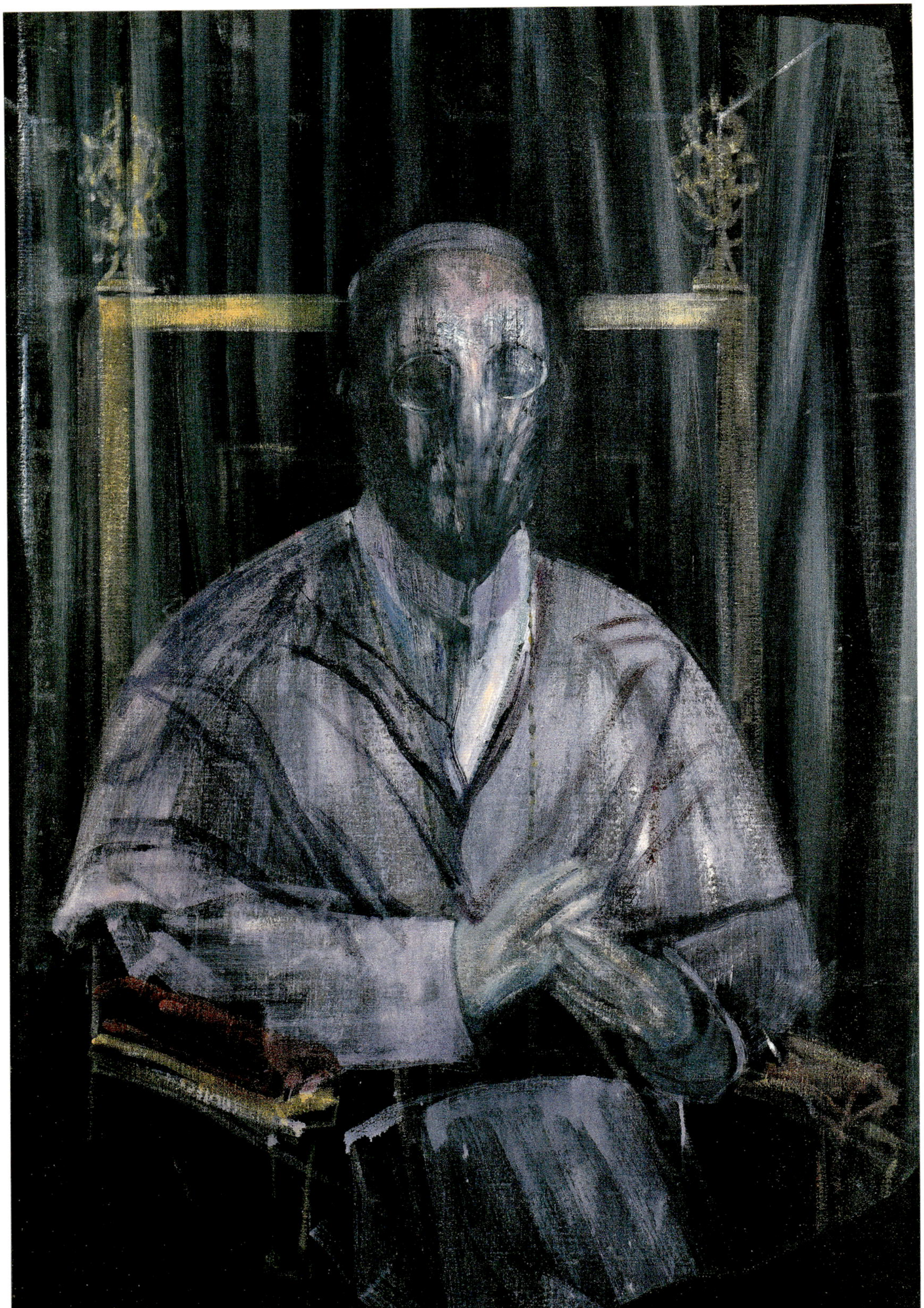

CAT 26 *Study (Imaginary Portrait of Pope Pius XII)*, 1955, 108.6 × 75.6 cm, oil on canvas.
Robert and Lisa Sainsbury Collection, University of East Anglia, Norwich.

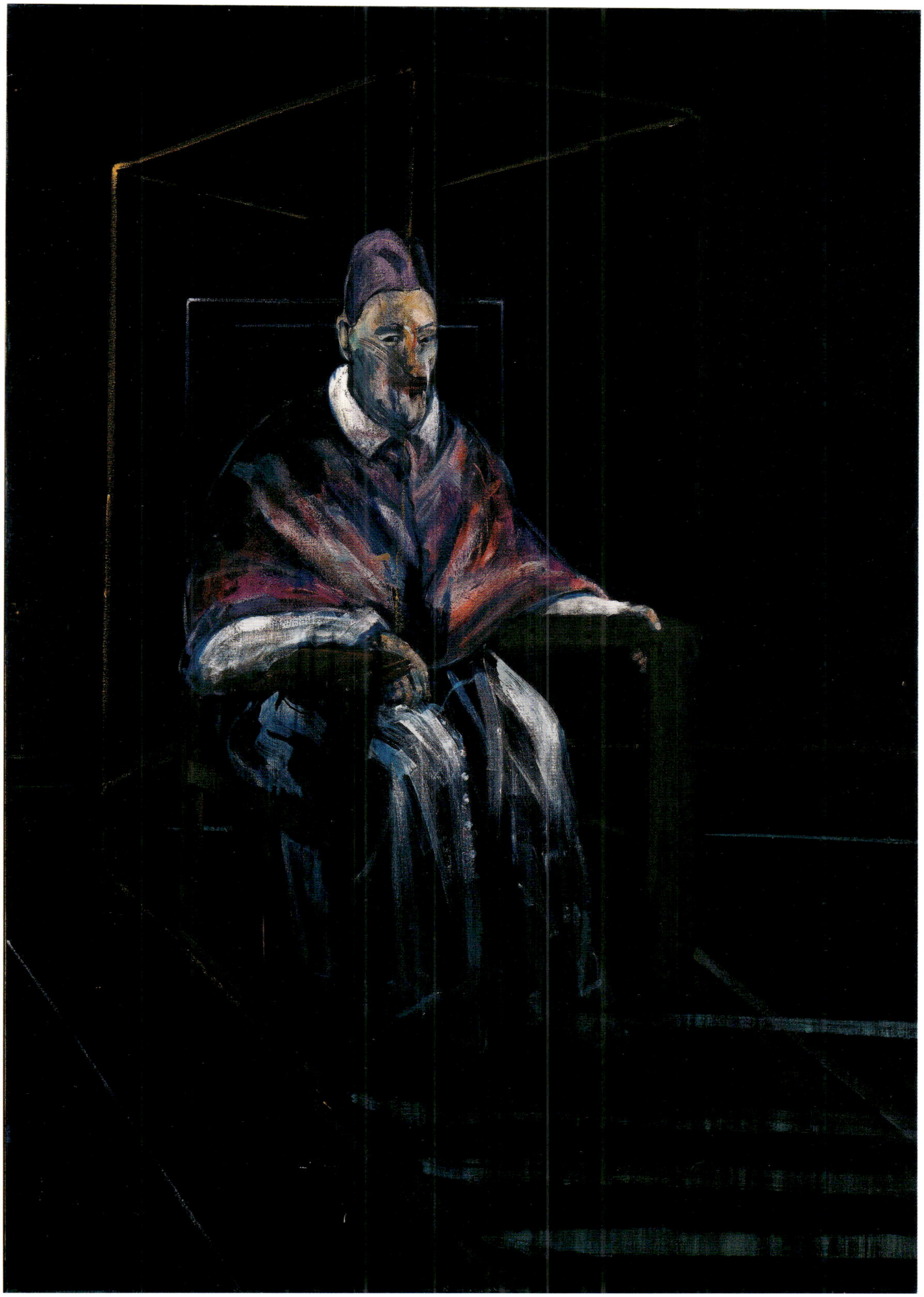

CAT 27 *Study for Portrait no. 1*, 1956, 216.2 × 160.5 cm, oil on canvas.
National Gallery of Canada, Ottawa. Purchased 1957.

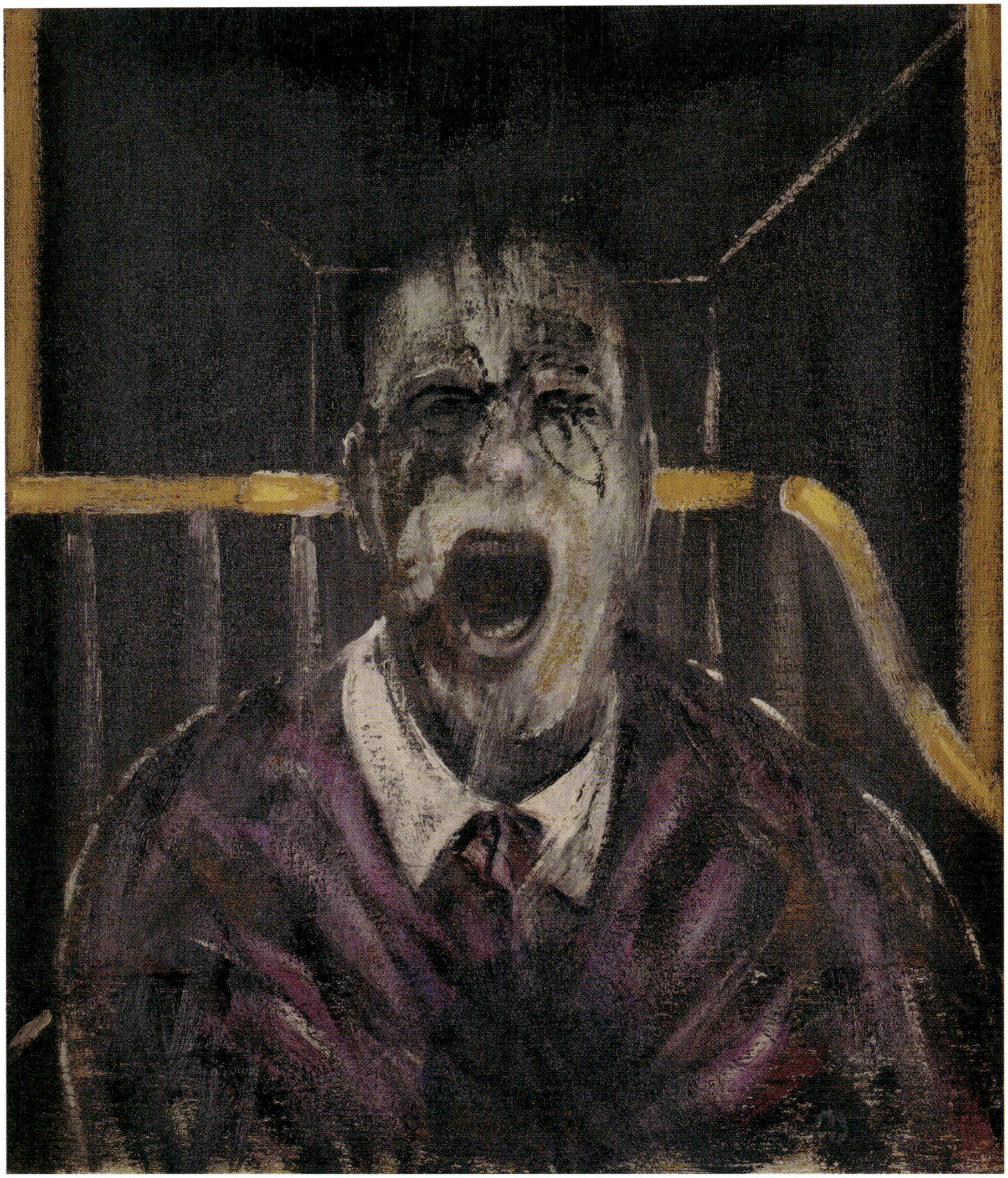

CAT 28 *Study for a Head*, 1952, 63.5 × 55.9 cm, oil on canvas. Collection Jane Lang Davis.

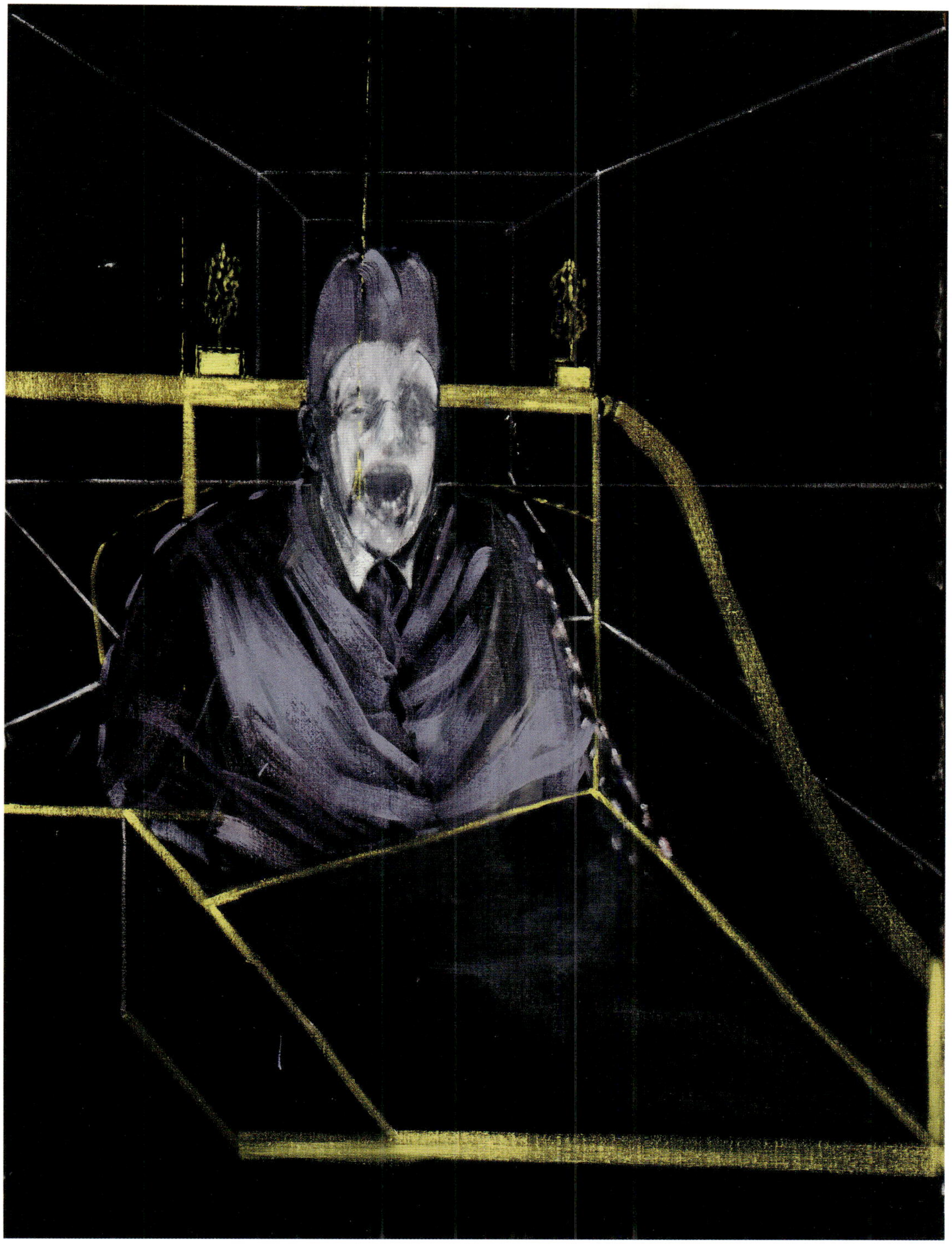

CAT 29 *Number VIII from Eight Studies for a Portrait*, 1953, 152 × 117 cm, oil on linen. The Museum of Modern Art, New York. Gift of Mr. and Mrs. William A. M. Burden.

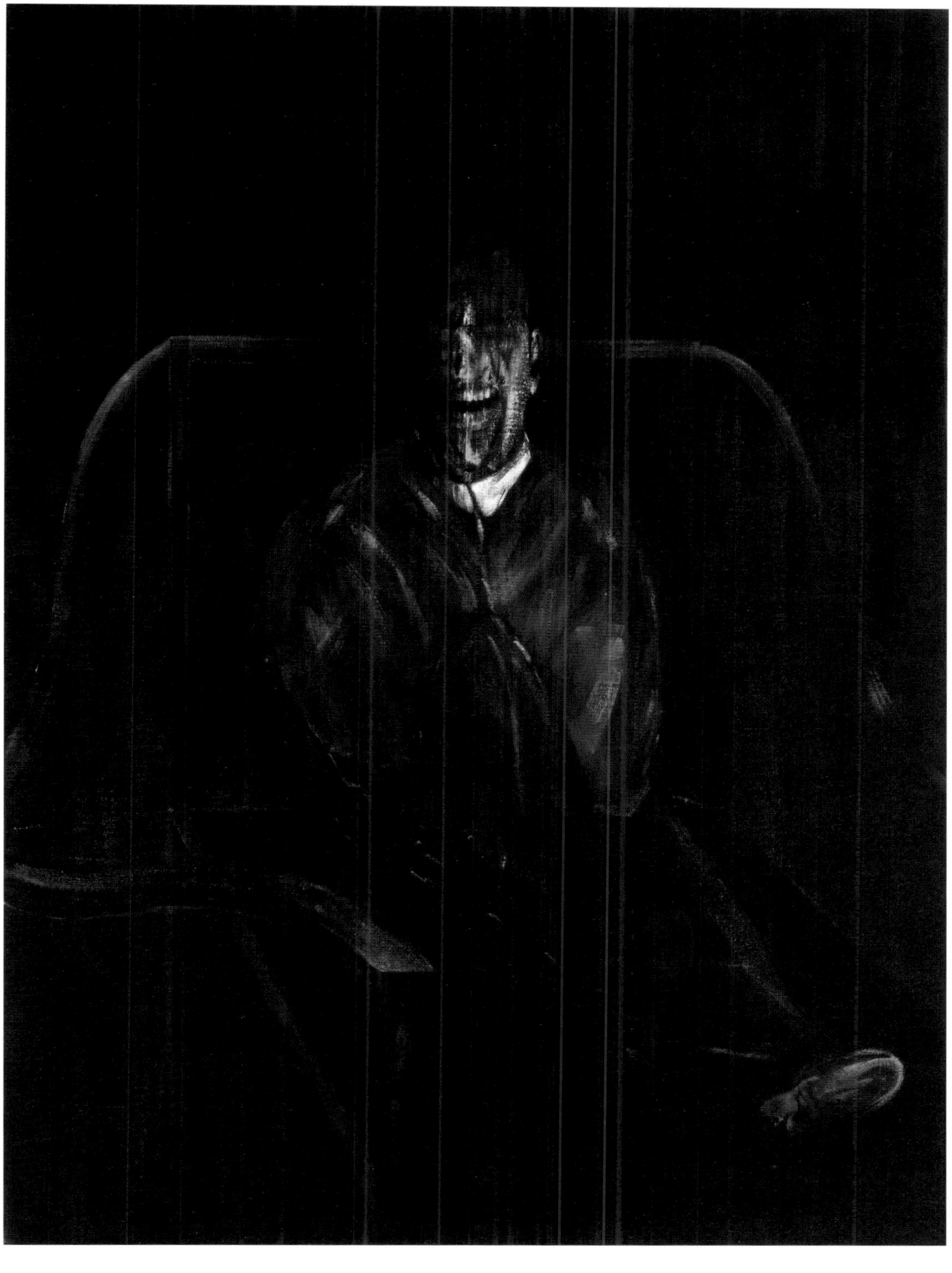

CAT 30 *Figure Seated (The Cardinal)*, 1955, 152 × 117 cm, oil on canvas.
Stedelijk Museum voor Actuele Kunst, Gent.

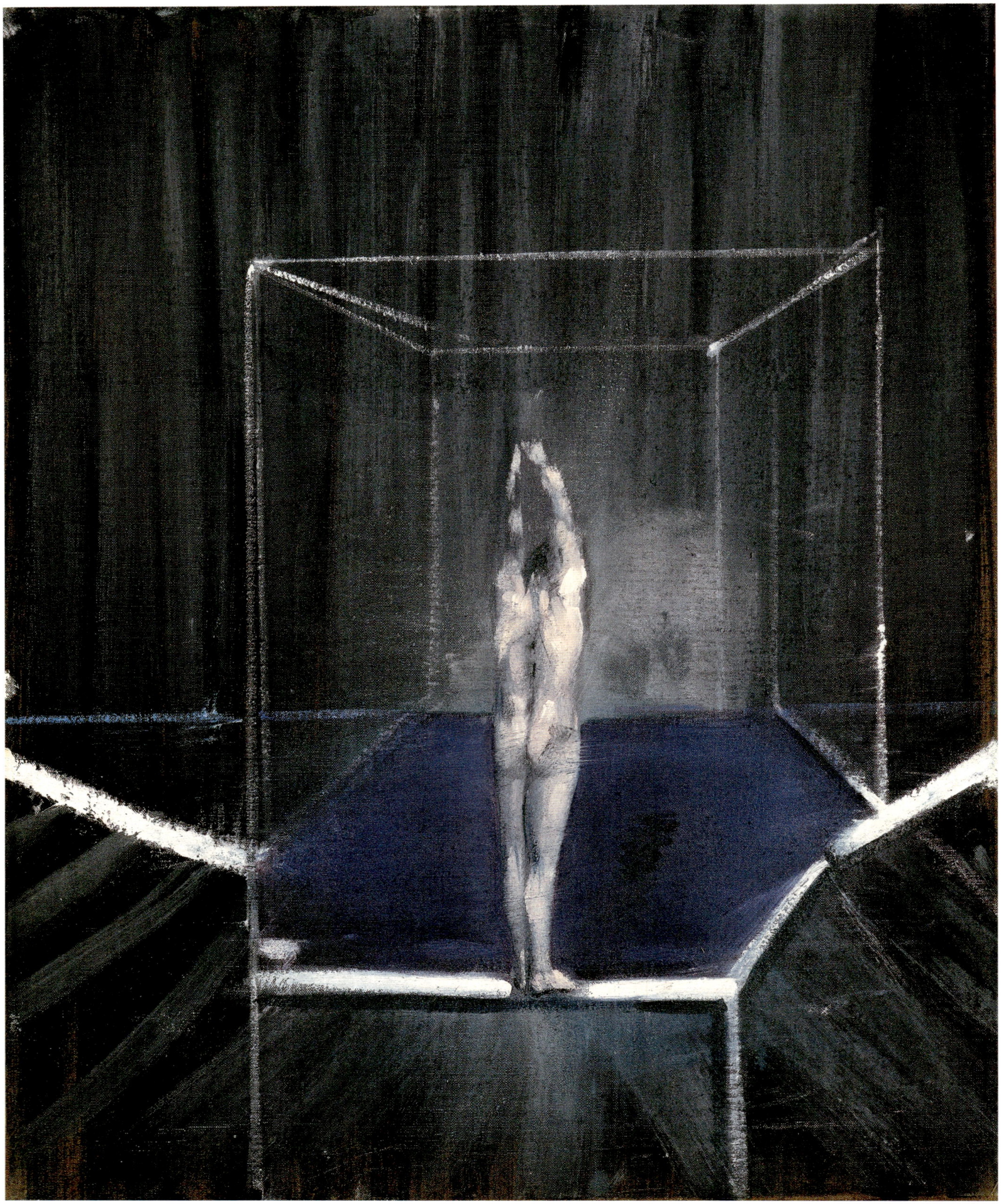

CAT 31 *Study of a Nude*, 1952, 59.7 × 49.5 cm, oil on canvas. Robert and Lisa Sainsbury Collection, University of East Anglia, Norwich.

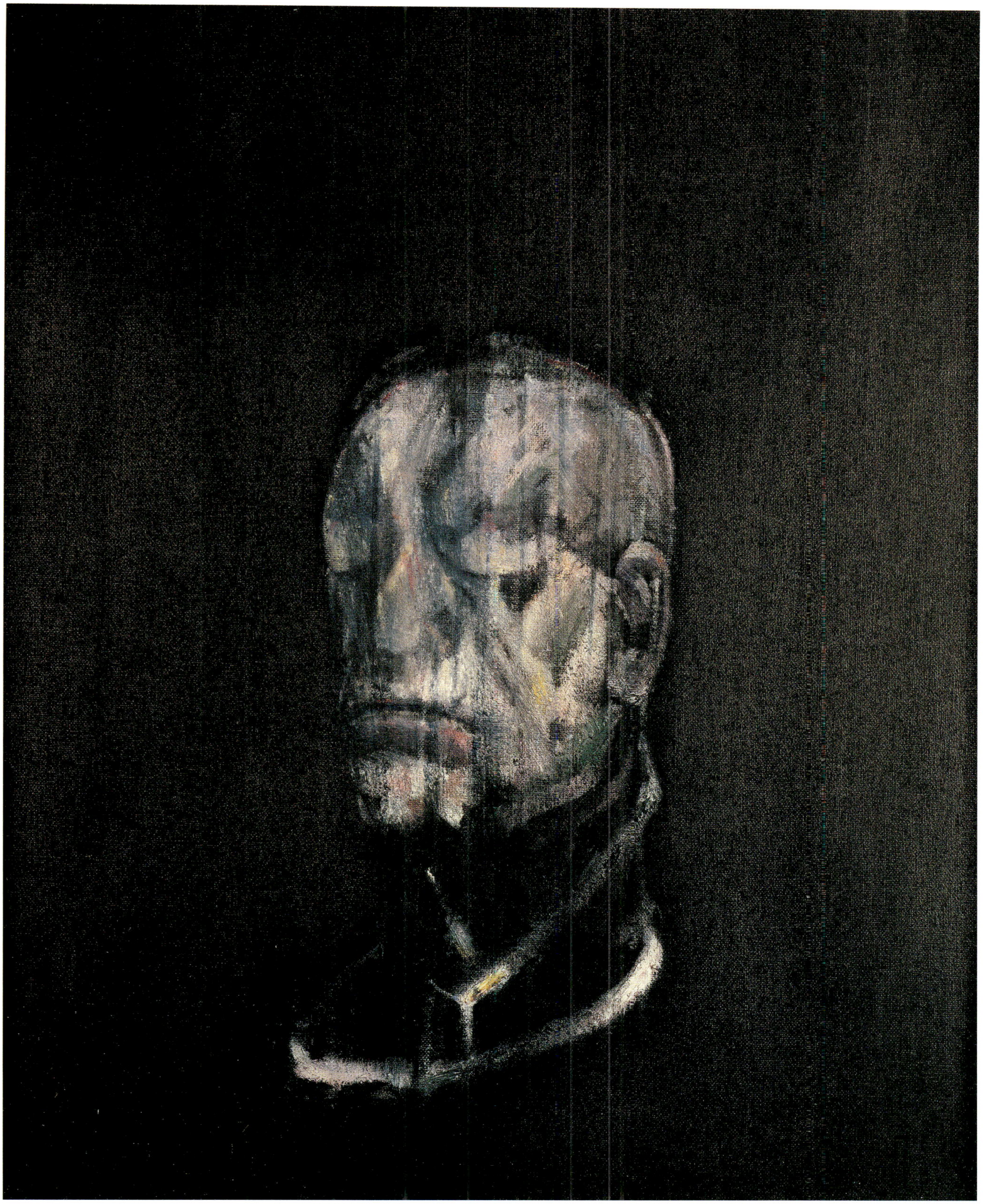

CAT 32 *Study for Portrait III (after Life Mask of William Blake)*, 1955, 78.5 × 69 cm, oil on canvas.
Private collection.

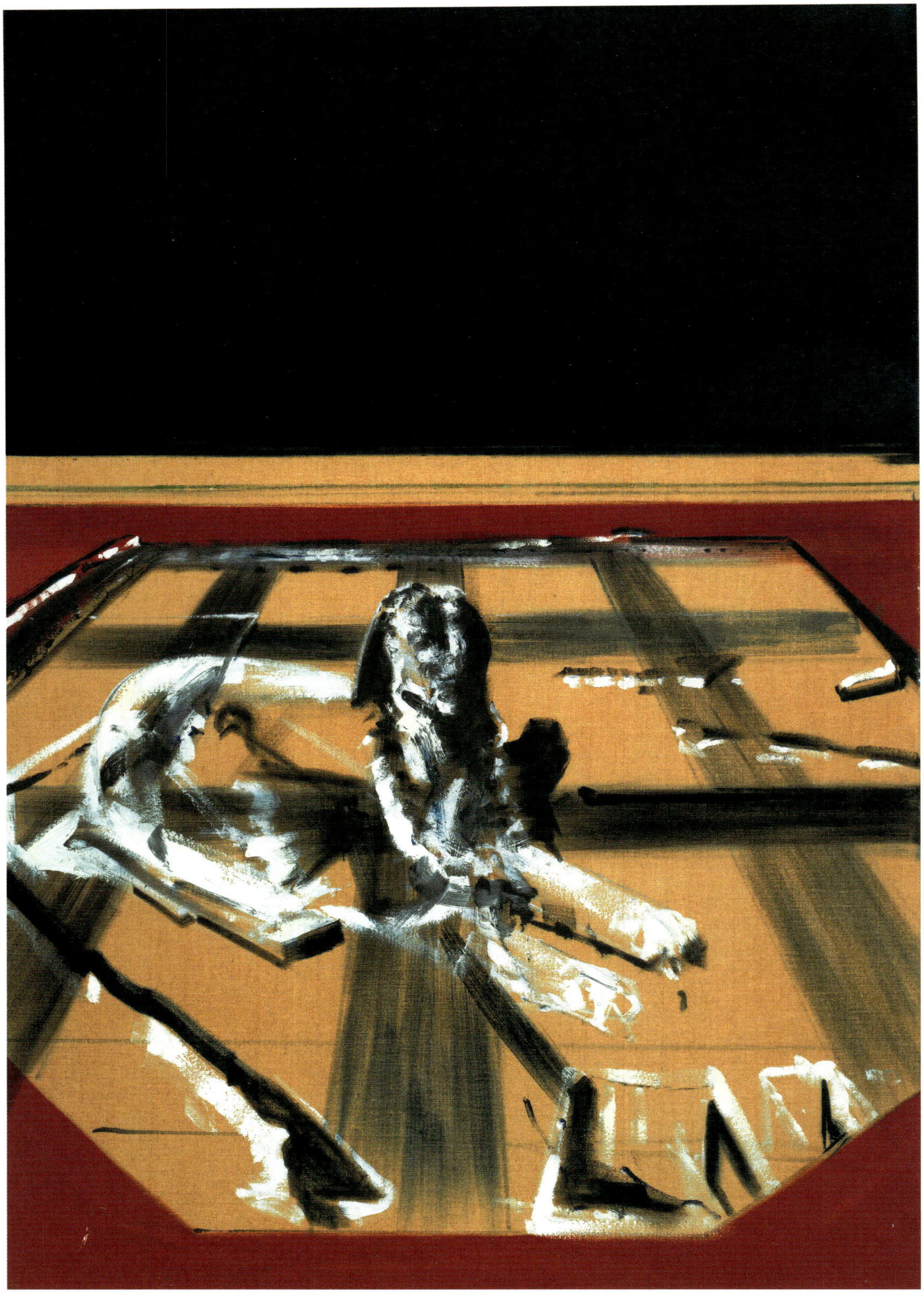

CAT 33 *Study of the Sphinx*, 1953, 198.4 × 137.1 cm, oil on canvas. Yale University Art Gallery, Gift of Stephen Carlton Clark, B.A., 1903.

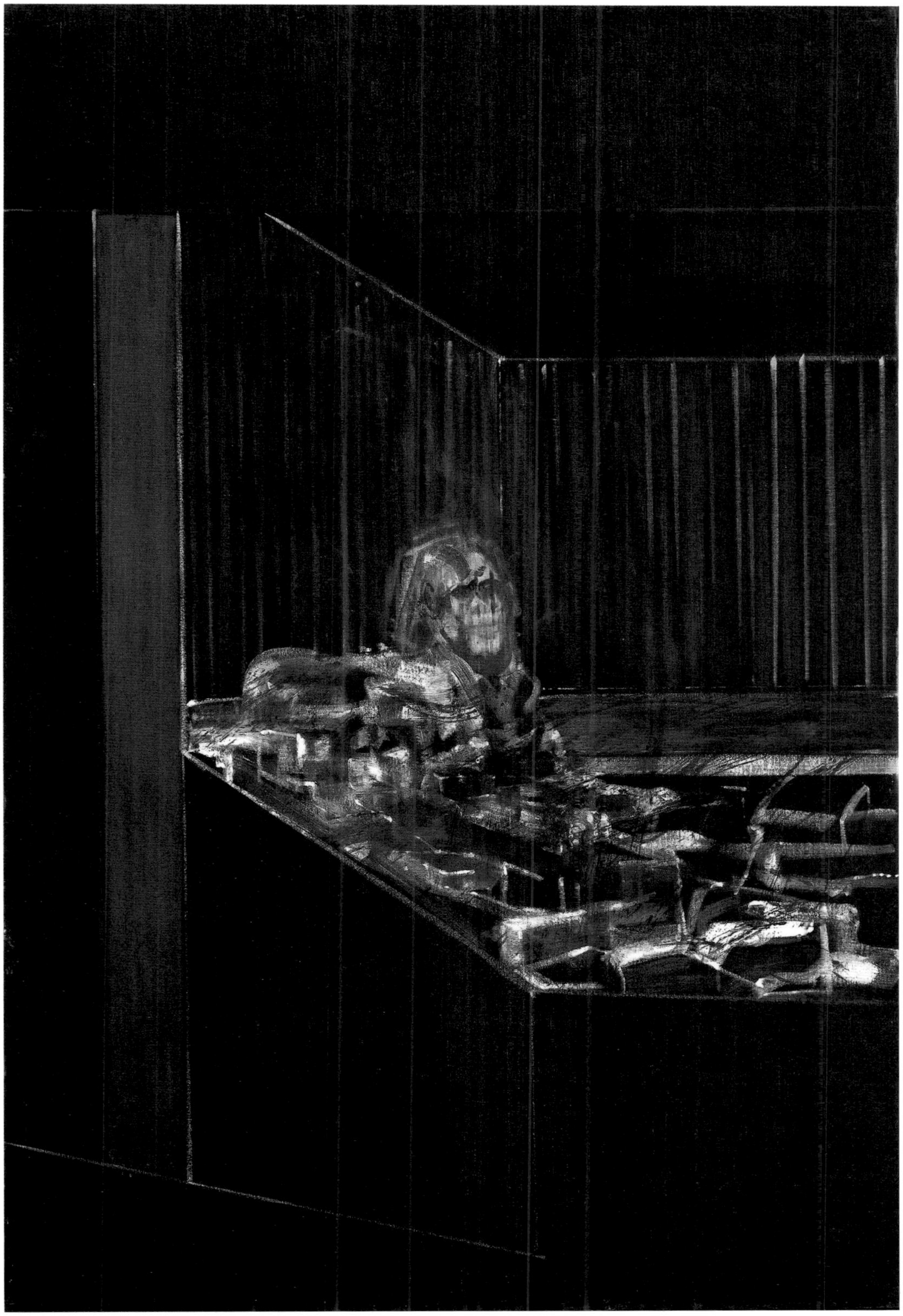

CAT 34 *Sphinx III*, 1954, 198.7 × 137 cm, oil on canvas. Hirshhorn Museum and Sculpture Garden, Smithsonian Institution, Gift of Joseph H. Hirshhorn, 1966.

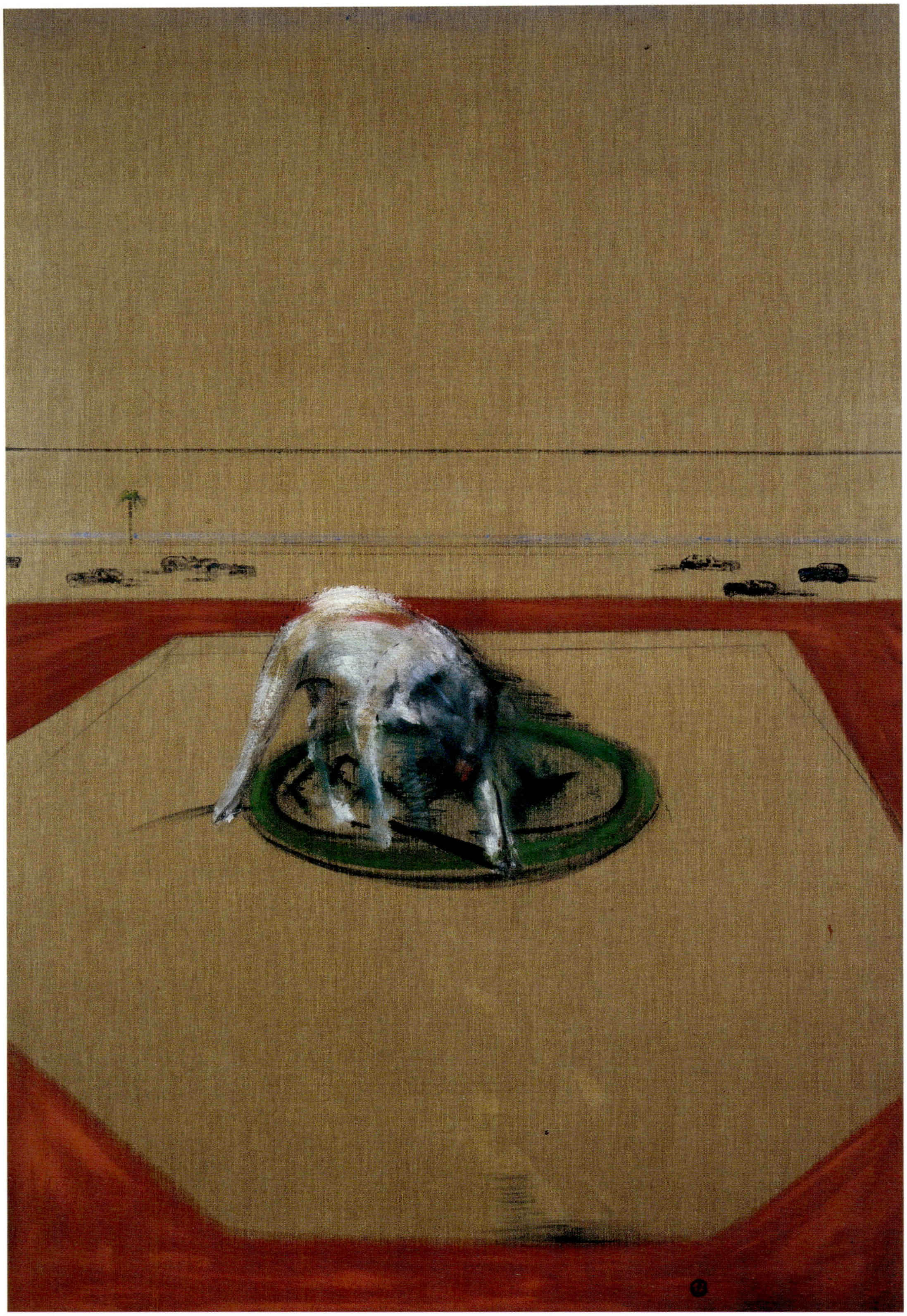

CAT 35 *Study of a Dog*, 1952, 198.1 × 137.2 cm, oil on canvas. Tate, London, presented by Eric Hall, 1952.

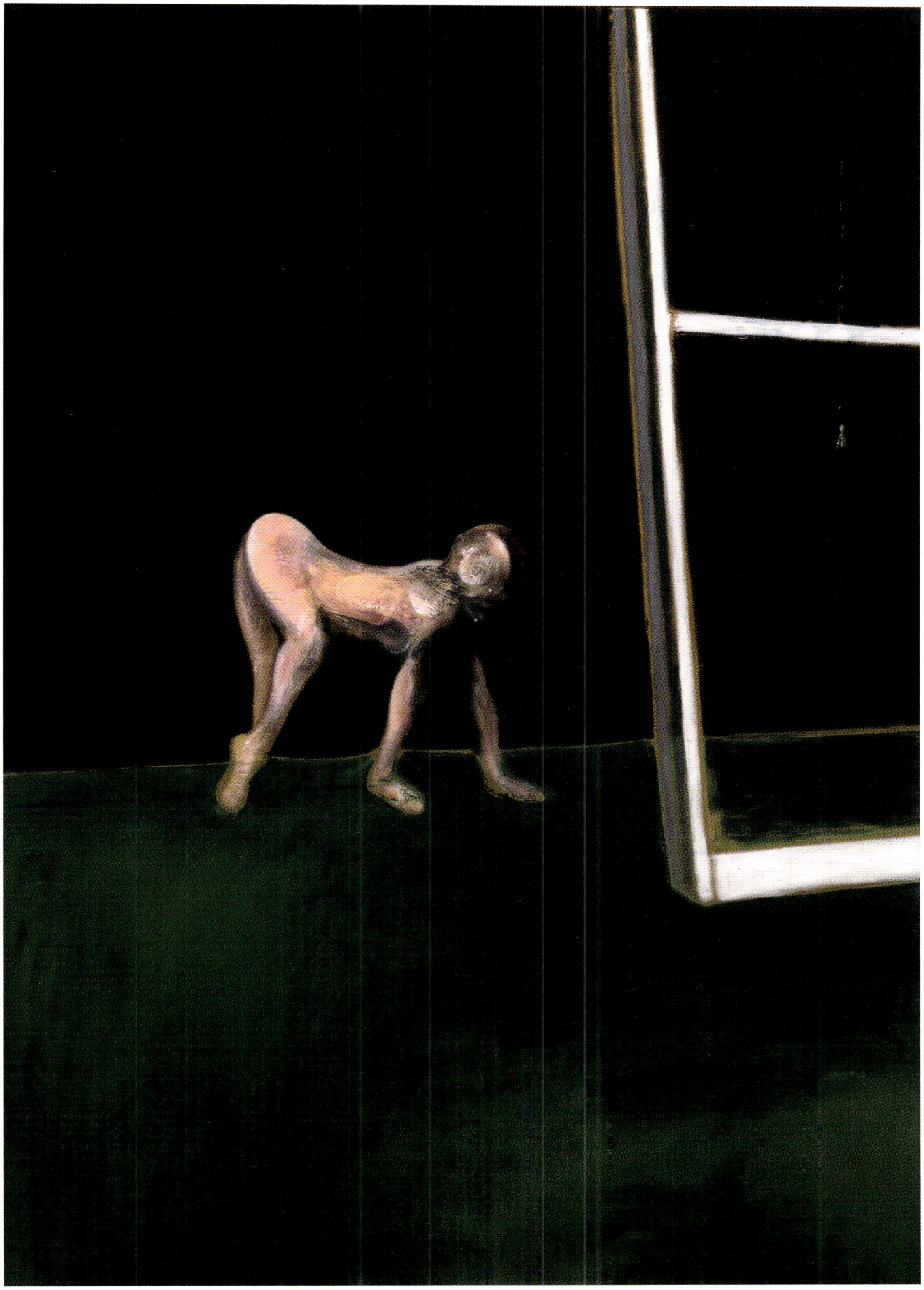

CAT 36 *Paralytic Child Walking on all Fours (from Muybridge)*, 1961, 198 × 142 cm, oil on canvas.
Collection of the Gemeentemuseum Den Haag.

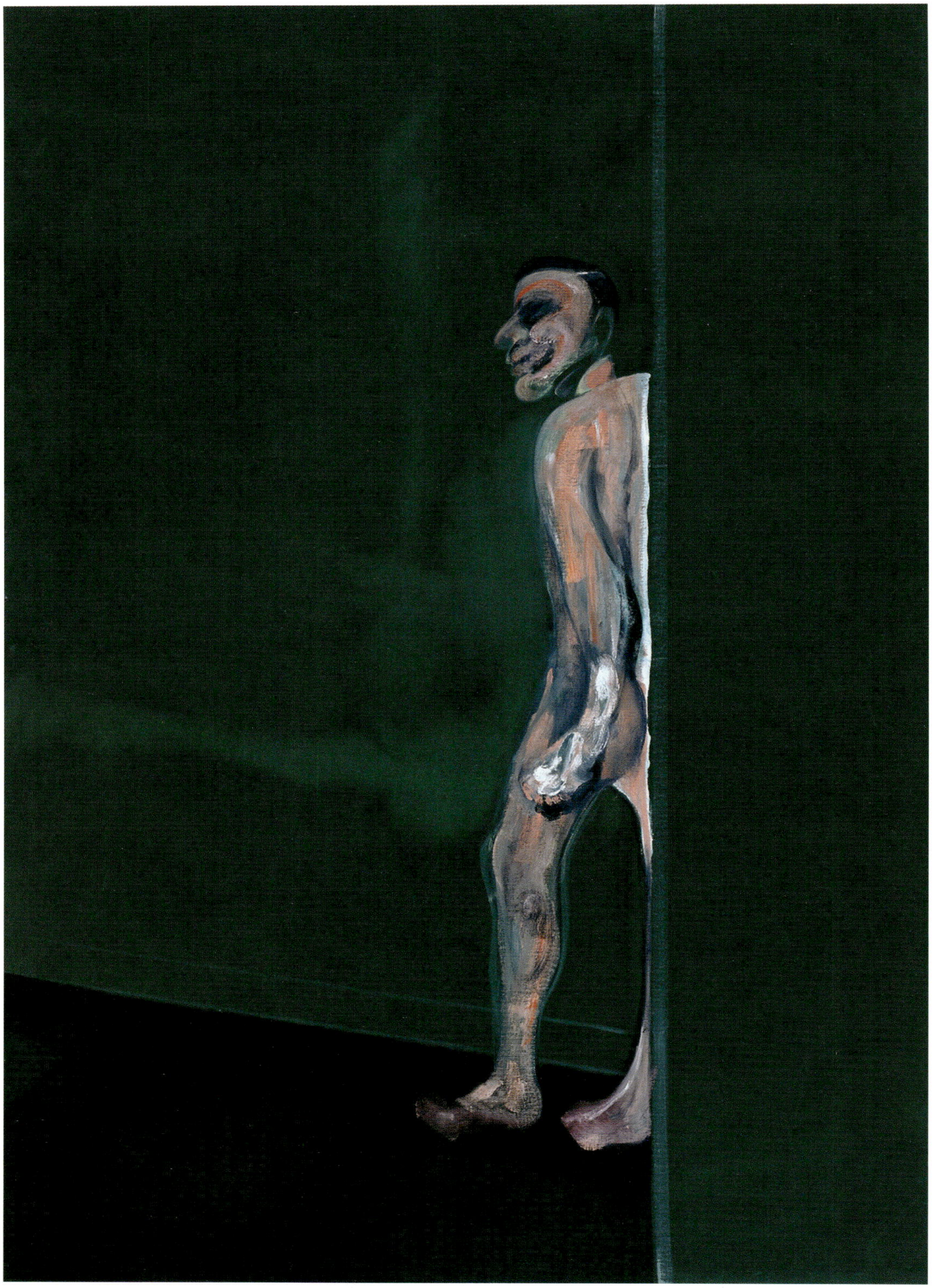

CAT 37 *Walking Figure*, 1959–60, 198 × 142 cm, oil on canvas, Dallas Museum of Art, Foundation for the Arts Collection. Gift of Mr. and Mrs. J. O. Lambert, Jr. and Mr. and Mrs. David Garrison.

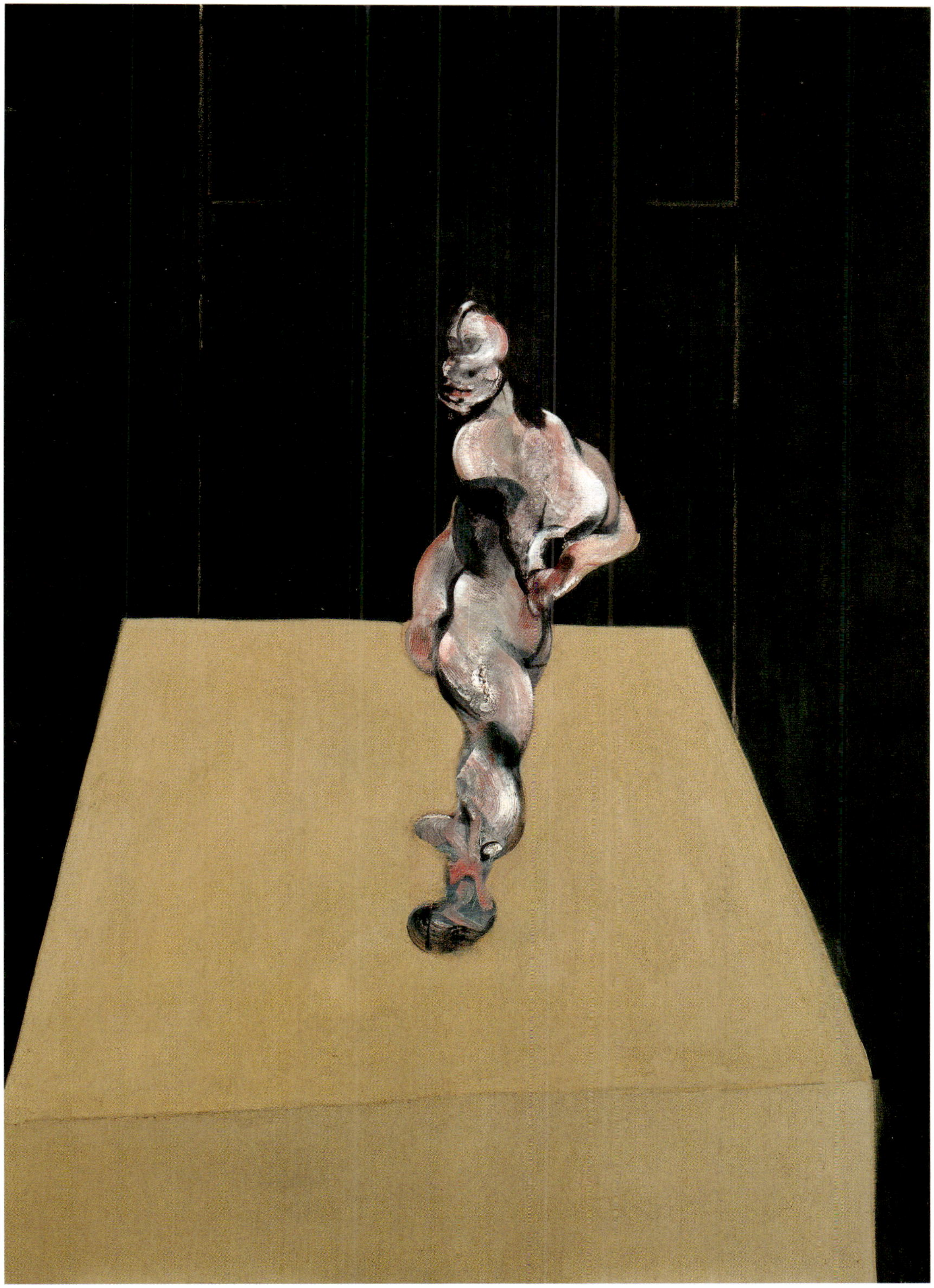

CAT 38 *Turning Figure*, 1962, 198 × 145 cm, oil on canvas. Private collection.

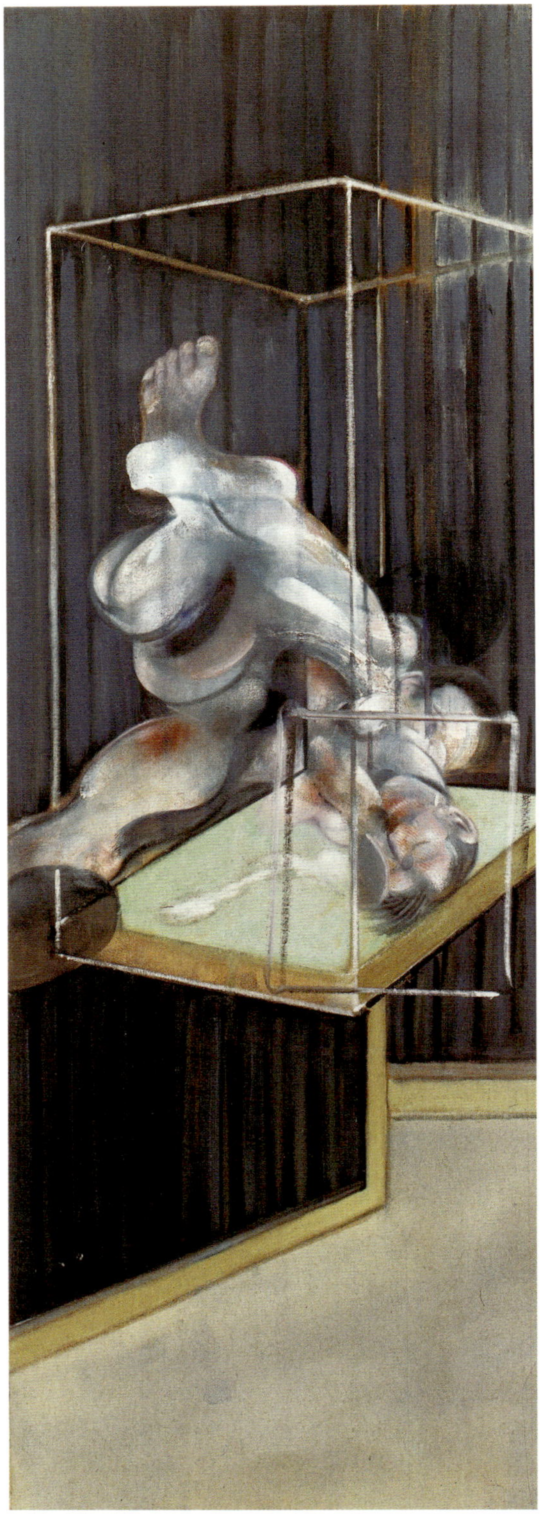

CAT 39 *Two Figures*, 1975, 190 × 70 cm,
oil on canvas. Private collection.

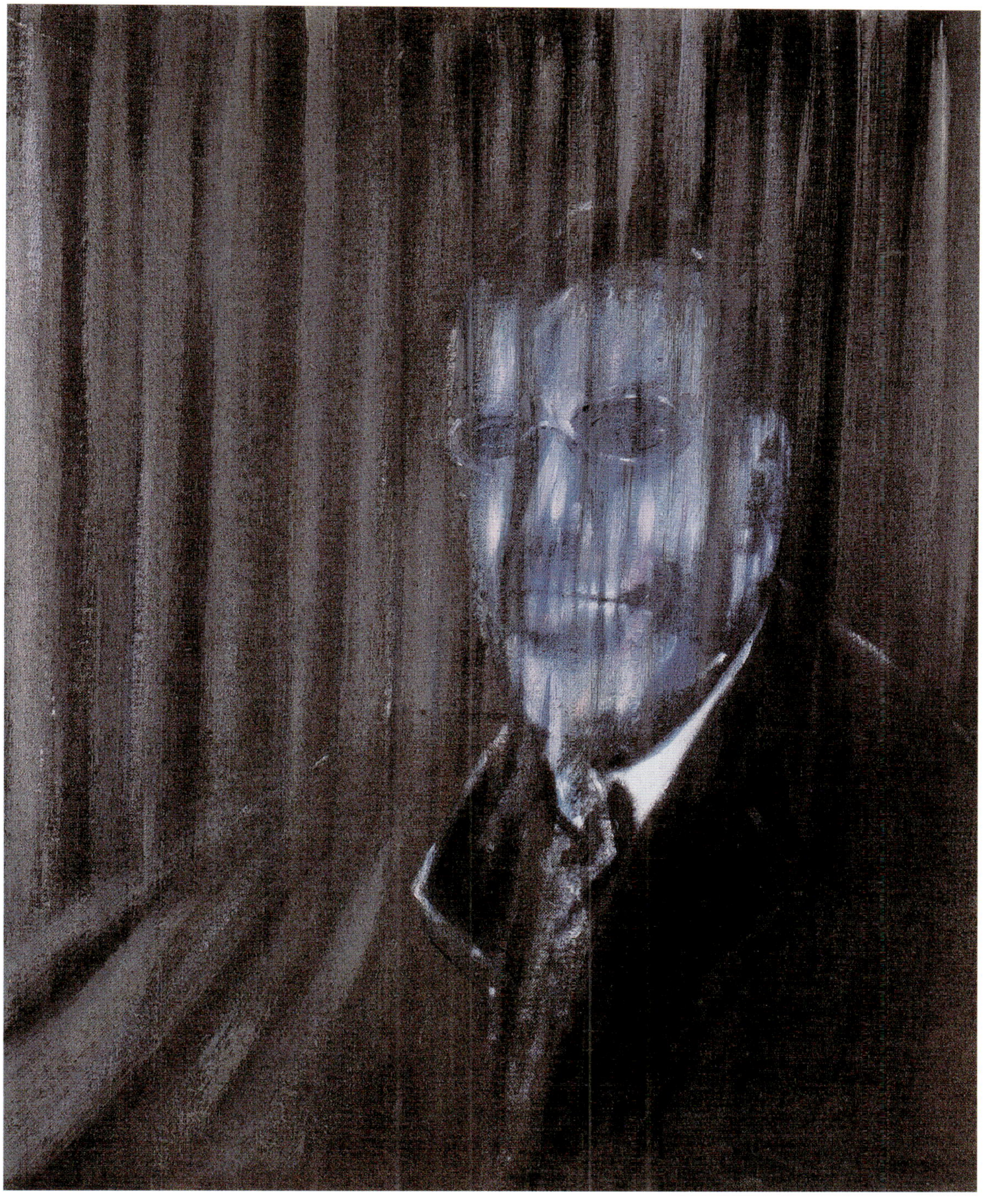

CAT 40 *Study of the Human Head*, 1953, 61 × 51 cm, oil on canvas. Private collection.

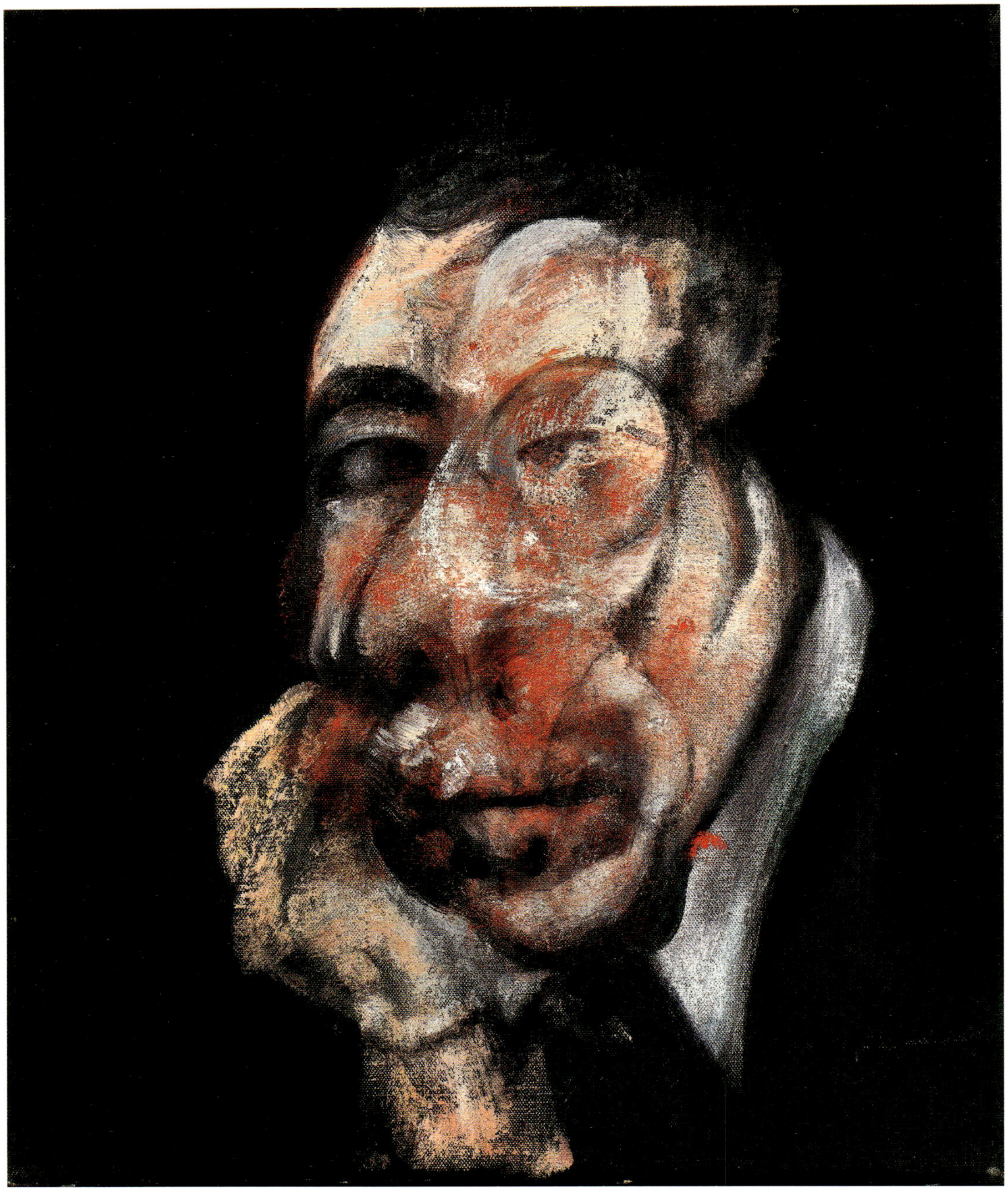

CAT 41 *Head III*, 1961, 50 × 45 cm, oil on canvas. Private collection.

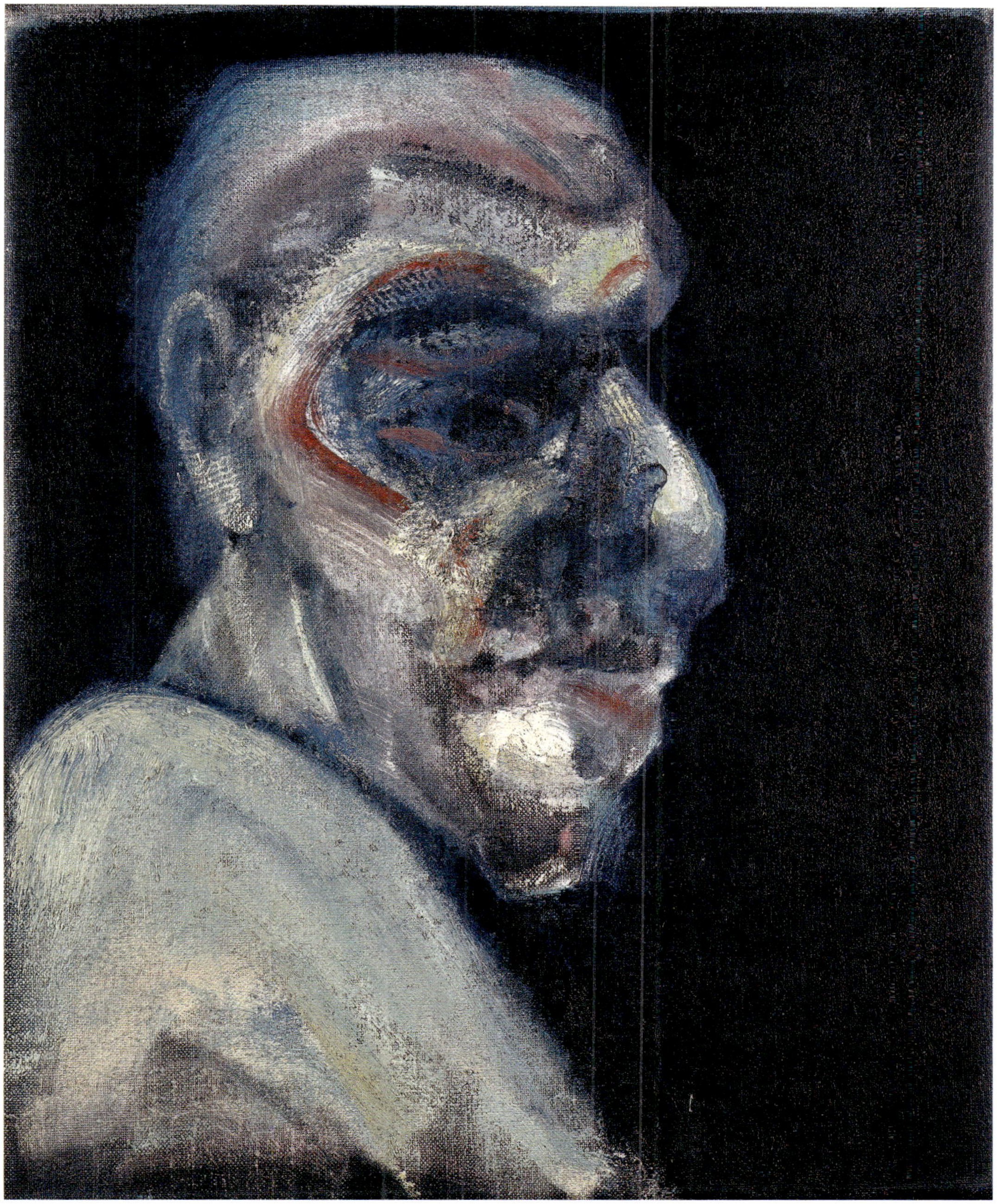

CAT 42 *Head of a Man no. 1*, 1960, 36.5 × 30.5 cm, oil on canvas. Robert and Lisa Sainsbury Collection, University of East Anglia, Norwich.

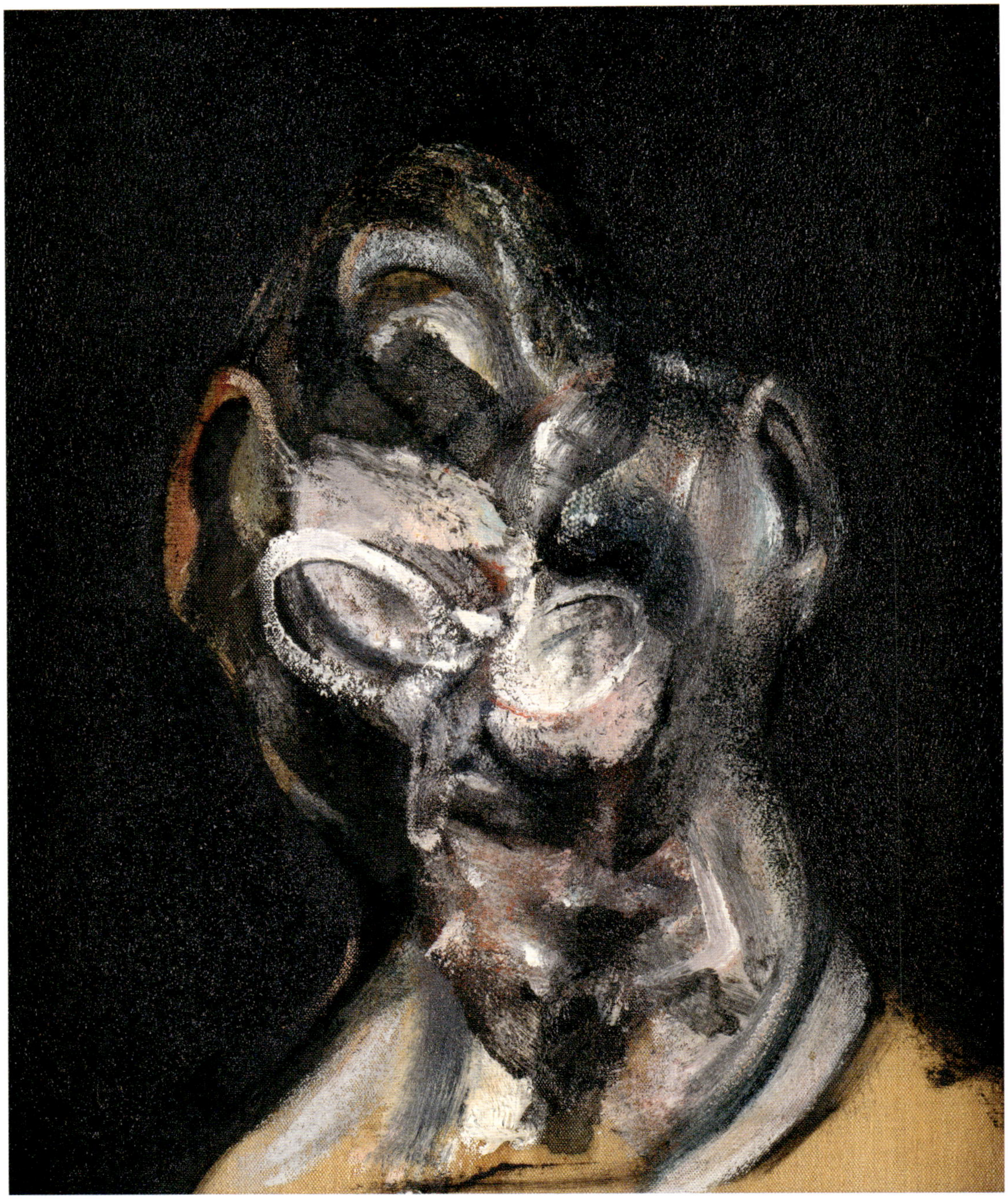

CAT 43 *Man with Glasses*, 1963, 28 × 35.6 cm, oil on canvas. Collection Jane Lang Davis.

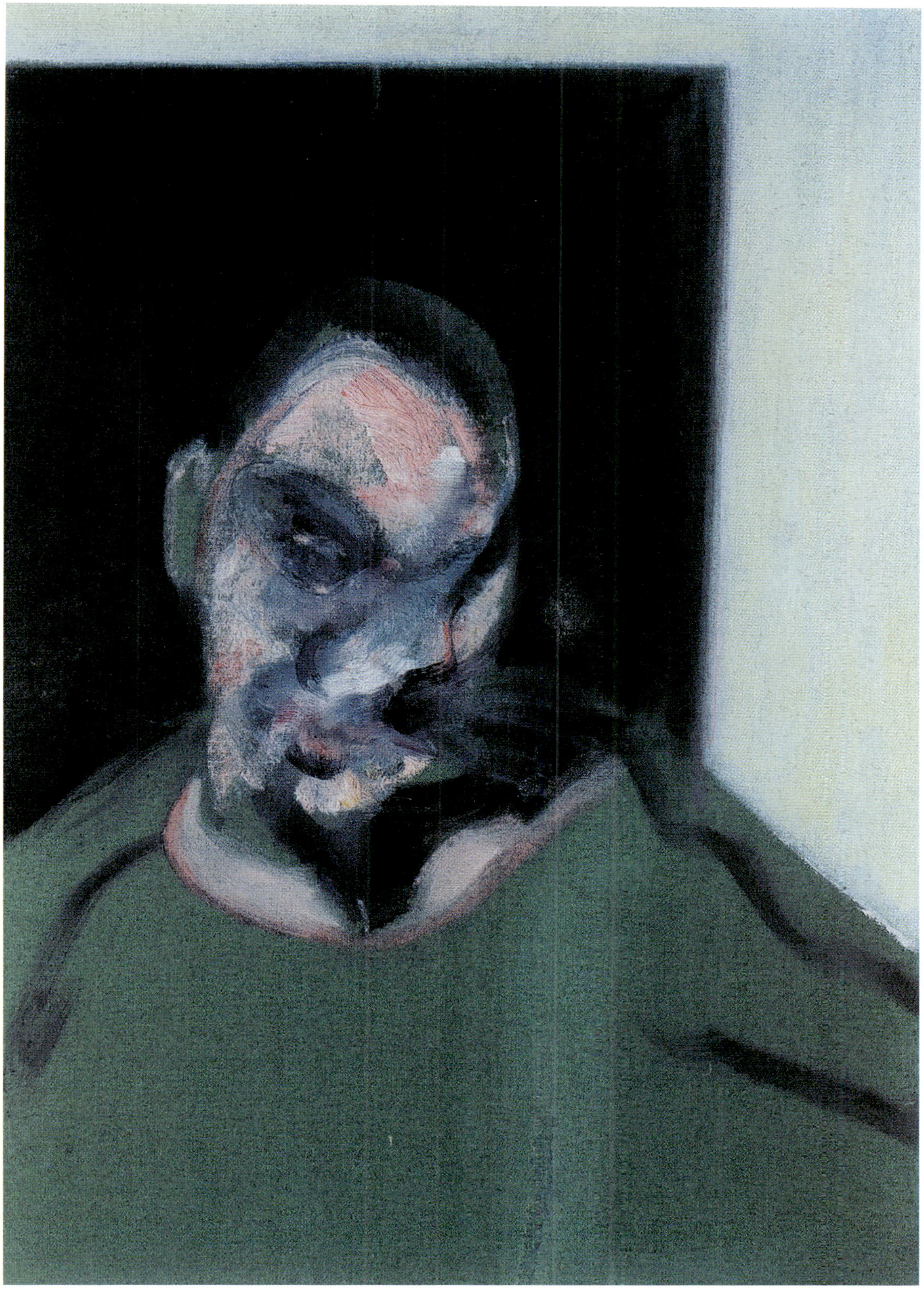

CAT 44 *Head of a Boy*, 1960, 61 × 44.5 cm, oil on canvas. Private collection.

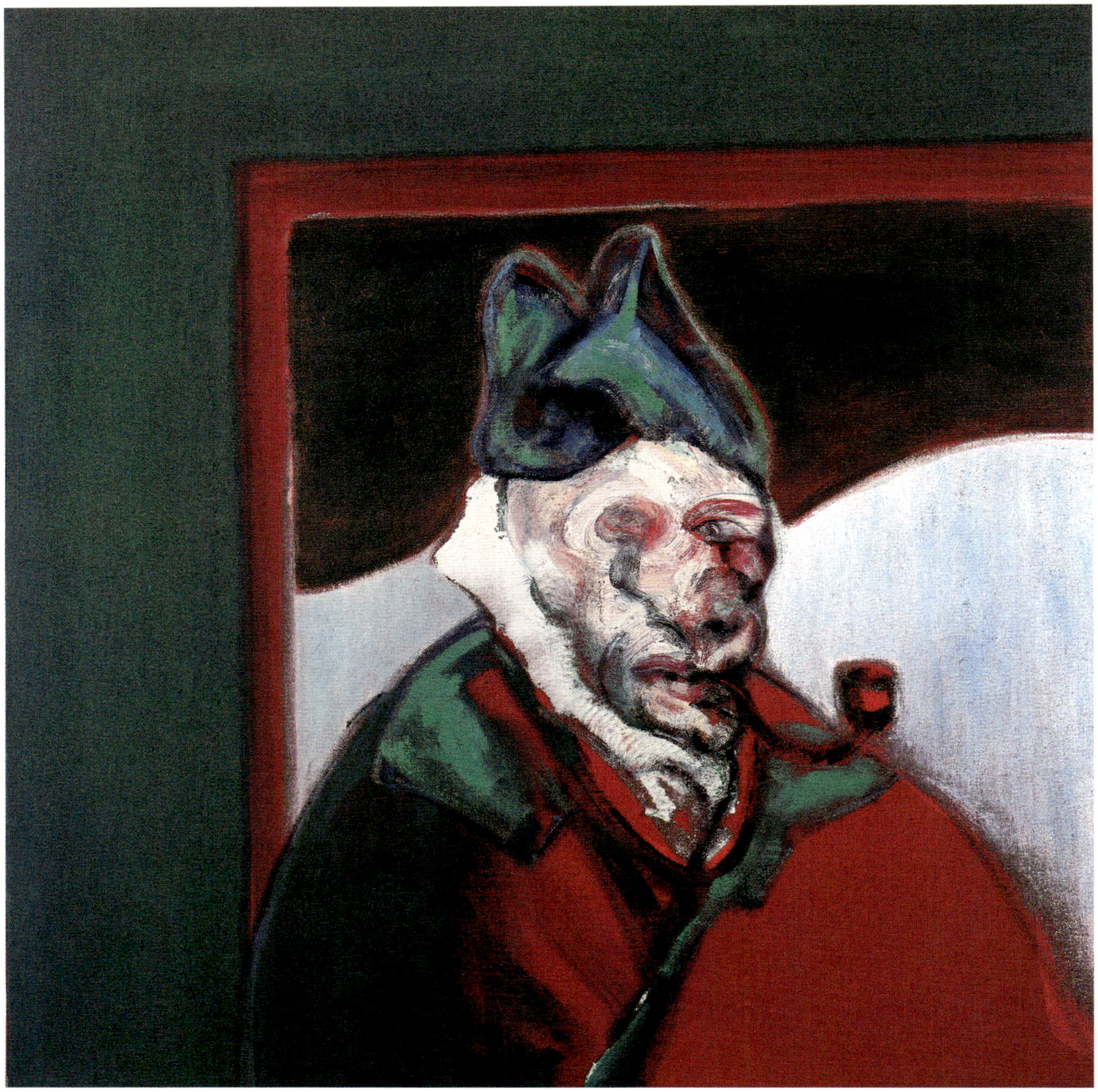

CAT 45 *Homage to van Gogh*, 1960, 86.5 × 86.5 cm, oil on canvas. Göteborgs Konstmuseum, Göteborg.

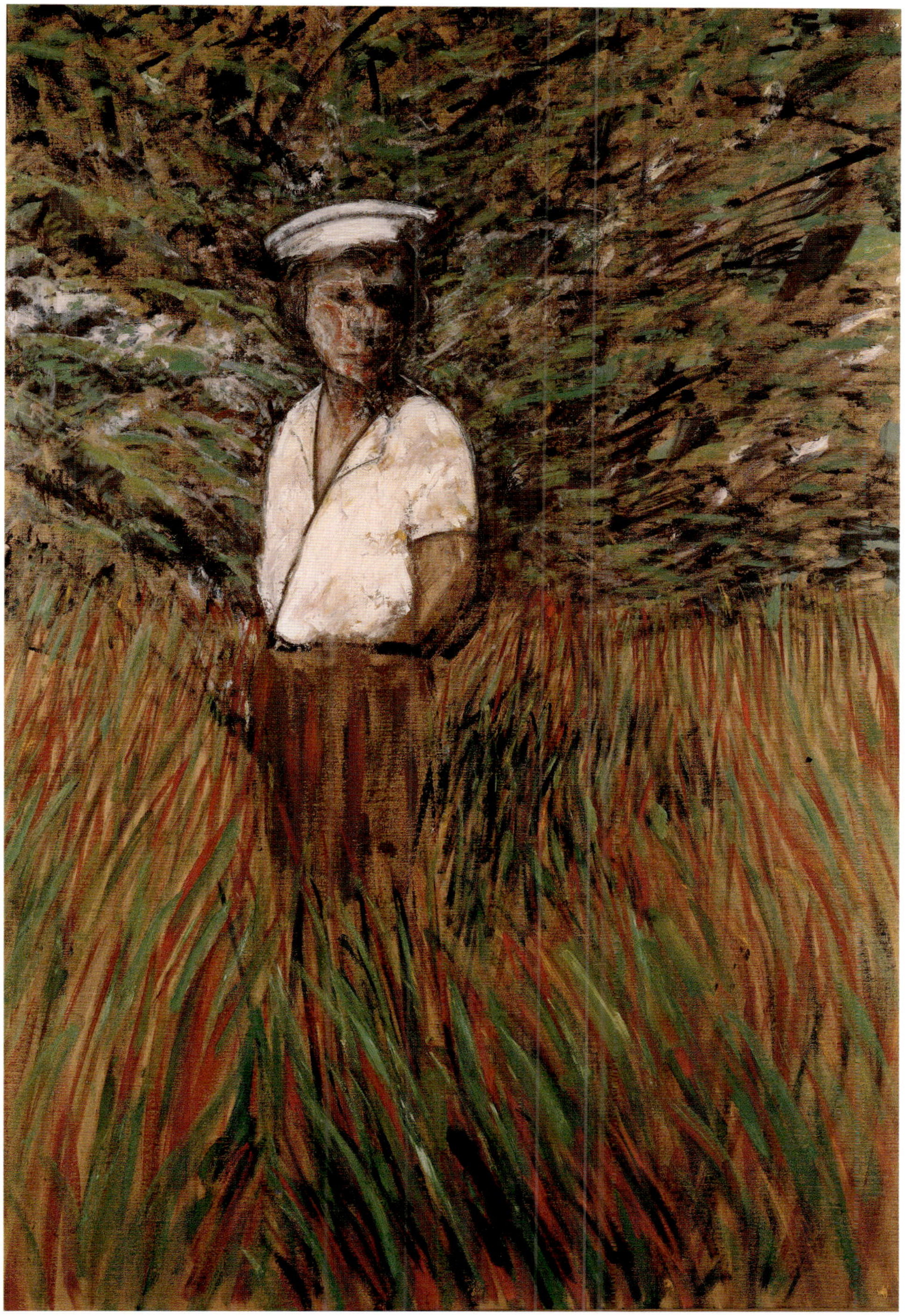

CAT 46 *Figure in a Landscape*, 1957, 198 × 137 cm, oil on canvas. Private collection.

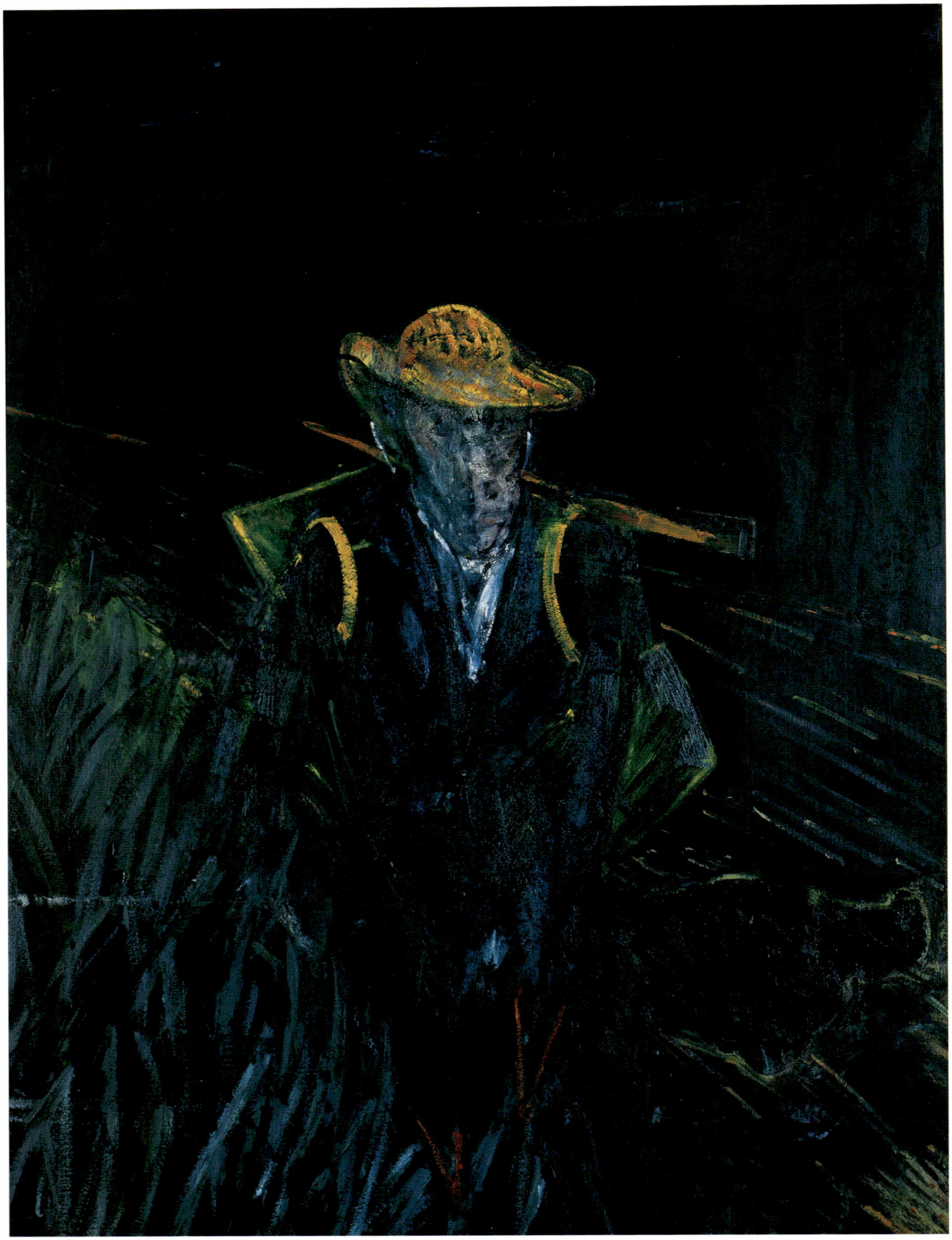

CAT 47 *Study for a Portrait of van Gogh I*, 1956, 154.1 × 115.6 cm, oil on canvas, Robert and Lisa Sainsbury Collection, University of East Anglia, Norwich.

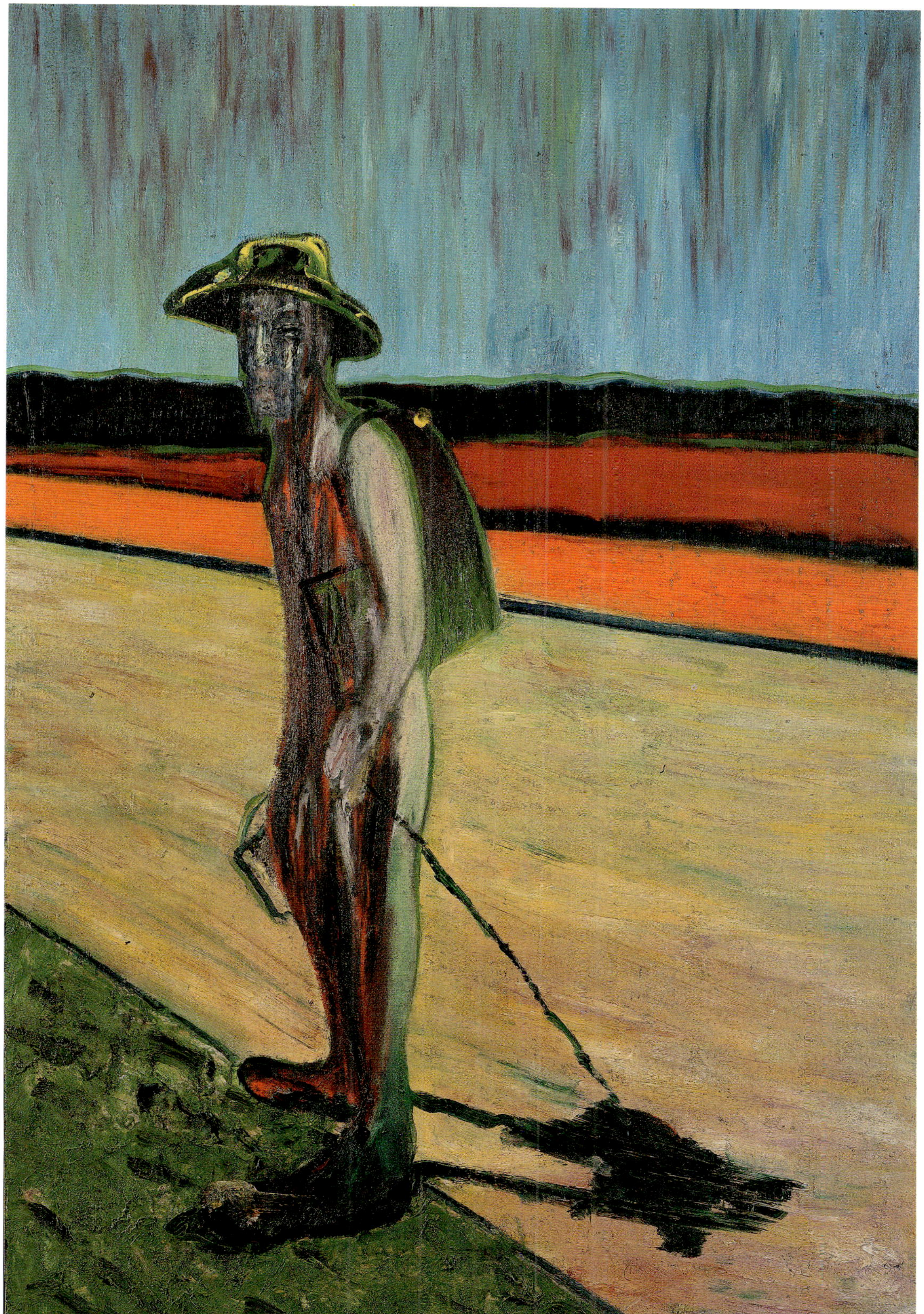

CAT 48 *Study for a Portrait of van Gogh V*, 1957, 198.7 × 137.5 cm, oil on canvas. Hirshhorn Museum and Sculpture Garden, Smithsonian Institution, gift of the Joseph H. Hirshhorn Foundation, 1966.

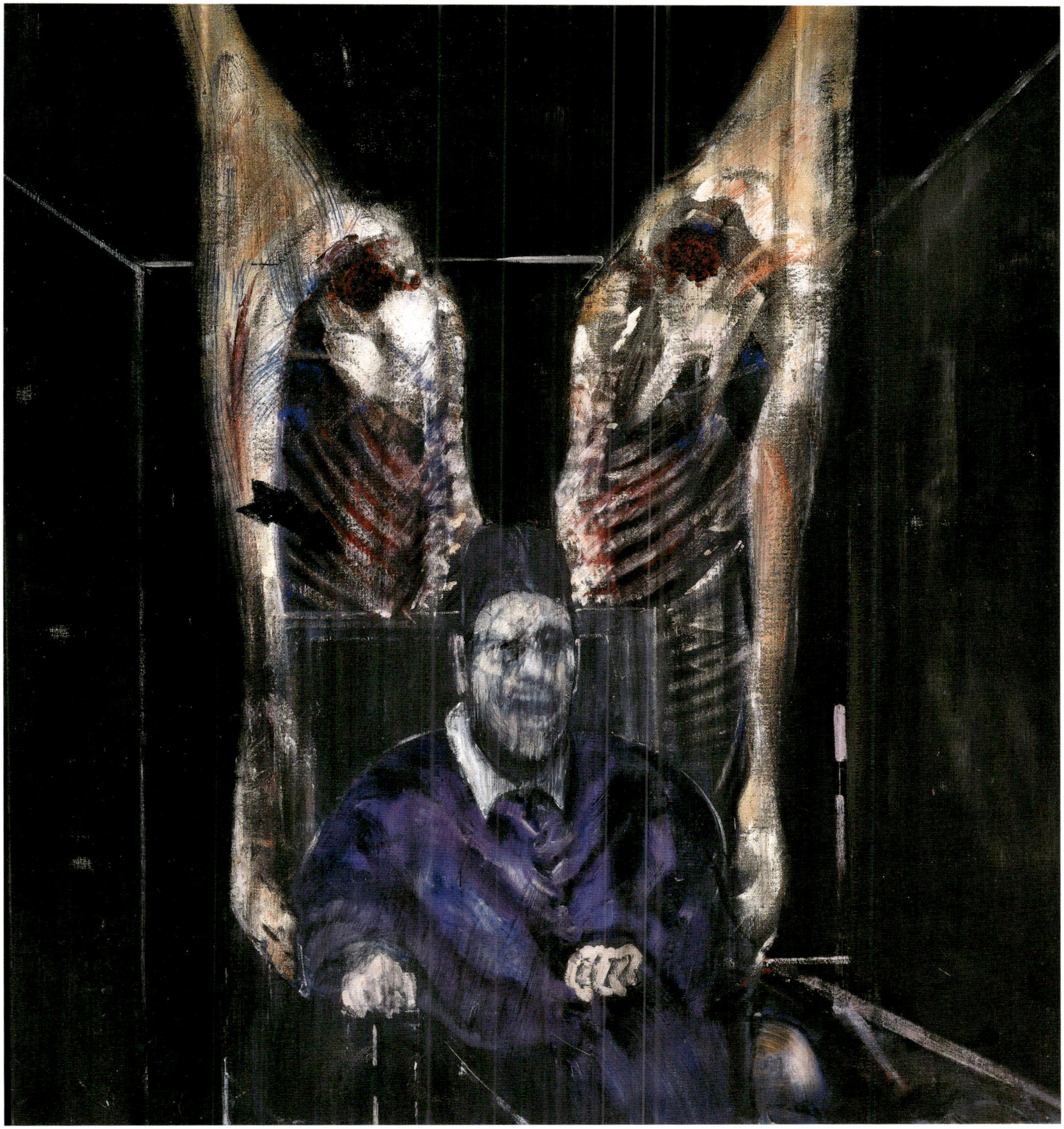

CAT 49 *Figure with Meat*, 1954, 129.9 × 121.9 cm, oil on canvas. The Art Institute of Chicago, Harriott A. Fox Fund, 1956.

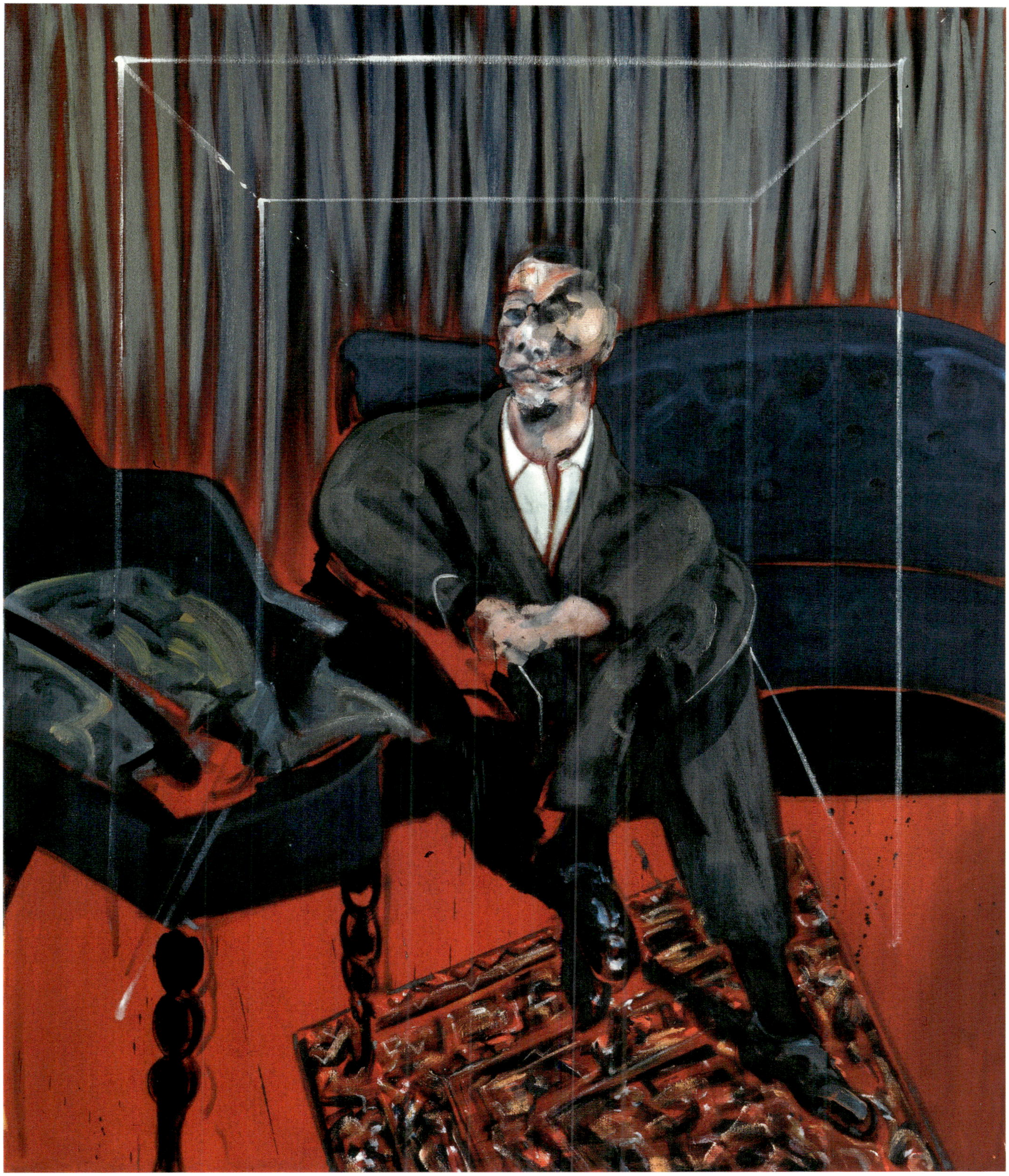

CAT 50 *Seated Figure*, 1961, 165.1 × 142.2 cm, oil on canvas. Tate, London, presented by J. Sainsbury, 1961.

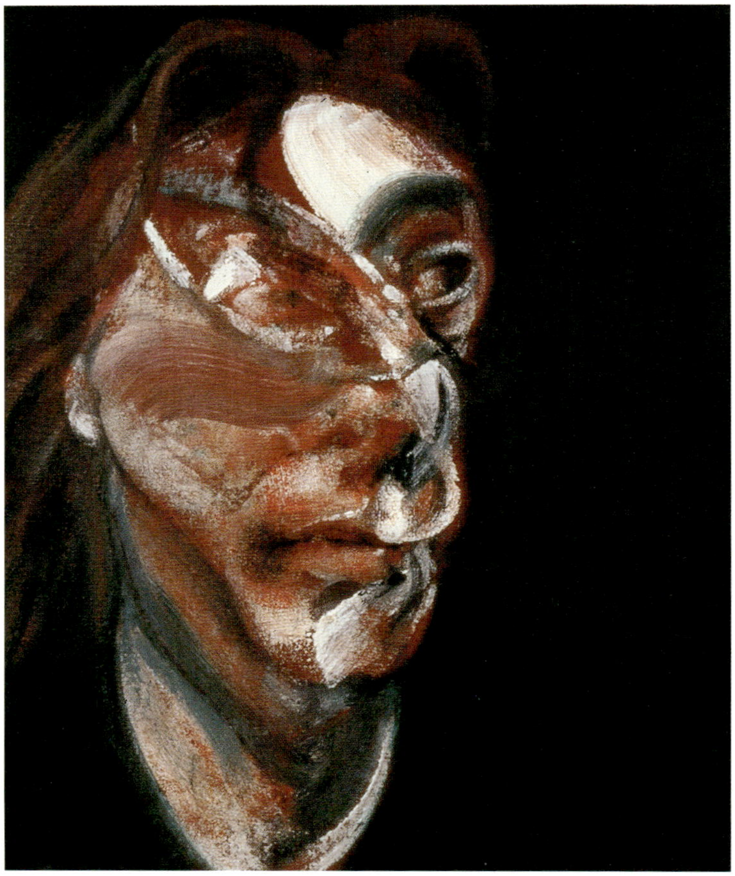

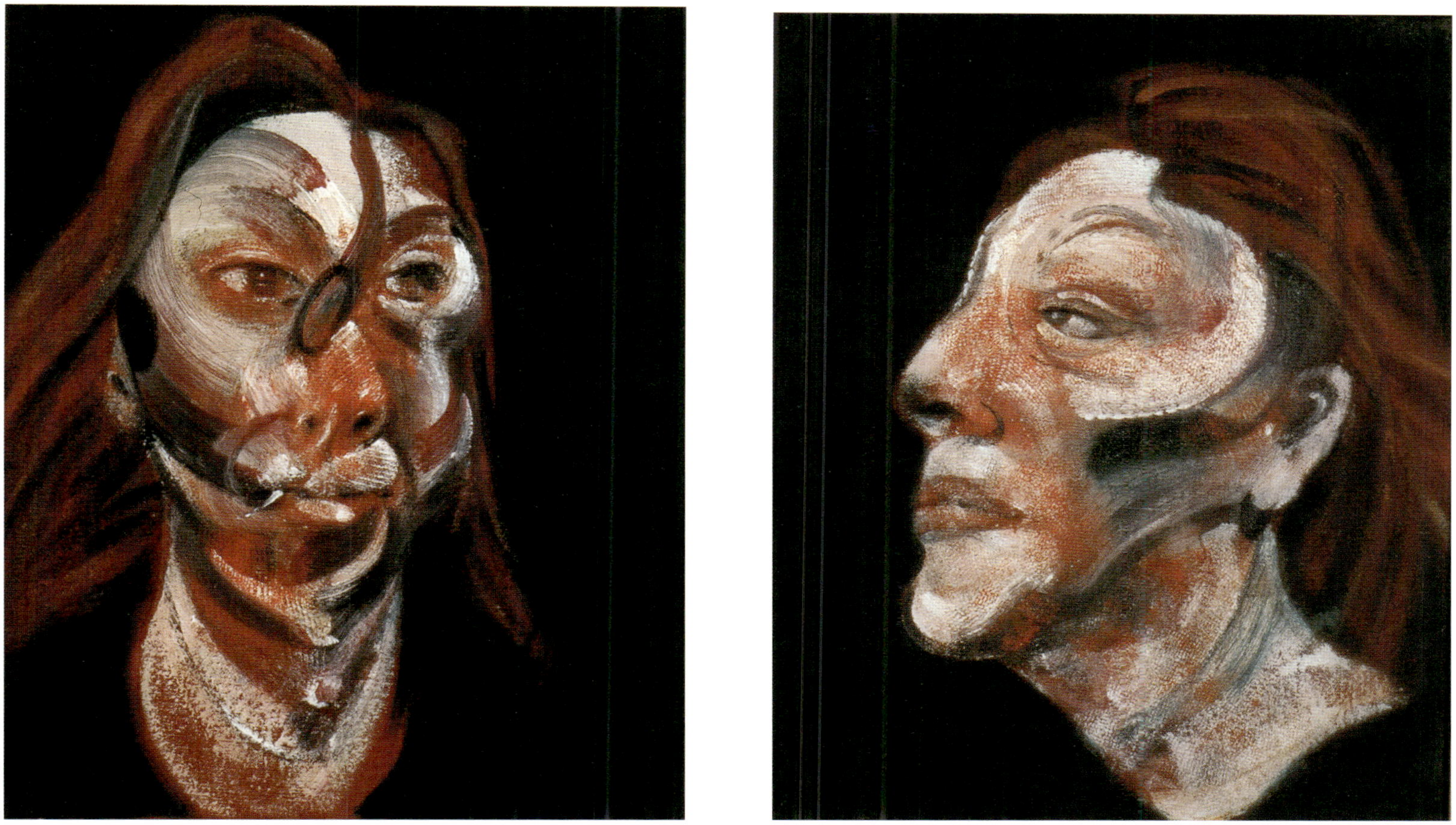

CAT 51 *Three Studies for Portrait of Isabel Rawsthorne*, 1965, 35.6 × 30.5 cm (each panel), oil on canvas.
Robert and Lisa Sainsbury Collection, University of East Anglia, Norwich.

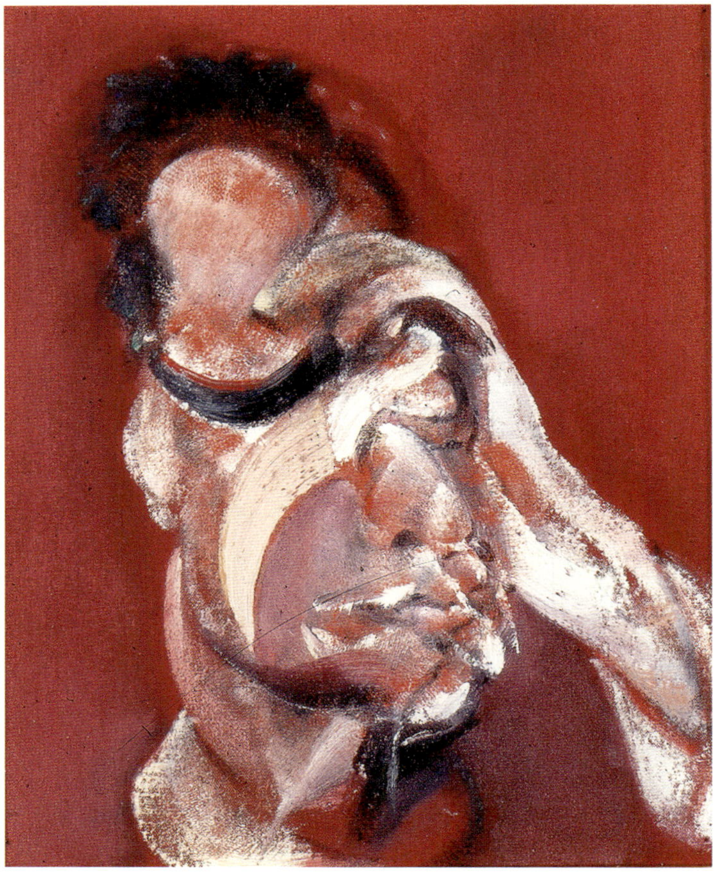

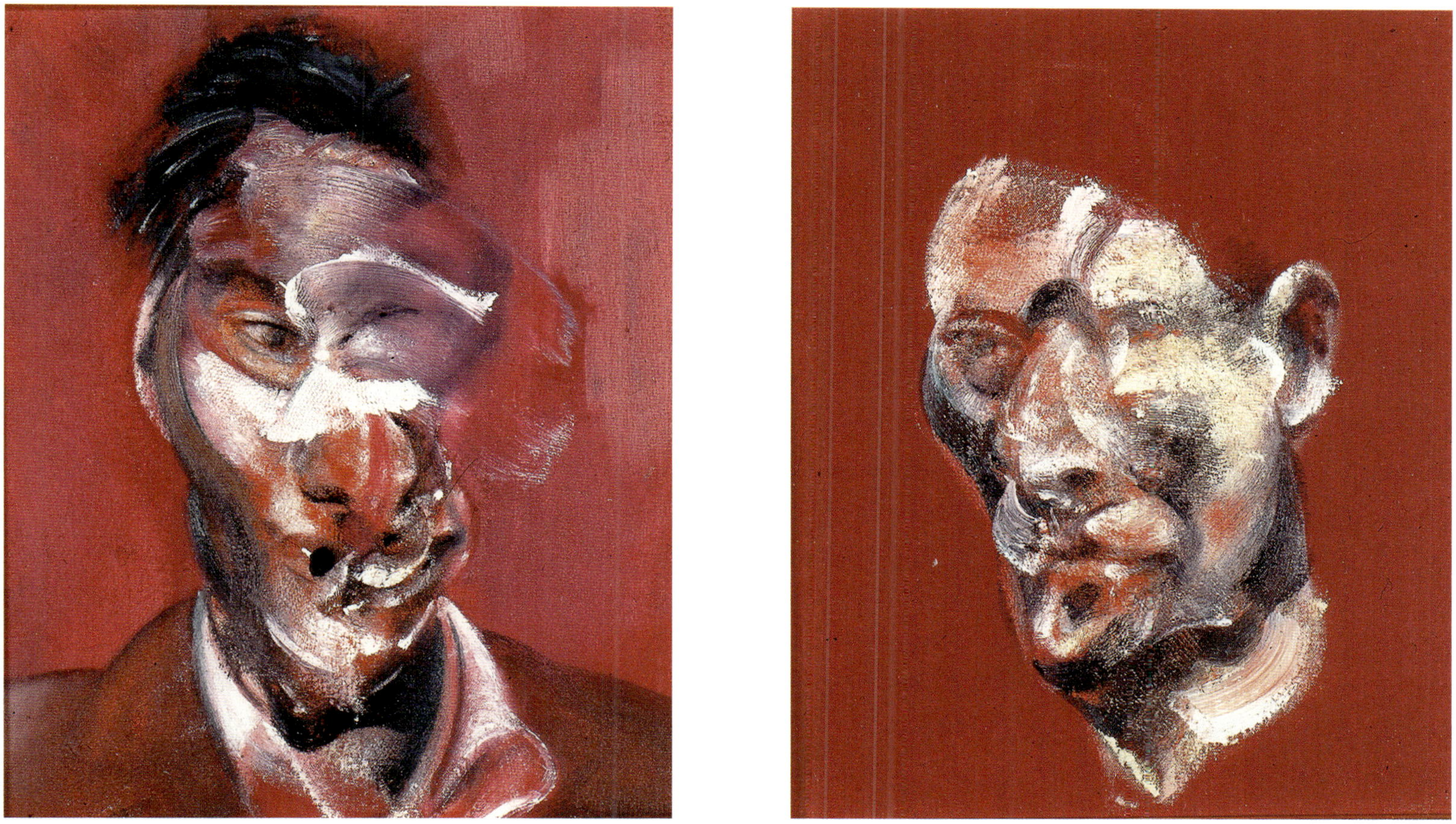

CAT 52 *Three Studies for Portrait of Lucian Freud*, 1965, 35.6 × 30.5 cm (each panel), oil on canvas.
Yageo Foundation, Taiwan.

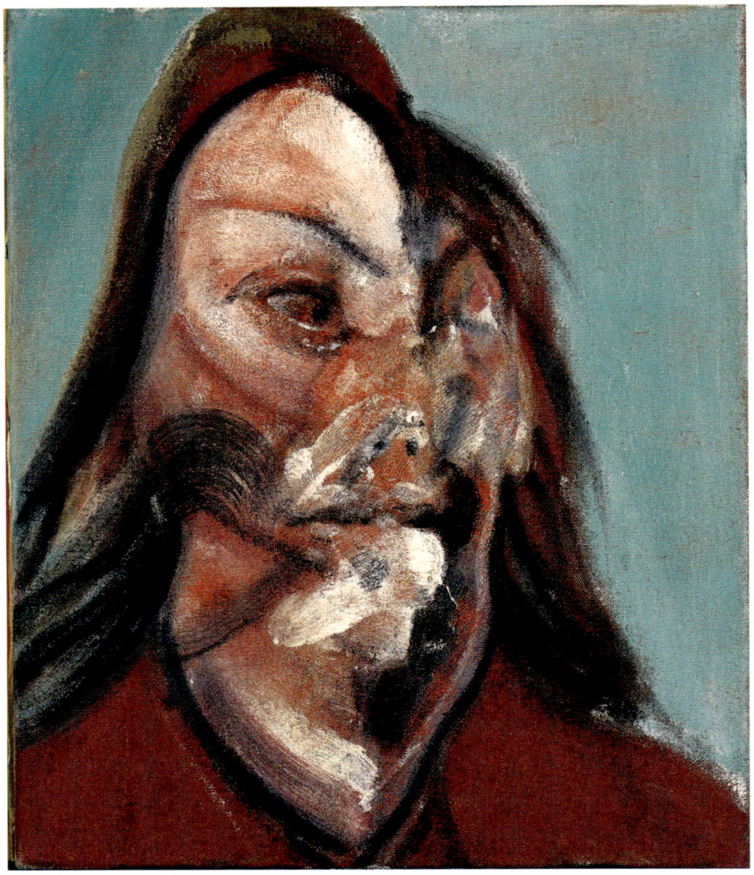

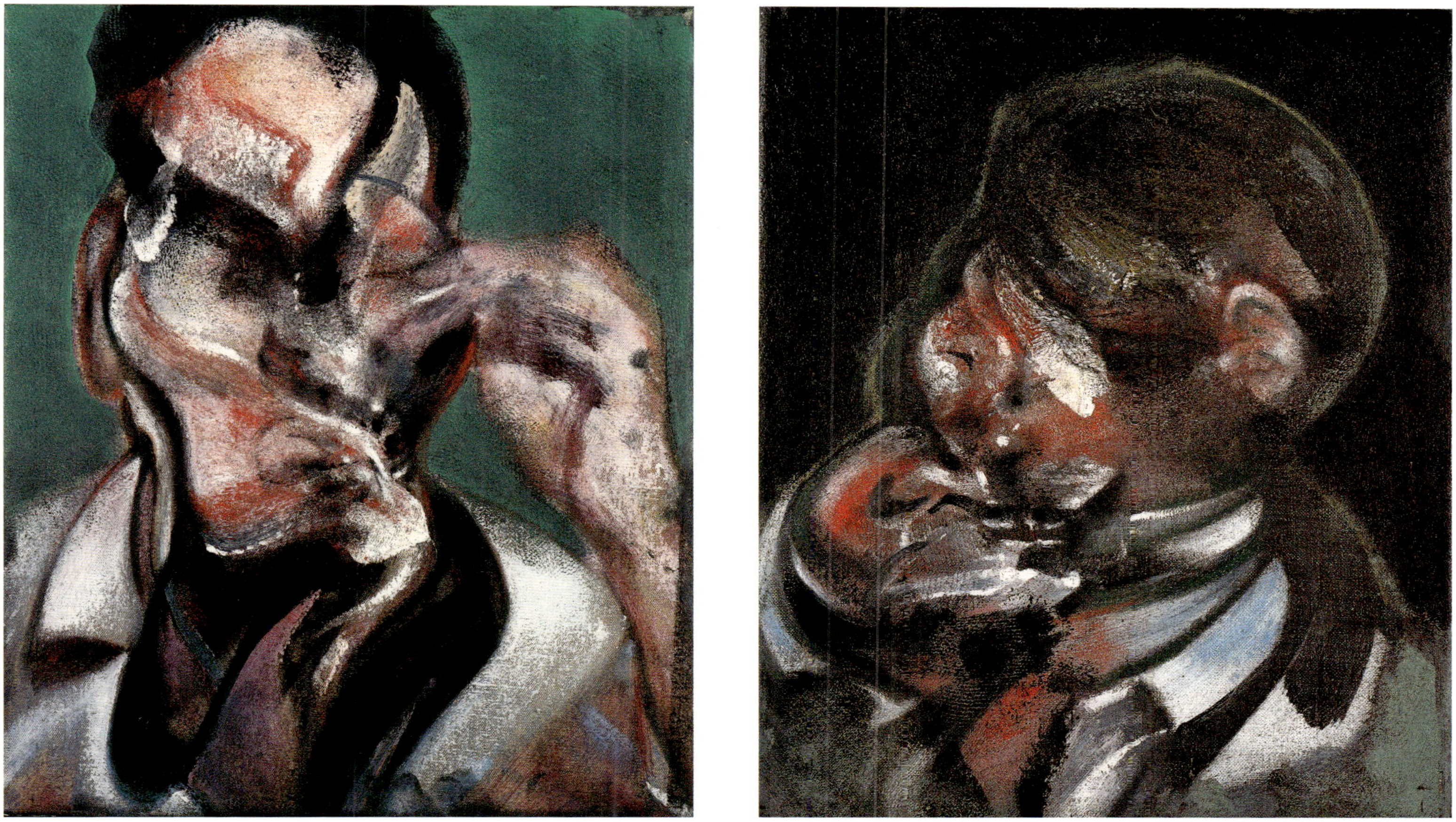

CAT 53 *Three Studies for Portraits: Isabel Rawsthorne, Lucian Freud and John Hewitt*, 1966, 34.5 × 29.3 cm (each panel), oil on canvas. Private collection.

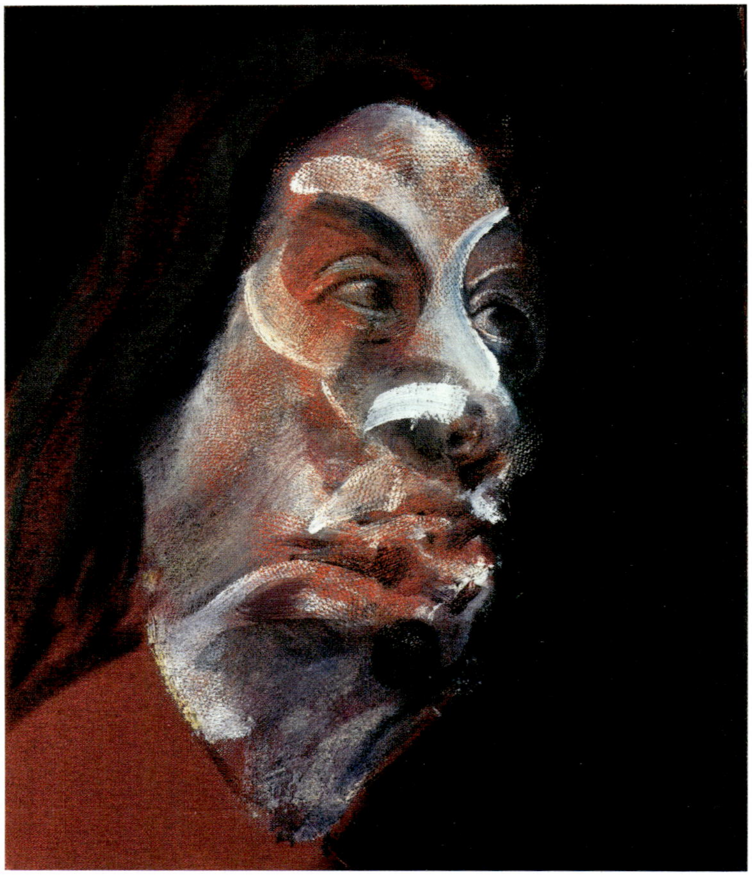

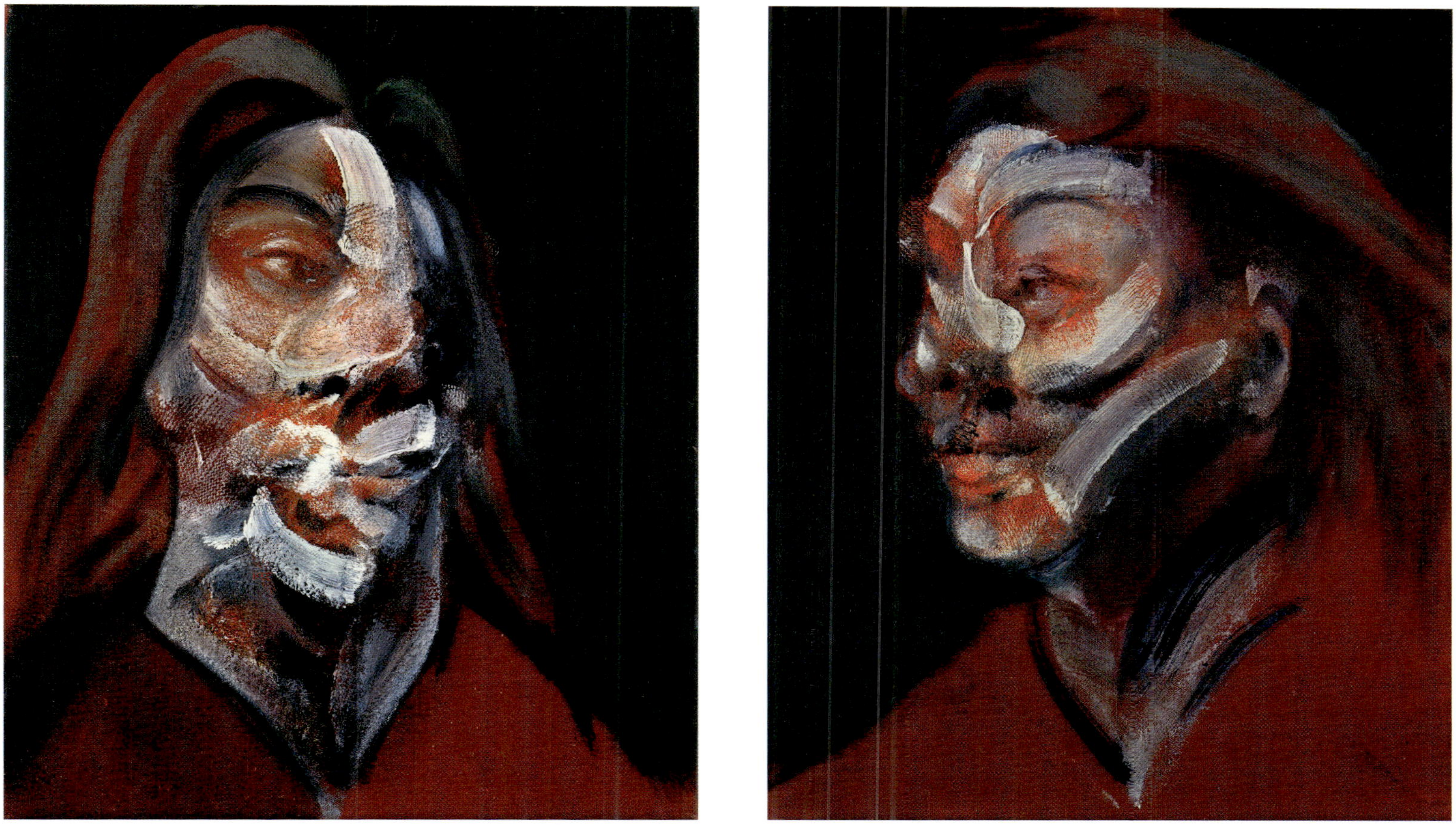

CAT 54 *Three Studies for Portrait of Isabel Rawsthorne*, 1966, 35.6 × 30.5 cm (each panel), oil on canvas. Private collection.

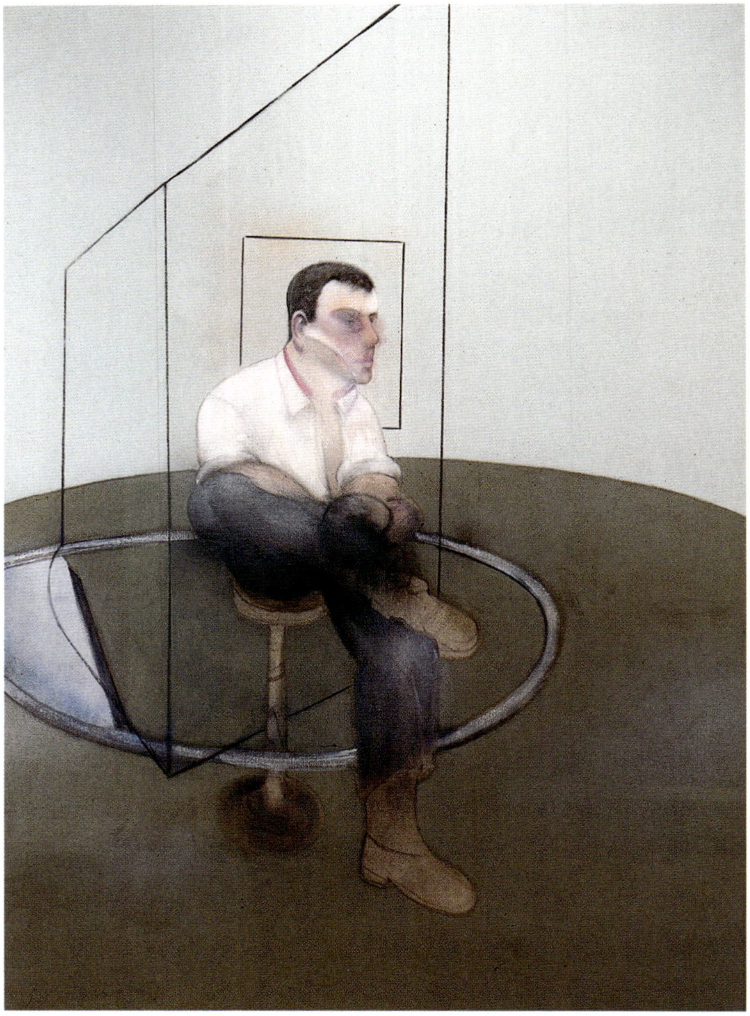

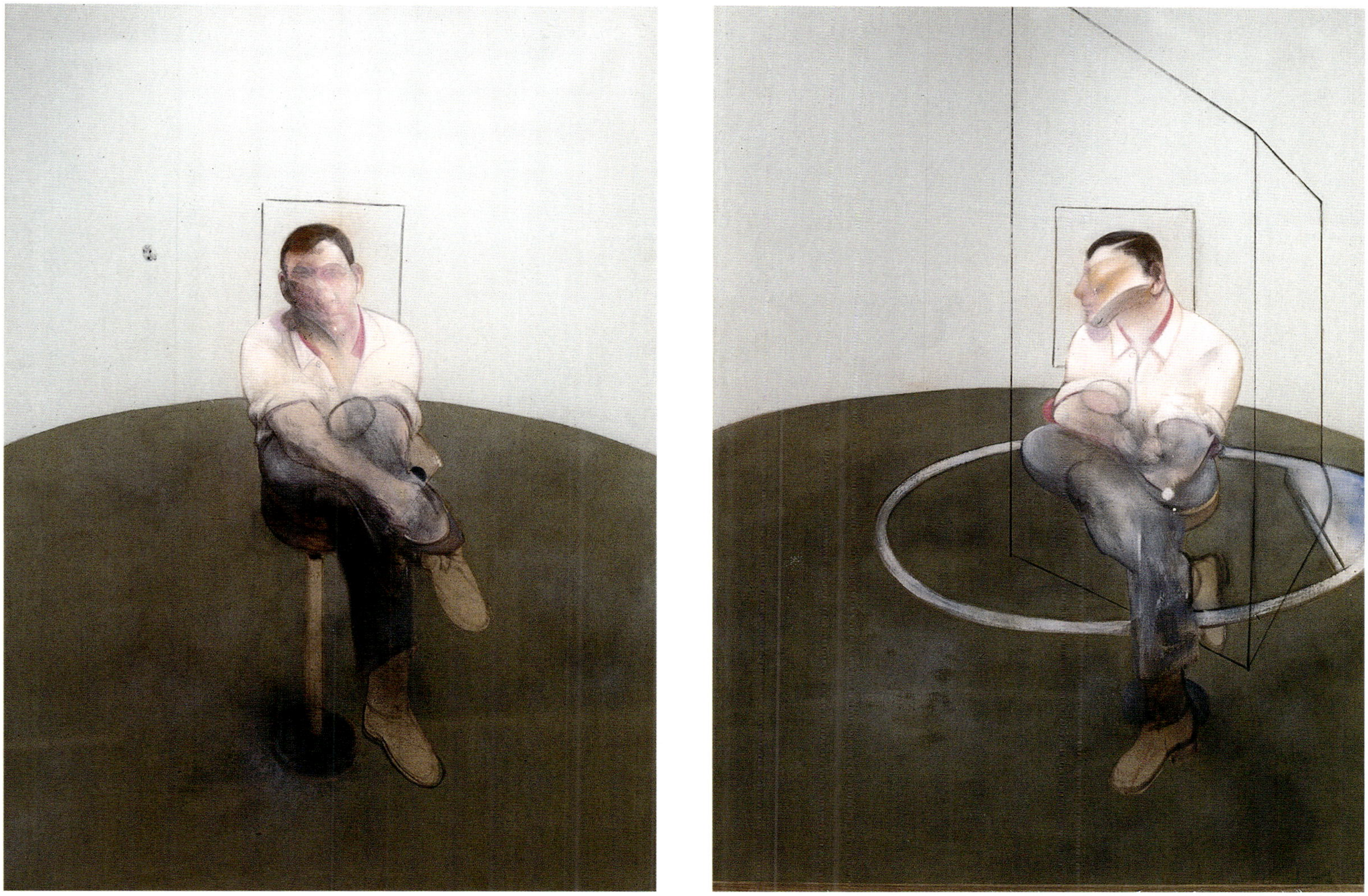

CAT 55 *Three Studies for Portrait of John Edwards*, 1984, 198 × 147.5 cm, oil on canvas.
Yageo Foundation, Taiwan.

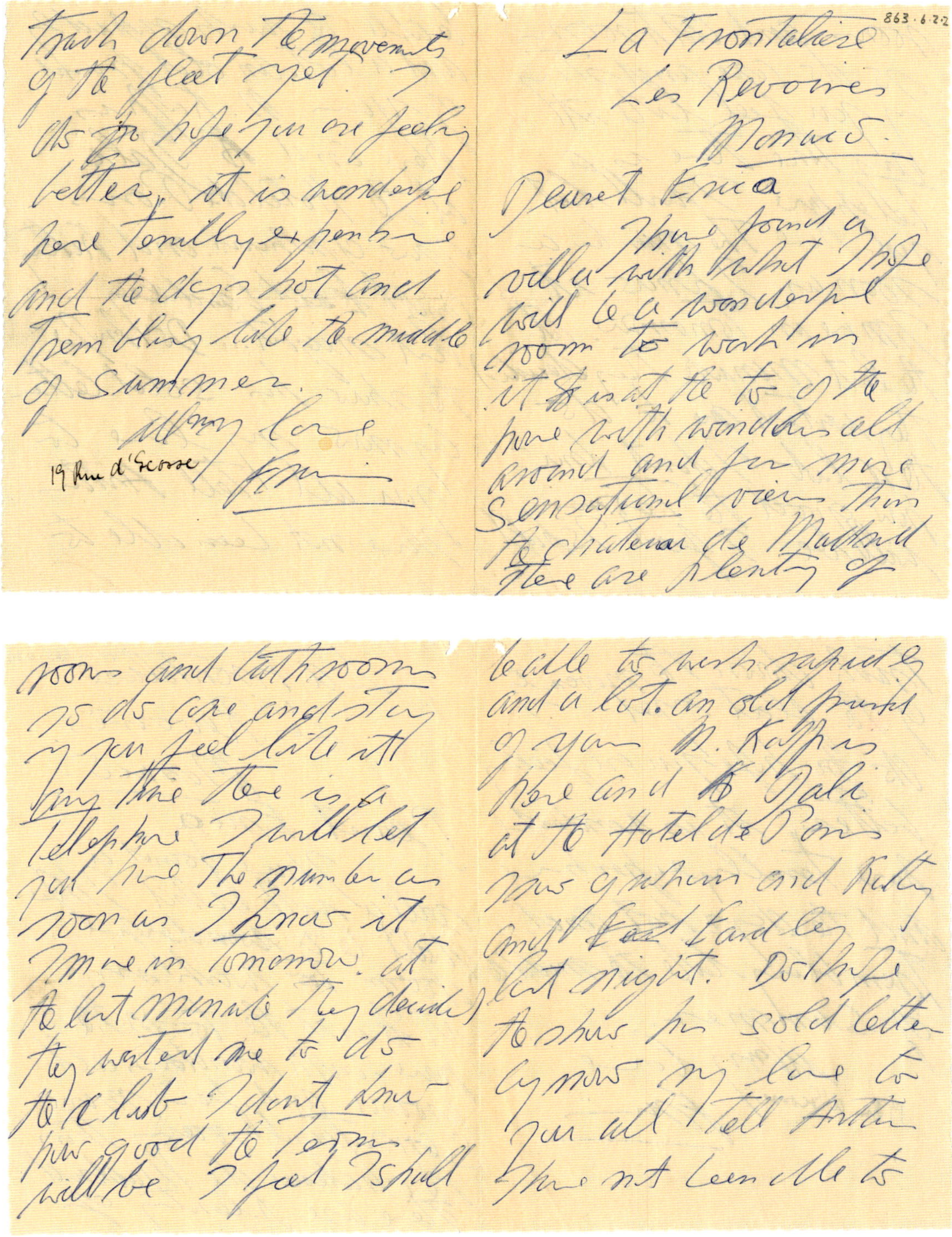
863.6.2.2

La Frontalière
Les Revoires
Monaco

Dearest Erica
I have found a villa with what I hope will be a wonderful room to work in it is at the top of the house with windows all around and far more sensational view than the Chateau de Madrid there are plenty of rooms and bathroom so do come and stay if you feel like it at any time there is a telephone I will let you have the number as soon as I know it I move in tomorrow. at the last minute they decided they wanted me to do the club I don't know how good the terms will be I feel I shall be able to work rapidly and a lot. an old friend of yours M. Kaff is here and Dali at the Hotel de Paris saw Graham and Kathy and Earl Eardley last night. Do hope to show him solid letters by now my love to you all tell Arthur I have not been able to track down the movements of the flat yet. I do hope you are feeling better, it is wonderful here terribly expensive and the days hot and trembling like the middle of summer.
Always love
Francis

19 Rue d'Ecosse

29 Letter from Francis Bacon to Erica Brausen, Hanover Gallery archive.

BACON'S LETTERS TO THE HANOVER GALLERY

Francis Bacon was not a natural or a gifted letter-writer. He tended to use letters for specific purposes: to settle some outstanding gallery or financial business, to make or to change appointments, or simply to express his thanks. Fluently and brilliantly as he talked (and in private he was wittier and more outrageous than in the interviews he gave), Bacon became automatically far less at ease once he put pen to paper. To some extent this may have been because he felt that his sporadic schooling had not provided him with the basic tools to write well – much as the lack of early artistic training prevented him from ever seriously trying his hand at drawing. And later in life Bacon made up his mind in his typically categorical way about both activities. Drawing could at best provide a rough, notational starting-point for a painting, while a letter served only to make a brief, almost telegraphic, point or two.

As a younger man, however, Bacon was more relaxed and occasionally even quite lyrical in the letters he wrote. Relatively few of these pages in their instantly recognizable, forward-sloping handwriting appear to have survived[1], and most forms part either of the correspondence Bacon had with his friend and one-time mentor Graham Sutherland (dating mainly from the mid-1940s), or the equally important one he maintained over some ten years with Erica Brausen, his dealer from the late 1940s to the late 1950s. The former has received some scholarly attention[2], while the latter has had next to none. This is in fact the first time that the complete correspondence has ever been published.

I have tried to establish what I think might be the most likely chronology for the letters, starting with a couple of short notes from Monte Carlo in the late 1940s to Brausen's short-lived financial partner, Arthur Jeffress, and ending on an acerbic, despairing, undated letter, sent from the Imperial Hotel in Henley-on-Thames which, I suspect, heralds the dramatic falling-out between painter and dealer that took place in October 1958. I have also added the few surviving letters from Erica Brausen, as and when they occurred, to bring the exchange into focus.[3]

Written over ten years (1947–57), these seventeen letters chronicle Bacon's frequent travels over the period. They follow him from his early stays in Monte Carlo through his trip to Southern Rhodesia (present-day Zimbabwe), back to Monaco, then to Tangier, from where the main body of the letters was written. They also record Bacon's visit to Rome and Naples, while the two last letters come from a friends' house in Wivenhoe and the Imperial Hotel at Henley-on-Thames (a key location for Bacon in the 1950s because he was allowed to paint in the room he had there). Significantly, not one of the letters comes from London, so it can be assumed that if Bacon had any business to discuss with Brausen while they were both in town, he would either telephone her or go directly to the Hanover Gallery to see her.

As with the letters to Bob and Lisa Sainsbury, Bacon's correspondence with Brausen centres around money matters. Although his paintings were highly priced, Bacon produced relatively little for sale (in part because he destroyed so much of his work). Since he also spent freely, whether at the gaming tables or in treating his friends to champagne and caviar, he was frequently hard up or in debt during the 1950s. It is likely, in fact, that if Bacon had not undergone frequent financial crises throughout the decade none of the following letters would have been written. But while he was angling for a payment of this or an advance of that, Bacon often added a brief sketch of his travels, insights into his state of mind and also, tantalizingly enough, references to the paintings he planned or had finished (sometimes, no doubt, to encourage his dealer to come up with the cash).

If Bacon provided these dashes of extra colour and information, it was mainly because he was genuinely fond of Brausen and wanted to maintain the rapport of mutual trust they had established. Several things had brought them close. First, Bacon was fully aware of the fact that Brausen had risked a great deal by taking him on at her gallery when he was still very little known; her admiration for his work and her commitment to his career never wavered. Secondly, the fact that they were both homosexual created a strong bond between them. Bacon was very at ease in lesbian circles, because he found it so natural to be attracted by people of one's own sex; and he was fascinated by the rites and ambience of lesbian clubs and bars. What's more, while Brausen would have been won over by the painter's social ease and seductive charm, Bacon was undoubtedly drawn to his dealer's cosmopolitan background[4] and her linguistic fluency (a gift he felt he himself did not possess but which he much admired in others; however, that did not prevent Bacon from gleefully imitating Brausen's Germanic accent in English when he discussed her with friends).

Brausen, for her part, appears both protective and slightly exasperated by her star artist in the occasional references she makes to him in her correspondence with other people.[5] Clearly at Bacon's behest, she remains very guarded about providing any biographical details about him. Thus requests for background information are met either with a rather mysterious: 'There is very little known about Francis Bacon', or the more trenchant: 'The artist will not allow the publication of any personal details.' Small wonder that Alfred Barr, the influential director of the Museum of Modern Art in New York (which had bought *Painting 1946*) remonstrated with Brausen about the lack of information concerning Bacon: 'You really ought to document thoroughly the work of England's most interesting painter! Who else will!'[6] Meanwhile, when writing to George Dix, Bacon's dealer at Durlacher Bros in New York, Brausen has a fond and nicely revealing grumble about Bacon: 'The paintings came back from Paris at the last moment and he kept altering the new ones – you know what he is like, so the catalogue could not be printed on time.'[7]

With these close bonds and the inevitable interdependence of artist and dealer, Bacon was clearly at ease to write whatever he felt in these brief missives back home. Although their prime purpose was usually to raise cash for another week or two abroad, the letters abound with amusing descriptions and unexpected insights. Arriving in southern Rhodesia, for instance, Bacon finds the cross-country journey to Zimbabwe 'like a continuous Renoir landscape'. On his return, he writes, he plans to take a boat to Port Sudan, make his way to Thebes (famous in the ancient world for its encouragement of pederasty) then 'rejoin the boat again at Alexandria to Marseille' (Bacon cannot have been unmindful of the way this echoes Rimbaud's wanderings). He ends this lively letter on a camp description of the Rhodesian police as 'too sexy for words starched shorts and highly polished leggings'. Some of the other letters, while more terse, wonderfully evoke the atmosphere of the place where Bacon happens to be, such as when he writes repeatedly from Tangier to ask Brausen to transfer funds into the account of the very louche-sounding 'Auto Gears and Spare Parts Co'; in this context, Somerset Maugham's summary of spots like Tangier as 'sunny places for shady people' assumes a new dimension.

Taken together, these letters also chart the whole course of Bacon and Brausen's relationship. While the early letters are full of charming banter, the later ones come more quickly to the point and the last sound a peremptory note. All in all, fragmentary and tantalizing as they are, the correspondence constitutes the most complete documentary source that we have for Francis Bacon in the 1950s.

Francis Bacon to Arthur Jeffress[8]

Saiha Hati [?], Blvd. des Moulins, Monte-Carlo

Dear Arthur

I have not written before as I did not think you would be back from Italy. Thank you so much for advancing the £200 on the show. The pictures seem to be going well I am at the moment working on some heads which I like better than any I have done before. I hope you and Erica will like them. I shall come over in November or December to bring some of the stuff over and leave with you. I am rather disturbed as to what to do about frames also when you know your plans for exhibitions could you let me know about what date you would like to show the things the later the better for me. I do hope you enjoyed Malta [?].

My best wishes to you all

Francis

Saiha Hati[?], Blvd. des Moulins, Monte-Carlo 30/9/48

Dear Arthur

Thank you very much for your letter. I would like the 12th of June to the 7th of July as all the stuff will be new it will give you a bit more time. I expect to be over about the middle of November and will leave some of it with you then. It is terribly quiet and deserted here which I quite like and lovely weather.

all best wishes

Francis

Francis Bacon to Erica Brausen

32a St. George St., Hanover Sq., London W1, England c/o Thos. Cook Salisbury[9] S. Rhodesia[10] 22/2/51

Dearest Erica

I got here about a week ago. I stayed at Zimbabwe[11] and the country from there to here is too marvelous it is like a continuous Renoir landscape and Zimbabwe itself is incredible. Robert Heber-Percy[12] has left and will be back in London soon. I have started to work it is so thrilling here and I met someone who has a farm near Zimbabwe and am going back there now that I have got rid of Robert. The work has started terribly well. I am going to try and do a set of 3 quickly – could the gallery possibly advance me £50 as now that I have left Robert I have practically no money. I have the return ticket by air which I am changing and trying to get a boat from Beira up the east coast they call in at all the ports and then I want to get off at Port Sudan and go to Thebes and rejoin the boat again at Alexandria to Marseilles. I am trying to get a passage on a boat that leaves Beira on the 18th of March and I should be home about the end of April. I would be terribly grateful if you could do this for me everyone is so terribly nice here. I don't like sponging on them all the time and paints and canvas are very expensive. You can send it from Thos. Cook in Berkeley St. to their branch here in Salisbury addressed to me by cable. I shall be in and out of Salisbury for the next 3 weeks. The men are too marvelous drinking lazing [?]

overfed - and rich - Champagne starts at 11 o'clock in the mornings. Tell Arthur the Rhodesian Police are completely him too sexy for words starched shorts and highly polished leggings – I feel 20 years younger we are mad to stay in England. I am certain you would adore this country.

All my love to you all

Francis

[Air Letter] c/o Thos. Cook & Sons, Salisbury S. Rhodesia 27/2/51

Dearest Erica,

I have since writing to you been able to fix a passage from Beira. I should arrive in Marseille about the 22nd of April. I am sorry to ask again but could you wire me the £50 immediately care of Cooks at the above address. I have done 3 small paintings which I am excited about. I hope you will like them – I terribly want to get off at Port Sudan and go to Thebes and get the boat again at Alexandria also I want to buy some more materials to try and work on the boat and it is so difficult having to ask all the time for little sums of money. As I did not come on with Robert I am without anything but my fare. I am enjoying being here terribly. I am not living in Salisbury but come in every few days. Could you cable the money here so that it arrives by or before the 10th of March. My love to you all lots of news when I see you.

Love and best wishes

Francis

La Frontalière, Les Revoires, Monaco [undated]

Dearest Erica

I have found a villa with what I hope will be a wonderful room to work in it is at the top of the house with windows all around and far more sensational views than the chateau de Madrid. There are plenty of rooms and bathrooms so do come and stay if you feel like it any time. There is a telephone I will let you know the number as soon as I know it. I move in tomorrow. at the last minute they decided they wanted me to do the club. I don't know how good the terms will be. I feel I should be able to work rapidly and a lot an old friend of yours M. Kapp is here and Dali at the Hotel de Paris. I saw Graham and Kathy and Eardley last night.[13] Do hope the show has sold better by now my love to you all tell Arthur[14] I have not been able track down the movements of the Fleet yet. I do hope you are feeling better, it is wonderful here, terribly expensive, and the days hot and trembling like the middle of Summer.

All my love

Francis

19 Rue d'Ecosse [in different ink, in a different hand, beside the signature]

13 Dec (1954?)[15]

My dear Erica

I am so sorry not to have written to you sooner – it has not been possible to get a place in Rome for 2 months as they are so expensive with the American invasion so I am living in Ostia as there are masses of appartments [sic] very cheap and it is very easy to get to Rome – but will you write to me at the Hotel Inghleterra [sic]

Via Bocca del Leone

Rome

as I am not sure if letters get here. The work is going very well I have finished 2 large ones. I don't think del Corso[16] wants to do a show unless he can get the stuff direct as of course he won't make enough. But I told him anything had to be done through you so I don't think he is interested. Cremonini[17] has a show on there now he is very nice but the stuff is purely modern academic at the moment but when he has a show with you why don't you get Wystan Auden to do an article as when I saw him in the summer he told me how much he liked it but as it is modern academy it will probably sell in any case. I have seen nothing modern here of any interest. But I love Rome not the social life the little I have seen but the Town. The Italians made me pay quite a lot of duty on the canvases. I hope it won't be the same taking them into England. I do hope you are well and things are going well my love to you and Toto and Mrs Dornbach.

best love and wishes

Francis

Hotel Inghilterra, Via Bocca del Leone, Rome. Dec 27th

My dear Erica

Thank you so much for your letter. I don't know what to say about a show here the Gallery is so small even Cremonini's work looked too large in it. I think perhaps it would be better to bring the pictures back with me. I think when I have a show there it would be better to show much smaller things which I hope I shall be able to do soon. I have been in Naples for a few days. I found it wonderful and would like to work there for a time. For me it is much more exciting than Rome. I expect I will be back about the end of January. I am leaving Henley and am going to try and find a place in London where I can really settle for a change and perhaps let when I go away. I am so sick of never having a permanent place. Thank you so much for sending the cheque on the 1st January to the bank

my love and very best wishes for the New Year

yours

Francis

Poste Restante, British Post Office, Tangiers [undated]

My dear Erica

I found France so expensive that I came over here and I have been very lucky as the Director of the museum in the Kasbah has lent me a room to work in. I have seen Yacoubi he says you want him to have a show in London.[18] I feel they would sell very well especially if he came over too. I have just started to work I will try and send some things back soon the Chelsea Art Stores will put them on stretchers if I send them rolled it is very cheap to live here and in lots of ways very exciting. All my love Francis

P.T.O

[on reverse]

I don't know if I shall get the work done for the show in Paris[19] that is to say it is a short time to do all new ones. Will you let me know where I can write to you when you go away

love

Francis

[written on an invitation to the private view of works by Bacon at the Galerie Rive Droite, February 1957][20]

Sunday morning

My dear Erica

I am so sorry about last night but everything went wrong and I couldn't get along. Thank you so much for the money it was so good of you. I do hope the show will go well. I hope to have some more good paintings for the show in London

all best love and thank you so much for everything

love Francis

[ps] They have made a mistake in the catalogue – it is not – Painting in a Rocky Landscape – but Figure in a Rocky Landscape.

April 9th [1957?]

My dear Erica – I would like to work on this series a bit longer before I let them go. I will let you know as soon as they are ready - is there any special exhibition you want to arrange if you could let me know what you plan I will let you know when I can have them ready – I am sorry not to be able to let you have them at the moment but I feel I can get them much better.

best love

Francis

Hotel Cecil, Tangier 29/ [May 1957?]

My dear Erica

If you want to get in touch with me will you write to this address. I hear from Achmid[21] that Toto[22] is coming out here. I would be so grateful if you could send the £100 you owe me by her. Achmid has done some very good new paintings and it should be a very good show. Hope you are all well.

All best wishes

Francis

Erica Brausen to Francis Bacon

[Typescript copy]

Francis Bacon Esq., Hotel Cecil, Tangier, 6th June 1957

Dearest Francis,

We have sent the £100 with Toto – I hope it will reach you safely.
George Dix[23] came in today; we talked about your show and he thinks that as you have had so much success lately it would be a good idea to have your American exhibition in the not too distant future. He would like to arrange it for April 1958. That would mean the pictures will have to be ready to leave here at the end of February 1958.
The bank has been paid - in fact everything is going very well.

With all my love

as ever [Erica]

Francis Bacon to Erica Brausen

Hotel Cecil, Tangier, Morocco, June 12th [1957]

My dear Erica

Thank you very much for your letter. About the show in America will you please try and arrange it for the autumn of 1958. I feel it is too soon to get the things ready by February. I do want to have a good show this time and not a rushed affair like last time. I really do not feel I can do it before the autumn of 1958.
Do hope you are well

all very best wishes

love Francis

PS Please write here by air mail as otherwise letters take about 3 weeks to arrive.

Erica Brausen to Francis Bacon

[Typescript copy] 16th July 1957

Francis Bacon Esq., Hotel Cecil, Tangier, Morocco

Dear Francis,

I was delighted to hear from Toto that you are well and happy.
I am going away tomorrow for my summer holiday and shall not be back until September 1st.
Should you need any money urgently in the meantime, provided it is not a very large sum, please get in touch with Margot at the Gallery and she will arrange it.

All my love

Yours [Erica]

[Typescript copy] 22 April 1958

Dearest Francis,

Thank you very much for your letter. I am so delighted to hear that you are working. The plans for you are Germany, Mexico and New York, and also we would like another show here next year! So do let me me know when you have something. As we have sold 4 paintings in Italy and as we are lending a group of work for an exhibition in Liverpool we shall have very little left to show.

With all my love as always [Erica]

How is Ahmed?

Mr Francis Bacon
Hotel Cecil, Tangier, Morocco

[Typescript copy] 29th May, 1958

Dearest Francis,

That old Durlacher is coming over in July to arrange the show for you next January, and I have literally nothing to show him.
So if you really have something ready, just send them by air, all charges forward, but remember to send a nominal invoice of their value so that I can clear the consignment through customs without trouble.
I was delighted to hear today from Eric Alport that A[24] had at last been set free. Saw Paul[25] the other day, and he seems very gay and happy.
But all I want is to hear from you.

All my love [Erica]

Francis Bacon Esq.
Hotel Cecil, Tangier, Morocco

Francis Bacon to Erica Brausen

Apartemento D. Piso 6eme, Blvd. Mohammed V. 105, Tangier, Morocco 8/6/58

My dear Erica

Thank you very much for your letter. About George I want to keep the pictures here until September or October as I am right in the middle of a lot of things which bear on one another. I hope to have at least 20 by the middle or end of September. I find I can work very well here now. I think they are much better and more concentrated than before. I wonder Erica if you could advance me £300 I am getting very short as I have to buy a lot of paint. I would be so grateful if you would do this for me. Could you please do it the following way just instruct your bank to send £300 to the Bank Credit Foncier D'Algerie et de Tunisie Gibralter [sic] to be paid into the account of Auto Gears and Spare Parts Co.
51 Main St.
Gibralter
There is no need for a letter.
Ahmed is out and well. I had a letter from Paul saying he is returning to America

I hope you are all well

love Francis

[On a separate sheet]
This is where the money should have been sent
For [address typed] AUTO GEARS AND SPARE PARTS COMPANY
The [address typed] CREDIT FONCIER D'ALGERIE ET DE TUNISIE
Gibralter

Erica Brausen to Francis Bacon

[typescript copy] 26th June, 1958

Dearest Francis,

Thank you for your telegram. I am sorry to hear that you haven't yet received the money, which our Bank notified us had been sent some days ago. Anyway, you should get it any day now.
I should very much like to know how you feel about having a show here in the Spring next year. I am trying to arrange the exhibitions for 1959, and you know that, apart from my sculpture shows, you are the one I love best.
If your work is going well at the moment, and you have some finished things that you are pleased with, do you think you could possibly send me a few paintings now so that I have at least something to show that old George Dix when he comes? I should be so very pleased if you could.
I do hope the money will have arrived by the time you receive this.

So with all my love [Erica]

Francis Bacon Esq., Apartemento D. Piso 6eme, Boulevard Mohammed V. 105, Tangier, Morocco.

Francis Bacon to Erica Brausen

[pencil note in another hand top right: 'Recently received/no date/ recently received/this note made 21.10.58; undated]

My dear Erica

Thank you for your telegram nothing has yet been received in Gibralter it was to be sent to the account of Auto Gears & Spare Parts Co. at the Credit Foncier D'Algerie et de Tunisie – Gibralter. I hope it was sent to the[re] please let me know if your bank transferred it correctly. I hope it will come soon but in any case thank you very much for sending it. Will you in future write to me c/o Hotel Cecil as I never seem to get letters here

Best love

Francis

Piso 6eme Appt. D., Blvd. Mohammed V. 105, Tangier

My dear Erica

Thanks so much for your letter it is amazing the pictures sold in Italy. I only wish they had been better ones. Anyhow I am working a lot here I have finished 4. I think 2 are the best thing I have done. I am doing two series one of the Pope with owls quite different from the others and a serial portrait of a person in a room. I am very excited about it. I hope to come back with about 20 or 25 pictures early in October do you think we could delay arranging exhibitions for a bit so that I can for once work in peace. I would like to have one next time of things I like especially in America. I feel full of work and believe I may do a few really good paintings now. This is my address now as I live and work here. I do hope you are well and Toto. Fondest love to you both

Francis

The Stone House, The Quay, Wivenhoe, Essex. Feb 9th

My dear Erica

I am staying down with Dennis and Dickey[26] for a few weeks and am working on some small canvases. I would be so grateful if you could send me £15 of next months allowance as I had to pay for a suit with the other and it has left me rather short. I am staying in a pub here and working in their home. It is going very well. I hope to have six small canvases by the end of the month. Do hope you are all well. Could you make out the cheque to Richard Chopping as he can cash it for me

love

Francis

[undated] Imperial Hotel, Henley-on-Thames, Oxon

My dear Erica

I am not able to finish any paintings at the moment so will you please put off the exhibitions. I am terribly sorry about this but as you know these things happen with work. I will let you have the paintings I owe you as soon as I possibly can but please do not have a show of the things you have got in the gallery of mine. I think it would be a great mistake to show them both for you and for me as you know. I want to replace most of them when I can. Also there have been too many shows of mine. I am desperate and completely broke and am going to try and get a job for a time. I am terribly sorry about this but will let you have the pictures as soon as possible I hope before the end of the year. Please forgive me but I cannot finish the work at the moment.

Best love

Francis

1 Since Bacon wrote regularly to several of his close friends, it is possible that in time more of his letters will become known.

2 Notably in Roger Berthoud, *Graham Sutherland*, London, 1982, and Martin Hammer, *Bacon and Sutherland*, London, 2005.

3 Erica Brausen kept typescript copies of some of her letters to Bacon which can be found with his in the Hanover Gallery archives at the Tate Gallery Archive.

4 Born in Düsseldorf in 1908, Brausen lived in Paris in the 1930s, then moved (out of admiration for Miró) to Majorca, before settling into the London art world and eventually opening her own gallery.

5 Brausen's general correspondence forms part of the Hanover Gallery archives that can be consulted at the Tate Archive.

6 Letter dated 5 July 1957. Barr was requesting photographs of Bacon's recent paintings for the MoMA's files.

7 Letter dated 1 April 1957. The show in Paris took place at the Galerie Rive Droite earlier that year.

8 Arthur Jeffress (1904–61) was a wealthy American collector and art dealer living in Europe. Jeffress briefly provided financial backing for Erica Brausen's Hanover Gallery as well as running a gallery of his own in London in the 1950s. He had a relationship with John Deakin, the acid-tongued photographer and wit who took so many remarkable portrait photographs for Bacon.

9 Present-day Harare.

10 Present-day Zimbabwe. Bacon's famiy had close ties with Rhodesia. His elder brother, Harley, joined the police force in Northern Rhodesia and died there while still young. Both his sisters went to live in Southern Rhodesia, while his mother settled in South Africa after his father's death.

11 The Great Zimbabwe ruins. The largest surviving stone monument south of the pyramids, it was the centre of a thriving Shona Empire during the 13th to 15th centuries.

12 Robert Heber-Percy (1911–86), nicknamed 'Mad Boy', was an upper-class, bisexual, English eccentric who agreed to pay for a trip he and Bacon decided to take to Southern Rhodesia. However, the two men soon quarrelled and parted.

13 Graham and Kathy Sutherland. 'Eardley' presumably refers to the painter Eardley Knollys (1902–91), who helped introduce the Sutherlands to France.

14 Arthur Jeffress had a noted penchant for the lower ranks in uniform.

15 In 1954 Bacon exhibited several works in the British Pavilion during the Venice Biennale. He visited Italy in the autumn of that year, without going to Venice, but travelling directly to Rome (where, notoriously, he did not go to see the Velázquez 'Portrait of Innocent X' of which he had made so many paraphrases and which he knew only from reproductions).

16 Gaspero del Corso ran the Galleria l'Obelisco in Rome where Bacon had a show (which had begun in Turin and Milan) in 1958.

17 Leonardo Cremonini (1925–), prominent Italian painter.

18 Yacoubi, who was one of the very rare people to be allowed to watch Bacon paint (in his studio in the Kasbah in Tangier) was given a show at the Hanover Gallery in 1957.

19 Bacon is presumably referring to his forthcoming show at the Galerie Rive Droite. This would date the letter as having been written before the opening of the Paris show in February 1957.

20 This was Bacon's first exhibition in Paris, which remained the city where he felt artistic recognition mattered most.

21 Ahmed Yacoubi (1931–85) was a Moroccan painter and story-teller. He became a close friend of the American writer Paul Bowles and later got to know Bacon, who taught him to paint in oils.

22 Toto Koopman, an exotically beautiful model and actress, had a long-standing relationship with Erica Brausen.

23 Co-director of Durlacher Bros, the gallery in New York which put on a show of Bacon's work (the first he ever had outside London) in 1953.

24 Ahmed Yacoubi had been imprisoned in Tangier on suspicion of having seduced a young German boy whose parents had complained to the police. He was later released.

25 Paul Danquah and Peter Pollock gave Bacon a room to live and work in their flat in Battersea during the 1950s.

26 The painter Dennis Wirth-Miller (1915– and the book illustrator Richard Chopping (1917–), two of Bacon's oldest and closest friends.

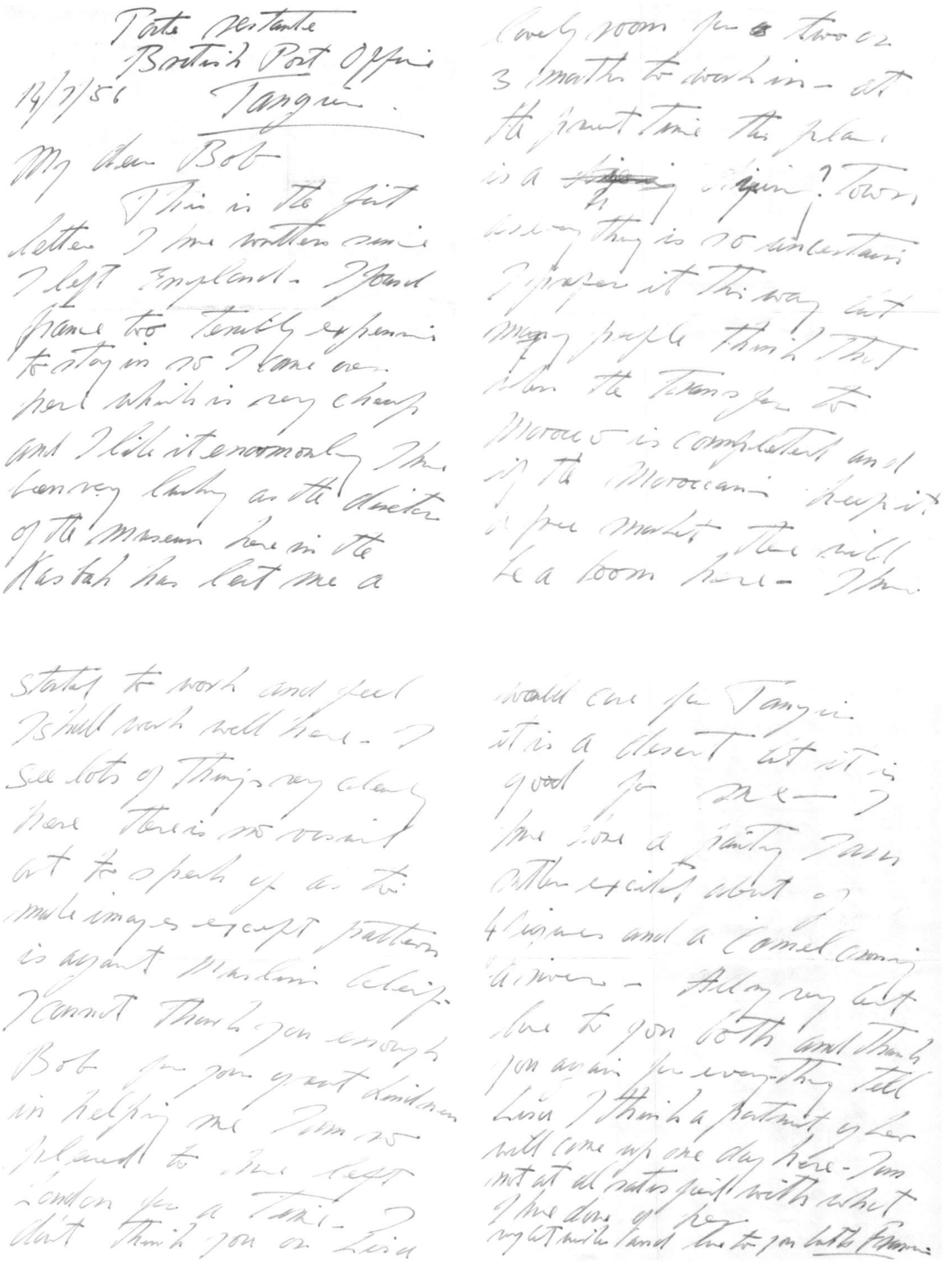

Poste restante
British Post Office
Tangier.
14/7/56

My dear Bob
This is the first letter I have written since I left England. I found France too terribly expensive to stay in so I came over here which is very cheap and I like it enormously. The very kindly as the director of the museum here in the Kasbah has lent me a lovely room for two or 3 months to work in – at the present time this place is a [illegible] town as everything is so uncertain. I prefer it this way but many people think that when the transfer to Morocco is completed and if the Moroccans keep it a free market there will be a boom here – I have started to work and feel I shall work well here – I see lots of things very clearly here there is no visual art to speak of as to make images except pattern is against Moslem religion. I cannot thank you enough Bob for your great kindness in helping me so quickly to leave London for a time – I don't think you or Lisa would care for Tangier it is a desert but it is good for me – I have done a painting I am rather excited about of 4 figures and a camel coming towards – All my very best love to you both and thank you again for everything. Tell Lisa I think a portrait of her will come up one day here – I am not at all satisfied with what I have done of her. My very best wishes and love to you both Francis

30 Letter from Francis Bacon to Robert Sainsbury, 14 July 1956. The Sainsbury Collection Archive, University of East Anglia, Norwich.

BACON'S LETTERS TO ROBERT AND LISA SAINSBURY

In 1953 Robert and Lisa Sainsbury bought their first painting by Francis Bacon, *Study of a Nude* (1952–53; CAT 31). In 1955 the collectors met the artist and became his patrons, first in the sense that they commissioned a portrait – *Portrait of Robert Sainsbury* (1955)[1] – from him; and secondly, because they continued to acquire works of his for several years thereafter and helped him at a critical moment in his career by lending him money, then guaranteeing an overdraft for him at his bank. The guarantee was never withdrawn, and many years later Bacon told the Sainsburys in jest that he might have need of it if his paintings became unfashionable and did not sell.

Always prompt to return a favour, Bacon made eight attempts at portraits of Lisa, of which he destroyed all but three. Bacon also gave the Sainsburys three of the thirteen paintings of his they came to own: *Study (Imaginary Portrait of Pope Pius XII)* (1955),[2] *Sketch for a Portrait of Lisa* (1956) and *Portrait of Lisa* (1957).[3]

Bacon's letters to Robert and Lisa Sainsbury record the development of an unusual artist–patron relationship and throw an interesting light on Bacon's situation and state of mind during the 1950s.

14 Beaufort Gardens, SW3

My dear Lisa,

I hope you will forgive me – but I feel too embarrassed to come to your party. I can never have a private view – do please excuse me – I am so glad you and Bob are pleased with it, it gives me great pleasure.

I do hope I will see you both soon.

Yours

Francis

Long Cottage, Hurst, Berkshire, Thursday

Dear Lisa,

I got a bad attack of flu and asthma am going up to London tomorrow. I am terribly sorry I had to discontinue the sittings for the portrait but when you come back from Paris I do hope you will have the time to come for a few more sittings. I do hope you and Bob are both well. I hope also to have some paintings to show you when you come back from Paris.

All best wishes to you both.

Francis

9 Overstrand Mansions, Prince of Wales Drive, SW11, December 3rd (1955)

Dear Bob,

I am in rather bad money difficulties for the next 3 months and I wondered if you could possibly lend me £400 until the beginning of April when I could repay you. I entirely understand if you cannot do this and I hate asking you. The trouble is that the work has not been coming off in the sense that I have not been able to finish things but I feel it is really getting better but in the meantime I have got terribly into debt. I could repay you in April without fail. It has been so good of Lisa to come and sit so often. I feel terribly depressed that the portrait has not come off but I would like to make another attempt after Christmas if she has the time.

Best wishes

Yours Francis

9 Overstrand Mansions, LONDON SW11, 19/12/55

My dear Bob,

I wanted to thank you very much for your great kindness in guaranteeing my account. It has been the most terrific help. I would like to make another attempt at Lisa's portrait in the New Year when she can spare the time. In the meantime all my very best wishes to you both.

Yours sincerely Francis

British Post Office, Poste Restante, Tangiers 14/7/56

My dear Bob,

This is the first letter I have written since I left England. I found France too terribly expensive to stay in, so I came over here which is very cheap and I like it enormously. I have been very lucky as the director of the museum here in the Kasbah has lent me a lovely room for two or 3 months to work in. At the present time this place is a dying town as everything is so uncertain. I prefer it this way but many people think that when the transfer to Morocco is completed and if the Moroccans keep it a free market there will be a boom here. I have started to work and feel I shall work well here. I see lots of things very clearly here. There is no visual art to speak of as to make images except patterns is against Muslim belief.
I cannot thank you enough Bob for your great kindness in helping me. I am so pleased to have left London for a time. I don't think you or Lisa would care for Tangiers. It is a desert but it is good for me. I have done a painting I am rather excited about of 4 figures and a camel crossing a river.
All my very best love to you both and thank you again for everything. Tell Lisa I think a portrait of her will come up one day here. I am not at all satisfied with what I have done of her.

My best wishes and love to you both, Francis

9 Overstrand Mansions, Prince of Wales Drive, SW11, June 1st 1956

My dear Bob,

I hope you will forgive me for bothering you at this time, but I have been in a bad way mentally and physically for the last few months and I simply cannot work and I feel the only hope is to try and get away for a few months, and perhaps if I get away I shall be able to start working again.
Could you possibly lend me £450 for a few months. It sounds a lot but I have an enormous bill for painting materials which I hope to pay before I go – about £150 - and the remaining money I could live on while I am trying to work for the show in Paris. I want to do the series on Van Gogh and a series of nudes but I feel I shall never work until I can get away from here. I have not told Erica I have written to you. She is very annoyed with me as I do not produce any pictures for her but I simply cannot. If you could possibly manage this it would be a godsend to me.

My very best wishes to you both

Francis

9 Overstrand Mansions, Prince of Wales Drive, SW11 (Postmark on envelope 22 Jan 1957)

My dear Bob,

I have been meaning to write to you and Lisa to thank you for all you have done for me. It will be wonderful to get free of debts. It will be almost the first time since I started painting. I am having a show with Erica on the 19th of March. They will be different from what went to Paris. A group of images I have wanted to do for a long time. I do hope you will both enjoy America. I long to hear about the Barnes collection if you get there. Thank you both again for all your kindness and help.

Very best wishes

Francis

Wivenhoe, ESSEX 15/5/78

Dear Bob,

I went to Norwich last week and saw your magnificent collection of sculptures. I think it has been superbly shown and the building is also really magnificent it is hardly possible to believe the same architect was concerned with Beaubourg which to me is a mess.
You and Lisa have really made a wonderful gift to the nation.

With all very best wishes to you both.

Yours

Francis

7 Reece Mews, LONDON SW7, 12/1/87

Dear Lisa,

Congratulations to you and Bob for your Golden Wedding. It is so nice of you to invite me but alas I have to be in France.

With all very best wishes to you both

Yours

Francis

1 The portrait was painted in a studio in Mallord Street, off the King's Road, that belonged to the prominent Tory politician, Michael Astor. Lisa Sainsbury remembers that the studio was very cold and that her husband sat to Bacon in his overcoat.

2 In an interview with David Sylvester, Lisa Sainsbury gave the following account of how she and her husband acquired their 'Pope' picture: 'We met Francis at a party at Erica Brausen's and Francis suddenly said: "I've been painting well today. I've done a Pope." We went back to the house together and I said: "Can we see the picture?" By that time he was saying that the picture was not quite as good as he had said earlier. And when we got to Prince of Wales's Drive he said the picture was awful. We argued. We spent an hour saying: "You can't destroy this picture." Then Bob said: "It's the most wonderful face ever." Francis said: "If you feel that, I will cut the face out and you can have it." And so he got a razor blade and cut out the Pope's face and shoulders and said "Take it away." So we took it away on the top of the car.' (David Sylvester, *Trapping Appearance – Portraits by Francis Bacon and Alberto Giacometti from the Robert and Lisa Sainsbury Collection*, exh. cat., Sainsbury Centre for Visual Arts, University of East Anglia, Norwich, 1996, p. 31.

In the same interview, David Sylvester asks Lisa Sainsbury about her experience of sitting to Bacon:

> DS: So how many portraits did he start on in the course of producing the three that escaped destruction?
>
> LS: He worked on eight. They were all done not as a commission but as an act of friendship.
>
> DS: And did you begin at Mallord Street or towards the end of the year, after Francis moved into Paul Danquah's flat in Battersea?
>
> LS: It was always there, at Prince of Wales's Drive. It was rather difficult to sit in that room. As you know, there was so much on the floor it was jolly difficult to get to the chair without being covered with paint. He dried his hands on the curtains but there were always things on the floor everywhere – tubes of paint, brochures . . .
>
> DS: Can you remember how many pictures Francis started before he kept one?
>
> LS: That I can't remember. But it was always the same thing. I would sit and then I might come back two or three times and suddenly there was this message saying it had gone. The most remarkable thing is that the final picture was painted very quickly. He worked at them again and again and destroyed them but the final one was done very quickly indeed. (Sylvester, ibid., p. 30).

3 The Sainsburys also bought four further Bacons from the Hanover Gallery and presented them to the Contemporary Art Society.

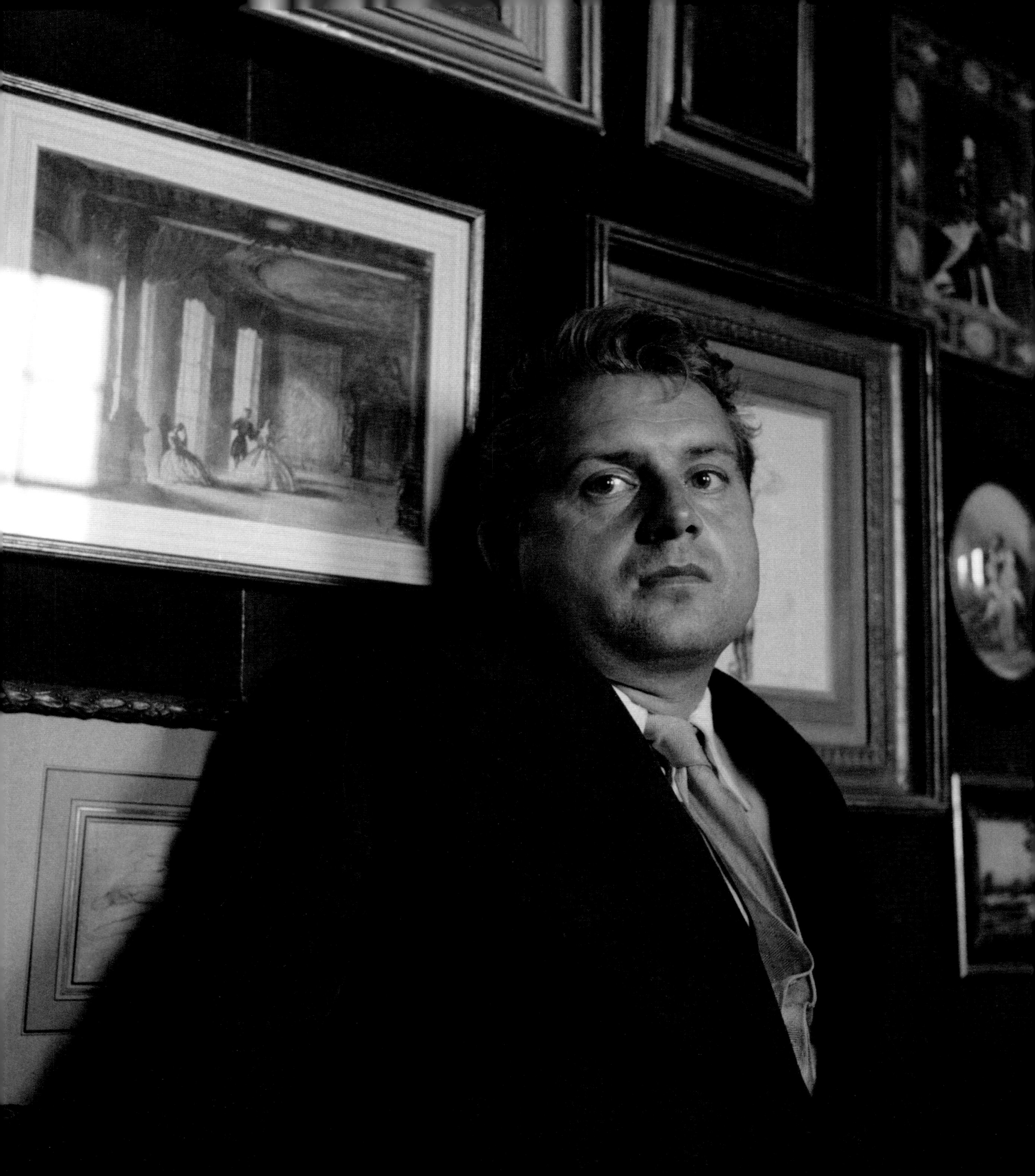

CHRONOLOGY

1909–1923

Francis Bacon is born on 28 October 1909 in a nursing home in Dublin to English parents, Christina Winifred Bacon (née Firth) and Captain Anthony Edward Mortimer Bacon. Francis's father (who claimed collateral descent from the Elizabethan philosopher, Francis Bacon) had retired from the British Army and moved with his much younger wife (an heiress to the Firth family's stainless steel business) to a large house, near the famous Curragh racecourse in County Kildare, where he set up as a racehorse trainer.

Francis is the second of five children; although considered the 'weakling of the family' because of his chronic asthma, he would far outlive his two brothers. During the First World War, the family went to London, where Captain Bacon took up a job at the War Office. Thereafter the Bacons move frequently between England and Ireland.

1924–1928

After sporadic local schooling, Francis is sent to Dean Close, a boarding school in Cheltenham, England. His time there (Autumn 1924–Spring 1926) ends when he is found 'going' (in Bacon's own words) with other boys. Tensions with his authoritarian father come to a head shortly thereafter when Francis is discovered trying on his mother's underwear. In 1926 Francis leaves

31 Francis Bacon, 1951, photo: Cecil Beaton, Cecil Beaton Studio Archive, Sotheby's

Ireland for London, where he makes his way with a weekly allowance from his mother as well as by various odd jobs and casual liaisons.

In 1927 Captain Bacon asks a relative to take Francis with him on a trip to Berlin in the hope that the experience will 'cure' the young man of his homosexuality. In Francis's version of events, the experience seriously misfires, with the young 'uncle' first seducing him, then abandoning him to Berlin's sophisticated range of sexual pleasures.

Bacon leaves Germany for France in Spring 1927, staying with a family near Chantilly, where he sees Poussin's *Massacre of the Innocents* at the Musée Condé. With his cultivated hostess, who helps him learn French, Bacon visits the Paris galleries and is deeply struck by a show of Picasso's classical drawings at the Galerie Paul Rosenberg; the slightly later biomorph images from Picasso's Dinard period were to have a decisive influence on the young Englishman's development. Bacon makes his first, serious experiments in drawing and watercolour. He buys a book containing hand-painted illustrations of diseases of the mouth. He also sees Eisenstein's film *Battleship Potemkin* for the first of many times and becomes riveted by the Odessa Steps sequence.

1929–1939

Bacon returns to London and establishes himself as a designer of furniture, tapestries and rugs. The speed and skill with which he has absorbed modernism in design will also characterize his early, self-taught attempts at oil painting. He receives numerous furniture commissions, notably from the collector Douglas Cooper and the writer Patrick White; 'The Studio' features his work in a survey entitled 'The 1930 Look in British Decoration'. Although Bacon would later dismiss his design work as wholly derivative of Le Corbusier, he regularly used variations on his own tubular structures as an effective way of presenting the distorted figures in his paintings. Bacon's other patrons at this time include the Australian artist Roy de Maistre, who gives him some tips and tutoring in painting techniques, and Eric Hall, a cultivated businessman who becomes Bacon's close companion for some fifteen years. In November 1930 Bacon exhibits some of his paintings and rugs in a group show held in the converted garage in South Kensington which he has turned into a studio.

He moves with his old nanny, Jessie Lightfoot, to a studio in Chelsea, where he will stay until 1936, and paints his first significant works, notably several *Crucifixions*, exhibited in two group shows (which include works by Paul Klee and Max Ernst) at the Mayor Gallery in the West End. The influential critic Herbert Read reproduces *Crucifixion* of 1933 in his book entitled *Art Now*. In February 1934 Bacon organizes his first one-man show of paintings in the basement of the decorator Arundell Clarke's house in Mayfair. Deeply discouraged by the lack of interest in the show, Bacon begins to paint less and to give himself over to gambling and other pleasures.

Exclusion of his work as 'insufficiently surrealist' from the International Surrealist Exhibition held in London in 1936 compounds Bacon's disappointment as an artist. He destroys a great deal of his existing works and paints very little until 1944.

1939–1948

Declared unfit for active service, Bacon joins Air Raid Precautions to help enforce the black-out in his area and rescue victims of air raids. Worsening asthma obliges him to live for a period in the countryside (which he loathed), before finding a new studio in a house in Cromwell Place, South Kensington, which had once belonged to the prominent Pre-Raphaelite painter John Everett Millais. His nanny and Eric Hall (who has meanwhile abandoned his wife and family) join Bacon there in a curious but contented *ménage à trois*. Bacon paints *Three Studies for Figures at the Base of a Crucifixion* in 1944, which causes an outcry when exhibited the following year at the Lefevre Gallery. Eric Hall purchases the triptych and eventually persuades the Tate Gallery to accept it as a gift.

After two impressive *Figure Studies*, Bacon completes his next major work, *Painting 1946*, which he would later describe as 'a series of accidents mounting on top of each other'. At the suggestion of their mutual friend, the painter Graham Sutherland, Erica Brausen visits Bacon's studio, buys the new picture (selling it to the Museum of Modern Art in New York), and becomes Bacon's dealer. With the proceeds from the sale, Bacon makes the first of several visits to Monte Carlo, where he finds the louche atmosphere congenial but the Mediterranean light too strong to allow him to paint successfully.

1949–1954

Bacon returns to London to complete a series of *Heads* for his first one-man show at Brausen's Hanover Gallery. *Head VI* morphs into Bacon's first variation on Velázquez's *Portrait of Pope Innocent X*; he is to return to this theme obsessively for some twenty years, producing around fifty *Popes*. The show attracts both fervent praise and fierce criticism.

He teaches briefly at the Royal College of Art as a stand-in for his friend, the painter John Minton. In 1951, after his beloved nanny's death, Bacon gives up the Cromwell Place studio and lives for brief periods in a series of rented rooms. He paints his first *Portrait of Lucian Freud* (originally sparked off by a photograph of Franz Kafka) and a series of three *Popes* for his second exhibition at the Hanover Gallery. He also makes two trips to South Africa, where his mother has re-established herself after his father's death in 1940. Stopping in Cairo on his way back, he is deeply impressed by Egyptian monuments and sculpture. The wild life he sees in South Africa also fascinates him. These experiences give rise to pictures as different as the *Sphinx* series and *Elephant Fording a River* (1952).

Freud paints a memorable portrait of Bacon, and John Deakin takes several unforgettable photographs of him. Describing a remarkable frontal portrait he took of Bacon, Deakin wrote: 'He's an odd one, wonderfully tender and generous by nature, yet with curious streaks of cruelty, especially to his friends. I think with this portrait I succeeded in capturing something of the fear that underlies his contradictory character.' Bacon begins a long, tortured love affair with Peter Lacy, a former fighter pilot, who becomes the centre of his life and the subject of numerous figure paintings and portraits.

In 1953 Bacon paints some twenty pictures, including *Study after Velázquez's Portrait of Pope Innocent X* and the series of eight paintings of Popes, *Study for Portrait I–VIII*. Five of the latter form part of Bacon's first show in the US at Durlacher Bros in New York. He also paints *Two Figures*, based on a Muybridge photograph of two wrestlers; the painting, which shows two naked men grappling on a bed, is judged so provocative that Erica Brausen, fearing a police raid, hangs it discreetly out of the way on the gallery's upper floor. During a stay at Henley-on-Thames Bacon meets a man who becomes the subject for a new series, *Man in Blue*, which he completes for a further show at the Hanover Gallery. He exhibits with Ben Nicholson and Lucian Freud in the British Pavilion at the 1954 Venice Biennale. He then visits Rome, at a difficult moment in his relationship with Lacy, but never goes to the Palazzo Doria Pamphilii to see the Velázquez portrait that has obsessed him for so long.

1955–1958

The first small retrospective of Bacon's work, consisting of thirteen paintings, takes place at the Institute of Contemporary Art in London. He receives a commission to make portraits of the collectors Robert and Lisa Sainsbury, who become good friends and lifelong supporters; the Sainsburys build up a collection of thirteen of his paintings, which they eventually donate to the Sainsbury Centre for Visual Arts at the University of East Anglia in Norwich. In May 1955 Bacon takes part in a group exhibition at the Museum of Modern Art in New York, contributing a statement to the catalogue which includes this striking definition: 'I would like my pictures to look as if a human being had passed between them, like a snail, leaving a trail of the human presence and memory trace of past events as the snail leaves its slime.'

Bacon begins a series of portraits based on the life mask of the poet and artist William Blake which he has seen at the National Portrait Gallery in London. He decides to have all his pictures put in heavy gilt frames and under glass. After years of wandering from lodging to lodging, Bacon shares the use of a flat overlooking Battersea Park with two close friends, Peter Pollock and Paul Danquah. Apart from frequent trips to Tangier in North Africa, this would become his home and his studio for the following six years.

Bacon paints the first of a series of eight pictures inspired by Vincent van Gogh's *The Painter on the Road to Tarascon* of 1888, destroyed in Germany during the Second World War and

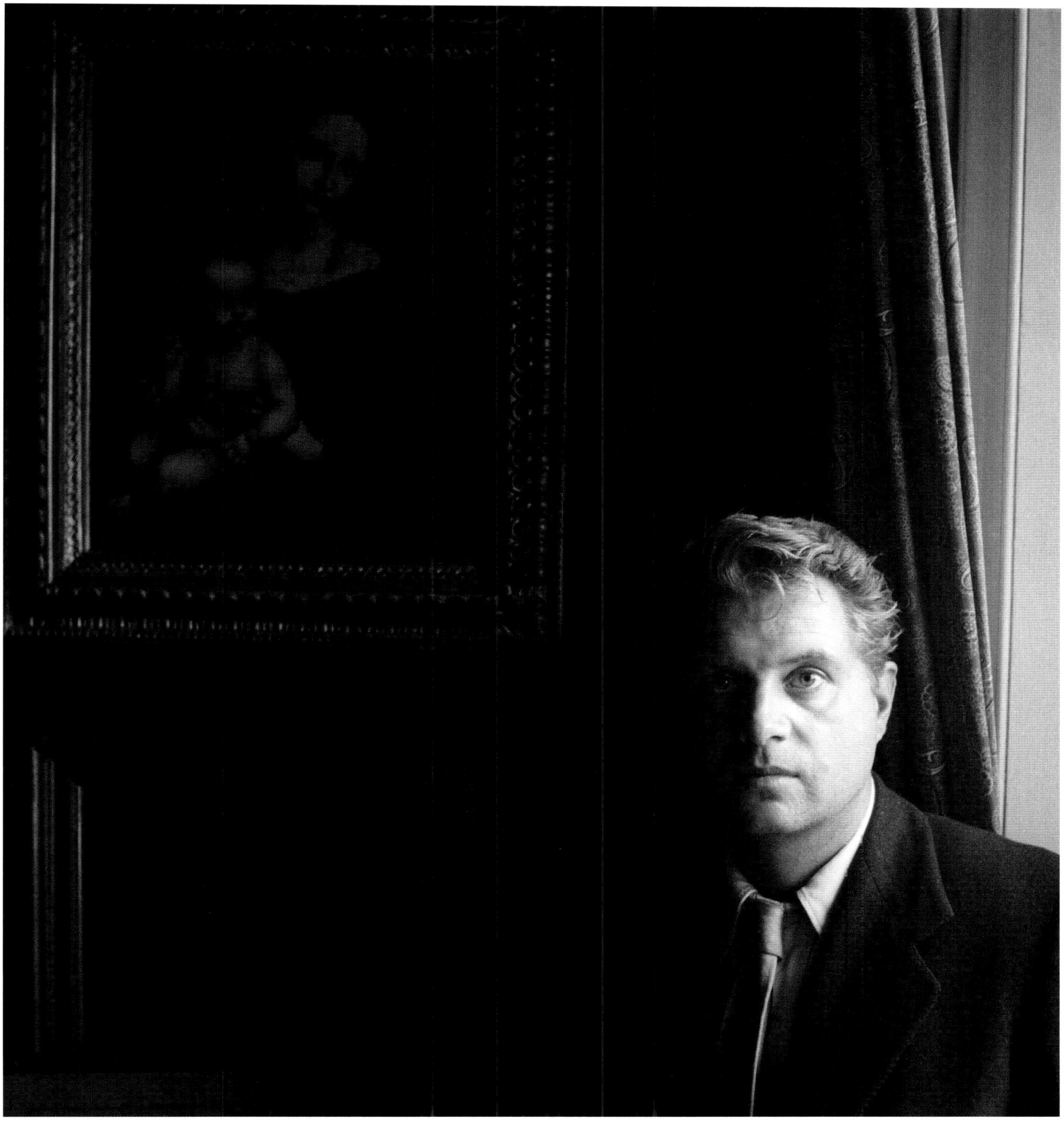

32 Francis Bacon, 1951, photo: Cecil Beaton, Cecil Beaton Studio Archive, Sotheby's.

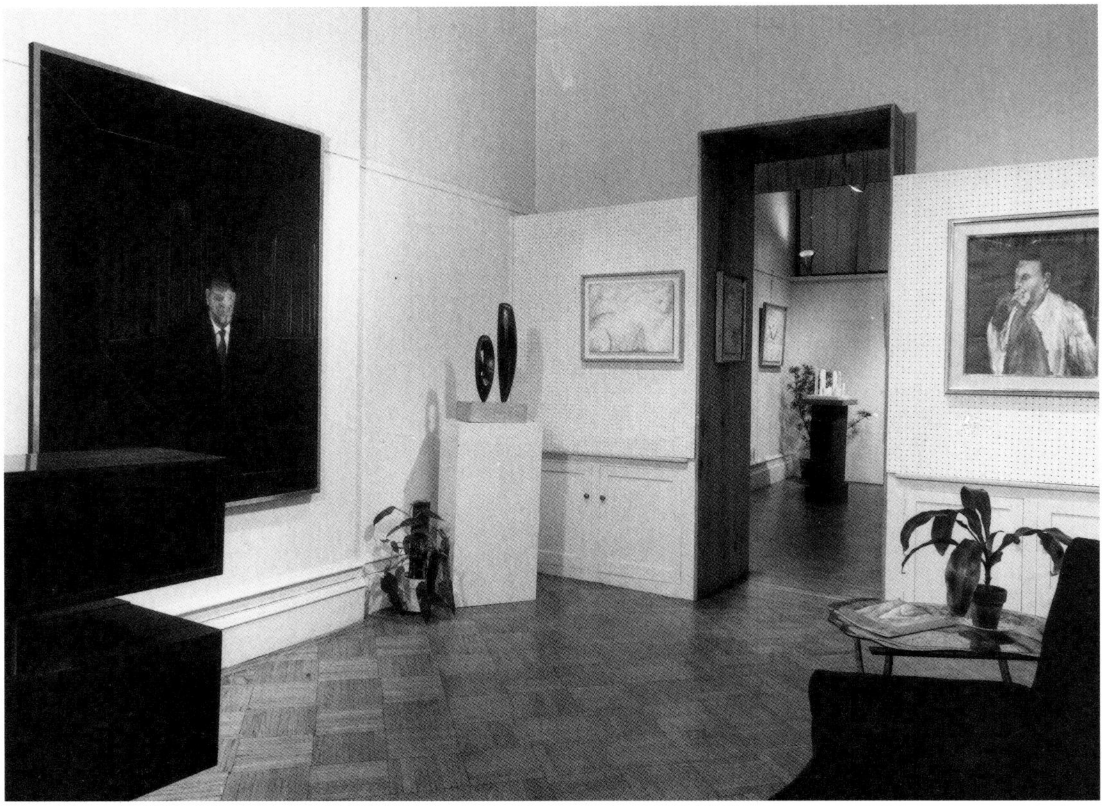

33 Installation shot of 'Three British Artists' exhibition, Martha Jackson Gallery, New York, 1954.

which Bacon knew, like the Velázquez *Pope*, only through reproductions. Bacon, who identified with van Gogh and constantly reread his *Letters*, described the artist in this picture as looking 'like a phantom of the road'.

Bacon spends part of summer 1956 in Tangier, visiting Peter Lacy who is working as a pianist in an expatriate bar. He gets to know the American writers Paul Bowles, Allen Ginsberg and above all William Burroughs, whose 'cut-up' technique interests Bacon. Other notable foreigners in Tangier at the time include Noel Coward, Ian Fleming and Tennessee Williams. As in Monte Carlo, Bacon finds the light too strong to allow him to paint successfully. *Man Carrying a Child*, clearly suggested by a Moroccan street scene, is executed on his return to London. Around this date he also paints his first *Self-Portrait*.

First one-man exhibition in Paris takes place at the Galerie Rive Droite in February 1957. This is followed by another show at the Hanover Gallery which presents six *Studies for a Portrait of van Gogh*; two of the pictures, painted at the last moment, are put on show while still wet.

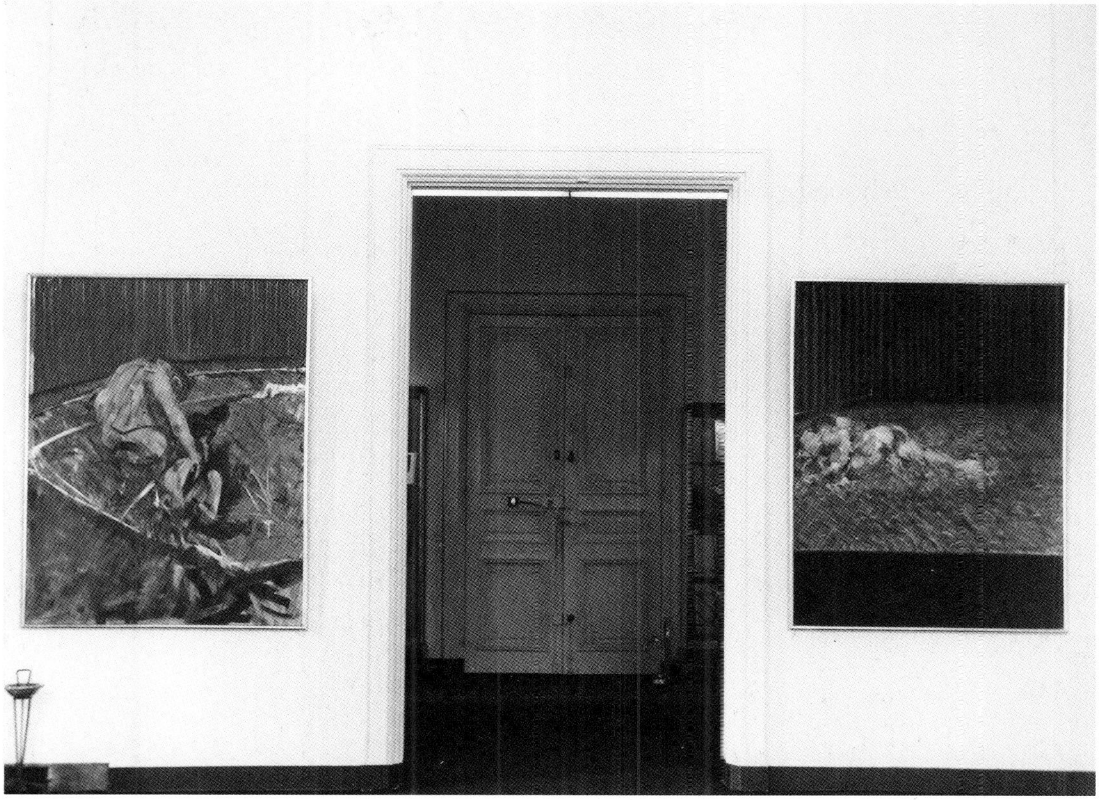

34 Installation shot of the Francis Bacon exhibition at Galerie Rive Droite, Paris, 1957.

Bacon's first solo show in Italy opens at the Galleria Galatea in Turin at the beginning of 1958, then travels to two other commercial galleries in Milan and Rome. Having decided abruptly to break with Erica Brausen and the Hanover Gallery, Bacon signs a contract with the directors of Marlborough Fine Art, who will remain his dealers for the rest of his life.

1959–1963

Eric Hall dies. Bacon has his last exhibition at the Hanover Gallery, and his first in Chicago (a small retrospective of twelve paintings) at the Richard Feigen Gallery. His works are featured at the Kassel Documenta and the São Paulo Biennial. From September 1959 to January 1960 Bacon rents a studio at St Ives, Cornwall, where he paints from memory a portrait of Muriel Belcher, a close friend and owner of his favourite drinking club, the Colony Room in Soho.
His first exhibition at Marlborough Fine Art in 1960 brings together over thirty recent paintings and is a notable success.

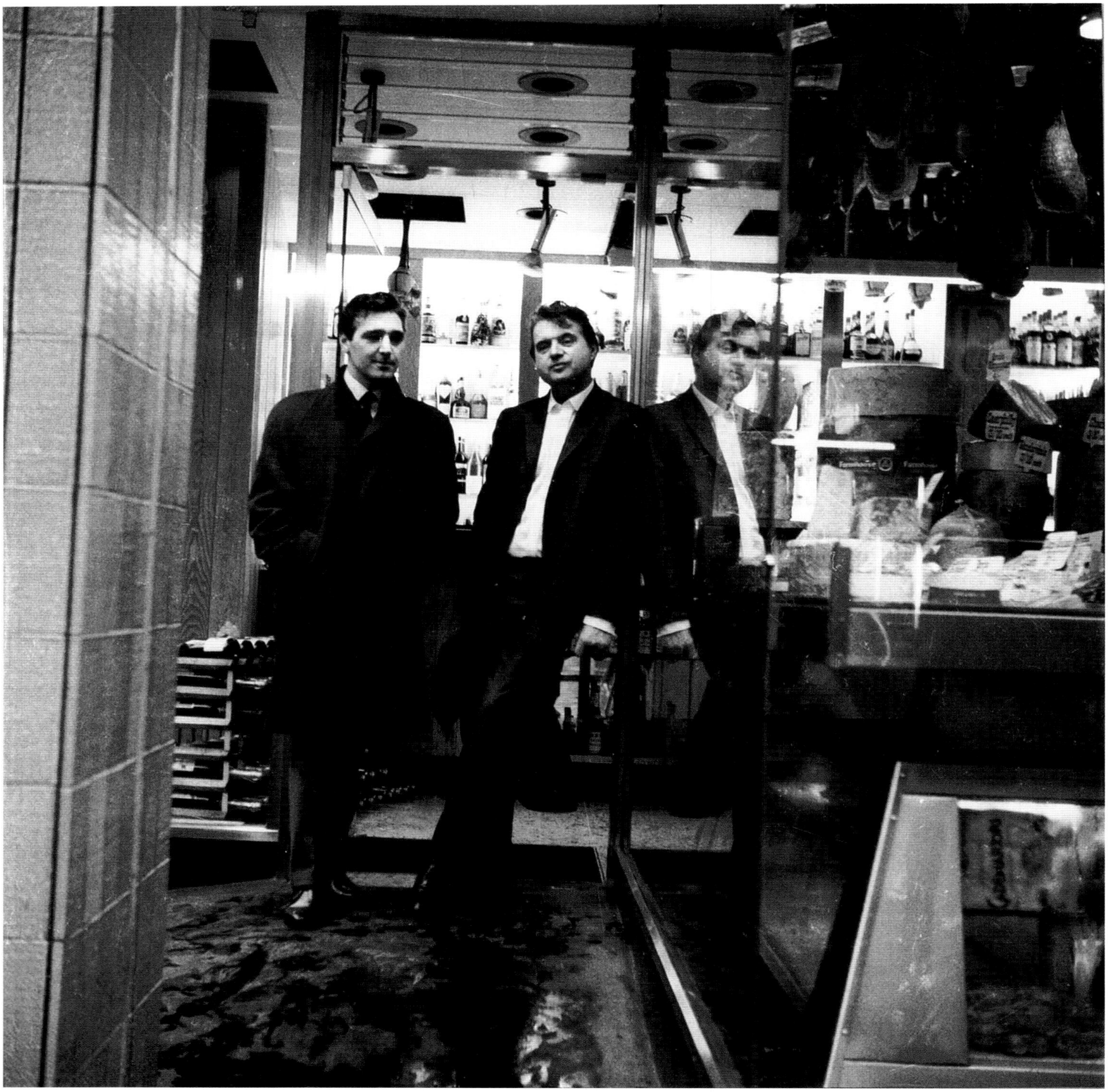

35 Francis Bacon and George Dyer, Soho, early 1960s, photo: John Deakin.

In 1961 Bacon moves to 7 Reece Mews, a row of converted stables in South Kensington. He uses one of the two modest rooms as a studio, and the other as living quarters. Although the quickly cluttered studio is barely big enough for him to paint more than one large-scale canvas at a time, Bacon prefers this to the many other, more commodious studios he is offered and continues to work there until his death. He paints *Paralytic Child Walking on All Fours (from Muybridge)*.

From May to July 1962 the Tate Gallery holds a retrospective of ninety-one paintings by Bacon (nearly half his total existing output), including his first large triptych, *Three Studies for a Crucifixion*. The exhibition confirms Bacon's growing reputation. On the day the retrospective opens, Bacon receives a telegram informing him that Peter Lacy has died in Tangier. The retrospective travels to Mannheim, Turin, Zurich and Amsterdam.

Through his friend Isabel Rawsthorne, Bacon meets Giacometti, whose drawings he particularly admires, and spends several memorable evenings with him.

Bacon talks about his work brilliantly and freely. In October 1962 David Sylvester records the first of several illuminating interviews with the artist. The following year Bacon begins a series of interviews with his future biographer, Michael Peppiatt.

Another friend, John Deakin, starts taking photographs of the handful of people whom Bacon will portray often during the 1960s, notably Henrietta Moraes, Isabel Rawsthorne and George Dyer, a young man from the East End who became Bacon's lover. With Deakin's revealing photos scattered over the floor of his studio, Bacon paints a *Portrait of Henrietta Moraes* and *Three Studies for a Portrait of George Dyer*. Bacon also paints a remarkable *Landscape near Malabata, Tangier* in memory of Peter Lacy, who has been buried in the area.

1964–1969

Bacon paints *Three Figures in a Room*, a large triptych later acquired by the Centre Georges Pompidou in Paris, and his first portrait of Isabel Rawsthorne (who has modelled for Epstein, Derain and Giacometti). A catalogue raisonné of Bacon's work by Ronald Alley, with a preface by John Rothenstein, director of the Tate, is published listing 221 paintings as well as thirteen 'abandoned' and nine 'destroyed' works (several of which later reappear on the market).

He completes the *Crucifixion* triptych, now at the Pinakothek der Moderne in Munich. Around this time he meets the poet and erstwhile Surrealist, Michel Leiris, a close friend of Picasso and Giacometti who will also write several key texts on Bacon.

A large exhibition at Galerie Maeght in Paris stimulates a growing interest in Bacon in France. 'If the French like my work,' Bacon says at the time, 'then I shall feel I have, to some extent, succeeded.'

Willem de Kooning and the artist meet in London. Accompanied by George Dyer, Bacon makes his first visit to the US for his show at the Marlborough Gallery in New York, which opens to widespread acclaim. The Hirshhorn Museum acquires *Triptych Inspired by T. S. Eliot's Poem 'Sweeney Agonistes'*.

Bacon paints three versions of *Study for a Bullfight*.

1970–1974

Bacon buys a house with a jetty overlooking the Thames in Limehouse in the East End and redecorates it in an updated version of his 1930s modernism. Tries to paint there but finds the light flickering on the river distracting, and eventually uses the house mainly to entertain.

A quarrel with George Dyer results in cannabis being planted in Bacon's studio and the police being alerted to the fact. The newspapers headline the story and the case is taken to court, but Bacon is acquitted of any wrongdoing.

In April 1971 Bacon's mother dies in South Africa. Later that year a major retrospective of over one hundred paintings, including eleven large triptychs, opens at the Grand Palais in Paris; Michel Leiris writes the catalogue essay. The event galvanizes Paris, and a poll to establish the ten most important living artists organized by a leading French art magazine puts Bacon first (Picasso being *hors concours*). Just before the exhibition opens, George Dyer dies from an overdose of drink and sleeping tablets in the hotel room where he and the artist have been staying. Later in the year Bacon paints *Triptych – In Memory of George Dyer*, the first in a series of powerful, sombre works commemorating Dyer's death and the artist's feelings of guilt and loss.

The highly successful retrospective, which remained Bacon's favourite presentation of his work, travels to Düsseldorf. John Deakin, photographer, wit and one of the artist's favourite drinking partners in Soho, dies of throat cancer. Bacon concentrates on self-portraits, making the remark that since his friends were dying all around him he only has himself left to paint.

Bacon buys a small house in Wivenhoe, near Colchester, where two of his oldest friends, Dennis Wirth-Miller and Dickie Chopping, had been living for years. John Edwards, whom the artist meets in an East End pub, becomes Bacon's favourite companion.

1975–1979

After the Metropolitan Museum in New York organizes a show of his recent work (1968–74), Bacon's reputation in America is resoundingly confirmed. Bacon spends ten days in New York and meets a number of artists, notably Andy Warhol and Robert Rauschenberg.

Bacon starts spending regular periods of time in Paris, living and working in a small apartment in a seventeenth-century building beside the Place des Vosges. He paints his first small head of Michel Leiris there in 1976. The exhibition of recent work put on at the Galerie Claude Bernard on the Left Bank draws such huge crowds that the police cordon off the street.

In 1977 Bacon makes a short trip to Rome to meet the painter Balthus and see the gardens of the Villa Medici (where Balthus was director) which Velázquez had painted. There are further exhibitions in Mexico City and Caracas, then in Madrid and Barcelona. Bacon completes *Painting 1978*, which he admits is inspired by two lines of Eliot's *Waste Land*: 'I have heard the key / Turn in the door once and turn once only.' As with previous honours and awards that have been offered to him, Bacon declines to accept the Max Beckmann prize from the city of Frankfurt.

After Muriel Belcher's death, Bacon paints *Sphinx – Portrait of Muriel Belcher*.

1980–1986

A show of recent work at the Marlborough Gallery in New York includes *Triptych – Studies of the Human Body* and the first version of *Jet of Water* as well as some small heads of John Edwards and the artist himself.

Bacon paints *Triptych Inspired by the Oresteia of Aeschylus*.

His younger sister, Winnie, dies.

The literature on Bacon becomes increasingly varied and voluminous. After John Russell's account of the artist's work and David Sylvester's interviews with him come Michel Leiris's essays ('Francis Bacon aujourd'hui', 'Bacon le hors-la-loi', 'Francis Bacon, face et profil') and Gilles Deleuze's subtle philosophical investigation, 'Francis Bacon – Logique de la sensation'.

Ingres, whose portraits in particular Bacon admired, provides a point of departure for two new paintings in 1982: *Study of the Human Body – from a Drawing by Ingres* and *Oedipus and the Sphinx after Ingres*.

The first exhibition of Bacon's work in Japan opens in Tokyo, then travels to Kyoto and Nagoya.

Bacon travels to Paris for a show at Galerie Maeght-Lelong and to New York for another exhibition at the Marlborough Gallery. Michel Leiris donates four heads by Bacon (one of the artist, two of himself and one of Isabel Rawsthorne) to the Centre Georges Pompidou in Paris.

The second retrospective is shown at the Tate Gallery in London, with 125 paintings dated between 1945 and 1984. Bacon is referred to in the catalogue as 'the greatest living painter'.

The exhibition travels to Stuttgart and Berlin. Bacon goes to the opening at the Nationalgalerie in Berlin. He visits the Pergamon with interest but is otherwise disappointed to find so little of what he remembered from his first, formative stay in the city sixty years earlier.

As part of an exhibition series entitled 'The Artist's Eye', Bacon is invited to make his own choice from the works at the National Gallery in London. His selection extends from an altarpiece by Masaccio through two Rembrandts to Manet, Seurat, van Gogh and Degas, but he declines to include any of his own paintings.

1987–1992

Bacon paints a large triptych on the theme of bull-fighting inspired by a poem by Lorca. Paintings of the 1980s, including the *Triptych Inspired by the Oresteia of Aeschylus*, shown at the Marlborough Gallery, New York, and in a small retrospective at the Galerie Beyeler, Basel. Twenty-two works by Bacon go on show at the Central House of Artists at the New Tretyakov Gallery in Moscow, marking the first time a living western artist has been shown in the Soviet Union. Asthma prevents Bacon from attending, but he writes a short text for the catalogue of the show saying how important seeing two of Eisenstein's films, *Strike* and *Battleship Potemkin*, had been in his development as a painter.

Bacon undertakes a *Second Version of Triptych 1944* when he is told that the early triptych in the Tate is too fragile to travel to Washington for his retrospective at the Hirshhorn Museum. This first Bacon retrospective in the US since the Guggenheim's in 1963 travels to Los Angeles before going to the Museum of Modern Art in New York.

Bacon, who has turned eighty, travels to Madrid to see the Velázquez exhibition at the Prado in 1990.

Paints *Study from the Human Body*, with John Edwards as his model.

On a trip to Madrid to visit his young Spanish lover, the artist is hospitalized with severe pneumonia. On 28 April 1992 Bacon dies in Madrid of a heart attack.

BIBLIOGRAPHY

CATALOGUES OF SOLO EXHIBITIONS

1955 *Francis Bacon*, exh. cat. (London: Institute of Contemporary Arts, 1955); intro. Max Clarac-Séroux.

1957 *Francis Bacon*, exh. cat. (Paris: Galerie Rive Droite, 1957); foreword by Roland Penrose and text by David Sylvester, ('Some Notes on the Paintings of Francis Bacon', n.p.).

1958 *Francis Bacon*, exh. cat. (Torino: Galleria Galatea, 1958); intro. Luigi Carluccio. Special edition for the Galleria dell'Ariete, Milan and Galleria L'Obelisco, Rome (1958) with intro. by Toni del Renzio.

1960 *Francis Bacon: Paintings 1959–1960*, exh. cat. (London: Marlborough Fine Art, 1960); text by Robert Melville ('Francis Bacon', n.p., first published in the catalogue of the Sao Paulo v Biennial, 1959).

1961 *Francis Bacon*, exh. cat. (Nottingham: Nottingham University, 1961); intro. Helen Lessore.

1962 *Francis Bacon*, exh. cat. (London: Tate Gallery, 1962); intro. John Rothenstein and catalogue entries by Ronald Alley. Bilingual German/English edition: *Francis Bacon* (Mannheim: Städtische Kunsthalle and Zürich: Kunsthaus Zürich, 1962); intro. Stephen Spender ('Francis Bacon', pp. 5–7) and letter from Francis Bacon ('Letter, 9 January', p.18). Italian edition: *Francis Bacon* (Torino: Galleria Civica d'Arte Moderna, 1962); intro. Luigi Carluccio. Dutch edition: *Francis Bacon* (Amsterdam: Stedelijk Museum, 1963); intro. Stephen Spender.1963 *Francis Bacon*, exh. cat. (New York: The Solomon R. Guggenheim Museum, 1963); intro. Lawrence Alloway ('Introduction to Francis Bacon', pp. 12–25) and bibliography by Maurice Tuchman.

1965 *Francis Bacon*, exh. cat. (Hamburg: Hamburger Kunstverein, 1965); intro. Ronald Alley. Swedish edition: *Francis Bacon, malningar 1945–1964* (Stockholm: Moderna museet, 1965). English edition: *Francis Bacon* (Dublin: Municipal Gallery of Modern Art, 1965).

1966 *Francis Bacon*, exh. cat. (Paris: Galerie Maeght, 1966). Text by Michel Leiris ('Ce que m'ont dit les peintures de Francis Bacon', pp. 7–11). English edition: *Francis Bacon* (London: Marlborough New London Gallery, 1967). Text by Michel Leiris ('What Francis Bacon's Paintings Say to Me', pp. 13–24) and interview by David Sylvester ('Francis Bacon', pp. 26–38).

1968 *Francis Bacon: Recent Paintings*, exh. cat. (New York: Marlborough-Gerson Gallery, 1968 Essay by Lawrence Gowing ('The Irrefutable Image', pp. 7–18) and handwritten notes by Francis Bacon ('A Note on Putting Glass over my Paintings'; 'I am very happy to be having this first exhibition in Japan').

1971 *Francis Bacon: Rétrospective*, exh. cat. (Paris: Galeries Nationales du Grand Palais, 1971); intro. Michel Leiris ('Francis Bacon aujourd'hui', pp. 3–16). German edition: *Francis Bacon* (Düsseldorf: Städtische Kunsthalle, 1972).

1975 *Francis Bacon: Recent Paintings 1968–1974*, exh. cat. (New York: The Metropolitan Museum of Art, 1975); intro. Henry Geldzahler (pp. 5–13). with a contribution from Peter Beard ('Francis Bacon: Remarks from an Interview with Peter Beard', pp. 14–20).

1976 *Francis Bacon: Oeuvres récentes*, exh. cat. (Marseille: Musée Cantini, 1976); intro. Gaëtan Picon ('Le cercle et le cri', n.p.).

1978 *Francis Bacon*, exh. cat. (Madrid: Fundación Juan March and Barcelona: Fundació Joan Miró, 1978); intro. Antonio Bonet Correa (pp. 5–13).

1980 Waldegg, Joachim Heusinger von, *Francis Bacon: Schreiender Papst, 1951*, exh. cat. (Mannheim: Städtische Kunsthalle, Coll. Kunst und Dokumentation, 1980).

1983 *Francis Bacon: Paintings 1945–1982*, exh. cat. (Tokyo: The National Museum of Modern Art in association with the Tokyo Shimbun, 1983); intro. Lawrence Gowing (pp. 10–19; English trans.,

'Francis Bacon', pp. 20–26) and essay by Masanori Ichikawa (pp. 100–104; English trans.: 'On Francis Bacon', pp. 105–109).

1984 *Francis Bacon: Peintures récentes*, exh. cat. (Paris: Galerie Maeght-Lelong, *Cahiers d'art contemporain*, no.10), 1984, foreword by Jaques Dupin ('Fragments dans les marges d'un texte de Michel Leiris', pp. 3–16) and interview by David Sylvester ('Francis Bacon and David Sylvester: An Unpublished Interview', pp. 21–32).

1985 Ades, Dawn, and Andrew Forge, *Francis Bacon*, exh. cat. (London: Tate Gallery and Thames & Hudson; and New York: Abrams, 1985). Essays by Dawn Ades ('Web of Images', pp. 8–23), Andrew Forge ('About Bacon', pp. 24–31) and Andrew Durham ('Note on Technique', pp. 231–33) and bibliography compiled by Krzysztof Cieszkowski. Supplement to the catalogue with essay by Richard Francis; German ed.: *Francis Bacon* (Stuttgart: Staatsgalerie and Berlin: Nationalgalerie, 1985).

1987 *Francis Bacon: Paintings of the Eighties*, exh. cat. (New York: Marlborough Gallery, 1987); interview by David Sylvester ('Francis Bacon and David Sylvester: An Unpublished Interview', pp. 170–83).

Francis Bacon: Retrospektive, exh. cat. (Basel: Galerie Beyeler, 1987). Essay by Werner Schmalenbach ('Die nackte Existenz des Bildes', n.p.).

Francis Bacon: Peintures récentes, exh. cat. (Paris: Galerie Lelong (Cahiers d'art contemporain no. 39) 1987), foreword by Jacques Dupin ('Notes sur les dernières peintures', pp. 3–14) and interview by David Sylvester ('Entretien de Francis Bacon avec David Sylvester', pp. 17–42).

1988 *Francis Bacon: Paintings*, exh. cat. (Tokyo: Marlborough Fine Art, 1988); intro. by John McEwen ('Francis Bacon', pp. 9–11).

Fréncis Békon, exh. cat. (Moscow: New Tretyakov Gallery and London: British Council and Marlborough Fine Art, 1988). Text by Grey Gowrie ('Francis Bacon', pp. 11–16, English trans.: pp. 22–27) and Mikhail N. Sokolov (Russian only; amended version: 'Tragedies without a Hero: The Art of Francis Bacon', reproduced in *Art Monthly*, London, no. 121, November 1988, pp. 3–5) and handwritten note by Francis Bacon ('It's a great honour to be invited to have an exhibition of paintings in Moscow . . .', p. 5).

1989 Demetrion, James T. (org.), *Francis Bacon*, exh. cat. (Washington DC: Hirshhorn Museum and Thames & Hudson, 1989. Foreword by Lawrence Gowing ('The Human Presence', pp. 11–26) and Sam Hunter ('Metaphor and Meaning in Francis Bacon', pp. 27–38).

1990 *Francis Bacon*, exh. cat. (London: The Tate Gallery Publications, 1990); contributions by Richard Francis ('Memory Traces', pp. 7–10) and Andrew Durham ('Note on Technique', pp. 11–12).

1992 Francis Bacon, *Pinturas 1981–1991*, exh. cat. (Madrid: Galeria Marlborough, 1992); interview by Richard Cork ('Entrevista a Francis Bacon', pp. 11–17) and text by Antonio Muñoz Molina ('El Gabinete del Doctor Bacon', pp. 9–10). English edition: *Francis Bacon: Paintings 1981–1991* (New York: Marlborough Gallery, 1993).

1993 Chiappini, Rudy (ed.), *Francis Bacon*, exh. cat. (Lugano: Museo d'Arte Moderna della Città di Lugano and Milano: Electa, 1993); essays by Ronald Alley ('Francis Bacon's Place in Twentieth-Century Art', pp. 15–30), Hugh M. Davies ('The Screaming Pope: Past and Present Reality', pp. 33–66), Michael Peppiatt ('A Vision Fulfilled', pp. 69–114), and Rudy Chiappini ('A Desperate Splendid Painting', pp. 117–30).

Francis Bacon 1909–1992. *Small Portrait Studies*, exh. cat. (London: Marlborough Fine Art, 1993); essay by William Feaver ('That's it', n.p.) and text by John Russell (extract from 'Francis Bacon').

Figurabile Francis Bacon, exh. cat. (Venice: Museo Correr and Milano: Electa, 1993); essays by David Sylvester ('Bacon's Course', pp. 19–86), David A. Mellor ('Francis Bacon: Affinities, Contexts and the British Visual Tradition', pp. 95–104), Gilles Deleuze ('The Logic of Sensation', pp. 105–11), Lorenza Trucchi ('The Delirium of the Body', pp. 113–20) and Daniela Palazzoli ('Bacon, Photography and the Invisible Man', pp. 121–26).

1994 *Francis Bacon: Einblicke in das graphische Werk*, exh. cat. (Berlin-Charlottenburg: Fine Art Rafaël Vostell, 1994).

1996 *Francis Bacon*, exh. cat. (Paris: Centre Georges Pompidou, 1996); essays by David Sylvester ('Un parcours', pp. 13–31), Jean-Louis Schefer ('Chair de la peinture', pp. 33–41), Jean-Claude Lebensztejn ('Notes sur Francis Bacon', pp. 43–53), Fabrice Hergott ('La chambre de verre', pp. 55–61), Hervé Vanel ('L'Imagination technique', pp. 63–71) and Yves Kobry ('Bacon, vu de France', pp. 73–77), plus an anthology of texts. German edition: *Francis Bacon* (Munich: Haus der Kunst, 1996); essays by

Jean-Louis Schefer and Yves Kobry replaced by contributions by Ernst van Alphen ('Die Dekonstruktion der Männlichkeit zur Körpersprache im Werk Francis Bacons', pp. 32–41) and Bernhardt Schwenk ('Francis Bacon aus heutiger Sicht', pp. 72–77).

1998 Sylvester, David, *Francis Bacon: The Human Body*, exh. cat. (London: Hayward Gallery and Berkeley: University of California Press, 1998).

Francis Bacon, exh. cat. (Humlebaek, Louisiana Museum, 1998); essays by Carter Ratcliff ('Francis Bacon – An exhibition', pp. 16–37) and Poul Erik Tøjner ('The Mysterious Heart of Realism', pp. 38–49).

Francis Bacon: Important Paintings from The Estate, exh. cat. (New York: Tony Shafrazi Gallery, 1998); contribution by John Edwards ('Eggs was a Diamond', p. 7) and essays by David Sylvester ('The Supreme Pontiff', pp. 24–27), Sam Hunter ('Francis Bacon's Endgame: Humanism Revisited', pp. 14 ff) and Michael Peppiatt ('Extracts from Francis Bacon: Anatomy of an Enigma', pp. 78–83).

1999 Farr, Dennis, *Francis Bacon: A Retrospective*, exh. cat. (New York: Harry N. Abrams, Inc., in association with The Trust for Museum Exhibitions, 1999. Contributions by Sally Yard ('Francis Bacon', pp. 8–17), Dennis Farr ('Francis Bacon in Context', pp. 18–24) and Michael Peppiatt ('Francis Bacon at Work', pp. 25–37; 'Three Interviews with Francis Bacon', pp. 38–50).

Francis Bacon: Paintings from the Estate, 1980–1991, exh. cat. (London: Faggionato Fine Arts, 1999); essay by Martin Harrison ('Points of Reference: Francis Bacon and Photography', pp. 11–23).

Gale, Matthew, *Francis Bacon: Working on Paper*, exh. cat. (London: Tate Gallery, 1999); intro. David Sylvester ('Bacon's Secret Vice', pp. 9–11), and essay by Matthew Gale ('Francis Bacon: Working on Paper', pp. 13–36).

Francis Bacon: Papes et Autres Figures, exh. cat. (Paris: Repères, no. 106, 1999); texts by David Sylvester ('Francis Bacon, "Les premiers Papes"', pp. 6–9), Louise Bourgeois ('Francis Bacon', pp. 21–23) and Antonio Saura ('Bacon et l'espace', pp. 29–33). English trans., pp. 41–47.

2000 Sylvester, David, *Francis Bacon in Dublin*, exh. cat. (Dublin: Hugh Lane Municipal Gallery of Modern Art and Thames & Hudson, 2000); contributions by Grey Gowrie ('Documentaries of Stress', pp. 13–20), Louis le Brocquy ('The Mystery of Fact', pp. 21–23), Anthony Cronin ('An Irish Fear of Death?', pp. 24–26) and Paul Durcan ('The King of Snails', pp. 27–32).

2001 Davies, Hugh Marlais, *Francis Bacon: The Papal Portraits of 1953*, exh. cat. (San Diego: Museum of Contemporary Art and Seattle: Marquand Books Inc., 2001); essay ('Bacon's Popes: Ex Cathedra to In Camera', pp. 11–19) and an interview with Francis Bacon (1973), pp. 27 ff.

Darley, Esther, and Hans Janssen, *Francis Bacon*, exh. cat. (The Hague: Gemeentemuseum Den Haag, 2001).

Dawson, Barbara, and Margarita Cappock, *Francis Bacon's Studio at the Hugh Lane* (Dublin: Hugh Lane Municipal Gallery of Modern Art, 2001).

Ogden, Perry, *7 Reece Mews, Francis Bacon's Studio* (London: Thames & Hudson, 2001); foreword by John Edwards.

2002 *Francis Bacon: Paintings*, exh. cat. (New York: Tony Shafrazi Gallery, 2002); intro. Carter Ratcliff ('Francis Bacon: "The Violence of Reality"', pp. 8–11).

Van Gogh by Bacon, exh. cat. (Arles: Actes Sud and Foundation Vincent Van Gogh, 2002); intro. Yolande Clergue and essays by Philippe Sollers ('Bacon with Van Gogh', pp. 19–20), David Alan Mellor ('Bacon's Van Gogh', pp. 21–29) and Alain Jouffroy ('Francis Bacon and his Doubles', pp. 58–59).

Francis Bacon: Paintings, exh. cat. (New York: Marlborough Gallery, 2002); essay by Robert Rosenblum ('Francis Bacon's Pulp Fictions', pp. 3–5).

Francis Bacon: Last Paintings, exh. cat. (London: Faggionato Fine Arts, 2002).

2003 *Francis Bacon: Caged – Uncaged* (Porto: Fundaçao de Serralves, 2003); essay and artist biography by Martin Harrison.

Francis Bacon und die Bildtradition, ed. Wilfried Seipel, Barbara Steffen and Christoph Vitali (Francis Bacon and the Tradition of Art), (Vienna: Kunsthistorisches Museum, 2003–4); essays by Barbara Steffen, Norman Bryson, Ernst van Alphen, Olivier Berggruen, Margarita Cappock and Michael Peppiatt. Interviews with Bacon by David Sylvester and Michel Archimbaud.

Francis Giacobetti: Francis Bacon, exh. cat. (London: Marlborough Gallery, 2003); photographic portraits of Bacon by Francis Giacobetti; includes an essay by Philippe Garner and reminiscence by Michel Archimbaud.

2004 *Lo sagrado y lo profano*, exh. cat. (Valencia: Institut Valencia d'Art Modern, 2003–4); exhibition curated by Michael Peppiatt; including essays by Kosme de Baranano, Hugh M. Davis, María Jesús Folch, Massimo Martino and Barbara Steffen. French version: *Francis Bacon – Le Sacré et le profane*, exh. cat. (Paris: Musée Maillol, 2004), intro. Dina Vierny ('Francis Bacon à Paris', p. 9), two essays by Michael Peppiatt ('Francis Bacon: Le Sacré et le profane', pp. 11–26; 'Portrait de l'artiste au travail', pp. 30–40), and three interviews with Francis Bacon by Michael Peppiatt (pp. 43–51).

2005 *Francis Bacon: Portraits and Heads*, exh. cat. (Edinburgh, National Galleries of Scotland in association with the British Council, 2005); essays by Richard Calvocoressi and Martin Hammer.

Heinrich, Christoph (ed.), *Francis Bacon: Die Portraits*, exh. cat. (Hamburg: Kunsthalle, 2005); contributions by Heinrich Dietz, Christoph Heinrich, Invar-Torre Hollaus, Andrea Rose and Claire Rose.

Francis Bacon: Studying Form, exh. cat. (London: Faggionato Fine Art, 2005); essays by David Sylvester and Martin Harrison.

INTERVIEWS

Archimbaud, Michel, *Francis Bacon: Entretiens avec Michel Archimbaud* (Paris: Jean-Claude Lattès, 1992). English trans.: *Francis Bacon: In Conversation with Michel Archimbaud* (London: Phaidon Press, 1993). Italian trans.: *Francis Bacon: In conversazione con Michel Archimbaud* (Genoa: recco, Le Mani, 1993).

Bacon, Francis, *Entretiens* (Paris: Ed. Carré, Coll. arts et esthétiques, 1996); foreword by Hervé Vanel.

Clair, Jean, 'Un entretien inédit avec Francis Bacon', *Le Monde*, Paris, 2 May 1992. Reprinted in 'Last Thoughts and Last Work', *The Art Newspaper*, London, no. 19, June 1992. Full-length reprint, 'Le pathos et la mort', *Corps crucifiés*, exh. cat. (Paris: Musée Picasso, 1992, pp. 132–144).

Clair, Jean, Maurice Eschapasse and Peter Malchus, 'Entretiens avec Francis Bacon', *Chroniques de l'art vivant* (Paris, no. 26, December 1971 – January 1972. pp. 4–7).

Duras, Marguerite, 'Marguerite Duras s'entretient avec Francis Bacon', *La quinzaine littéraire*, Paris, 16–30 November 1971, pp. 16–17. Reprinted in 'Conversación con Francis Bacon', *Arte en Colombia*, Bogotá, no. 1, June 1976, pp. 44–46, and Marguerite Duras, *Outside, Papiers d'un jour* (Paris: Albin Michel, Coll. Illustrations, 1981), pp. 265–70.

Gonzalez Bermejo, Ernesto, 'El optimismo es una forma de imbecilidad: intervista con Francis Bacon', *Cuadernos para el Dialogo*, Madrid, 8 April 1978, pp. 51–53.

Giacobetti, Francis, 'Francis Bacon: I painted to be loved', *The Art Newspaper*, London, XIII, June 2003, pp. 28–29.

Huser, France. 'Falstaff 1984: Un entretien avec Francis Bacon', *Le nouvel observateur*, Paris, 3 February 1984, pp. 72–73.

Maubert, Franck, 'Francis Bacon, sa dernière interview: "Je poursuis la peinture car je sais qu'il n'est pas possible de l'arrêter"', *Paris-Match*, Paris, no. 2242, 14 May 1992, pp. 92–93.

Michel, Jacques, 'Entretien avec un portraitiste de l'inimaginable', *Le Monde*, Paris, 3 November 1971, p.15.

Peppiatt, Michael, 'From a Conversation with Francis Bacon', *Cambridge Opinion*, Cambridge, no. 37, January 1964, pp. 48–49. (Condensed passages in *Francis Bacon: A Retrospective*, exh. cat. (New York: Harry N. Abrams, Inc. in association with The Trust for Museum Exhibitions, 1999, pp. 41–42.)

Peppiatt, Michael, 'Francis Bacon: Reality Conveyed by a Lie', *Art International*, Paris, Autumn 1987, pp. 36–37. Reprinted in *Francis Bacon: A Retrospective*, exh. cat. (New York: Harry N. Abrams, Inc. in association with The Trust for Museum Exhibitions, 1999), pp. 42–45.

Peppiatt, Michael, 'An Interview with Francis Bacon: Provoking accidents, prompting chance', *Art International*, Paris, Autumn 1989, pp. 28–33. Reprinted in *Francis Bacon: A Retrospective*, exh. cat. (New York: Harry N. Abrams, Inc. in association with The Trust for Museum Exhibitions, 1999, pp. 46–50). Spanish trans.: 'Incitando accidents, provocando el destino: entrevista – Francis Bacon', *Reverso*, Madrid, no. 1, Spring 1990, pp. 71–73.

Pergolani, Michael, 'Playmen intervista: Francis Bacon, conversazione senza complessi con un grande pittore intrattabile', *Playmen*, no. 10, October 1970, pp. 17 ff.

Saraben, Jacques, 'Francis Bacon: To make a Sahara of the mouth' (interview with the artist), *Art Press*, Paris, no. 215, July/August 1996, pp. 20–26.

Spender, Stephen, '"Der Tradition eine neue Wendung geben": ein Gespräch mit dem Maler Francis Bacon', *Die Weltwoche*, Zürich, 19 October 1962, p. 27.

Sylvester, David, 'Francis Bacon Talking to David Sylvester'. Taped on 21 October 1962; broadcast by the BBC on 23 March 1963. Transcribed in 'The Art of the Impossible', *The Sunday Times Supplement*, London, 14 July 1963, pp. 13–18. Résumé in Francis Bacon, exh. cat. (London: Marlborough New London Gallery, 1963, pp. 3–5). Reprinted in 'Ce qu'a dit Francis Bacon à David Sylvester', *Derrière le miroir*, Paris, Galerie Maeght, no. 162, November 1966, pp. 17–26, and in David Sylvester, *Interviews with Francis Bacon*, 1975, pp. 8–29 (interview 1).

Sylvester, David, 'Francis Bacon', interview, BBC Television for *Sunday Night*, dir. Michael Gill, May 1966, first transmitted on 18 September 1966. Transcribed in *Francis Bacon: Recent Paintings*, exh. cat. (London: Marlborough Fine Art, 1967, pp. 26–38), and David Sylvester, *Interviews with Francis Bacon*, 1975, pp. 30–67 (interview 2).

Sylvester, David. 'Interview de Francis Bacon par David Sylvester', *Le petit journal des grandes expositions*, Paris, CNAC, 27 October 1971.

Sylvester, David, *Interviews with Francis Bacon* (London: Thames and Hudson and New York: Pantheon Books, 1975). Interview 1: October 1962, first broadcast on 23 March 1963, first published 14 July 1963; interview 2: May 1966, first transmitted on 18 September 1966 (embodied in Michael Gill's film *Fragments of a Portrait*), first published March 1967; interview 3: taped December 1971, July 1973 and October 1973; interview 4: taped September 1974. Swedish trans.: Samtal med Francis Bacon, Stockholm: Forum, 1976; includes also interview 5, based on a videotape recording made by The London Weekend Television on 23 April 1975 (transmitted in Aquarius, 30 November 1975) and a private recording from June 1975. Spanish trans.: *Entrevistas con Francis Bacon* (Barcelona: Ediciones Polígrafa, 1977); includes interviews 1–5.

Sylvester, David, 'Exhilarated Despair of Francis Bacon', *Art News*, New York, LXXIV, May 1975, pp. 26–31 (extracted from David Sylvester, Interviews with Francis Bacon, London/New York, 1975).

Sylvester, David, *Interviews with Francis Bacon 1962–1979*. London: Thames and Hudson, 1980 (2nd, enlarged edition). Includes interviews 1–7 (interviews 6 and 7: taped in March, August and September 1979). German trans.: *Gespräche mit Francis Bacon* (Munich: Prestel-Verlag, 1982). Extracts reprinted in *Du*, Zürich, no. 9, 1982, pp. 6, 8, 11, 13.

Sylvester, David, 'An Interview with Francis Bacon', *The Times Literary Supplement*, London, 21 November 1980, pp. 13–18 (extract from David Sylvester, Interviews with Francis Bacon 1962–1979, 1980).

Sylvester, David, *The Brutality of Fact: Interviews with Francis Bacon* (third expanded ed., London: Thames & Hudson, 1987). Interviews 1–9; interview 8: based on a recording made by Lecon Arts in March 1982, first released in a series of cassettes and slides, Artists Talking, in 1985; interview 9 first published in *Francis Bacon: Paintings of the Eighties*, exh. cat. (New York: Marlborough Gallery, 1987), based on transcripts from Michael Blackwood's film, *The Brutality of Fact*, recorded in March 1984, and from notes made after conversations in 1985–86. Reprinted 1993 and 1999 (interview 8 supplemented in the latter edition with remarks confirmed by the artist and with passages derived from the transcriptions of recordings from Blackwood's film).

MONOGRAPHS

Alley, Ronald, and John Rothenstein, *Francis Bacon: Catalogue raisonné* (London: Thames & Hudson and New York: Viking Press, 1964).

Alphen, Ernst van, *Francis Bacon and the Loss of Self* (London: Reaktion Books Ltd., 1992).

Anzieu, Didier, and Michèle Monjauze, *Francis Bacon ou le portrait de l'homme désespéré* (Vevey: L'Aire and Paris: Archimbaud, 1993).

Anzieu, Didier, 'La peau, la mère et le miroir dans les tableaux de Francis Bacon', *Le corps de l'Œuvre* (Paris: Gallimard, 1981), pp. 333–39.

Archimbaud, Michel (ed.), *Bacon: Portraits et autoportraits* (Paris: Les Belles Lettres/Archimbaud, 1996). English edition: *Bacon: Portraits and Self-Portraits* (London and New York: Thames & Hudson, 1996). Essays by Milan Kundera ('The Painter's Brutal Gesture', pp. 8–18) and France Borel ('Francis Bacon: The Face Flayed', pp. 187–202). German edition: *Francis Bacon: Portraits und Selbstportraits* (Munich: Schirmer/Mosel, 1996).

Baldassari, Anne, *Bacon Picasso: The Life of Images* (Published on the occasion of an exhibition held at the Musée Picasso, Paris, 2005).

Brighton, Andrew, *Francis Bacon* (London: Tate Gallery, 2001).

Calhoun, Alice Ann, *Suspended Projections: Religious Roles and Adaptable Myths in John Hawkes's Novels, Francis Bacon's Paintings and Ingmar Bergman's Films*, PhD dissertation, University of South Carolina, 1979 (Ann Arbor: University of South Carolina, Microfilm International, 1979).

Cappock, Margarita, *Francis Bacon's Studio* (London: Merrell, 2005).

Charras, Pierre, *Francis Bacon: Le ring de la douleur* (Paris: Ramsay/Archimbaud, 1996).

Dagen, Philippe, *Francis Bacon* (Paris: Cercle d'Art, 1996).

Davies, Hugh Marlais, *Francis Bacon: The Early and Middle Years, 1928–1958*, PhD dissertation, Princeton University, 1975 (New York and London: Garland Publishing Inc., 1978).

Davies, Hugh M. and Sally Yard, *Bacon* (New York: Abbeville Press and Munich: C. J. Bücher, 1986).

Deacon, David Thomas, *The Nature and Development of the Theme-Form Violation within Containment in Harold Pinter's Plays and Francis Bacon's Paintings*, PhD dissertation, Ohio University, 1982 (Dissertation Abstracts International, no. DA8221887).

Deleuze, Gilles, *Francis Bacon: Logique de la sensation* (Paris: Éditions de la Différence, 1981; revised edition 1984). English trans.: *Francis Bacon: The Logic of Sensation* (New York: Portmanteau Press, 1992; London: Continuum, 2003).

Domino, Christophe, *Francis Bacon* (Paris: Gallimard and Centre Georges Pompidou, 1996). English trans.: *Francis Bacon: 'Taking Reality by Surprise'* (London: Thames & Hudson, 1997); and *Francis Bacon: Painter of a Dark Vision* (New York: Harry N. Abrams, 1997).

Dückers, Alexander, *Francis Bacon: 'Painting 1946'* (Stuttgart: Philipp Reclam Jr., 1971).

Farson, Daniel, *The Gilded-Gutter Life of Francis Bacon* (London: Century and New York: Pantheon Books, 1993; Vintage, 1994); French trans.: *Francis Bacon, aspects d'une vie* (Paris: Le Promeneur, Gallimard, 1994).

Ficacci, Luigi, *Francis Bacon 1909–1992* (Cologne and London: Taschen, 2003).

Fusini, Nadia, *B & B* (Milano: Garzanti, 1994).

Goyens de Heusch, Serge, *Francis Bacon: Un Génie Nietzschéen des profondeurs* [s.l., s.n.], 1980.

Guin, Pierre, et al., *Une oeuvre de Bacon* (Marseille: Muntaner, 2000), essays on Bacon's self-portrait painting in the Musée Cantini, Marseille.

Hammer, Martin, *Bacon and Sutherland* (London: Yale University Press, 2005).

Harrison, Martin, *In Camera: Francis Bacon: Photography, Film and the Practice of Painting* (London: Thames & Hudson, 2005).

James, N. P. et.al., 'Francis Bacon seminar: a discussion of the artist', CV/Visual Arts Research no. 31, 2004.

Leclercq, Stéfan, *L'expérience du mouvement dans la peinture de Francis Bacon* (Paris: L'Harmattan, 2002).

Leiris, Michel, *Francis Bacon, ou la vérité criante* (Montpellier: Fata Morgana/Scholies, 1974).

Leiris, Michel, *Francis Bacon, face et profil* (Paris: Albin Michel; Munich: Prestel-Verlag; Milan: Rizzoli; Barcelona: Ediciones Poligrafa, 1983). English trans.: John Weightman, *Francis Bacon, Full Face and in Profile* (Oxford: Phaidon, and New York: Rizzoli, 1983; revised edition: Paris: Albin Michel, 1987, 1988, 2004; New York: Rizzoli, 1988. Japanese trans. 1989).

Leiris, Michel, *Francis Bacon ou la brutalité du fait* (Paris: L'Ecole des lettres/Seuil, 1995).

Micheli, Mario de, *Il Disagio Della Civiltà e le Immagini: Bacon, Giacometti, Cremonini, Ipousteguy* (Milan: Jaca Book, 1982).

Monsel, Philippe (ed.), *Bacon 1909–1992* (Paris: Cercle d'Art, 1994).

Nixon, John William, 'Francis Bacon, Paintings 1959–1979: Opposites and Structural Rationalism', PhD dissertation, Ulster: University of Ulster, 1986.

Nogueira, Luís Carlos, 'Francis Bacon: Corpos, Esgares e Silêncios. Ensaio-sumário', PhD dissertation, Covilha: Universidade de Beira Interior, 1999.

Peppiatt, Michael, *Francis Bacon: Anatomy of an Enigma* (London: Weidenfeld & Nicholson, 1996; New York: Farrar, Straus & Giroux, 1997; Barcelona: Editorial

Gedisa, 1999; Cologne: DuMont Buchverlag, 2000; Paris: Flammarion, 2004; Tokyo: Shinchosha, 2004).

Peppiatt, Michael, *Entretiens avec Francis Bacon* (Paris: L'Echoppe, 1998).

Peppiatt, Michael, *Francis Bacon à l'atelier* (Paris: L'Echoppe, 1999).

Peppiatt, Michael, *Le regard de Bacon* (Paris: L'Echoppe, 2004).

Peppiatt, Michael, *L'amitié Leiris Bacon: une étrange fascination* (Paris: L'Echoppe, 2006).

Rothenstein, John, *Francis Bacon* (Milano: Fratelli Fabbri Editori, 1963; London: Purnell and Sons, Coll. The Masters, no. 71; Paris: Hachette, 1967).

Russell, John, *Francis Bacon* (London: Methuen and Co. Coll. Art in Progress, 1964).

Russell, John, *Francis Bacon* (London: Thames and Hudson; Greenwich, Connecticut: New York Graphic Society; Paris: Les Éditions du Chêne; Berlin: Propyläen Verlag, 1971. Revised edition: London: Thames and Hudson, Coll. World of Art Series, 1979; New York: Oxford University Press, Coll. World of Art, 1985. Revised and updated, London 1993; Paris 1994).

Schilling, Jürgen, *Etudes pour un portrait de Van Gogh par Francis Bacon* (Paris: Editions de la Maison des sciences de l'homme, 2005).

Schmied, Wieland, *Francis Bacon: Vier Studien zu einem Porträt* (Frankfurt-am-Main: Fischer Taschenbuch, 1985).

Schmied, Wieland, *Francis Bacon: Commitment and Conflict* (Munich and New York: Prestel-Verlag, 1996).

Schreiner, Richard Gus, *The Concrete Imagination: A Perspective on Selected Works of Francis Bacon and Edvard Munch*, PhD, New York: Teacher's College, Columbia University, 1980 (Ann Arbor, University Microfilms International, 1980).

Sinclair, Andrew, *Francis Bacon: His Life and Violent Times* (London: Sinclair–Stevenson, 1993).

Sladen, Mark, *Bacon's Eye: Works on Paper Attributed to Francis Bacon from the Barry Joule Archive* (London, 2001. Published on the occasion of an exhibition held at the Barbican Art Gallery, 2001). Includes an interview with Barry Joule.

Sollers, Philippe, *Les Passions de Francis Bacon* (Paris: Éditions Gallimard, 1996).

Sylvester, David, *Looking Back at Francis Bacon* (London and New York: Thames & Hudson, 2000).

Trucchi, Lorenza, *Francis Bacon* (Milan; Fratelli Fabbri Editori, 1975). English trans.: John Shepley (New York: Harry N. Abrams, 1975, and London: Thames & Hudson, 1976).

Wyzinska, Edyta, 'Critical reception of Francis Bacon's painting in Britain 1945–1962', MA thesis, London, Courtauld Institute of Art, 1990.

Zimmermann, J., *Francis Bacon Kreuzigung: Versuch, eine gewalttätige Wirklichkeit neu zu sehen* (Frankfurt-am-Main: Fischer Taschenbuch, 1986). Reprinted 1992.

GENERAL

Coke, Deren van, *The Painter and the Photographer from Delacroix to Warhol* (Albuquerque: University of New Mexico Press, 1964), pp. 112–17, 166–70.

Conde, Teresa del, *Tres Maestros* (Mexico: Universidad Nacional Automnoma de Mexico, 1997).

Hooper, Steven, *Robert and Lisa Sainsbury Collection Catalgoue*, (London: Yale University Press, 1997).

Moore, Andrew and Charlotte Crawley, *Family and Friends: A Regional Survey of British Portraiture* (London: HMSO, 1992).

Muir, Robin, *John Deakin Photographs* (London: National Portrait Gallery and Munich: Schirmer Mosel, 1996. Reprinted Vendome Press, 1997).

Peppiatt, Michael, *L'Ecole de Londres* (Paris: L'Echoppe, 2006).

Read, Herbert, *Art Now: An Introduction to the Theory of Modern Painting and Sculpture* (London: Faber and Faber, 1933 . Revised and enlarged edition, 1960.

Read, Herbert, *Contemporary British Art* (Harmondsworth, Baltimore: Penguin Books, 1951), pp. 27, 33–35, 40.

Read, Herbert, *A Concise History of Modern Painting* (New York: Praeger and London: Thames & Hudson, 1959), p. 144.

Ronte, Dieter, *Hess Collection, Berne* (Stuttgart: Paul Haupt, 1989).

Usherwood, Nicholas, *The Bible in Twentieth Century Art* (London: Pagoda, 1987).

PERIODICALS

Acha, Juan, 'Francis Bacon: acción expresionista, silencio, ambientales', *Artes Visuales*, Mexico, no. 16, Winter 1977.

Adams, Parveen, 'The Violence of Paint', Benjamin, Andrew (ed.), *Journal of Philosophy and the Visual Arts, London, Special Issue: The Body*, 1993, pp. 52–59.

Alberge, Dalya, 'Bacon film hit by dispute over who owns artist's words', *The Times*, 9 May 1997, p. 13.

Alberge, Dalya, 'Experts divided over "Francis Bacon" cast-offs', *The Times*, 1 August 1998, p. 6.

Alberge, Dalya, 'Artist and hero are divided by Bacon's last tapes', *The Times*, 3 March 2001, p. 3.

Alberge, Dalya, 'Tate brings home a £20m Bacon collection', *The Times*, 19 January 2004, p. 10.

Alphen, Ernst van, 'The Body Unbound: The Post-Modern Aesthetics of Francis Bacon', *Word and Image*, London, VII, no. 1, January–March 1971, pp. 71–84.

Alley, Ronald, 'Francis Bacon', *Cimaise*, Paris, X, no.63, January–February 1963, pp. 12–25.

Alley, Ronald, 'Bacon X-Rayed', *Studio International*, London, April 1972, p. 144.

Alloway, Lawrence, 'Notes on Francis Bacon', *Art News and Review*, London, VII, no. 27, 5 February 1955, p. 4.

Alloway, Lawrence, 'Art News from London', *Art News*, New York, LIV, March 1955, pp. 17, 59–60.

Alloway, Lawrence, 'Charm', *Art News and Review*, London, VII, no.12, 9 July 1955, p. 7.

Alloway, Lawrence, 'Art News from London: Style and Bacon', *Art News*, New York, LVI, May 1957, pp. 48, 58.

Alloway, Lawrence, 'Exhibitions in London', *Art International*, Zürich, II, no. 4–5, May–June 1958, p. 44.

Alloway, Lawrence, 'Francis Bacon', *Art International*, Zürich, IV, no. 2–3, 1960, pp. 62–63.

Alloway, Lawrence, 'Dr. No's Bacon', *Art News and Review*, London, XII, 9 April 1960, pp. 4–5.

Alloway, Lawrence, 'Francis Bacon. A Great, Shocking, Eccentric Painter', *Vogue*, New York, CXLII, 1 November 1963, pp. 136–39.

Alloway, Lawrence, 'Bacon, le convulsif ou l'angoisse sied aux héros', *XXe Siècle*, Paris, no. 23, May 1964, pp. 27–34.

Alvard, Julien, 'Des gorilles et des hommes', *Le nouvel observateur*, Paris, no. 107, 30 November 1966, p. 43.

Alvard, Julien, 'Paris: The Grand Inquisitor', *Art News*, New York, LXVI, January 1967, pp. 24–25.

Alvard, Julien, 'Francis Bacon', *Art et architecture d'aujourd'hui*, Paris, January 1967, pp. 186–87.

Alvarez Diez, L., 'Francis Bacon: contradicciones sublimadas', *Goya*, Madrid, no. 189, November–December 1985, pp. 156–58.

Alvaro, Edígio, 'Carta de Paris: Picasso–Bacon', *Artes e Letras*, Lisbon, Ano XII, no. 630, 30 March 1967.

Apuleo, Vito, 'Personale alla Marlborough: i personaggi di Bacon', *La Voce Repubblicana*, Rome, 27 January 1967.

Artner, Alan G., 'Anguish comes into Vogue in Bacon's Theater of Cruelty', *Chicago Tribune*, European ed., Paris, 7 November 1962, p. 6.

Ashton, Dore, 'Notes on Francis Bacon', *Arts & Architecture*, Los Angeles, January 1964, pp. 6–7, 32.

Assouline, Pierre, 'Quand un peintre rencontre un écrivain', *Lire*, Paris, no. 183, December 1990.

Bacon, Francis, 'Turner at the Academy', letter to the editor, *The Times*, London, 26 September 1974, p.15.

Bacon, Francis, 'Mieux que personne Michel Leiris', *L'Ire des vents*, autour de Michel Leiris, no. 3–4, 1981, p. 139.

Bailey, Anthony, 'Francis Bacon: "I Wanted to Paint the Scream"', *New York Times*, New York, 16 March 1975, section 8, pp. 1, 34.Bailey, Martin, 'The Estate of Francis Bacon drops legal action against Marlborough', *The Art Newspaper*, no.123, March 2002, p. 7.

Bailey, Martin, 'Bacon Estate forces museum to banish Joule material to basement', *The Art Newspaper*, April 2005, p. 8.

Baron, Jeannine, 'Francis Bacon: un univers en marge de la réalité et de la beauté', *La Croix*, Paris, 15 November 1971.

Barotte, René, 'Brutalité et tendresse de Bacon', *Paris–press–l'intransigeant*, Paris, 17 November 1966.

Barrière, Gérard, 'Bacon, la chute des corps', *Décoration Internationale*, Paris, October 1987, pp. 101–12, 130.

Batache, Eddy, 'Francis Bacon ou les ultimes convulsions de

l'humanisme', *Opus International*, Paris, no. 60, Summer 1978, pp. 32–34. English trans.: 'Francis Bacon and the Last Convulsion of Humanism', *Art and Australia*, Summer 1985, XXIII, no. 2, pp. 222–25.

Battcock, Gregory, 'Francis Bacon First Major New York Gallery Show', *Arts*, New York, XLIII, no. 2, November 1968, pp. 46–47.

Beckett, Wendy, 'Spiritual Insight', *Antique Collector*, UK, LXIII, no. 1, December 1991–January 1992, pp. 78–79.

Beckett, Wendy, 'The Flaying of Freud', *Modern Painters*, London, VI, no. 4, Winter 1993, pp. 24–27.

Beek, Marius Vaan, 'De "schaterende pausen" van Francis Bacon', *De Tijd*, Rotterdam, 16 June 1962.

Beek, Marius Vaan, 'Francis Bacon: tocht door een absurde wereld', *Museumjournaal*, Otterlo, VIII, February 1963, pp. 147–54.

Behr, Edward, 'I only Paint for Myself', *Newsweek*, New York, 24 January 1977, pp. 48–49.

Bellony-Rewald, Alice, 'Francis Bacon', *Beaux-Arts*, Paris, no. 10, February 1984, pp. 28–33.

Berger, John, 'Francis Bacon', *New Statement and Nation*, London, 5 January 1952, pp. 11–12.

Berger, John, 'The Worst is Not Yet', *New Society*, London, XLIII, 6 January 1972, pp. 22–23. Reprinted in Paul Barker, *Arts in Society*, London: Fontana/Collins, 1977, pp. 66–73 and, under the title 'Francis Bacon and Walt Disney', in John Berger, *About Looking, London: Writers and Readers*, 1980, pp. 111–18.

Berger, John, 'Bed on Dais', *Studio International*, London, March 1972.

Bertolon, Liana, 'Il Maestro della Nuova Figurazione', *Grazia*, Milan, 9 February 1967.

Bertrand, Anne, 'A la manière de Bacon', *Libération*, Paris, 13 May 1993.

Biasion, Renzo, 'Francis Bacon dipinge gli orrori della Guerra', *Oggi*, Milan, 18 October 1962.

Biedrzynski, Richard, 'Anatomie des Schrechkens', *Stuttgarter Zeitung*, Postausgabe, Stuttgart, 20 July 1962.

Blanch, Maria-Teresa, 'Bacon, la subliminación de la convulso', *Batik*, Madrid, no. 42–43, May–June 1978, pp. 10–11.

Boles, Bernard, 'Mostly Bacon', *Art News and Review*, London, VI, no. 11, 26 June 1954, p. 4.

Bonaventura, Paul, 'An Equal Match?', *Modern Painters*, London, VII, no. 2, Summer 1994, pp. 58–60.

Bone, Stephen, 'Works which Play on the Nerves', *The Manchester Guardian*, Manchester, 20 January 1955.

Bone, Stephen, 'Horrors and Abstracts', *Time and Tide*, London, XXXVI, 29 January 1955, pp. 134–35.

Bonet, Juan Manuel, 'Francis Bacon: el arte como obsessión', *La Calle*, Madrid, 11–18 April 1978, pp. 52–53.

Bonnefoi, Geneviève, 'Une horreur superbe', *Les lettres nouvelles*, Paris, March–April 1967, pp. 146–48.

Bonnefoi, Geneviève, 'Francis Bacon ou l'intensité', *Les cahiers du chemin*, Paris, January 1972.

Bosquet, Alain, 'Francis Bacon ou la terreur de soi', *Le Quotidien de Paris*, Paris, 15 October 1987.

Bosquet, Alain, 'Francis Bacon, la terreur d'être', *Le Figaro*, Paris, 30 April 1992.

Boston, Richard, 'Humanity and Horror', *Peace News*, London, 15 June 1962, p.5.

Boston, Richard, 'Meat and Poison', *The Guardian*, London, 15 November 1971.

Boudaille, Georges, 'Une "nouvelle figuration": un simple slogan?', *Cimaise*, Paris, 1964, pp. 24–36.

Boudaille, Georges, 'Tête-à-tête avec Francis Bacon', *Les lettres françaises*, Paris, no. 1158, 24–30 November 1966, pp. 31–32.

Boudaille, Georges, 'Francis Bacon: figure en crise', *Les lettres françaises*, Paris, 10 November 1971, pp. 24–25.

Bouisset, Maïten, 'Francis Bacon sur fond de peinture', *Le Matin*, Paris, 4–5 February 1983.

Bouisset, Maïten, 'La rencontre Leiris/Bacon', *Le Matin*, Paris, 9 December 1983, p. 33.

Bouisset, Maïten, 'Francis Bacon: je prends la réalité en sténo', *Le Matin*, Paris, 19 January 1984, pp. 27–28.

Bouisset, Maïten, 'Bacon: 'Je suis juste un homme qui fait des images', *Le Matin*, Paris, 1 October 1987, pp. 16–17.

Bouisset, Maïten, 'Espace théâtral, espace construit dans l'œuvre de Francis Bacon', *Artstudio*, Summer 1990, no. 17, pp. 70–81.

Bouyeure, Claude, 'Au Grand Palais: Francis Bacon pose ses pièges', *Les lettre françaises*, Paris, 15 October 1971.

Bouyeure, Claude, 'Francis Bacon ou la réalité piégée', *Jardin des Arts*, Paris, no. 204, November 1971, pp. 6–7.

Bowness, Alan, 'London: Bacon's turning point', *Arts*, New York, XXXIV, May 1960, pp. 20–21.

Brett, Guy, 'Francis Bacon's Imagery: Less Intense', *The Times*, London, 15 March 1967, p. 10.

Brett, Guy, 'Francis Bacon in Paris: Figures in a Room', *The Times*, London, 27 October 1971, p. 17.

Briganti, Giuliano, 'Ridono di paura i mostri di Bacon', *L'Espresso*, Rome, no. 47, 1965.

Brighton, Andrew, 'Why Bacon is a Great Artist', *Art Monthly*, July–August 1985, no. 88, pp. 3–6.

Brin, Irène, 'Francis Bacon e la maschera del dopoguerra', *La Fiera Letteraria*, Rome, 24 January 1965.

Brogan, Patrick, 'Francis Bacon paintings boost Britain', *The Times*, 11 January 1972, p. 5.

Brown, Mick and Caroline Davies, 'Gallery accused of exploiting Britain's most celebrated artist over 30 years', *Daily Telegraph*, London, 22 March 2000,

Brown, Mick, 'Eggs, Bacon and jellied eels', *Daily Telegraph*, London, 19 February 2002, p.15.

Burn, Guy, 'Francis Bacon', *Arts Review*, London, XIV, no. 10, 2 June 1962, p. 7.

Burr, James, 'The Baconian Van Gogh: Hanover Gallery', *Art News and Review*, London, IX, no. 5, 30 March 1957, p. 6.

Burr, James, 'Horror and Harmony', *Apollo*, London, July 1965, p. 63.

Burr, James, 'London Galleries: Convulsion of Mind and Body', *Apollo*, London, March 1967, p. 225.

Butler, Barbara, 'Paris: Chadwick, Hitchens and Bacon featured in an artistic "Entente Cordiale"', *Arts*, New York, CXXXI, April 1957, pp. 18–19.

Butler, John F., 'Anti-Religious Art', *Mosaic*, London, October 1965, pp. 118–23.

Butler, Joseph T., 'The American Way with Art: Francis Bacon, Recent Paintings', *The Connoisseur*, London, April 1969, pp. 270–71.

Cabanne, Pierre, 'Bacon, une dialectique du paroxysme', *Combat*, Paris, 15 November 1971.

Campbell, Lawrence, 'Francis Bacon', *Art News*, New York, November 1963, p.13.

Cappock, Margarita, 'Works on paper by Francis Bacon in the Hugh Lane Gallery, Dublin', *The Burlington Magazine*, London, v.145, February 2003, pp.73–81.

Cappock, Margarita, 'A Clear Compositional Link: Francis Bacon's Works on Paper', *Irish Arts Review Yearbook 2002*, XVIII, 2002, pp. 153–63.

Cara, Domenico, 'Francis Bacon e le sue figure exumane', *Italia Moderna Produce*, Milan, November 1962, pp. 51–53.

Carluccio, Luigi, 'Un mondo di paura e di ceneri', *Gazzetta del Popolo*, Turin, 11 September 1962.

Catling, Patrick Skene, 'A precious collection of debris', *The Spectator*, London, 19 May 2001.

Catzeflis, Paul, 'Francis Bacon, le grand sorcier de la peinture', *Le Figaro*, Paris, 10–11 July 1976.

Chabrun, Jean-François: 'Da-da, Yéyé et les monstres mous: Francis Bacon', *Les Arts*, Paris, 11 December 1966, p. 58.

Chalumeau, Jean-Luc, 'Pourquoi Bacon?', *Opus International*, Paris, no. 68, Summer 1978, p. 10.

Chalumeau, Jean-Luc, 'Sur les Crucifixions', *Opus International*, Paris, no. 68, Summer 1978, pp. 16–17.

Chao, Ramon, 'Conversación con Bacon', *Guadalimar*, Madrid, no. 12, May 1978, pp. 46–47.

Chapsal, Madeleine, 'Francis Bacon et la joie', *L'Express*, Paris, 7–13 February 1977, pp. 10–13.

Charliat, Hélène, 'Bacon, merveilleux et terrifiant', *La tribune des nations*, Paris, 26 November 1971.

Choay, Françoise, 'La peinture scandaleuse de Francis Bacon', *La quinzaine littéraire*, Paris, 16–30 November 1971, pp. 15–16.

Clair, Jean, 'La coquille et la toile', *L'Arc*, Aix-en-Provence, no. 73, 1978, pp. 12–20.

Clair, Jean, 'Visages des dieux: visage de l'homme à propos des Crucifixions de Francis Bacon', *Artstudio*, Paris, no. 17, Summer 1990, pp. 22–37.

Clarac-Sérou, Max, 'Les personnages de Bacon', *Opus International*, Paris, no. 68, Summer 1978, p. 12.

Clark, Kenneth, 'The New Romanticism in British Painting', *Art News*, New York, XLV, February 1947, pp. 29, 58.

Clay, Jean, 'Entretien avec Michel Leiris: Bacon, le peintre de la détresse humaine', *Réalités*, Paris, no. 250, November 1966, pp. 106–107.

Conil-Lacoste, Michel, 'Les paroxysmes de Bacon', *Le Monde*, Paris, 2 December 1965.

Conil-Lacoste, Michel, 'Francis Bacon: le paradoxe du tragique et du suave', *Le Monde*, Paris, 3 November 1971, p. 15.

Connolly, Dominic, 'Francis Bacon's multi-million pound works head for the US', *Evening Standard*, London, 28 August 1998, p. 3

Coplans, John, 'British Art Today', *Artforum*, New York, I, no. 7, December 1962, p. 28.

Cork, Richard, 'When the Copying Had to Stop', *Evening Standard*, London, 16 September 1971.

Cork, Richard, 'Why Bacon Will Paint His Life Story', *Evening Standard*, London, 4 October 1971, p. 19.

Cork, Richard, 'Bacon and the Road to Grand Guignol Glory', *Evening Standard*, London, 11 November 1971, p. 12.

Cork, Richard, 'Beware the Feeble Forties', *Evening Standard*, London, 23 November 1972.

Cork, Richard, 'Home Thoughts from an Incurable Surrealist', *The Times Saturday Review*, London, 16 March 1991, pp. 16–17.

Cork, Richard, 'Le portrait moderne en Grande Bretagne: innovation et tradition', *Artstudio*, Paris, no. 21, Summer 1991, pp. 50–57.

Cork, Richard, 'Face to Face with a Dog of War', *The Times*, London, 8 May 1992, p. 3.

Cork, Richard, 'Diving Deep into Darkness', *The Times*, London, 6 February 1998,

Courcelles, Pierre, 'Bacon: le corps en friche', *Révolution*, Paris, 10–16 February 1984, pp. 48–49.

Darwent, Charles, 'Sketches of Pain', *New Statesman*, London, 19 February 1999, p.36.

Davies, Douglas, 'Swatches of Bacon', *Newsweek*, New York, 31 March 1975, p. 49.

Davies, Hugh Marlais, 'Bacon's Black Triptychs', *Art in America*, New York, LXIII, no. 2, March–April 1975, pp. 62–68.

Debailleux, Henri-François, 'Bacon à l'orange', *Libération*, Paris, 29 September 1987, pp. 30–31.

Degutsi, Yuko, 'Francis Bacon no "ningen tatsi"', *Mizue*, Tokyo, no. 927, Summer, 1983, pp. 48–71.

Deleuze, Gilles, 'Francis Bacon: The Logic of Sensation', *Flash Art*, Milan, no. 112, May 1983, pp. 8–16.

Deleuze, Gilles, 'A New Power of Laughter for the Living: Interpretations of the Body', *Art International*, Paris, VIII, Autumn 1989, pp. 34–40.

Deleuze, Gilles, 'Interpretaciones del cuerpo: el nuevo poder de la risa para los vivos', *Reverso*, Madrid, I, Spring 1990, pp. 74–79.

Delubac, Jacqueline, 'C'était un monsieur d'une douceur infinie', *Paris-Match,* Paris, May 1992, p. 93.

Denny, Robin, 'A Note on Henry Moore and Francis Bacon', *Art International*, Lugano, VII, 25 September 1963, pp. 49–52.

Dippel, R. M., 'Van Gogh en Bacon', Museumjournaal, *Otterlo*, no. 14, April 1969, pp. 99–101.

Dorment, Richard, 'The Body and Soul of Francis Bacon', *The Daily Telegraph*, London, 4 February 1998, p. 18.

Dorment, Richard, 'A Fresh Side of Bacon', *The Daily Telegraph*, London, 22 June 2005, p. 17.

Dreyfus, Alain, 'Freud et Bacon, bien saignant', *Libération*, Paris, 18 September 1995, p. 40.

Edelmann, Frédéric, 'Francis Bacon: peindre le cri', *Le Monde*, Paris, 8 August 1985, p. 11.

Elgar, Frank, 'Le corps humain tel que le voient l'anglais Bacon et l'américain Wesselmann', *Carrefour*, Paris, no. 1159, 30 November 1966.

Elgar, Frank and Joseph-Emile Muller, 'Francis Bacon: le plus important des artistes vivants', *Carrefour*, Paris, 10 November 1971, p. 13.

Elgar, Frank and Joseph-Emile Muller, 'Œuvres récentes de Francis Bacon: "Peindre le cri plus que l'horreur"', *Carrefour*, Paris, 17 February 1977.

Ellison, Michael, 'Show that brings home the Bacon to a new market', *The Guardian*, 2 November 1998.

Esteban, Claude, 'Francis Bacon ou la peinture à vif', Nouvelle revue française, Paris, March 1972, no. 231, pp. 12–41. Reprinted in 'Francis Bacon o la pintura en carne viva', *Goya*, Madrid, no. 179, March–April 1984, pp. 284–87.

Fallon, Brian, 'Bacon entre Angleterre et Irlande', *Artstudio*, Paris, no.17, Summer 1990, pp. 116–24.

Farson, Daniel, 'Freudian analysis', *Art Review*, XLV, October 1993, pp. 47–52.

Feigen, Richard L., 'Bacon Paintings Could Shock or Haunt Viewers', *Chicago Tribune*, Chicago, 2 February 1964.

Fernandez, Jesse, 'Reportage: Bacon dans son atelier', *Opus International*, Paris, no. 68, Summer 1978, pp. 34–42.

Ford, Russell, 'Francis Bacon', *The Journal of Aesthetics and Art Criticism*, Pennsylvania, LXIII, no. 4, Fall 2005, pp. 392–94.

Forge, Andrew, 'Bacon: The Painter of Screams', *Art News*, New York, LXII, no. 6, October 1963, pp. 38–41, 55–56.

Forge, Andrew, 'Painting of the Month: Seated Figure by Francis Bacon', *The Listener*, London, 9 December 1965, pp. 964–65.

Forge, Andrew, 'Tearing the Human Image to Bits: Andrew Forge, Francis Bacon and Michael Levey talk about Titian', *The Listener*, London, 16 March 1972, pp. 334–35.

Fowler, Rebecca, 'Legacy of a Bohemian', *The Times*, London, 5 September 1993.

Frankenstein, Alfred, 'The Tortured Figures of Francis Bacon', *Examiner & Chronicle*, San Francisco, 20 April 1975.

French, Philip, 'A Whiff of Bacon', *Observer Review*, London, 20 September 1998, p.6.

Fried, Michael, 'Bacon's Achievement', *Arts*, New York, XXXVI, September 1962, pp. 28–29.

Frigério, Simone, 'Léger ou Bacon. . .', *Colóquio Artes*, Lisbon, 2nd series, no. 6, February 1972, pp. 6–9.

Fuller, Peter, 'Interviews with Francis Bacon', *The Connoisseur*, London, June 1975, p. 166.

Fuller, Peter, 'Francis Bacon: Ludic Hope', *Vanguard*, Canada, XIII, no. 3, April 1984, pp. 10–14.

Fuller, Peter, 'London: Francis Bacon', *The Burlington Magazine*, London, August 1985, CXVII, no. 989, pp. 553–54.

Fuller, Peter, 'Nature and Raw Flesh', *Modern Painters*, I, no. 1, Spring 1988, pp. 21–27.

Gaizo, Vittorio del, 'La maschera nuda di Bacon', *La Fiera Litteraria*, Rome, 7 September 1965.

Gaizo, Vittorio del, 'Solitudine e vuoto nei quadri di Francis Bacon', *La Fiera Litteraria*, Rome, 9 February 1967.

Gallego, J. M., 'Madrid', *Cóloquio Artes*, Lisbon, no. 32, April 1977, pp. 22–29, 86–87.

Gauthier, Xavier, 'L'homme insulté de Bacon', *La Galerie*, Paris, November 1971, p. 68.

Gauville, Hervé, 'Francis Bacon, la fin des sensations', *Libération*, Paris, 29 April 1992.

Gayford, Martin, 'The Brutality of the Facts', *Modern Painters*, London, Autumn 1996, pp. 43–49.

Gayford, Martin, 'Surprise Faults and Virtues', *The Spectator*, London, 14 February 1998, pp.36–7.

Gayford, Martin, 'Sketchy about the details', *The Daily Telegraph*, London, 13 February 1999, p.7.

Genauer, Emily, 'The Art of Francis Bacon's Utterly Defeated Flesh', *New York Herald Tribune*, New York, 17 October 1963.

Genauer, Emily, '*The Times* and the Work of Francis Bacon', *International Herald Tribune*, New York, 29 March 1975.

Gérard, Michel, 'L'espace du cri', *Opus International*, Paris, no. 68, Summer 1978, pp. 25–27.

Gibson, Michael, 'The Ambiguous Appeal of Francis Bacon's Work', *International Herald Tribune*, New York, 30–31 December 1971, p. 7.

Gilder, Joshua, 'I think About Death Every Day', *Saturday Review*, New York, September 1981, p. 39. Reprinted in Flash Art, Milan, no. 112, May 1983, pp. 17–21.

de Giorgi, Franco, 'Vivo in una fogna dorata: intervistato a Londra il pittore che ha preso il posto di Picasso', *Gente*, Milan, 5 September 1974, pp. 28–31.

Glazebrook, Mark, 'Doodles do not drawings make', *The Spectator*, London, 5 June 1999.

Glozer, Lazlo, 'Zum Beispiel das Fleisch', *Süddeutsche Zeitung*, Munich, 20 November 1971.

Glueck, Grace, 'Bacon Speaks About Pain and Painting', *New York Times*, New York, 20 March 1975, p. 46.

Goldberg, Itzhak, 'Bacon Picasso: au nom du Pair', *Beaux-Arts*, Paris, no.251, May 2005, pp. 60–1.

Golding, John, 'Lust for Death', *New Statesman and Nation*, London, LIII, 6 April 1957, p. 438.

Gooding, Mel, 'Francis Bacon: Full Face and in Profile', *Art Review*, London, 25 November 1983.

Goodman, Jonathan, 'Francis Bacon', *Arts Magazine*, New York, LXIV, no. 5, January 1990, p. 85.

Gorsen, Peter, 'Die Revision des Porträts durch Francis Bacon', *Das Kunstwerk*, Stuttgart, August–September 1963, pp. 4, 18–21, 33.

Gosling, Nigel, 'Report from the Underworld', *Observer Weekend Review*, London, 27 May 1962, p. 27.

Gosling, Nigel, 'Bacon: A Generation in his Spell', *Observer*, London, 5 March 1967.

Gosling, Nigel, 'Francis Bacon: Man Not Nude but Naked', *Observer Colour Supplement*, London, 5 March 1967, pp. 16–24, 27–28.

Gosling, Nigel, 'Bacon Talking', *Observer*, London, 6 April 1975.

Gowing, Lawrence, 'Another Look at Francis Bacon', *Observer*, London, 11 August 1963, p.18.

Gowing, Lawrence, 'Positioning in Representation', *Studio International*, London, January 1972, CLXXXIII, no. 940, pp. 14–22. French trans.: 'La position dans la représentation: Réflexions sur Bacon et la figuration du passé et du futur', Cahiers du MNAM, Paris, no. 21, September 1987, pp. 79–102.

Gowrie, Grey, 'Francis Bacon: Artist of Endgame', *The Sunday Times Magazine*, London, 19 May 1985, pp. 48–53.

Gowrie, Grey, 'Question of Bacon's Private Life', *The Independent*, London, 28 September 1988.

Gowrie, Grey, 'Bacon in Moscow: a Small Gloss on Glasnost', *Modern Painters*, London, 1, no. 4, Winter 1988–89, pp. 33–35, 37–39.

Graham, Hugh, 'Art: Francis Bacon', *The Spectator*, London, CCVIII, 8 June 1962, pp. 753–54.

Graham-Dixon, Andrew, 'A Side of Bacon', *Sunday Telegraph Magazine*, London, 28 January 2001, pp. 30–33.

Greenwood, Michael, 'Ape and Bacon', *Granta*, Cambridge, LV, 8 March 1952, pp. 20–21.

Griffin, Howard, 'Francis Bacon: Case-History Painting', *Studio*, London, CLXI, May 1961, pp. 164–69.

Grimes, Nancy, 'Francis Bacon: Marlborough', *Art News*, New York, October 1987, p. 167.

Gross, Miriam, 'Bringing Home Bacon', *Observer*, London, 30 November 1980, pp. 29–30. Reprinted in 'Confessione di un genio disperato: un colloquio col grande pittore Francis Bacon', *Gente*, Milan, 1981, pp. 174, 179, 182–84.

Gruen, John, 'Francis Bacon: A Night's Journey and a Day', *Vogue*, London, 15 October 1971, pp. 86–89. Reprinted in *The Artist Observed: 28 Interviews with Contemporary Artists 1972–1987* (Chicago: Chicago Review Press, 1991, pp. 1–11).

Guercio, Antonio del, 'Bacon è il pittore della disumanizzazione dell'età contemporanea', *Italia Moderna*, Milan, November 1962.

Gurrini, Rosanna, 'Il pittore maledetto che vale millioni', *Il Tempo*, Milan, no. 6, February 1965.

Guzzi, Virgilio, 'Disperazione di Bacon', *Il Tempo*, Milan, 28 January 1967.

Haase, Amine, 'Francis Bacon: Das Echo des Schreis', *Kunstforum International*, Mainz, no. 119, 1992, pp. 147–50.

Hale, Jane Alison, 'The Impossible Art of Francis Bacon and Samuel Beckett', *Gazette des Beaux-Arts*, Paris, no. 1431, CXI, April 1988, pp. 268–74.

Harlow, John, 'Bank vault art hoard reveals Bacon's big lie', *The Sunday Times*, London, 19 July 1998, p.19.

Harriman, Virginia, 'A Disquieting Nude by Francis Bacon', *Bulletin of the Detroit Institute of Arts*, Detroit, XXXVI, no 1, 1956–57, pp. 16–18.

Harrison, Jane, 'Dissent on Francis Bacon', *Arts Magazine*, New York, XXXVIII, December 1963, pp. 18–23.

Harrison, Martin, 'Francis Bacon: Lost and Found', *Apollo*, London, CLXI, March 2005, pp. 90–7.

Henning, Edward. B., 'A Painting by Francis Bacon', *The Bulletin of the Cleveland Museum of Art*, Cleveland, November 1983, LXX, no. 9, pp. 354–59.

Heron, Patrick, 'London: Francis Bacon, Life and Work', *Art in America*, New York, LXXXII, no. 12, December 1994, pp. 31–35.

Hoare, Philip, 'Demon Lover', *Independent on Sunday*, London, 13 March 2005, pp.7–9.

Hobhouse, Janet, 'Francis Bacon: Retrospective at the Grand Palais', *Arts Magazine*, New York, XLVI, no. 4, February 1972, pp. 36–38.

Hoctin, Luce, 'Francis Bacon et la hantise de l'homme', *XXe Siècle*, Paris, new series, no. 11, Christmas 1958, pp 53–55.

Hoge, Warren, 'A legal wrangle over Francis Bacon's estate', *International Herald Tribune*, New York, 25 March 1999, p. 24.

Hughes, Robert, 'Out of the Black Hole', *Time*, New York, 13 December 1971, p. 66.

Hughes, Robert, 'Screams in Paint', *Time*, New York, 7 April 1975, pp. 54–57.

Hughes, Robert, 'Singing within the Bloody Wood: At the Tate, a Second Celebration of Francis Bacon', *Time*, New York, 1 July 1985, pp. 54–55.

Hunter, Sam, 'Francis Bacon: The Anatomy of Horror', *Magazine of Art*, Washington D.C., XLV, January 1952, pp. 11–15.

Hunter, Sam, 'Francis Bacon: An Acute Sense of Impasse', *Art Digest*, New York, XXVIII, 15 October 1953, p. 16.

Hunter, Sam, 'The Art of Exhilarated Despair', *Elle*, Paris, October 1988, pp. 208–14.

Huser, France, 'Un univers de désespérance', *Le nouvel observateur*, Paris, 24 August 1976, p. 52.

Hyman, Timothy, 'Under Bacon's Black Sun', *Art International*, Lugano, no. 8, Autumn 1989, pp. 41–44.

Inui, Yoshiaki, 'Francis Bacon, Portraits of Humanity in Collapse'. *Bijutsu Techo*, Tokyo, no. 8, 1970.

Hollaus, Invar, 'Francis Bacons Selbstbildnisse – Der Rausch der Vitalität', *Zeitschrift für Kunstgeschichte*, Munich, v.66, no.3, 2003, pp. 409–24.

Ironside, Robin, 'England's Poets in Paint', *Art News*, New York, XLIX, October 1950, pp. 21, 67.

Jabès, Edmond, 'Les métamorphoses de Bacon', *Les nouvelles littéraires*, Paris, no. 20, 7 January 1977.

Jabès, Edmond, 'Le corps innervé de la peinture', *Art et Culture*, Belgium, VIII, no. 4, December 1993, pp. 14–15.

James, Geoff. 'Francis Bacon', Isis, Oxford, 6 June 1964.

Janssen, Pierre. 'Bacon zet ouschuld voor aap in Spiegel', *Het Parrol*, Amsterdam, 19 January 1963.

Januszczak, Waldemar. 'La Grand Parade', *Studio International*, London, CXCVIII, no. 1009, 1985, pp. 36–39.

Jeffrey, Ian. 'Francis Bacon by Lorenza Trucchi', *Art Review*, London, 17 September 1976, p. 493.

Jenkis, Peter. 'Francis Bacon at 80', *Modern Painters*, London, II, no. 4, Winter 1989–90, pp. 41–43.

Johnston, John. 'The Figure, the Body, Sensation', *Art Papers*, USA, XV, no. 6, November–December 1991, pp. 63–65.

Joly, G. 'Francis Bacon', *L'Aurore*, Paris, 22 November 1966, p. 9a.

Jones, Jonathan. 'The beast within', *The Guardian*, London, 9 August 2005, pp.12–13.

Joppolo, Giovanni. 'Fortune de Francis Bacon', *Opus International*, Paris, no. 68, Summer 1978, pp. 23–34.

Joppolo, Giovanni. 'Histoires de Crucifixion', *Opus International*, Paris, no. 130, Winter 1993, p. 51.

Joyce, Conor. 'Bacon, Deleuze and the Way of all Flesh', *Circa*, Belfast, no. 24, September–October 1985, pp. 23–27.

Jury, Louise. 'Art world torn over Bacon's sketches', *The Independent on Sunday*, London, 14 February 1999, p. 3.

Jury, Louise. 'Too risqué for Iran, Bacon's "lost" painting goes on show', *The Independent*, London, 18 June 2004, p. 9.

Kay, Jane Holtz. 'A Painter Whose Source is Film', *Christian Science Monitor*, 1 August 1975.

Kenedy, R. C. 'Francis Bacon', *Art International*, Lugano, X, no. 10, December 1966, pp.24, 28–29.

Kent, Sarah. 'Elegantly Wasted', *Time Out*, London, 11–18 February 1998, p.46.

Killer, Peter. 'Leitfossilien. Die Zeitkunst 1945–1973', *Du*, Zürich, April 1973, p.231.

Kimmelman, Michael, 'Unnerving art', *The New York Times Magazine*, New York, 20 August 1989.

Kimmelman, Michael, 'Francis Bacon, Master of Macabre', *International Herald Tribune*, New York, 31 October 1989.

Kimmelman, Michael, 'The Writhing Images of Francis Bacon', *International Herald Tribune*, New York, 30 April 1992.

Kitaj, R. B., 'Bacon in the Nut House Again', *London American*, London, 7–13 April 1960, p. 14.

Kladnik, Dirk, 'Die Aesthetik des Kadavers: zu den Kreuzigungen von Francis Bacon', *Kunstforum International*, Mainz, no.153, January/March 2001, pp.144–151.

Klokov, Sergei, 'Letter from Moscow: Francis Bacon', *Apollo*, London, no. 128, December 1988, pp. 428–29.

Kramer, Hilton, 'The Problem of Francis Bacon', *The New York Times*, New York, 17 November 1968. Reprinted in Hilton Kramer, *The Age of the Avant-Garde: An Art Chronicle of 1956–72* (New York: Farrar, 1973 and London Secker & Warburg, 1974), pp. 374–77.

Kulterman, Udo, 'Van Gogh in Contemporary Art', *Voice/South*, November–December 1978, pp. 51–55.

Kuspit, Donald, 'Francis Bacon: The Authority of Flesh', *Artforum*, New York, Summer 1975, XIII, no. 10, pp. 50–59.

Kuspit, Donald, 'Hysterical Painting', *Artforum*, New York, XIV, no. 5, January 1986, pp. 55–60.

Kuspit, Donald, 'Francis Bacon', *Artforum*, New York, XXIX, no. 3, November 1990, pp. 162–63.

Kuspit, Donald, 'The Decline, Fall and Magical Resurrection of the Body', *Sculpture*, XIII, no. 3, May–June 1994, pp. 20–23.

Kuspit, Donald and Linda Nochlin, 'Flesh for Phantasy: Lucian Freud', *Artforum*, New York, XXXII, no. 7, March 1994, pp. 54–59.

Laessøe, Rolf, 'Francis Bacon and T. S. Eliot', *Hafnia: Copenhagen Papers in the History of Art*, Copenhagen, no. 9, 1983, pp. 113–30.

Laessøe, Rolf, 'Francis Bacon's Crucifixions and Related Themes', *Hafnia: Copenhagen Papers in the History of Art, Copenhagen*, no. 11, 1987, pp. 7–38.

Laessøe, Rolf, 'Francis Bacon 'Man and Child' – Self-projektion of Katharsis', *Tidsbilleder*, Copenhagen, no. 5, pp 8–18. Reprinted in Kjeld Kjeldsen and Charlotte Sabroe (eds), *The Evolution of a Collection* (Humlebaek: Lousiana Museum, 1988, pp. 35–39).

Lambert, Helen, 'Aesthetic Emotion: Criticism of Excess in UK shows', *New York Herald Tribune*, New York, 13 June 1962.

Lascault, Gilbert, 'Les visages de Bacon', *Chroniques de l'art vivant*, Paris, no. 26, December 1971– January 1972.

Lascault, Gilbert, 'Sécurité et insécurité dans l'œuvre de Bacon', *Paris–Normandie*, Rouen, 12 January 1972.

Lascault, Gilbert, 'Francis Bacon', *La revue d'esthétique*, Paris, 1972, p. 254.

Lascault, Gilbert, 'Francis Bacon: Les chefs-d'œuvre reconnus', *xxe Siècle*, Paris, no. 45, December 1975, pp. 20–27.

Lascault, Gilbert, 'Francis Bacon, la tradition picturale et sa perturbation', *Centre nationale de documentation pédagogique*, Paris 1978, pp. 13–17. Reprinted 1991, Coll. Actualité des Arts Plastiques.

Lascault, Gilbert, 'Peindre la viande', *L'Arc*, Aix-en-Provence, no. 73, 1978, pp. 21–24.

Lascault, Gilbert, 'Bacon et le récit', *Artstudio*, Paris, Summer 1990, no. 17, pp. 90–98.

Lauris, François, 'L'enfer de Bacon', *Beaux-Arts*, Paris, 9–15 November 1966, pp. 32–33.

Le Bot, Marc, 'Espaces', *L'Arc*, Aix-en-Provence, no. 73, 1978, pp. 56–61.

Le Bot, Marc, 'Francis Bacon: Personnage écrivant, refleté dans le miroir', *Art Press*, Paris, no. 110, January 1987, pp. 84–85.

Le Bot, Marc, 'Les enjeux actuels de l'art', *Colóquio Artes*, Lisbon, XXXIII, no. 90, September 1991, pp. 5–11.

Le Bot, Marc, 'Francis Bacon/Lucian Freud: Violences jumelles', *Cimaise*, Paris, no. 236, June–August 1995, pp. 25–34.

Le Buhan, Dominique, 'La chair des visages de Francis Bacon', *Opus International*, Paris, no. 68, Summer 1978, pp. 13–15.

Léger, Jack Alain, 'Francis Bacon', *Art Press*, Paris, no. 39, July–August 1980, p. 13.

Leider, Philip, 'Francis Bacon by John Rothenstein and Ronald Alley', *Artforum*, New York, January 1965, p. 51.

Leiris, Michel, 'Figures de haute tension: une nouvelle exposition Francis Bacon à Paris', *L'Humanité*, Paris, 25 January 1977.

Leiris, Michel, 'Le grand jeu de Francis Bacon', *XXe Siècle*, Paris, December 1977, no. 49, pp. 16–20. English trans.: 'The Art of Francis Bacon', *Times Literary Supplement*, London, 18 March 1977, p. 309. Reprinted in Michel Leiris, *Bacon le hors-la Loi*, Éditions Fourbis, 1989.

Leiris, Michel, 'Bacon le hors-la loi', *Critique*, Paris, tome 36, no. 408, May 1981, pp. 519–25. Reprinted in Michel Leiris, *Bacon le hors-la Loi*, Paris, Éditions Fourbis, 1989.

Lemaire, Gérard-Georges, 'L'Entrée en matière', *Opus International*, Paris, no. 68, Summer 1978, pp. 20–22.

Lennon, Peter, 'A Brush with Ebullient Despair: *The Times* Profile, Francis Bacon', *The Times*, London, 15 September 1983, p. 8.

Leonardini, Jean-Pierre, 'Le regard touche la viande: Gilles Deleuze devant Francis Bacon', *L'Humanité*, Paris, 22 April 1982.

Lessore, Helen, 'A Note on the Development of Francis Bacon's Painting', X, *A Quarterly Review*, London, II, no. 1, March 1961, pp. 23–26.

Lessore, Helen, 'Francis Bacon', *Goya*, Madrid, July–August 1975, pp. 27–33.

Lévêque, Jean-François, 'Bacon', *L'Information*, Paris, 26 November 1966.

Lévêque, Jean–François, 'A Marseille. Bacon: La mort aux trousses', *Le Quotidien de Paris*, Paris, 31 July 1976.

Levey, Michael, 'Body Language', *Art News*, New York, LXXXIX, no. 6, Summer 1990, pp. 148–51.

Levick, L. E., 'Figures do the Twist in Bacon's Realism', *Art and Artists*, New York, 19 October 1963.

Llosa, Mario Vargas, 'L'homme de Bacon: Le musée égoïste, *Le Nouvel Observateur*, Paris, 28 June–4 July 1985, pp. 11–14.

Lombard, Suzanne, 'Francis Bacon et l'angoisse moderne', *Beaux-Arts*, Brussels, February 1955.

Lubbock, Tom, 'Francis Bacon: the man who put the pain into painting?', *The Independent*, London, 10 February 1998, p. 10.

Lubbock, Tom, 'Bacon: The Rough Guide', *Independent Tuesday Review*, London, 2 March 1999, p. 10.

Lubbock, Tom, 'Past master of just past it?', *The Independent*, London, 20 June 2005, p. 43.

Lupien, Jocelyne, 'Le corps morcelé', *Espace*, Canada, no. 23, March–May 1993, pp. 25–29.

Marchiori, Giuseppe, 'Une nouvelle figuration en Europe et en Amérique', *XXe Siècle*, Paris, no. 29, December 1967.

Marshall, Lee, 'A Question of Attribution', *The Independent on Sunday*, London, 3 May 1998, pp. 6–8.

Meades, Jonathan, 'Francis Bacon', *New Statesman*, London, 6 February 1998, pp. 38–39.

McCrystal, Cal, 'Hunt for 'missing' works of Francis Bacon', *Independent on Sunday*, London, 12 March 2000, p. 5.

McEwen, John, 'Francis Bacon: New Transmutations of an Autumn Rose', *Studio International*, London, CXCVIII, no. 1010, 1985, pp. 3–13.

McEwen, John, 'Sensation, awe and unease', *Sunday Telegraph*, London, 6 August 2000, p. 9.

McLaughlin, Brighid, 'Life in a Gilded Gutter', *Sunday Independent* (Ireland), Dublin, 13 September 1998.

Melville, Robert, 'Francis Bacon', *Horizon*, London, XX, no. 120–21, December 1949–January 1950, pp. 419–23.

Melville, Robert, 'The Iconoclasm of Francis Bacon', *World Review*, London, new series, no. 23, January 1951, pp. 63–64.

Melville, Robert, 'A Note on the Recent Paintings of Francis Bacon', *World Review*, London, new series, no. 36, February 1952, pp. 31–32.

Melville, Robert, 'Der Maler Francis Bacon', *Werk*, Winterthur, XLVIII, January 1961, pp. 30–32.

Mennekes, Friedhelm, 'Francis Bacon: Distanzierung vom Augenschein: Transformation des Mythischen', *Kunst und Kirche*, Darmstadt, no. 1, 1986, pp. 31–37.

Meuris, Jacques, 'Francis Bacon ou la peinture resuscitée', *Clés pour les Arts*, Brussels, no. 16, December 1971, p. 18.

Micha, René, 'L'imaginaire de Bacon', *Art International*, Lugano, March–April 1977, pp. 51–52.

Micha, René, 'Le 'Francis Bacon' de Gilles Deleuze', *Art International*, Lugano, May–June 1982, pp. 109–16.

Michel, Jacques, 'Les métaphores de Francis Bacon', *Le Monde*, Paris, 6 August 1976, pp. 12–13.

Michel, Jacques, 'Francis Bacon dans et autour de la peinture: "Je voudrais casser les styles"', *Le Monde*, Paris, 26 January 1984, pp. 12–13.

Millet, Nick, 'The Fugitive Body', *Journal of Philosophy and the Visual Arts*, London, Special Issue: The Body, 1993, pp. 40–51.

Milner, Catherine, 'Court cuts gallery's ties with Francis Bacon', *The Sunday Telegraph*, London, 4 April 1999, p. 13.

Mongenthaler, H., 'Der Mensch in Bacons Schreckenskammer', *Badische Neueste Nachrichten*, Karlsrühe, 21 July 1962.

Moorhouse, Paul, 'The Crucifixion in Bacon's Art: A Magnificent Armature', *Art International*, Paris, no. 8, Autumn 1989, pp. 23–27. Spanish trans.: 'La Crucifixion en las obras de Bacon: Un arma zon magnifico', *Reverso*, Madrid, no. 1, Spring 1990, pp. 67–70.

Morgan, Stuart, 'Body Language', *Frieze*, London, no. 6, September–October, 1992, pp. 28–34.

Moulin, Raoul-Jean, 'Francis Bacon: la figure en souffrance', *L'Humanité*, Paris, 10 February 1984.

Mullaly, Terence, 'Bacon Looks at Man: The Veneer is Stripped Away', *The Daily Telegraph*, London, 30 March 1960, p. 15.

Mullaly, Terence, 'Sincerity of Francis Bacon: Rewarding Show at Nottingham', *The Daily Telegraph*, London, 20 February 1961.

Mullaly, Terence, 'Bacon's Works Shock Viewer: Painter with Eye to Realities', *The Daily Telegraph*, London, 24 May 1962.

Mullaly, Terence, 'Age Mirrored in Bacon's Art: Distortion Used to Shock Viewer', *The Daily Telegraph*, London, 19 July 1963.

Mullaly, Terence, 'Magicians of Art Still Surprise Us', *The Daily Telegraph*, London, 16 July, 1965.

Mullaly, Terence, 'Two Artists with Power in Common', *The Daily Telegraph*, London, 16 December 1971.

Munro, Eleanor C., 'Bacon, Hepworth, Scott', *Art News*, New York, LIII, October 1954, pp. 51–52.

Muray, Philippe, 'Les cadavres dans le triptyque', *Art Press*, Paris, no. 59, May 1982, pp. 15, 18–20.

Nahara, Y., 'Francis Bacon: A Confined Human', *Mizue*, Tokyo, September 1976, pp. 10–21.

Nash, John M., 'The Private Obsessions of Francis Bacon', *The Yorkshire Post*, Leeds, 25 May 1962.

Newton, Eric, 'An Unhappy Genius', *The Sunday Times*, London, 7 September 1950.

Newton, Eric, 'Paintings of Visual Nausea', *The Guardian*, London, 24 March 1960.

Nungesser, Michael, 'Des Mensch als Tater und Opfer: Das malerische Werk von Francis Bacon', *Bildende Kunst*, Berlin, XXXV, no. 7, 1987, pp. 308–10.

Nurisdany, Michel, 'Francis Bacon: face à face avec la solitude', *Le Figaro*, Paris, 29 September 1987.

Nurisdany, Michel, 'Un écorché vif amateur de scandales', *Le Figaro*, Paris, 29 April 1992.

O'Doherty, Brian, 'On the Strange Case of Francis Bacon', *The New York Times*, New York, 20 October 1963, p. 17.

Ofield, Simon, 'Wrestling with Francis Bacon', *Oxford Art Journal*, Oxford, XXIV, no. 1, 2001, pp. 113–30, 179.

Oliver, Georgina, 'Living Dangerously on and off Canvas', *The Paris Metro*, 2 February 1977, pp. 17–18.

Oliver, Georgina, 'Et après Bacon?', *Connaissance des Arts*, Paris, no. 304, June 1977, pp. 96–103.

Oliver, Paul, 'Francis Bacon', *Arts Review*, London, 18 March 1967, pp. 80–81.

Peppiatt, Michael, 'Francis Bacon's New Paintings', *Art International*, Lugano, XII, no. 10, 20 December 1968, pp. 35–38.

Peppiatt, Michael, 'The Art of Francis Bacon', *Mundus Artium*, Ohio University, Winter 1968.

Peppiatt, Michael, 'Francis Bacon: The Last Seven Years', *Art Spectrum*, Lugano, I, no. 3, March 1975, pp. 16–21.

Peppiatt, Michael, 'Francis Bacon au Metropolitan Museum de New York', *Le Monde*, 3 April 1975.

Peppiatt, Michael, 'Francis Bacon's Recent Paintings', *Financial Times*, 26 April 1975, p8.

Peppiatt, Michael, 'Les rêves décomposés de Francis Bacon', *Connaissance des Arts*, Paris, no. 351, May 1981, pp. 48–57.

Peppiatt, Michael, 'Francis Bacon: The Studio as Symbol', *The Connoisseur*, London, September 1984, pp. 84–93.

Peppiatt, Michael, 'Francis Bacon: The Anatomy of Enigma', *Art International*, Lugano, September–November 1984, XXVII, no. 4, pp. 4–18. French trans. in Art Studio, Paris, no. 17, Summer 1990.

Peppiatt, Michael, 'Sono come un triatutto', *Arte*, Milan, XV, no. 153, June 1985, pp. 36–43.

Peppiatt, Michael, 'Francis Bacon', *Kunst og Kultur*, Norway, LXVIII, no. 1, 1985, pp. 66–69.

Peppiatt, Michael, 'Six New Masters', *The Connoisseur*, London, no. 217, September 1987, pp. 79–85

Peppiatt, Michael, 'In Francis Bacon's Studio', *Art International*, Paris, no. 8, Autumn 1989, pp. 16–22. Spanish trans.: 'En el studio de Francis Bacon', *Reverso*, Madrid, no. 1, Spring 1990, pp. 62–66.

Peppiatt, Michael, 'Bacon aux sources', *Artstudio*, Paris, no. 17, Summer 1990, pp. 126–38.

Peppiatt, Michael, 'Think of ju-ju', *The Times Literary Supplement*, London,19 March 1999.

Peppiatt, Michael, 'Bacon/Picasso', *The Burlington Magazine*, London, v.147, May 2005, pp. 345–46.

Pierrard, Jean, 'Francis Bacon: une superbe vie de chien', *Le Point*, Paris, 7 May 1993.

Pierre, José, 'Francis Bacon: l'enfer avec sortie de secours', *Cimaise*, Paris, September 1987, pp. 81–84.

Pincus-Witten, Robert, 'New York', *Artforum*, New York, VII, no. 5, January 1969, pp. 56–57.

Platschek, Hans, 'Francis Bacon: Alle Kunst ist Instinkt', *Art: das Kunstmagazin*, Hamburg, no. 10, October 1984, pp. 30–36, 38.

Poirson, Alain, 'Une peinture de l'hystérie', *Révolution*, Paris no. 97, 8–14 January 1982, pp. 44–45.

Polac, Michel, 'Bacon: 'Don't make me say it . . .' *Cimaise*, Paris, no. 43, September/October 1996, pp. 109–12.

Pontual, Roberto, 'Carta de Kassel: Documenta, a grande celebraçao', *Colóquio Artes*, Lisbon, XXXIV, no. 94, September 1992, pp. 62–64.

Pozo, Justo del, 'Francis Bacon o el Goya de la era atómica', *Goya*, Madrid, no. 70, January/February 1965, pp. 228 ff.

Pradel, Jean-Louis, 'Velázquez-Bacon', *Opus International*, Paris, no. 68, Summer 1978, pp. 18–20.

Prenderville, Brendan, 'Varying the Self: Bacon's Versions of van Gogh', *Oxford Art Journal*, Oxford, XXVII, no.1, 2004, pp.25–42.

Rabino, Max, 'I sei ermiti della scuola di Londra', *Arte*, Milan, no. 208, XX, June 1990, pp. 68–75.

Ragon, Michel, 'Francis Bacon: un individualiste chef de file', *La galerie des arts*, Paris, December 1966, no. 39, pp. 4–7.

Ragon, Michel, 'Francis Bacon, il selvaggio', *Arte*, Milan, February 1972.

Raillard, Georges, 'Un bon objet pour Gilles Deleuze', *La quinzaine littéraire*, Paris, 1 March 1984.

Read, Herbert, 'Le due tendenze inglesi, Ben Nicholson, Francis Bacon e Lucian Freud al Padiglione della Gran Bretagna', *La Biennale di Venezia*, Venice, no. 19–20, April–June 1954, pp. 53–57.

Reichart, Jasia, 'Les expositions à l'étranger: Londres', *Aujourd'hui*, Bologna, VI, June 1962, p. 50.

Reichart, Jasia, 'Developments in Style V: Francis Bacon', *The London Magazine*, London, new series, June 1962, II, no. 3, pp. 38–44.

Reichart, Jasia, 'Some Aspects of the Human Image', *Metro*, Milan, no. 8, January–March 1963, pp. 8–11.

Reichart, Jasia, 'Francis Bacon: Realism as violence and vice versa', *Artfactum*, Belgium, II, no. 11, November 1985–January 1986, pp. 24–27, 76, 80, 83.

Richardson, John, 'Grunts from the Underworld', *Show*, New York, III, October 1963, pp. 46, 123.

Robyn, Denny, 'A Note on Henry Moore and Francis Bacon', *Art International*, Lugano, 25 September 1963, pp. 49–52.

Rosenberg, Harold, 'Aesthetics of Mutilation', *New Yorker*, New York, 12 May 1975, pp. 122–26.

Roskill, Mark, 'Francis Bacon as a Mannerist', *The Listener*, London, 25 July 1963, p. 127. Reprinted in *Art International*, Lugano, VII, 25 September 1963, pp. 44–48.

Rothenstein, John, 'Francis Bacon', *Vogue*, London, May 1964, pp. 109–11.

Rouve, Pierre, 'Francis Bacon and Robin Ironside', *Art News and Review*, London, I, 19 November 1949, p. 3.

Rozhin, Alexander, 'Francis Bacon in Russia', *Arts Review*, London, 23 September 1988, pp. 646–47.

Rubin, Frank, 'Francis Bacon', *Kunst*, Copenhagen, II, February 1955, pp. 142–47.

Russell, John, 'Art Galleries: Reality Plus', *The Sunday Times*, London, 14 December 1952.

Russell, John, 'Across the Channel', *The Sunday Times*, London, 24 February 1957.

Russell, John, 'A Private Mythology', *The Sunday Times*, London, 24 March 1957.

Russell, John, 'Art News from London: Francis Bacon', *Art News*, New York, LIX, Summer 1960, pp. 52, 68.

Russell, John, 'Titian Crossed with Tussaud', *The Sunday Times*, London, 27 May 1962.

Russell, John, 'On Bacon's Own Terms', *The Sunday Times*, London, 21 July 1963.

Russell, John, 'Francis Bacon, Peer of the Macabre', *Art in America*, New York, no. 5, October 1963, pp. 100–103.

Russell, John, 'Francis Bacon', Aujourd'hui, *Paris*, July 1965, pp. 64–67.

Russell, John, 'On Bearable Terms with the Worst', *The Sunday Times*, London 11 July 1965.

Russell, John, 'Art News from London', *Art News*, New York, LXIV, no. 5, September 1965, pp. 50–51.

Russell, John, 'The Human Presence', *The Sunday Times*, London, 12 March 1967.

Russell, John, 'London: Simultaneous Bacon', *Art News*, New York, May 1967, p. 8.

Russell, John, 'Bacon's Universal Room', *The Sunday Times*, London 17 November 1968.

Russell, John, 'Francis Bacon at Sixty', *Art in America*, New York, LVIII, no. 1, January–February 1970, pp. 106–11.

Russell, John, 'Francis Bacon', *Ver Sacrum*, Vienna, 1970.

Russell, John, 'Francis Bacon: A Retrospective and a Preview', *Horizon*, New York, XIII, no. 4, Autumn 1971, pp. 79–95.

Russell, John, 'Art of a New Francis Bacon is at Met', *The New York Times*, New York, 20 March 1975, p. 46.

Russell, John, 'Bacon's art copes with loss of love', *The New York Times*, New York, 20 March 1975.

Russell, John, 'Bacon's New Creativity', *The Times*, London, 31 August, 1981, p. 5.

Russell, John, 'Art: Recent Paintings by Francis Bacon', *The New York Times*, New York, 4 May 1984.

Russell, John, 'Time Vindicates Francis Bacon's Searing Vision', *The New York Times*, New York, 9 June 1985.

Sakai, T., 'Nächtlicher Besuch: Ein Bekenntnis von Francis Bacon', *Mizue*, Tokyo, July 1972, pp. 7–41.

Sammler, Michael, 'Gegen Inhumanität: Bilder von Francis Bacon, Kompromisslos und Aktuell', *Deutsche Volkszeitung*, Düsseldorf, 11 May 1972.

Sara, Mary, 'The Pursuit of the Real: British Figurative Painting from Sickert to Bacon', *Green Book*, UK, III, no. 5, 1990, pp. 40–42, 54–55.

Saraben, Jacques, 'Francis Bacon', *Instants*, Bordeaux, no. 2, 25 March 1972, pp. 2–3.

Saura, Antonio, 'Glosas en memoria de Francis Bacon', *El País*, Madrid, 29 April 1992, p. 29.

Sawyer, Patrick, 'Gallery sued in '£30m' Francis Bacon claim', *Evening Standard*, 25 April 2001, p.5.

Schefer, Jean-Louis, 'Le vague au corps', *Artstudio*, Paris, no. 17, Summer 1990, pp. 10–20.

Schipp, Horace, 'Current Shows and Comments: The Dark is Light Enough, Francis Bacon at the Marlborough', *Apollo*, London, April 1960, p. 92.

Schnayerson, Michael, 'Francis Bacon's Tangled Web', *Vanity Fair*, New York, August 2000, pp. 74–80, 106–12.

Schneider, Pierre, 'The Savage God', *Observer*, London, 10 October 1971.

Schulze, Franz, 'Bacon's Burden', *Art News*, New York, November 1976, pp. 130, 132.

Scroppo, Filippo, 'I personaggi del pittore Bacon', *L'Unit*, Naples, 11 September 1962.

Searle, Adrian, 'This too, too squalid flesh', *The Guardian*, London, 4 February 1998, p.10.

Searle, Adrian, 'Me, Myself and Eye', *The Guardian*, London, 28 August 1998, p. 2.

Seckler, Dorothy Gees, 'Review and Preview: Francis Bacon', *Art News*, New York, November 1953, pp. 42–43.

Sewell, Brian, 'Sizzling Saga of the Rarest Bacon', *Evening Standard*, London, 1 February 1996, pp. 27–28.

Sewell, Brian, 'This is the way Bacon sliced it', *Evening Standard*, London, 25 February 1999.

Sewell, Brian, 'How Bacon became a cottage industry', *Evening Standard*, London, 16 February 2001, p.22.

Shepherd, Michael, 'Francis Bacon in Russia', *Arts Review*, London, 23 September 1988, p. 646.

Shone, Richard, 'Francis Bacon in 1930: An Early Exhibition Rediscovered', *The Burlington Magazine*, London, CXXXVIII, April 1996, pp. 253–55.

Shone, Richard, 'Swastika plus cricket pad equals art', *Observer*, London, 9 July 2000.

Silverthorne, Jeanne, 'Reviews: Francis Bacon', *Artforum*, New York, XIX, no. 2, October 1980, pp. 81–84.

Sinclair, Andrew, 'Last Days of the Rage', *The Sunday Times*, London, 5 September 1993, pp. 23–26.

Smiley, Xan, 'An Alien Culture Comes to Moscow', *The Daily Telegraph*, London, 24 September 1988.

Snookes, Rory, 'Relative Presences: A Roomful of Bacon at the Tate', *Apollo*, London, November 1991, pp. 350–51.

Soby, James Thrall, 'Mr Francis Bacon', *Saturday Review*, New York, XXXVI, 7 November 1953, pp. 48–49. Reprinted in *Modern Art and the New Past*, Norman: University of Oklahoma Press, 1957, pp. 126–30.

Soby, James Thrall, 'Reg Butler and Francis Bacon', *Saturday Review*, New York, XXXVIII, 7 May 1955, pp. 60–62.

Sokolov, Mikhail Nikolavich, 'Tragedies without a Hero: The Art of Francis Bacon', *Art Monthly*, Killara, no. 121, November 1988, pp. 3–5. Amended version of the essay first published in *Francis Bekon*, exh. cat. (Moscow: New Tretyakov Gallery and London: British Council & Marlborough Fine Art, 1988.

Sollers, Philippe, 'Francis Bacon dans le vif du sujet', *Beaux-Arts*, Paris, no. 80, June 1990, pp. 94–106.

Sontag, Susan, 'Francis Bacon: About Being in Pain', *Vogue*, New York, March 1975, pp. 136–37.

Southall, Derek, 'Bed or Dais', *Studio International*, London, CLXXXIII, no. 942, March 1972, p. 139.

Soutif, Daniel, 'Bacon couleur chair', *Libération*, Paris, 26 January 1984, pp. 27–28.

Spencer, Charles, 'Bacon Becomes Detached', *New York Times*, New York, 14 March 1967.

Spencer, Charles, 'Non sono mai riusciuto a dipingere un sorriso', *Bolaffiarte*, Turin, November 1971, pp. 45–49.

Spender, Stephen, 'English Artists vs. English Painting', *Art News*, New York, LII, November 1953, p. 14, 48–49.

Spender, Stephen, 'English Painting in the Fifties', *The New Republic*, Washington D.C., CXXX, 19 April 1954, pp. 16–17.

Spender, Stephen, 'As Bacon Sees Us', *Observer*, London, 27 March 1960, p. 24.

Spender, Stephen, 'Francis Bacon', *Quadrum*, Brussels, no. 11, December 1961, pp. 47–58.

Spiegelman, Arthur, 'Soft Words from a Painter of Screams', *Vancouver Sun*, Vancouver, 26 March 1975.

Stringham, Robin, 'Francis Bacon: The Fifties', *Arts Magazine*, New York, LX, no. 2, October 1985, pp. 84–87.

Sutton, Denys, 'Man at the Centre', *Art News and Review*, London, II, 20 June 1959, pp. 1, 8.

Sutton, Denys, 'Francis Bacon', *Kunst og Kultur*, Norway, LV, no. 2, 1972, pp. 93–104.

Sylvester, David, 'Les problèmes du peintre: Paris-Londres 1947 III', *L'Age nouveau*, Paris, no. 31, 1948, pp. 107–10.

Sylvester, David, 'The Paintings of Francis Bacon', *The Listener*, London, XLVII, 3 January 1952, pp. 28–29.

Sylvester, David, 'Realism Old and New', *Britain Today*, London, January 1953, pp. 10–13.

Sylvester, David, 'Francis Bacon', *Britain Today*, London, no. 214, February 1954, pp. 23–26.

Sylvester, David, 'At the Tate Gallery', *The Encounter*, London, VII, September 1956, p. 67.

Sylvester, David, 'Francis Bacon', *Konstrevy*, Stockholm, XXXII, no. 5–6, 1956, pp. 206–7

Sylvester, David, 'In Camera', *The Encounter*, London, VIII, April 1957, pp. 22–24.

Sylvester, David, 'Francis Bacon', *New Statesman and Nation*, London, LXIII, 22 June 1962, pp. 915–16.

Sylvester, David, 'Der sensationelle Maler', *Deutsche Zeitung mit Wirtschaftszeitung*, Cologne and Stuttgart, 25 July 1962.

Sylvester, David, 'Dark Sunlight', *The Sunday Times Colour Magazine*, London, 2 June 1963, pp. 3–14.

Sylvester, David, 'Enter Bacon, with the Bacon Scream', *New York Times Magazine*, New York, 20 October 1963, pp. 24–25, 57–59, 62–64.

Sylvester, David, 'A Kind of Grandeur', *The Sunday Times Magazine*, London, 23 March 1975, pp. 22–27, 29–30, 32.

Sylvester, David, 'Francis Bacon: Triptych/Figure', *Arts Magazine*, New York, LXIX, April 1975, pp. 60–61.

Sylvester, David, 'Francis Bacon: "Kreuzigung"', *Kunst und Kirche*, Darmstadt, no. 1, 1981, pp. 20–22.

Sylvester, David, 'Francis Bacon', *Modern Painters*, London, V, no. 2, Summer 1992, p. 110–11.

Sylvester, David, 'Bacon's Course', *Modern Painters*, London, VI, no. 2, Summer 1993, pp. 14–21 (first published in *Figurabile Francis Bacon*, exh. cat., Venice: Museo Correr and Milan: Electa, 1993, pp. 19–86).

Sylvester, David, 'Notes on Bacon', *Connaissance des Arts*, Paris, 1996. Reprinted in David Sylvester, *Looking Back at Francis Bacon* (London: Thames & Hudson 2000).

Sylvester, David, 'A Note on Francis Bacon and Poetry', *Independent on Sunday*, London, 1 February 1998. Reprinted in David Sylvester, *Looking Back at Francis Bacon*, London: Thames & Hudson, 2000.

Sylvester, David, 'My Brushes with Bacon', *Observer*, London, 21 May 2000, pp.30–33.

Tadini, Emilio, 'Il Goya dell'Era Atomica', *Sucesso*, Milan, November 1962, pp. 108, 112.

Tasset, Jean Marie, 'Le jour où je m'arrêterai de peindre, ce sera l'heure de ma mort', *Le Figaro*, Paris, 29 April 1992, p. 18.

Taylor, Basil, 'Bacon v. Van Gogh', *The Spectator*, London, 5 April 1957, p. 443.

Teshuva, Jacob-Baal, 'Bacon', *Jardin des Arts*, Paris, April 1975, pp. 70, 72–74.

Testori, Giovanni, 'Ecce Bacon', F.M.R., Milan, no. 34, June–July 1985, pp. 73–88.

Tourigny, Maurice, 'Francis Bacon: le hasard et l'odeur de la mort', *Vie des Arts*, Canada, XXXV, no. 139, June 1990, pp. 16–19.

Trichon-Milsane, Evrydike, 'O Francis Bacon kai o anthropos', *Eikastika*, Greece, no. 28, April 1984, pp. 19–23.

Trucchi, Lorenza, 'Bacon: la fotografia come supplemento di verità', *Qui Arte Contemporanea*, Milan, no. 8, June 1972.

Trucchi, Lorenza, 'Dix paragraphes pour Francis Bacon', *L'Arc*, Aix-en-Provence, no. 73, 1978, pp. 4–11.

Tully, Judd, 'Bacon Estate sues Marlborough: Rothko revisited?', *Art & Auction*, XXII, no.6, 15 April 2000, pp. 18–22.

Vanday, Patrick, 'Ecrit à vue: Deleuze-Bacon', *Critique*, Paris, no. 426, November 1982, pp. 956–64.

Varga, Miklos N., 'Francis Bacon: L'uomo in rivolta come artista', *Terzo Occhio*, Bologna, XIX, no. 2, June 1993, pp. 11–14.

Vaskovicova, Hana, 'Francis Bacon', *Vytvarny Zivot*, Czechoslovakia, XXXIV, no. 8, 1989, pp. 34–37.

Visser, M., 'Francis Bacon: Virtuoos schilder van het tragische', *De Waarheid*, Amsterdam, 26 January 1963.

Viviant, Arnaus, 'Une journée dans la vie de Bacon', *Libération*, Paris, 8 January 1993.

Vogel, Carol, 'Gallery accused of cheating prominent artist', *New York Times International*, New York, 22 March 2000.

Wadia, Bettina, 'Henry Moore et Francis Bacon', *Arts Review*, London 27 July–10 August 1963, pp. 2, 19.

Wagner, Monika, 'Duell mit Van Gogh', *Kunstforum International*, Mainz, no. 111, January–February 1991, pp. 122–31.

Walker, John A., 'The Van Gogh Industry', *Art and Artists*, New York, 1976, pp. 4–7.

Walker, John A., 'In the Face of Death', *The Times Literary Supplement*, London, 21 July 2000, p.20.

Wallis, Neville, 'Francis Bacon', *Observer*, London, 24 September 1950.

Waring, David, 'Hanover Gallery', *Art News and Review*, London, 27 December 1952, p. 5.

Willing, Victor, 'Icarus or the Walking-Wounded', *Modern Painters*, London, V, no. 3, Autumn 1992, pp. 69–71.

Whitfield, Sarah, 'Francis Bacon: Vienna and Basel', *The Burlington Magazine*, London, CXLVI, May 2004, pp. 351–53.

Wright, W. Martyn, 'Hanover Gallery: Francis Bacon and Hilly', *Art News and Review*, London, II, 23 September 1950, p. 4.

FILM

Francis Bacon: Paintings 1944–62, film made for the Arts Council of Great Britain and Marlborough Fine Art, London, by Samaritan Films, London; concept and dir. David Thompson, music by Elizabeth Lutyens. Distributed by Gala Films. 1962/63.

Francis Bacon, produced by Alexandre Burger for Radio Télévision Suisse Romande, Geneva; dir. Pierre Koralnik, 1964.

Francis Bacon, interview with David Sylvester, BBC Television (London) for *Sunday Night*; dir. Michael Gill, 1966.

Francis Bacon, Grand Palais 1971, BBC Television (London) for Review; dir. and interview Gavin Millar, prod. Colin Nears, 1971.

Francis Bacon, Interview with Maurice Chapulis, dir. J. M. Berzosa for ORTF, Paris, 1971 (on the occasion of the retrospective at the Grand Palais).

Portrait of Francis Bacon, NDR Television, Hamburg; dir. Thomas Ayck, screened 1974.

Interviews with Francis Bacon by David Sylvester, Aquarius, London Weekend Television, 1975.

Fenêtre sur . . . peintres de notre temps: Francis Bacon, Antenne 2; interview with Michel Lancelet and Edward Behr; dir. Georges Paumier, 1977, prod. Michel Lancelet.

Regards Entendus: Francis Bacon, Antenne 2 for the Institut National de l'Audiovisuel. Text by Michel Leiris; prod. Constantin Jelenski, Bry-sur-Marne, 1983.

Francis Bacon. Drei Studien, from the series '100 Masterpieces', BBC London, WRD Cologne, RM Productions, Munich, 1983/84.

Après Hiroshima . . . Francis Bacon? Interview with Pierre Daix, Antenne 2 for Désirs des arts, ORTF, Paris; dir. Pierre-André Boutang, P. Collin; screened 5 Feburary 1982.

Die Gewalttätigkeit des Wirklichen – Francis Bacon, dir. Michael Blackwood and David Sylvester; Michael Blackwood Productions for the Saarländischen Rundfunk, Saarbrücken, 1984.

The Brutality of Fact, interview with David Sylvester, BBC Television (London) for Arena; dir. Michael Blackwood, prod. Alan Yentob, 16 November 1984.

Francis Bacon, London Weekend Television, South Bank Show. Interview and ed. Melvyn Bragg; prod. and dir. David Hinton, 1985.

In the Name of the Father, BBC2 television documentary, for the series *The Works*, presented by Darian Leader; dir. David Stewart, exec. prod. Andrea Miller, 1996.

Love is the Devil, feature film directed by John Maybury. Coproduced by the British Film Institute and BBC Films, 1998; screenplay based in part on *The Gilded Gutter Life of Francis Bacon*, by Daniel Farson.

Francis Bacon: le sacré et le profane, documentary produced by Naïve Visions in conjunction with the exhibition 'Francis Bacon: le sacré et le profane' at the Musée Maillol, Paris, 2004.

Francis Bacon's Arena, dir. Adam Low; prod. BBC Arena and the Estate of Francis Bacon, 2005.

PHOTOGRAPH CREDITS

Every effort has been made to seek permission to reproduce those images in this catalogue whose copyright does not reside with the Sainsbury Centre for Visual Arts, and we are grateful to the individuals and institutions who have assisted in this task. Any omissions are entirely unintentional and the details should be addressed to the Sainsbury Centre for Visual Arts, University of East Anglia, Norwich.

All works by Francis Bacon © Estate of Francis Bacon 2006. All rights reerved, DACS, London 2006

All Francis Bacon Studio material images (figs 2, 3, 4, 5, 12, 13, 14, 16, 24, 26): © The Estate of Francis Bacon Collection: Dublin City Gallery, The Hugh Lane.

p. vi: photo: Irving Penn, copyright © 1963 by Condé Nast Publications Inc, New York; 1, 6, 18, 31, 32: photo: Cecil Beaton. Copyright © Cecil Beaton Studio Archive, Sotheby's; 7: Arts Council Collection, Hayward Gallery, London; 8, 10: © 2005 Digital image, The Museum of Modern Art/Scala, Florence; 9: Collection Van Abbe museum, Eindhoven, The Netherlands; 11: Kunsthalle Mannheim, Germany; VG Bild-Kunst, Bonn 2006; 15: Städelsches Kunstinstitute, Frankfurt am Main, Germany; 17: Photo: Michael Tropea, Chicago. Transparency © by the Des Moines Art Center; 19: Bochum Museum, Bochum; 20: © MUMOK, Museum Moderner Kunst Stiftung Ludwig Wien; 21, 33: © 2003 The Estate of Francis Bacon/ARS, New York/DACS, London; 22: Photograph by Lee Stalsworth; 23, 29, 34, 35: © photo Tate Archive; 25: Musee d'art Moderne, Centre Georges Pompidou, Paris; 27: Museo Thyssen-Bornemisza, Madrid; 28: Solomon R. Guggenheim Museum, New York; 30: Sainsbury Collection Archive, University of East Anglia, Norwich.

EXHIBITION IMAGES

cat 1: Yale Center for British Art; cat 2: courtesy Huddersfield Art Gallery; cat 3: The Whitworth Art Gallery, University of Manchester; cat 4: Walker Art Center, Minneapolis; cat 7, 8, 13, 16, 20, 21, 22, 23, 26, 31, 42, 47, 51: Photo: James Austin; cat 12: courtesy Crane Kalman Gallery, London; cat 14: Hatton Gallery, University of Newcastle; cat 17: Aviva PLC; cat 18: Collection of Samuel and Ronnie Heyman; cat 19: courtesy Galerie Beyeler, Basel; cat 24: Photo: Patrick Goetelen, Geneva; cat 25, 52, 55: Yageo Foundation, Taiwan; cat 27: National Gallery of Canada, Ottawa; cat 29: © 2005 Digital Image, The Museum of Modern Art/Scala, Florence; cat 30: Photo: Dirk Pauwels; cat 33: Yale University Art Gallery; cat 34: Photo: Lee Stalsworth; cat 35, 50: photo Tate archive, London; cat 36: Collection of the Gemeentemuseum Den Haag, The Netherlands; cat 37: Dallas Museum of Art, Foundation for the Arts Collection; cat 28, 43: Photo: Eduardo Calderon; cat 45: Göteborgs Konstmuseum, Göteborg; cat 48: Photo: Lee Stalsworth; cat 49: The Art Institute of Chicago.

INDEX